Ármann Jakobsson

A SENSE OF BELONGING

Morkinskinna and Icelandic Identity, c. 1220

Translated by

Fredrik Heinemann

UNIVERSITY PRESS OF SOUTHERN DENMARK
2014

© The Viking Collection and Ármann Jakobsson
Typesetting by Florian Grammel, Copenhagen
Printed by Special-Trykkeriet Viborg a-s
ISBN 978-87-7674-845-6
ISSN 0108-8408

To Jakob Ármannsson (1939–1996)
and Signý Thoroddsen (1940–2011)

Contents

7

Prologue

I have been studying *Morkinskinna* for the last 20 years, and this is my third book about it. *Staður í nýjum heimi*, my doctoral thesis, appeared in 2002, and my edition of *Morkinskinna* for the *Íslenzk fornrit* series was published in 2011. The present book covers much of the same ground but has been fashioned to suit the needs of an international audience. Furthermore, it also reaps the rewards of both hindsight and further work with the text.

I would like to repeat my thanks to the people who assisted me in the making of the earlier book, in particular my doctoral committee: Bjarni Guðnason, Ásdís Egilsdóttir and Davíð Erlingsson. My opponents at the defence were Sverrir Tómasson and Bergljót S. Kristjánsdóttir, whom I also thank. Among others to whom I owe large or small debts are Sverrir Jakobsson, Erna Erlingsdóttir, Robert Cook, Kari Ellen Gade, Theodore M. Andersson, Stefanie Gropper, Susanne Kramarz-Bein, Birna Bjarnadóttir, Svava Jakobsdóttir, Hrefna Róbertsdóttir, Hulda Egilsdóttir, Kristrún Heimisdóttir, Jóhannes Bjarni Sigtryggsson, Katrín Jakobsdóttir, Soffía Guðný Guðmundsdóttir, Valgerður Erna Þorvaldsdóttir, Yelena Sesselja Helgadóttir, Gunnvör Karlsdóttir, Magnús Lyngdal Magnússon, Alex Speed Kjeldsen, Jóhannes Nordal, Jónas Kristjánsson and Þórður Ingi Guðjónsson. In the making of the English version of this book, I received important assistance from Christopher Crocker, Andrew Wawn, Þórdís Edda Jóhannesdóttir and Viðar Pálsson, along with Margaret Clunies Ross, one of the editors of the Viking Collection, and an anonymous reviewer. But above all, I wish to thank my translator, Fredrik Heinemann. My collaboration with him is a saga in its own right and our correspondence, if it were ever to be published by some very unlucky person, would probably fill more pages than the present volume.

I also want to thank the Rannsóknamiðstöð Íslands, the Rannsóknasjóður Háskólans, the Íslenzka fornritafélagið, Den Arnamagnæanske

9

Prologue

Kommission, Den Arnamagnæanske Samling, Stofnun Árna Magnússonar and Landsbókasafn Íslands. Each of these institutions has been a source of great support to me, as has been my own employer these last few years, Háskóli Íslands.

My greatest debt, as before, is to Finnur Jónsson who edited Morkinskinna in 1932 and who is truly the giant of Old Norse scholarship on whose shoulders we all stand. I dedicated the Icelandic book to him but I dedicate this version to my parents, neither of whom ever published a book but who indirectly must have the honour or shoulder the blame for my own efforts.

Introduction

Morkinskinna, an Icelandic Kings' saga

Morkinskinna is a thirteenth-century Icelandic saga that portrays the kings who ruled Norway from 1030 to 1157.[1] It emerged during a particularly fertile period of composition of Icelandic kings' sagas, around 1220, and marks a key moment in the genre's development. Most twelfth-century kings' sagas are much shorter than *Morkinskinna*, incorporating Norwegian epitomes in which the deeds of many Norwegian kings are mentioned: *Historia de antiquitate regum Norwagiensium* 'The Ancient History of the Norwegian Kings', *Historia Norvegiae* 'History of Norway' and *Ágrip af Noregs konungasǫgum* 'A Summary of the Sagas of the Kings of Norway'. There are lengthier sagas in which one king is the main narrative concern, such as the sagas of Óláfr Tryggvason, Óláfr the Saint and King Sverrir. But *Morkinskinna* is the first extant work in Old Norse in which a saga dealing with many kings is narrated in such detail; it may even be the case that it is the first kings' saga in Old Norse concerned with the lives of more than a single king. And *Morkinskinna* differs considerably from earlier kings' sagas: it is longer and more detailed; it includes more skaldic verse than earlier sagas; and its structure is also idiosyncratic, virtually without parallel among Old Norse kings' sagas. Even *Flateyjarbók*, considerably later in date and in some ways its heir, is a very different kind of work.

Thus, for many reasons, *Morkinskinna* offers important material for research. Yet scholars of Icelandic have paid little attention to the saga and indeed detailed research is fraught with difficulties, two of which stand out. Firstly, the origins of *Morkinskinna* are hard to account for, and,

---

1   As discussed further below, the name *Morkinskinna* was first given to the thirteenth-century manuscript now preserved in the Royal Library in Copenhagen (GKS 1009 fol). Later the name was also applied to the text contained within the manuscript and to the saga contained therein. In this study the whole text of *Morkinskinna* is regarded as a single saga comprising many parts.

11

secondly, the saga has always been somewhat overshadowed by *Heimskringla*. *Morkinskinna* is the principal source for the final third of that work, even though the treatment of the material is very different and, where the sagas overlap, the texture of *Morkinskinna* is considerably denser and more extended than *Heimskringla*. *Morkinskinna* has attracted analysis because of its connection to other kings' sagas but almost never in its own right. As a result, scholarly attitudes towards the saga have long been mixed. The main objective of the present study is to redress the balance somewhat and to try as far as possible to illuminate the nature and purpose of the work.

The following discussion represents the first attempt to explore the saga as a unified whole. But before we address broader concerns, it may be helpful to analyse a short episode in which several of the saga's leitmotifs can be identified and a sense of its manner and style observed. This episode (*Msk.* II, 134–137)[2] occurs within the story of King Sigurðr Jórsalafari 'the Crusader'[3] and begins when the king goes straight to vespers from a

2 All references to *Morkinskinna* in this book marked simply '*Msk.*' are to the Íslenzk fornrit edition.
   Translator's note: all translations of the Old Icelandic are the translator's (FJH). On many occasions I have profited from Theodore M. Andersson and Kari Ellen Gade, *Morkinskinna: The Earliest Icelandic Chronicle of the Norwegian Kings (1030–1157)*. Translations of other quotations, namely in the footnotes, are also the translator's unless otherwise noted.

3 King Sigurðr Jórsalafari, though often referred to as Sigurðr the Crusader, is also sometimes called Sigurðr the Jerusalem-Farer. Similarly, King Haraldr harðráði is usually referred to as 'Hardrada', 'Hard-rule' or 'Hard-ruler' but – like 'Jerusalem-farer' – these are not proper English words. Indeed they exist only in connection with these individuals, and the same applies to some other traditional sobriquets originating in the nineteenth-century tradition of translating Old Icelandic that delighted in archaisms and 'Norseisms'. The preference of the present author is to actually translate such epithets, along with many others, as is the custom with most medieval kings. The statement that I wish to make with this action is that Norwegian medieval kings should be treated just like other European rulers, Louis the Pious or Charles the Fat for example, and not as outlandish figures with incomprehensible semi-Icelandic epithets. In the end, 'the Severe' was chosen because it seems more neutral than 'the tyrant' or 'the despot'. As for 'Crusader, while it remains a topic for debate whether Sigurðr's journey constituted a Crusade or an armed pilgrimage – one beyond the scope of the present study – it remains that scholars (Gary B. Doxey, 'Norwegian Crusaders and

drinking session; his men are *drukknir ok kátir* 'intoxicated and merry'. Near the church they happen upon an Icelander named Þórarinn stuttfeldr 'Short-cloak' who is not identified by family. He greets the king, who in turn invites the Icelander to visit him the next day. On his way to the king's court Þórarinn encounters a man named Árni fjǫruskeifr 'Shore-skewed', who tells Þórarinn that the king wishes the Icelander to compose a verse about one Hákon Serksson. Þórarinn is, in addition, instructed to call Hákon mǫrstrútr 'lard-arse', a nickname that should be worked into the verse. The Icelander recites his poem about Hákon, complete with nickname, but it turns out, not unexpectedly perhaps, that Þórarinn is the butt of the joke. Hákon and his retainers take vengeance on Árni later when Þórarinn composes a verse about Árni in which his vulgar nickname occurs. Sigurðr is placated and gives Þórarinn leave to compose a poem about the king himself, the so-called *Stuttfeldardrápa* 'Short-cloak's praise-poem'. Afterwards Þórarinn receives enough money to journey south to Rome, and the king promises him honour upon his return, *En hér greinir eigi um hvárt þeir fundusk síðan* 'But here it is not said whether they ever met again' (*Msk.* II, 137).

This narrative contains three stanzas and a couplet in the context of a frame narrative about drinking, poetic composition and competition among retainers. The tale rather peters out, but otherwise is in many respects typical of *Morkinskinna*. Firstly, the narrative material is commonplace, and characteristic of the saga as a whole: it is an *exemplum*, an episode used to illustrate a certain general principle or moral point. Secondly, it contains a portrait of the king that has wider reference to the power of kings and how they conduct their business. Thirdly, neither Þórarinn's identity as an Icelander nor as a poet is coincidental, bearing the mark of a consciously constructed narrative. Fourthly, the episode depicts a community that places importance on people's values and customs. Finally, three archtypical characters dominate the action: the king, the trusty retainer, and the outsider, an Icelander. All of these features are characteristic of *Morkinskinna*.

the Balearic Islands', pp. 156–159 and Jonathan Riley-Smith, *The First Crusade and the Idea of Crusading*, p. 132) have offered evidence that it was the former rather than the latter.

The principal elements in this episode are the customs of the king's retinue, the outsider and the king. The plot lacks density and any narrative significance in the saga as a whole. The episode does not occur in a definite year but rather at some unspecified time during the reign of a specific king. Þórarinn is associated with no particular family, farm or region in Iceland. That such seemingly trivial matter is introduced into his narrative by the author of a king's saga, let alone – as attested below – numerous episodes of this kind, is surprising and raises the question as to their function in such a work. In order to explore this point, we need to think about the entire context of *Morkinskinna*, a far from simple undertaking.

Like the example above, it will be shown in this study how the relationship between Icelanders and Norwegian kings is a theme that is frequently addressed in *Morkinskinna*. The saga offers important testimony about how Icelandic identity was defined in the Middle Ages. There is an even more striking exchange about royal power just before the story about Þórarinn Short-cloak. In this incident the kings Eysteinn and Sigurðr compare their respective qualities (*Msk.* II, 131–34). This exchange helps to define in just a few words the complex role of a king in society by comparing a crusade to the building of a harbour (see part IV, chapter 2). The nature of royal power is an important theme in a work that delves more deeply into such issues than do most other medieval sagas, but there are many other elements of interest in *Morkinskinna.*

In this study attention will be focused on those issues that are of particular importance for an overall understanding of *Morkinskinna.* As we have seen in the episode devoted to Þórarinn Short-cloak, kings are not alone in the saga. In the background is *a faire felde ful of folke*, as the narrator of *Piers Plowman* more than a century later puts it. *Morkinskinna* portrays a society that is courtly and densely populated – very different from the one in which the saga author must have grown up. We find trading and other peaceful activities; joyful occasions are frequent; it is a colourful society, while, in the distance, a vast and intriguing world beckons and is occasionally experienced. But despite the splendour and refinement, daily life is also rough and raw, involving a constant struggle for power and influence.

This study primarily constitutes a close reading of a single text and not a comparison of *Morkinskinna* with other sagas. And, of course, in the end the social context of the saga will be examined. Though a truism, it should not be forgotten that all saga writing is a product of its own time and surroundings. Moreover, it cannot be understood without reference to an authorial figure, although his identity will not be sought in this work.

Among the nearly five hundred characters named in *Morkinskinna*, two archetypical roles dominate the action: the king and the retainer, and those roles are filled by a myriad of these characters. More than twenty kings appear in the saga and a host of retainers, but they all fit the mould of these two basic types, and it is the dealings between these two character types that define both them as individuals and their functions. All the kings in the saga are in a sense one king, and the same is true of the retainers. Some retainers though have a special status, and the relationship between these Icelandic retainers and their kings is of great importance.

Morkinskinna is paradoxical. It depicts kings and Icelanders, a new courtly world of stone-built halls and decorative objects, old customs and contemporary sports, distant lands and home pastures, and, always, the omnipresent fellowship of retainers. It is sublime yet commonplace. It is austere yet exuberant and cheerful. It is spiritual yet worldly. Its perspectives are Icelandic; it revels in all things foreign. This kings' saga takes us on a journey to a foreign country and to a new world. In some ways this saga world is close to the daily experience of its thirteenth-century audience, but in others it is quite alien.

Even the name *Morkinskinna* is problematical. The name itself involves a certain semantic difficulty since it was first applied to the manuscript that preserves the oldest extant version of the text, and only later has the name has come to refer to the saga itself. Here it will be used as the name of a kings' saga, just as the name *Heimskringla* is used of another kings' saga.[4] The end and perhaps the beginning of the saga are missing,

---

4 It has been customary to refer to the large kings' sagas such as *Morkinskinna* and *Heimskringla* as 'compilations', dating back to an era when scholars believed that the writing of king' sagas had started with sagas of individual kings. The word 'compilation' describes well the art of writing a large saga, given that a saga is a work of history, where several sources, oral and written, are joined in a single unit. On the other hand, I would not want to suggest that *Heimskringla* and *Morkinskinna* are

and any attempt to interpret it without knowing what once filled these lacunae may be regarded, like the saga itself, as incomplete. The origins of the saga have been much debated, and although many leading scholars have offered solutions to this riddle, it will always remain unsolved in the absence of further evidence.

It remains, however, when dealing with *Morkinskinna*, that the first step is to address the question of its origins. Earlier studies concentrated on this issue in great detail, and merit discussion here before we turn to literary analysis. Every interpretation of a medieval text must be based on a clear view as to its origins. It seems unlikely that it will ever be possible to know for sure when and how *Morkinskinna* came into existence, a condition that applies to most texts from the thirteenth century. For now we have to deal with probabilities rather than certainties. Earlier scholars tended to pick sagas apart and compare them to a conjectured historical reality in order to infer the form and content of long-lost original texts, while recent scholars rather concentrate on extant texts and are reluctant to speculate about lost works without having firm support from comparative analysis. The question of the origins of *Morkinskinna* must be revisited in some detail, as the conjectures formulated eighty or ninety years ago were based on premises that differ from those informing scholarship of Old Norse literature today. While some scholars have recently retreated from older inferences without examining their premises, I will begin by summarising the earlier discussion, explaining the bases behind the conjectures about the saga's origins and then articulate a new position. I will show that earlier ideas about the saga's origins were based on a weak foundation – for the most part those that depend upon an inadequate appreciation of the saga's structure, which, given its complexity, is not surprising. The saga has often been considered peculiar, and its eccentricities have been drawn into the discussion of its origins. Throughout the nineteenth century and into the first half of the twentieth century, little thought was given to *Morkinskinna*'s structure, which, when judged by the aesthetic theories developed in the renaissance, was regarded as de-

fundamentally different from, for example, *Brennu-Njáls saga*, *Egils saga* or *Grettis saga* in this respect and thus I use 'saga' throughout, meaning a narrative that is in its very nature the joining of diverse source material (including fully fledged smaller narratives) in a single unit.

fective. But in recent decades scholarly understanding of the structure of many medieval works has become more nuanced. Perspectives that have emerged in relation to medieval literatures other than Old Norse can be used to help us to comprehend the structure of *Morkinskinna*. Though this initial attempt cannot hope to solve all the saga's structural problems, the present discussion seeks to initiate a fruitful and on-going debate. The complexity of *Morkinskinna* is a challenge for any scholar seeking to explore the work. In re-examining both the theories about its origins and their premises, and the aesthetics underpinning *Morkinskinna* it should be easier to address the substance of the overall saga, especially its organising themes: these include courtly society, royal power, the role of Icelandic retainers and the status and function of poetry in that society. This study is first and foremost a literary analysis of *Morkinskinna*, generally a rare undertaking in kings' saga studies. In 1985, Theodore M. Andersson noted the paucity of literary commentary in research on kings' sagas.[5] Despite the fact that much has been done since 1985, particularly in the last twenty years, it remains that the lion's share of the editorial and scholarly work focused upon the kings' sagas has concerned attempts to illuminate political conflicts and historical circumstances rather than conducting literary analysis. This apparent reluctance to treat the kings' sagas as literature may derive, to some degree, from the complex interconnections between several extant narratives of the same events. Scholars have understandably concentrated on these issues, perhaps causing them to lose sight of the sagas themselves. At the same time it may be that the kings' sagas have been deemed inferior to, say, the *Íslendingasögur* 'Sagas of Icelanders', because most of the material in a kings' saga can be found elsewhere, even though this is also the case with some of the Sagas of Icelanders. It should be noted, however, that there is also much material in king's sagas that cannot be found elsewhere. This is certainly true of the material in *Morkinskinna*, a considerable portion of which is unique to that saga. This is not to say that *Morkinskinna* was created out of nothing, without sources. On the other hand, it should not be more difficult to treat the saga as an inde-

---

5   'Most of the critical effort devoted to the kings' sagas has gone into establishing the sources of a given text. As a consequence, the nonexpert will be surprised at the relative absence of general literary comment' ('King's Sagas [Konungasögur],' p. 197).

pendent work than, say, *Brennu-Njáls saga* or *Grettis saga*. Another cause
for the relatively limited interest in kings' sagas, at least in Iceland, could
simply be that they deal with foreign kings. The kings' sagas are a co-
operative Norwegian-Icelandic project, and thus have never been entirely
taken under the wing of either country. Nor has it helped their cause that
some kings' sagas (among them *Morkinskinna*) have only recently been
edited for the general reading public.

Although the connection between kings' sagas is an important subject,
the time is ripe for an examination of the nature and artistic achievement
of each individual work. The textual relationships of *Morkinskinna* will,
of course, not be ignored, but the main focus in what follows will be on the
interpretation of the text. The approach will thus be historical but not to
the exclusion of all else. Although other sagas will be referred to briefly,
comparison with other sagas is not the main priority of this investigation,
which involves a close reading of the *Morkinskinna* text. The saga is interpreted as a work of literary art, in much the same way as scholars approach
contemporary narrative texts, but with an awareness of those elements that
distinguish medieval texts from more modern ones. It is the saga text itself
that matters, though its thirteenth-century origins and the circumstances
of its creation will not be ignored.

In the subsequent analysis I will speak of kings and other historical figures appearing in *Morkinskinna* more or less as characters in a story. The
narrative is not contemporary with the events depicted and characters in a
given narrative do not have a will of their own, except within the artistic
illusion of the narrative in question. They rather represent the author of the
narrative, in this case the author of *Morkinskinna*, although the concept of
saga authorship, in itself, is far from unproblematic. Furthermore, there is
considerable uncertainty as to how much of the material in the saga is original, as it is in many cases much more extensive than any older versions
of a given narrative. When it comes to historical narrative, there is always
a gap of uncertainty between the actual event and the earliest extant narrative in which it is related. In *Morkinskinna*, there is a gap of some hundred
years or two between the event and the account, and this gap must have
been filled by some kind of narrative tradition. Most of the sources, oral
and possibly written, have been lost, although some that remain appear to
be closer to the actual events, including the poetry contained within the

narrative, and clearly provide the saga with some of the material of the narrative.[6] All of these poems are purported to be contemporary, but they are mostly attested for the first time in *Morkinskinna*. In some instances, there are also nearly contemporary foreign sources that may be closer to 'what actually happened' but this study is not much concerned with that. And yet the kings of *Morkinskinna* are never only saga characters. It remains that some of their energy must come from the individual that lived a century or two before the narrative was composed, accounts and anecdotes that must have served as the author's material for creating the kings who appear as characters in the saga.

My reading of *Morkinskinna* seeks to draw attention to the elements that matter most for the saga as a whole – to its main point and purpose as revealed throughout the work. The ultimate goal is to identify the heart of the saga and to offer an interpretation of what, in another context, Sir Thomas Malory referred to as 'the hoole book'.

---

6 The skaldic poetry found in *Morkinskinna* has recently been published in *Skaldic Poetry of the Scandinavian Middle Ages II: Poetry from the Kings' Sagas 2*, ed. Kari Ellen Gade.

Part I.

ORIGINS

1. The Morkinskinna Manuscripts

Manuscripts and editions

The folio manuscript classified as GKS 1009 fol and often known as *Morkinskinna* has been in the Royal Library (Det Kongelige Bibliothek) in Copenhagen since the seventeenth century. Despite its name (*morkin*, 'rotten') the manuscript is far from being in an advanced state of decay. Those leaves that have best survived the ravages of time are in splendid condition and confirm that the manuscript was once one of the great literary treasures of its day.

In the seventeenth century the manuscript was in the possession of Bishop Brynjólfur Sveinsson in Skálholt (1605–1675), who, more than most, had both the means and the opportunity to acquire old and rare vellums. In 1662, a royal envoy, Þormóður Torfason (often referred to as Torfæus), visited Bishop Brynjólfur and returned to Copenhagen with seven valuable vellums, a gift to the king from the Bishop of Skálholt, as well as other manuscripts that he had acquired for himself. The oldest manuscript containing the text of *Morkinskinna*, and thus carrying the same name – as discussed above – was included in this batch and has remained in the Royal Library ever since. Little is known of the history of the manuscript before it came into the Bishop's possession although, as will be discussed below, *Morkinskinna* was almost four centuries old when it left Iceland.[1] In the autumn of 1662 a catalogue of manuscripts newly arrived in Copenhagen includes a reference – 'Regum qvorundam

---

1   On the Bishop's manuscript and his dealings with the King, see Jón Helgason, 'Bókasafn Brynjólfs biskups'; Jón Helgason, *Handritaspjall*, pp. 83–86; Þórhallur Guttormsson, *Brynjólfur biskup Sveinsson*, pp. 69–75; Finnur Jónsson, ed. *Morkinskinna*, p. iii; Jonna Louis-Jensen, *Kongesagastudier: Kompilationen Hulda-Hrokkinskinna*, p. 62; Jón Helgason, ed., *Morkinskinna. MS. No. 1009 fol. in the Old Royal collection of The Royal Library Copenhagen*, p. 1; *Katalog over de oldnorsk-islandske håndskrifter*, pp. xl–xli and 19; Einar Gunnar Pétursson, *Eddurit Jóns Guðmundssonar lærða. Samantektir á Eddu og Að fornu í þeirri gömlu norrænu köll-*

Norvegorum historia' – to *Morkinskinna*.[2] Shortly thereafter, Þormóður Torfason was sent to Norway and there in the summer of 1682 was appointed court historian. He later reappeared in Copenhagen and returned to Norway with several Icelandic manuscripts owned by the King. He kept these until 1704, occupying himself with historical writing, especially *Historia rerum Norvegicarum*, which was printed in 1711.

In Stangeland in Norway the manuscript received the somewhat unflattering Icelandic name that renders Þormóður's Latin ('putrida membrana'); the term occurs first in a letter to Árni Magnússon in 1691 and later in Þormóður's history of the Orkney Isles.[3] In his history of Norway, Þormóður states that he saw fit to give the manuscript this name because of its age and generally squalid state.[4] But the name is not entirely appropriate. Some leaves have suffered damage from damp, especially at the bottom, in others there are holes, and the first leaf is so dark and torn that it is difficult to read. The manuscript is nevertheless in unusually good condition with respect to the standards of other early Icelandic manuscripts. However, *Morkinskinna* may well have suffered in comparison to the other manuscripts that Þormóður had borrowed, namely *Kringla*, *Fagrskinna*, *Jöfraskinna* and *Gullinskinna*. These vellums are unusually fine and perhaps by this time were showing their age to a lesser extent than was *Morkinskinna*; *Gullinskinna* was a considerably younger manuscript, and *Kringla* and *Jöfraskinna* were in better condition by virtue of their having been sent from Iceland to Norway well before *Morkinskinna*.

uðust rúnir bæði ristingar og skrifelsi: Þættir úr fræðasögu 17. aldar. I. Inngangur, pp. 27–55.

2 *Katalog over de oldnorsk-islandske håndskrifter*, p. xli; Guðbrandur Vigfússon, ed. *Sturlunga saga*, Vol. I, pp. cxlv–cxlvi. The list survives in a single copy made by Árni Magnússon in 1712: 'Manuscriptorum in pergamenta Catalogus. Cla. Episcopus Schalholtiæ hos misit: suntqve.' Among other manuscripts listed are *Hrokkinskinna*, *Tómasskinna* and *Flateyjarbók* (which the King had acquired a few years previously). The *Morkinskinna* manuscript is there said to be from Brynjólfur byskup and it could be that he had previously (*Katalog over de oldnorsk-islandske håndskrifter*, pp. xxiii, xliii) lent it to his friend, the book collector and librarian Jørgen Seefeld.

3 Árni Magnússon, *Brevveksling med Torfæus (Þormóður Torfason)*, p. 133; Þormóður Torfason, *Orcades*, p. 80.

4 Þormóður Torfason, *Historia rerum Norvegicarum*, C verso: 'ob vetustatem et sqvalorem.'

Þormóður may well have been referring to the binding rather than the manuscript itself when he gave *Morkinskinna* and *Hrokkinskinna* (GKS 1010 fol) their respective names.[5] We cannot know this for certain, since the bound version of *Morkinskinna* from Þormóður's time no longer exists. The present binding of these two manuscripts dates from the reign of Christian VII of Denmark (1766–1808), but when *Morkinskinna* was bound around 1800 the pages were arranged out of order. In 1927 it was rebound, with the old binding preserved and the correct order of pages reestablished.[6]

In its present condition, GKS 1009 fol now consists of thirty-seven leaves. In all likelihood, 1009 originally consisted of fifty-three leaves, but leaves 2–7, 14, 17, 34, 41 and 48–53 have been lost, sixteen leaves in all. With two scribal hands easily distinguishable, the handwriting in the manuscript is mostly quite legible and the letters elegant and regular. The manuscript is neat and, for the most part, easy on the eye, as attested by the 1934 facsimile edition.[7] Where leaves are missing in the manuscript, there are, of course, lacunae, as in the stories of Magnús the Good and Haraldr the Severe (leaves 2–7, 14 and 17), Sigurðr the Crusader (34) and Haraldr Gillikrist 'Gilchrist' (41)[8]. In addition, the conclusion to *Morkinskinna* is missing, as GKS 1009 fol breaks off in the middle of the narrative of the death of Eysteinn Haraldsson. Since no other manuscript contains the last part of the saga, it is only possible to speculate about its conclusion. Because *Morkinskinna* was used as a source for both *Fagrskinna* and *Heimskringla*, these two sagas may provide a clue as to the conclusion of *Morkinskinna*; both continued until the year 1177, whereas the *Morkinskinna* narrative continues only to 1157.

5 Þormóður Torfason, *Series dynastarum et regum Daniæ*, p. 46: 'pergamenti, qvibus ab involucro hæc nomina indidi.' See also Louis-Jensen, *Kongesagastudier*, p. 62, note 3.
6 *Katalog over de oldnorsk-islandske håndskrifter*, p. 19; *Morkinskinna*, ed. Finnur Jónsson, p. iv.
7 *Morkinskinna: MS. No. 1009 fol.* Pages from Morkinskinna are printed in *Palæografisk Atlas* (no. 28) and the illustrated text in Hreinn Benediktsson, *Early Icelandic Script as Illustrated in Vernacular Texts from the Twelfth and Thirteenth Centuries*, p. xxxviii. See also Finnur Jónsson, ed. *Morkinskinna*, p. iii.
8 *Gilli* is a Celtic word meaning 'servant', and thus Haraldr's sobriquet Gillikrist (and the modern surname Gilchrist) means 'servant of Christ' (*Msk.* II, p. 142 note 2).

ORIGINS

A version of the *Morkinskinna* text also appears in both the *Hulda* (AM 66 fol) and *Hrokkinskinna* (GKS 1010 fol) manuscripts, the former from the late fourteenth century and the latter from the early fifteenth century, both of which differ somewhat from 1009.[9] Because those manuscripts are closely related to GKS 1009 fol, this version of the saga provides good evidence for the missing material in the first lacunae, but not for the lacuna in the tale of Haraldr Gilchrist, since that text is a mixture of *Morkinskinna* and *Heimskringla*.[10]

Flateyjarbók was written between 1387 and 1394, but in the later part of the fifteenth century three quires were added containing the tales of Magnús the Good and Haraldr the Severe (more than half of *Morkinskinna*), texts that obviously derive from the same source as 1009.[11] *Flateyjarbók* is a detailed narrative of the history of Norway from the earliest times and contains, most importantly, four lengthy kings' sagas: *Óláfs saga Tryggvasonar*, *Óláfs saga helga*, *Sverris saga* and *Hákonar saga Hákonarsonar*. At first the years between Óláfr and Sverrir (1030–1177) were not covered in *Flateyjarbók* but in the late fifteenth century, the then owner of *Flateyjarbók*, probably Þorleifur Björnsson at Reykhólar (c. 1439–c. 1486), had three quires added that served partially to fill this 'lacuna'.[12]

9 See Jón Helgason, ed. *Morkinskinna*, p. 11. A careful discussion of this text can be found in Louis-Jensen, *Kongesagastudier,* pp. 62–108. In Rafn's Fornmannasögur (*Fornmanna sögur eptir gömlum handritum útgefnar að tilhlutun hins Kónungliga norræna fornfræða fèlags* 6–7), Hulda is the main text. Hulda can be found as Volume 8 (1968) in the *Early Icelandic Manuscripts in Facsimile* series published in Copenhagen. Jonna Louis-Jensen's edited but as yet unpublished text may be consulted in Det Arnamagnæanske Institut in Copenhagen.

10 See the debate between Eivind Kvalén (*Den eldste norske kongesoga: Morkinskinna og Hryggjarstykki*, pp. 125–128), Gustav Storm (*Snorre Sturlassöns Historieskrivning: En kritisk undersögelse*, pp. 71–72) and Bjarni Aðalbjarnarson (*Om de norske kongers sagaer*, pp. 166–68) on the gaps at the beginning of the saga of Haraldr Gilchrist.

11 To be found on pages 251–400 in the 3rd volume of Unger's 1868 *Flateyjarbók* edition. On the differences, see Indrebø, *Fagrskinna*, p. 11; Finnur Jónsson, 'Flateyjarbók,' pp. 185–189; Bjarni Aðalbjarnarson, *Om de norske kongers sagaer*, pp. 135–136; Finn Hødnebø, 'Morkinskinna,' p. 704; Louis-Jensen, *Kongesagastudier*, p. 65.

12 Finnur Jónsson, 'Flateyjarbók,' pp. 185–189; Louis-Jensen, *Kongesagastudier*, p. 65. Compare Louis-Jensen, ed., *Hulda. Sagas of the Kings of Norway 1035–1177: Manuscript no. 66 fol. in the Arnamagnæan Collection*, pp. 14–15; Louis-Jensen, 'Den

Two extant manuscript fragments, AM 325 IV β 4to and AM 325 XI, 3 4to, each containing two leaves and considered to be from the latter part of the fourteenth century, are regarded by Louis-Jensen as remnants of an early manuscript of this more recent part of *Flateyjarbók*. This lost source probably contained the tales of Magnús the Good and Haraldr the Severe. These sagas alone would have occupied 150 leaves in the quarto fragment, so that the whole manuscript is unlikely to have contained much more material. Whoever added this text to *Flateyjarbók* must have intended to remedy the absence of any treatment of the history of Norway during the period 1030–1177. The most likely reason for the absence of further additions is that sagas about other kings were not included in the lost source.[13] Episodes from *Morkinskinna* have also been inserted into other kings' sagas, for example, the fourteenth-century *Óláfs saga Tryggvasonar en mesta*, the y-manuscript group of *Heimskringla*, and the *Codex Frisianus*, all of which are used in the latest edition of the saga.[14]

To return to GKS 1009 fol, its history begins in Iceland, where the manuscript is likely to have been written.[15] The manuscript preserves a habit of omitting 'h' before 'r' and 'l' and even 'n', as was customary in Norwegian at the time. This, however, does not mean that the manuscript is Norwegian, for there are many examples of Norwegian linguistic influence in Icelandic manuscripts. We may simply be talking about professional scribes who were experienced in copying manuscripts sent to Norway. Though the manuscript was copied before the export of such manuscripts began in earnest, it can still be dated to a period after Icelanders had become retainers of the King of Norway.[16] Most scholars

yngre del af Flateyjarbók'; Louis-Jensen, 'Et forlæg til Flateyjarbók? Fragmenterne AM 325 IV β og XI,3 4to.'

13 Louis-Jensen, *Kongesagastudier*, p. 66. If the manuscript had contained all of *Morkinskinna*, then it would have consisted of 200–300 quarto leaves, but we know of no quarto manuscript with more than 170 leaves.

14 For more information about the manuscripts containing the Morkinskinna text, see the introduction to *Íslenzk fornrit* 23, pp. vi–xiv.

15 Finnur Jónsson believed that it was written in the south or the southwest, but did not go into the matter further (see Finnur Jónsson, ed., *Morkinskinna*, p. iii). Louis-Jensen (*Kongesagastudier*, p. 64 note 1) points out that supporting evidence is lacking.

16 See Finnur Jónsson, ed., *Morkinskinna*, p. vii; Stefán Karlsson, 'Islandsk bogeksport til Norge i middelalderen'; 'Om norvagismer i islandske håndskrifter.'

consider that the manuscript was written in the latter part of the thirteenth century, around 1275–1280, a date that places it among the earliest medieval Icelandic manuscripts.[17] The history of the editions of *Morkinskinna* can be briefly summarised. In 1832 GKS 1009 fol was used during the preparation of the sixth and seventh volumes of Carl Christian Rafn's *Fornmanna sögur* edition; Þorgeir Guðmundsson transcribed the manuscript and Rasmus Christian Rask then checked his transcription. Although 1009 was not the principal manuscript used for the editorial work, the *Fornmanna sagna* volumes may still be thought of as a *Morkinskinna*-derived edition since one of the younger redactions of *Morkinskinna*, that found in *Hulda* (AM 66 fol), did serve as the base text. The Norwegian Carl Richard Unger's 1867 Christiania edition of *Morkinskinna* was essentially an edition of the main manuscript, 1009, a project funded through a grant from the Norwegian parliament. In 1928–1932 Finnur Jónsson edited *Morkinskinna* for the *Samfund til udgivelse af gammel nordisk litteratur* text series. Unlike Unger, who had used 1009 alone, Finnur filled in lacunae with material from *Flateyjarbók*. Thus, his edition seeks to provide a more complete picture of the original contents of *Morkinskinna*. In 1934 Jón Helgason produced a facsimile edition of GKS 1009 fol, for the Corpus codicum Islandicorum medii aevi series.

All of these editions were intended mainly for specialist readers. The Unger and Finnur Jónsson volumes are diplomatic editions. The publication in 2000 of a careful translation by Theodore M. Andersson and Kari Ellen Gade represents the first readily accessible version of the saga, and *Morkinskinna* was not available for a non-specialist Icelandic readership until the *Íslenzk fornrit* edition appeared in 2011, the edition that is used in this book.[18]

---

17 See, among other works, *Katalog over de oldnorsk-islandske håndskrifter*, p. 19; Storm, *Snorre Sturlassöns Historieskrivning*, p. 28; Finnur Jónsson, ed., *Morkinskinna*, p. iv; Bjarni Aðalbjarnarson, *Om de norske kongers sagaer*, p. 135; Gustaf Lindblad, *Det isländska accenttecknet: En historisk-ortografisk studie with an English summary*, p. 115; Hreinn Benediktsson, *Early Icelandic Script*, p. xxxviii; Louis-Jensen, 'Morkinskinna,' p. 419.

18 *Morkinskinna* I–II, ÍF 23–24, ed. Ármann Jakobsson and Þórður Ingi Guðjónsson.

Lacunae, dating and provenance

As indicated above, there is great uncertainty concerning both the beginning and the ending of *Morkinskinna*. Many have believed that, as with *Fagrskinna* and *Heimskringla*, material relating to the history of Norway up until 1177 had once been included in *Morkinskinna*. We read, for instance, that Ormr Ívarsson had become a *mikill hǫfðingi, sem síðan mun getit verða* (*Msk.* II, 214) 'a great chieftain, as will be taken up later'. Scholars have thought that this statement must refer to events that occurred during the reign of Magnús Erlingsson (1161–1184), and have concluded that this period must have been covered in the saga. It seemed likely that the saga would thus have concluded upon dealing with the same period as those sagas (*Fagrskinna* and *Heimskringla*) that later made use of it as a source.[19]

It is also uncertain how the original version of *Morkinskinna* began. Gustav Indrebø thought it may have started with the fall of Óláfr the Saint in 1030, since it is stated when Haraldr the Severe first appears in the saga that he had been *á Stiklastǫðum, sem fyrr var sagt, með Óláfi konungi* (*Msk.* I, 83) 'at Stiklastaðir, as was said before, with King Óláfr'.[20] Although worthy of consideration, this evidence does not prove that *Morkinskinna* originally included a long narrative dealing with the fall of Óláfr. It is possible, however, that the saga had always begun as it now stands. Let us assume this possibility in the absence of stronger evidence to the contrary. Once again, there is really no way to resolve the matter. We are dealing with the extant text of *Morkinskinna*; that which no longer exists will not feature here as part of the discussion.

For the last century, it has generally been consented that *Morkinskinna* is younger than *Ágrip af Nóregskonunga sǫgum* but older than both *Fagrskinna* and *Heimskringla*. Jón Þorkelsson believed that *Morkinskinna* had

19 Among those who have assumed this are Jón Helgason (*Morkinskinna*, p. 11), Bjarni Aðalbjarnarson (*Om de norske kongers sagaer*, p. 135), Gustav Indrebø ('Nokre merknader til den norröne kongesoga,' pp. 62–63) and Louis-Jensen (*Kongesagastudier*, p. 65). Indrebø considered the sentences about Ormr to be part of the interpolated chapters in *Morkinskinna*, but nevertheless agreed with the conclusions.
20 See Indrebø, 'Nokre merknader til den norröne kongesoga,' pp. 62–63. Finnur Jónsson (*Morkinskinna*, p. xvi) considered this reference to be a clumsy interpolation in *Morkinskinna*.

been written within the period 1217–1237 because it refers to Skúli Bárðarson as *jarl* 'earl' (*Msk*. I, 327), a title he held during that time.[21] In addition, Gustav Storm noted that Skúli's lineage is traced back to Sørkvir, King of Sweden, who is said to be *faðir Jóans konungs* (*Msk*. I, 106) 'the father of King Jón'. Jóan Sørkvisson was King of the Swedes from 1216–1222. The family of Saxi in Vík is also traced back to Jón from Austrátt, *er átti Sigríði, systur Inga konungs Bárðarsonar* (*Msk*. II, 113–114, at 114) 'who married Sigríðr, the sister of King Ingi Bárðarson'. This Jón died in 1214 whereas Ingi was king from 1204 to 1217. Storm thought that the lineage ended with Jón because the author did not yet know about the marriage of his daughter to Ásólfr jarlsfrændi 'Earl's kinsman' at Austrátt. In Storm's view the work was thus written after 1217, when Skúli became an earl, but before 1222, when Jóan Sørkvisson died and Ásólfr inherited Austrátt. This agrees with the fact that *Morkinskinna* was a source for *Fagrskinna* and *Heimskringla*, which were probably written a little after 1222.[22]

Many scholars have posited that the text in GKS 1009 fol contains several interpolations from 1220–1280 (compare part I, chapter 2). All discussion about the age of the text needs to address the issue of interpolations in the saga. Bjarni Aðalbjarnarson pointed out that although Earl Skúli is mentioned in the extant *Morkinskinna*, he is not named in the corresponding place in *Fagrskinna*. It is thus by no means certain that this passage was present in what he called the **Older Morkinskinna*. However, Bjarni believed that it probably was present since Skúli is mentioned (though he is called *hertogi* 'commander') in the corresponding place in *Heimskringla*. Jóan Sørkvisson is mentioned in the same place in *Fagrskinna* as in *Morkinskinna*, but not in *Heimskringla*.[23]

Finnur Jónsson considered that the linguistic archaisms of the manuscript indicate that the **Older Morkinskinna* dates from earlier than 1220. He thought he could identify behind it old sagas of individual kings that had been written down around 1170. Jonna Louis-Jensen was not convinced by this argument,[24] whereas Tor Ulset regarded the old linguistic word-forms as so numerous and important that it was impossible to think

---

21 As mentioned in a review by Jón Þorkelsson, 'Morkinskinna,' p. 66.

22 Storm, *Snorre Sturlassöns Historieskrivning*, pp. 28–29.

23 Bjarni Aðalbjarnarson, *Om de norske kongers sagaer*, pp. 136–137.

24 Louis-Jensen, *Kongesagastudier*, pp. 63–65.

in terms of an original version from the first part of the thirteenth century.[25] But additional arguments suggest that *Morkinskinna* was written around 1220. At one point a certain Þorgils is mentioned as telling a story that he said he had heard from Goðríðr, the daughter of Gothormr, the son of Steigar-Þórir, and Þorgils claims that he had seen the costly objects that Haraldr the Severe had given to Steigar-Þórir in 1046 (*Msk.* I, 125, 128).[26] If we further recall Storm's arguments, the textual relationship with *Fagrskinna* and the linguistic archaisms, the evidence all points to the same conclusion: *Morkinskinna* should be dated to around 1220.[27]

Morkinskinna expresses a marked interest in Iceland and all things Icelandic. Nowhere is this more apparent than in the story of the fall of Magnús blindi 'the Blind', where an account of important men killed in battle concludes with the observation: *Þá fellu tveir íslenzkir menn* (*Msk.* II, 205) 'Then two Icelandic men were killed'. The nationality of these two anonymous casualties seems like an incidental detail, but for the *Morkinskinna* author it is as if no detail relating to his fellow countrymen should be regarded as incidental – as if this almost incidental fact, in another theoretical telling of the tale, would constitute the main point of the incident. Similarly, mention is sometimes made of the Icelandic region from which people come, as with Auðun from the Westfjords (*Msk.* I, 217) and Sneglu-Halli *norðlenzkr at ætt* (*Msk.* I, 270) 'from the north of Iceland', as if being from Iceland was not sufficient information about ordinary people in a saga chiefly concerned, at least on the surface, with the history of Norwegian kings. *Morkinskinna* also includes many stories involving Icelanders, though these tales are often regarded as interpola-

25 Ulset, ed., *Utvalgte þættir fra Morkinskinna*, p. ii. No one has yet shown that archaisms feature more prominently in some parts of the saga rather than others or sought to conclude from any such evidence that different sections date from different periods.
26 Steigar-Þórir was born around 1030. His son's daughter could have been born about 1100 and could thus have been an old woman when she told the story to Þorgils around 1170. A few decades later he told the tale to the author of *Morkinskinna*.
27 It has to be added that Theodore Andersson considers *Morkinskinna*, in its present version, to have been written between 1215 and 1220. He links it to the disputes between Icelanders and Norwegians at this time. See Andersson, 'Snorri Sturluson and the saga school at Munkaþverá'; 'The Politics of Snorri Sturluson'; 'The Literary Prehistory of Eyjafjǫrðr'; 'The Unity of Morkinskinna'; Andersson and Kari Ellen Gade, ed. and trans., *Morkinskinna*, pp. 64–72. This point will be discussed in part IV, chapter 4.

tions. It should thus be noted that although the saga has generally been considered Icelandic, evidence for this view often derives from these potentially interpolated sections. This paradox may well have encouraged Gustav Indrebø to seek to show that *Morkinskinna* was Norwegian,[28] and yet its Icelandic provenance has rarely been called into question. Eivind Kvalén argued that the *Morkinskinna* author's knowledge of the island's geography proved that he was born and bred in Iceland.[29] Although Kvalén and Finnur Jónsson agreed on few matters, they were here of the same opinion. Finnur claims: 'The manuscript is in every respect like the other saga literature of Iceland and belongs to it from the beginning to the end'.[30] Theodore Andersson agrees and considers that *Morkinskinna* was largely 'written from an explicitly Icelandic point of view' that creates a definite distance from Norwegian society.[31]

It has seemed less certain where in Iceland *Morkinskinna* was created. Jón Þorkelsson thought it likely that 'one of the Sturlungs, or someone close to them' had compiled it, on the grounds that identifiable Icelanders (among others, Oddr Gellisson, Úlfr Óspaksson and Halldórr Snorrason) were all from the north or west of the country.[32] Finnur Jónsson thought, however, that since certain short episodes about Icelanders within the saga called *þættir* – which will be discussed at greater length below – had not

28 Indrebø, 'Nokre merknader til den norröne kongesoga,' 72. See part I, chapter 2. Indrebø's premature death in 1942 prevented him from carrying out his plan.
29 Eivind Kvalén, *Den eldste norske kongesoga: Morkinskinna og Hryggjarstykki.*
30 'Msk. slutter sig i et og alt til den øvrige sagalitteratur på Island og tilhører den fra først til sidst.' Finnur Jónsson, ed. *Morkinskinna,* p. xxxix.
31 Andersson, 'Snorri Sturluson and the saga school at Munkaþverá,' p. 16. He considers this point to apply most to the *þættir*: 'But a more palpable index is the omnipresence of the *þættir*, which consistently focus the stories of Norwegian kings through an Icelandic lens' (Andersson, 'The Unity of *Morkinskinna*,' p. 5). Andersson links this with the character descriptions of individual kings (compare part IV, chapter 2). See also Andersson and Gade, *Morkinskinna,* pp. 64–72.
32 Jón Þorkelsson, 'Morkinskinna', 66. In *Morkinskinna* Oddur is cited as an authority: *Sá maðr var þar með konungi er Oddr hét ok var Gellisson. Hann hefir sagt suma hluti frá þessum tíðendum (Msk.* I, 60) 'A man whose name is Oddr was there with the king, and he was the son of Gellir. He related some parts of these events'. Oddr is not known from other sources, but he might have been the son of Gellir Þorkelsson, the son of Guðrún Ósvífrsdóttir. Már Húnröðarson from Húnavatn is identified as an eyewitness later in the saga *(Msk.* I, 88).

been in the **Older Morkinskinna*, it would be difficult to use them as evidence.[33] On the other hand, Andersson has recently sought to identify the roots of *Morkinskinna* in Eyjafjörður and the 'saga writing school' at Munkaþverá.[34]

There is persuasive evidence to support the idea of an Icelandic provenance for *Morkinskinna*. Firstly, the earliest extant manuscript GKS 1009 fol is Icelandic and seems to have been in the country until 1662. Secondly, the literary and political themes are to a considerable extent Icelandic in nature, and much interest in Icelanders and things Icelandic is shown. This applies, of course, only to the extant *Morkinskinna*.

---

33 Though he noted that in 'Hreiðars þáttr' there is a reference to *norðr í Svarfaðardal* (*Msk.* I, 164) 'north in Svarfaðardalr'. See Finnur Jónsson, ed., *Morkinskinna*, p. xxxviii–xxxix; Bjarni Aðalbjarnarson, *Om de norske kongers sagaer*, p. 171, note 1.
34 See, for example, Andersson, 'Snorri Sturluson and the saga school at Munkaþverá,' pp. 17–23; Andersson, 'The Literary Prehistory of Eyjafjǫrðr.'

2. The Search for the Origins of *Morkinskinna*

A century of *Morkinskinna* studies

> With the sources at our disposal the question as to the genesis of the *Morkinskinna* is insoluble.
>
> *Jón Helgason[1]*

> The attempt of scholars to distinguish clearly all of the additions from the core of a work have yielded relatively little, and it is unlikely that this enterprise will ever sufficiently succeed.
>
> *Bjarni Aðalbjarnarson[2]*

Near the middle of the twentieth century, after nearly a century of scholarly discussion concerning the origins of *Morkinskinna* both Jón Helgason and Bjarni Aðalbjarnarson appeared very pessimistic as to whether the doubts associated with the married issues of origins and interpolations could ever be eliminated. The discussion has certainly been expressive and convoluted, and though the results have largely – as both Jón and Bjarni seem to agree – proven negative there is still much to be gained from examining these early scholarly approaches, not least the opportunity to move beyond questions that are ultimately unanswerable.

---

1   *Morkinskinna: MS. No. 1009 fol. in the Old Royal collection of The Royal Library,* Copenhagen, p. 14.
2   *viðleitni fræðimanna að greina alla íaukana með vissu frá stofni ritsins hefir borið fremur lítinn árangur, og örvænt má kalla, að það muni nokkru sinni takast til hlítar* (*Heimskringla* III, p. vi).

ORIGINS

The origins of *Morkinskinna* research[3] can be traced back to the Norwegian scholars C.R. Unger, whose pioneering edition of the manuscript appeared in 1867 and who also produced an edition of *Flateyjarbók*,[4] and Gustav Storm, whose 1873 *Heimskringla* study included a discussion of *Morkinskinna*.[5] In the respective works of these scholars, two contrasting views emerged: Unger posits an earlier version of *Morkinskinna*, no longer extant and very different to the text that survives in GKS 1009 fol, while Storm believes that those same two versions must have been very similar. In 1901, Finnur Jónsson espouses the former view and clearly thinks of *Morkinskinna* as two works: the version in 1009, and one he calls the 'original saga', from which much of the material now included in 1009 was absent, including the short episodes (the *þættir*) about Icelanders which characterise the saga.[6]

Gustav Indrebø's study of *Fagrskinna*, published in 1917, proved to be very influential in the *Morkinskinna* research of the twentieth century.[7] Whereas Storm had chiefly discussed *Heimskringla*, Indrebø concentrates on *Fagrskinna* – it has been *Morkinskinna*'s fate to be drawn into research on other kings' sagas without its own merits attracting sufficient recognition. Indrebø compares *Morkinskinna* and *Fagrskinna* in order to try to establish definitively which saga had borrowed from which. His discussion lent support to (then) current ideas about the age of these two works. Indrebø rejects Finnur Jónsson's idea that the textual similarities between *Morkinskinna* and *Fagrskinna* could be explained in terms of their use of putative common sources, notably those lost sagas of individual kings that Finnur considered to be the core of *Morkinskinna*.[8] Indrebø's conclusion is that *Morkinskinna* has to be the earlier work; its purpose had clearly been to collect within a single text as much information as possible about the kings of Norway. Though *Fagrskinna* offers less detail, it still includes

3   On the history of *Morkinskinna* research, see Ármann Jakobsson, 'Um uppruna Morkinskinnu: Drög að rannsóknarsögu,' a somewhat fuller account than the one presented here.
4   *Flateyjarbok: En Samling af norske Konge-sagaer med indskudte mindre Fortællinger om Begivenheder i og udenfor Norge samt Annaler* 3.
5   Gustav Storm, *Snorre Sturlassöns Historieskrivning: En kritisk undersögelse.*
6   Finnur Jónsson, *Den oldnorske og oldislandske Litteraturs Historie* 2, p. 627.
7   Gustav Indrebø, *Fagrskinna: Avhandlinger fra Universitetets historiske seminar.*
8   Ibid., p. 14.

material that the *Morkinskinna* author would hardly have ignored had he known it. From this Indrebø concludes that *Fagrskinna* must have drawn on *Morkinskinna* rather than the other way round.

Indrebø believes, firstly, that there must have been two *Morkinskinna* versions – the **Original Morkinskinna*, and the (extant) 1009 text; and, secondly, that the one used by the author of *Fagrskinna* is not the same as the 1009 version. Commenting on the **Original Morkinskinna*, Indrebø says:

> This older, more original version we can call *the oldest Morkinskinna*. It differed from the extant *Morkinskinna* in the following ways:
>
> 1. The text, the choice of words was somewhat different.
>
> 2. It lacked:
>
>   a) all the borrowings from *Ágrip*;
>
>   b) one of the versions of how Haraldr the Severe returned to Norway?
>
>   c) a few *þættir* (episodes) without stanzas?
>
>   d) some direct speech (and dialogues).[9]

Indrebø points out the verbal differences between *Fagrskinna* and *Morkinskinna* in clearly related parts of the text. He thinks it more likely that the author of the later version of *Morkinskinna* would have changed the wording, rather than the author of *Fagrskinna* – such changes would have been against his nature.[10]

Indrebø notes that the *Morkinskinna* 'borrowings' from *Ágrip af Nóregskonunga sǫgum* were consistently absent from *Fagrskinna*. He discusses them in greater detail than any other putative differences between the **Oldest Morkinskinna* and the extant text. The 'borrowings' that he

---

9 *Denne eldre, upphavlegare tilemningi kann vi kalla* den eldste Mork. *Ho har skilt seg fraa den kjende Mork. paa fylgjande punkt: 1. Teksten, sjølve ordvalet har vore noko annleis. 2. Ho har vanta a) alle laan fra Ágr; b) denn eine versjonen om koss Harald Hardraade kom til Noreg? c) nokre tætter utan vers? d) ymis direkte tale (og samtalar).* Ibid., p. 19.

10 Ibid., p. 20.

identified were of a different nature, mostly very short pieces of text, which suggest a clear relationship between *Ágrip* and *Morkinskinna*. Indrebø concludes that since those same episodes are absent from *Fagrskinna*, they must have been interpolated into a later version of *Morkinskinna*. Indeed, Indrebø claims that even though the *Fagrskinna* author knew *Ágrip*, he would have needed to compare the texts very carefully in order to eliminate all traces of these episodes. Indrebø thought it more likely, therefore, that they were later additions to *Morkinskinna*.[11]

For example, *Morkinskinna* has two versions of Haraldr the Severe's arrival in Norway. Indrebø regards them as contradictory (see part II, chapter 3 and part IV, chapter 1), and believes that only one version was in the **Oldest Morkinskinna*.[12] He also reckons that the 'digressions' (some of which are called *þættir*) were not present in the original. A metafictional reference in *Morkinskinna* refers to an account of Sveinn Úlfsson's dealings with an old woman as *gamans frásǫgn ok eigi sǫguligt eins kostar* 'a story told for pleasure and not particularly historical' (*Msk.* I, 252). Indrebø regards this remark as evidence that the author of the **Oldest Morkinskinna* did not think such tales belonged in an historical work, and that such a view was at odds with the inclusion of so many *þættir* in the extant *Morkinskinna* (in GKS 1009 fol and later manuscripts).[13] Indrebø also believes that the **Oldest Morkinskinna* may have contained less direct speech than does the extant version.

In his brief discussion of the passages in the extant *Morkinskinna* that he considers to be interpolations from *Ágrip*, Indrebø for the most part agrees with Finnur Jónsson's view. Storm, by contrast, had claimed that *Heimskringla* emerged from the melting pot of the verbose *Morkinskinna* and the more reticent *Fagrskinna*. As we have seen, various so-called *þættir* are included in Indrebø's list of additions to the original saga. Although his discussion of the 'borrowings' from *Ágrip* is very detailed, his view that the *þættir* were interpolations rests primarily on the assumption that the author of *Fagrskinna* would not have completely omitted material from *Ágrip*. Items 2 (b) and (c) in his list are actually followed by ques-

---

11   Ibid., pp. 22–31 and 34–43.
12   Indrebø, *Fagrskinna*, p 31.
13   Ibid., pp. 31–33.

tion marks, and he does not identify the 'few *þættir*' referred to in 2 (c). Finally, his claim that direct speech has frequently been added is based only on comparison with *Fagrskinna*, which he considers to be closer to the *Oldest Morkinskinna than the extant text in GKS 1009 fol.[14]

Although his ideas do not differ significantly from those of Finnur Jónsson, Indrebø assumes the existence of an authored work, the *Oldest Morkinskinna, which was closer to *Fagrskinna* than to the extant *Morkinskinna*. Finnur viewed *Morkinskinna* as a saga compilation and seems to have regarded its redactor as having interpolated the material that Indrebø regarded as superfluous and contradictory. In Finnur's view, *Morkinskinna* did not have a *forfatter* 'author', only a *bearbejder* 're-dactor', and that individual (or those individuals) failed to remove all the contradictions from the narrative. Indrebø and Finnur agree that such a failure argues against the existence of a single author – a 'real author' would have removed such contradictions.

In the two decades after Indrebø developed his ideas about *Morkin-skinna* the saga attracted a greater degree of scholarly attention, including the largely ignored work of Eivind Kvalén in 1925.[15] In 1928, in a contri-bution to a festschrift for Finnur Jónsson, Indrebø revisits his view that the *þættir* are interpolations. His main argument is that the characterisation of Haraldr the Severe in the main narrative – where he '(like Magnús) is a hero' – differs from that in the *þættir* where 'he is a villain'.[16] Indrebø sees this as one example of the 'self-contradictions' in *Morkinskinna* that suggest that the *þættir* are subsequent scribal interpolations. He emphas-ises that the *Oldest Morkinskinna must have been a *tour de force*: 'The *Morkinskinna*-master – the original author – was a greater author than he ever receives credit for'.[17] It is possible, he argues, to come close to the ori-ginal master-work by removing later scribal additions, identifiable by the

14 Ibid., pp. 33–34.
15 Eivind Kvalén, 'Tilhøvet millom Morkinskinna, Fagrskinna, Ágrip og Orkneyinga saga.'
16 'Harald Hardraade i Morkinskinna,' p. 177. Compare Andersson, 'The Politics of Snorri Sturluson'; Ármann Jakobsson, 'The Individual and the Ideal: The Repres-entation of Royalty in Morkinskinna.'
17 'Morkinskinna-meisteren – originalforfatteren – hev vore ein större forfattar enn han jamleg fær ære for.' Indrebø, 'Harald Hardraade i Morkinskinna,' p. 179.

contradictions that they create in the narrative, as in the characterisation of Haraldr.[18]

Finnur Jónsson's edition of *Morkinskinna* (1928–32)[19] soon established itself as a standard edition of the work. In it he made use of the younger part of *Flateyjarbók* to fill in the lacunae in GKS 1009 fol. In the introduction Finnur goes further than before in determining what may have been originally present in the saga and what was interpolated. Finnur, like Indrebø, speaks about the **Oldest Morkinskinna* as being different from the extant version.[20] He assumes, on the other hand, that the **Oldest Morkinskinna* was itself a transitional version, behind which lay independent sagas about individual kings that had been assembled by a redactor.[21] In line with these conclusions Finnur discusses in detail those underlying sagas, and he cites examples of narratives that must have been interpolated later. He claims that such narrative material either contradicts, is incompatible with, or serves no obvious purpose in the 'main saga': for Finnur it is narrative consistency that helps to determine what is original. He assumes that his own judgments were in harmony with those of the great authors of the saga age, and he clearly sees the extant texts as close to his ideal of saga composition, in which only the main events, those that nineteenth-century historians considered important in the life of every king, are treated.[22] On the other hand, a 'redactor' could have added material that had no place in the saga and could thus have created contradictions.

The main difference between Finnur's and Indrebø's views concerns the proposition that 'original sagas' lay behind the **Oldest Morkinskinna*. Indrebø has less faith in this notion than does Finnur. The two scholars do, however, agree that the *þættir* in the saga, those concerning Icelanders and others, are additions. Finnur believes in the 'organic unity' of a literary work, a notion that implies the existence of a coherence and unity in the

---

18 See the more detailed discussion in part IV, chapter 2.

19 Copenhagen, 1932.

20 Finnur Jónsson, ed. *Morkinskinna*, p. ix.

21 Ibid., p. xl.

22 For further detail, see Ármann Jakobsson, 'Den kluntede afskriver: Finnur Jónsson og Morkinskinna.'

kings' sagas that the *þættir* violate.[23] He imagines an idealised narrative structure, from which the 'interpolations' are recognisable as deviations. He claims that the *þættir* are 'in and of themselves ... peculiar and entertaining enough, but they fall outside a royal biography'.[24] In short there is a better way of composing a kings' saga. The yard-stick for that better way is to be found in other medieval sagas – notably, for Finnur, *Heimskringla*.

Finnur discusses what he considers to be the rather haphazard working habits of the redactor in making use of many *þættir* and of other material available to him.[25] He does not believe that a single author was responsible for the saga – many copyists could have been involved. 'Interpolations' can be identified not only by keeping the narrative's overall logic in mind but also by paying attention to elements of repetition, contradiction and textual scars. Finnur finds such elements throughout the saga, as, for example, in an episode about Karl inn vesali 'the Luckless', a Norwegian merchant, which seems to offer two contradictory descriptions of Magnús the Good's arrival in Norway. Such awkwardness, in Finnur's mind, was the result of a redactor's maladroit inclusion of this episode;[26] its inconsistencies confirm that it could not be a part of the original **Magnúss saga góða*. The interpolation reflects the tendency of *Morkinskinna* to lose touch with its historical core. Finnur's view is that the original narratives are not only more coherent but also 'more authentic' than the interpolated 'unhistorical matter'. His basic premise is that truth, the real course of events, is by nature consistent. The closer a saga stands to historical reality, the more coherent it is.

Although Finnur's analysis of interpolations is dominated by a discussion of repetition, incoherence and lack of taste, he also seeks support from textual comparison. He points out that some *þættir* in *Morkinskinna* are either absent from, or present only in very different forms, in the more recent part of *Flateyjarbók* (that is, the tales of Magnús the Good and Haraldr the Severe), although in other respects this text is closer to the one in 1009. The missing or altered *þættir* are the tales of Hreiðarr the Simple, Halldórr Snorrason, Auðun of the Westfjords, Brandr inn ǫrvi

23 Finnur Jónsson, ed. *Morkinskinna*, pp. xxxv–xxxvi.
24 Ibid., p. xl.
25 Ibid., p. xxxvi.
26 Ibid., p. xi.

'the Bountiful', an anonymous storytelling Icelander and Sneglu-Halli –
all of them tales about Icelanders. Finnur does not believe that these ab-
sences or differences are the result of lacunae in the original work used
for the composition of *Flateyjarbók*,[27] and considers that evidence derived
from textual comparison alone cannot be conclusive when discussing the
origins of *Morkinskinna*. Such evidence can, however, offer support for
conclusions that derive from careful analysis of the narrative contradictions and clumsiness in the extant saga.

In 1936 Bjarni Aðalbjarnarson made his initial contribution to the debate on the origins of *Morkinskinna*. While accepting Indrebø's ideas
about the influence of *Morkinskinna* on *Fagrskinna*, he disagrees that the
Fagrskinna text is generally closer to the **Oldest Morkinskinna* than the
Morkinskinna text. By textual comparison he shows that the versions in
Morkinskinna and *Heimskringla* often agree with each other rather than
with *Fagrskinna*, but that in other instances *Fagrskinna* and *Heimskringla*
represent 'more original' texts. His conclusion is that '*Msk.* [*Morkinskinna*] and *Fsk.* [*Fagrskinna*] each in turn depart from the earliest *Msk.*
text'.[28]

In this way Bjarni challenged Indrebø's notions about the development of *Morkinskinna*, since, as noted earlier, Indrebø was convinced that
the text of *Fagrskinna* was closer to the **Oldest Morkinskinna* than was
Morkinskinna. But Bjarni, like Indrebø, claimed that the **Oldest Morkinskinna* was very different from the extant version. He looked to go further, however, by dealing in great detail with its sources. He posited the
existence of *spesialsagaer* 'sagas about individual kings' as had Finnur
Jónsson, but nevertheless saw no reason to assume an independent saga
for every king.[29] Bjarni did not set much store by Finnur's linguistic and

27 Finnur Jónsson, ed. *Morkinskinna*, pp. ix–x. See also Finnur Jónsson, 'Flateyjarbók,'
   pp. 185–189.
28 '*Msk. og Fsk.* vekselvis viker av fra den eldste *Msk.*'s tekst.' Bjarni Aðalbjarnarson,
   Om de norske kongers sagaer, pp. 172–173.
29 This emerges even more clearly in Bjarni's introduction to his *Heimskringla* edition
   (Íslenzk fornrit, 26–28 [Reykjavík, 1941–51]): *Má hvort tveggja vera, að verk höf-
   undarins hafi verið í því fólgið, að steypa saman eldri sögum, og hitt, að hann hafi
   frumsamið eftir sögnum og vísum* (*Heimskringla* I, ÍF 26, p. xvii) 'It is possible that
   the author's work involved both stitching together earlier sagas and original composition based on available narratives and verses'.

literary arguments with respect to these sagas. The best evidence lay in 'compositional mistakes that could be understood as scars from the process of suturing together the individual sagas'.[30] Under 'compositional mistakes' he listed repetition, incoherence, clumsiness, and breaches of taste, along with the contradictions that also featured prominently in both Finnur's and Indrebø's works.

Bjarni's discussion of the role played by *þættir* is more detailed than that of Indrebø. He identifies sixteen *þættir* that could have had an independent existence before their introduction into *Morkinskinna*.[31] For Bjarni these *þættir* are comparable with Finnur's individual sagas – they were the narrative building blocks of *Morkinskinna*. His analysis of them is an integral part of his overall exploration of the saga. His main argument is that the *þættir* are insufficiently important to merit inclusion in kings' sagas.[32] Like Finnur, Bjarni has a definite aesthetic in mind – as attested by the word *komposisjonsfeil* – that determines what belongs in a saga and what does not.

The search for independent *þættir* carries the spirit of both Finnur and Indrebø. Bjarni regarded the presence of material in a *þáttr* that has already appeared in *Morkinskinna* as evidence that the *þáttr* had once enjoyed an independent existence prior to its incorporation in the saga. Some *þættir* had definitely not been included in the **Oldest Morkinskinna* – for example, those which, as Finnur had pointed out, were either not in *Flateyjarbók* or appeared there in much altered form. Bjarni, on the other hand, did not suggest a new way of identifying those *þættir* that had not been part of the **Oldest Morkinskinna*.[33] Along with many scholars of his generation he thought that the *þættir* served no useful purpose in the saga, and also violated good taste. They were 'fragments that do nothing to strengthen the substance of the sagas, and which could be excised without leaving any scar'.[34] But Bjarni also maintained that it is the *þættir* of least importance for the saga that were least likely to have had an independent

---

30 *Om de norske kongers sagaer*, p. 169. For Bjarni's discussion of the sources of *Morkinskinna*, see pp. 151–72.
31 *Om de norske kongers sagaer*, p. 154.
32 Ibid., p. 155.
33 Ibid., pp. 154–59.
34 Ibid., p. 157.

existence. Therein lay a clear contradiction at the heart of his argument. The main argument in support of the proposition that the *þættir* do not belong in the saga is that they are not important enough to be included. At the same time it appears that much of the material that might be excised from the saga must have been in the **Oldest Morkinskinna*, since those sections could scarcely have been independent.

Like Finnur, Bjarni dealt not only with the **Oldest Morkinskinna* but also with sagas of individual kings that, he believed, lay behind that work. In most respects Bjarni accepted Indrebø and Finnur's view that the *þættir* are mainly interpolations, but he hedged his bets in indicating that the matter was difficult to resolve – he disagreed with Finnur that 'there is no doubt that all of this is interpolated'.[35] Bjarni assumed that many (though not all) *þættir* were present in the **Oldest Morkinskinna*, and yet he felt that such material scarcely belongs in the saga.

Bjarni also discussed those chapters that have parallels in *Ágrip*, and, unlike Kvalén, he believed that they derive from this work. Bjarni considered that these 'borrowings' were interpolations, using the same arguments previously deployed by Indrebø, namely, that the chapters are missing from *Fagrskinna*. He focused on the clumsiness behind the repetitions and contradictions. Where such maladroitness seems scribal rather than authorial, 'the loans' from *Ágrip* were not to be found in the **Oldest Morkinskinna*. The main point, however, is that they are not in *Fagrskinna*. Nevertheless, Bjarni was not quite in step with Indrebø in determining what narrative material represents a 'borrowing' from *Ágrip*, in that he identified many more interpolations than Indrebø had done.[36]

Returning to these issues in a 1939 essay,[37] Indrebø noted that while Bjarni had made a good case for the borrowings from *Ágrip* as 'secondary interpolations', he had stopped short in his conclusions about the difference between the **Oldest Morkinskinna* and the extant saga. Indrebø was convinced that it should be possible to remove the secondary material from the extant saga and identify its original core, but declared this to be a project for a later day.[38] Turning his attention to the **Oldest Morkin-*

35 Ibid., p. 158.
36 *Om de norske kongers sagaer*, pp. 137–51. Compare Indrebø, 'Aagrip,' pp. 25–40.
37 Indrebø, 'Nokre merknader til den norröne kongesoga,' pp. 63–64.
38 Ibid., p. 62.

skinna, Indrebø took the beginning of the extant saga, in which several contradictions were apparent, as an example of how a close reading can help distinguish between original and interpolated material.[39] There were, for example, two contradictory ideas about the circumstances of Magnús's return to Norway, which became a cornerstone of Indrebø's conjectures.[40]

Though Indrebø regarded Bjarni Aðalbjarnarson as too cautious in classifying *þættir* as interpolations, he himself said almost nothing about the *þættir* in *Morkinskinna*, except for the tale of Karl the Luckless, which, he believed, does not belong in the **Oldest Morkinskinna*.[41] He made no attempt to explore this further, however; he did not explain what he meant by 'semi-independent entities'; and he spoke warily about problems and uncertainties. Indrebø believed that if the interpolations were left out, *Morkinskinna* would make more sense and also be a better saga – the work of an author and not a jumble created by a scribe.[42] He argued that the **Oldest Morkinskinna* might perhaps more appropriately be called *Ur-Fagrskinna*, because it was so unlike the extant *Morkinskinna*, and he considered that saga to be an 'original work' rather than a 'compilation'.[43] Herein lies his main disagreement with Finnur Jónsson. Bjarni Aðalbjarnarson had, like Finnur, assumed that older sagas lay behind *Morkinskinna*. While Indrebø did not deny this possibility, he emphasised the absence of admissible evidence.[44] In Indrebø's opinion the **Oldest Morkinskinna*, the work of one author, had little in common with the extant *Morkinskinna*.

These exchanges between Finnur Jónsson, Indrebø and Bjarni Aðalbjarnarson left several loose ends. Indrebø thought that *Morkinskinna* deserved to be treated as an independent saga, and in this view the critical

---

39 For discussion, see ibid., pp. 63–71.
40 *Forteljingi no i Mork. er soleis heller ihopp-lappa. Og samanstöypingi hev tydeleg valda vanskar. Ymis sjölvmotsegjing og ujamnskap stend att til minne um det. Mork. no grunngjev soleis på tvo ulike måtar at nordmennene for til Gardarike* (Ibid., 70) 'The present narrative of *Morkinskinna* is very patchy. And linking of the sections has clearly not been without its problems. Various contradictions and unevenness attest to this. *Morkinskinna* in its present form has two versions of how the Norsemen went to Gardariki'.
41 Ibid., p. 72.
42 Ibid.
43 Ibid., pp. 72–76.
44 Ibid., p. 76.

consensus was on his side.[45] No one followed up the suggestion of both Finnur and Bjarni in searching for independent tales behind the saga. On the other hand, both Finnur and Bjarni clearly assumed the existence of interpolations; in this matter Bjarni had many doubts, Finnur had none, and Indrebø had, after all, discussed only one episode in detail – the arrival of Magnús the Good in Norway.

Indrebø realised more than anyone that considerable research was needed and urged others to scrutinise the origins of the saga closely. In his edition of *Heimskringla* Bjarni appears to draw closer to Indrebø's position. He comments on the **Oldest Morkinskinna*: '*Fagrskinna* must to some extent be the best representative of the saga, but it has by no means preserved all of its substance'.[46] It is hard to tell from this remark whether he is questioning his earlier conclusion that both *Fagrskinna* and the extant *Morkinskinna* differ in various ways from the text in the **Oldest Morkinskinna*. However, he clearly believed that not enough pertinent research had been undertaken: 'Scholars have tried to clarify how *Morkinskinna* originated and what changes it has undergone – but much remains to be done'.[47]

Few new studies dealing with the origins of *Morkinskinna* were published in the years immediately after 1940. Scholarly interest in kings' sagas, apart from *Heimskringla*, declined, and exploration of their development came to a virtual standstill, although most of the controversial issues relating to the origins of *Morkinskinna* remained unresolved. In 1968, however, Alfred Jakobsen closely examined the relationship between *Fagrskinna* and *Morkinskinna*. He considered it by no means impossible that the redactor of *Morkinskinna* had omitted material mentioned in *Fagrskinna* and cautioned against drawing too many conclusions from relatively unimportant stylistic features, as Indrebø had also done.

---

45 The idea of 'independent sagas' has not been well received (Eyvind Fjeld Halvorsen, 'Fagrskinna,' pp. 139–40; Finn Hødnebø, 'Morkinskinna,' pp. 703–704; Jonna Louis-Jensen, 'Morkinskinna,' pp. 419–420; Theodore M. Andersson, 'King's Sagas (*Konungasögur*),' pp. 197–238, 218–220, 223, 226; Sverrir Tómasson, 'Konungasögur,' pp. 383–386).

46 Bjarni Aðalbjarnarson, ed. *Heimskringla* III, ÍF 28, p. v.

47 Ibid. On the sources of *Morkinskinna*, see Theodore M. Andersson and Kari Ellen Gade (*Morkinskinna*, pp. 11–65) and Ármann Jakobsson and Þórður Ingi Guðjónsson (*Msk.* I, pp. xxxiv–xxxviii).

Textual comparison led him to conclude that some elements in *Fagrskinna* had been borrowed from *Morkinskinna* and subsequently shortened. Jakobsen also agreed with Finnur Jónsson that in *Morkinskinna* the language is more comprehensively archaic than that in *Fagrskinna* and thought it likely that the younger version would have had a more modern linguistic profile.[48] Jakobsen's analysis thus serves to strengthen Indrebø's important conclusion that *Morkinskinna* is older than *Fagrskinna*.[49]

Following this, Heinrich Gimmler eventually took up the subject of the *þættir* in *Morkinskinna* in his 1972 doctoral dissertation. He sought to identify the *þættir* that had existed independently and had been interpolated into the saga, and to distinguish them from *þættir-ähnliche Stücke* '*þættir*-like entities' that had never existed outside the work. He agreed with Bjarni Aðalbjarnarson that not everything loosely connected to the 'main saga' need be thought of as an interpolation and claimed that Finnur Jónsson went too far in regarding all such material as interpolated. Gimmler, like Bjarni, assumed that there had been *þættir* and 'þættir-like' matter in the **Oldest Morkinskinna* but did not agree with him about how many of the saga's *þættir* were interpolations, identifying twelve independent *þættir* to Bjarni's sixteen.[50]

In 1977 Jonna Louis-Jensen offered the first detailed comparative investigation of GKS 1009 fol and other manuscripts in which the *Morkinskinna* text appears – that is, the younger part of *Flateyjarbók*, *Hulda* and *Hrokkinskinna* and the manuscript fragments AM 325 IV β 4to and AM 325 XI 3 4to.[51] She had previously argued that these fragments were remnants of an earlier manuscript of the more recent part of *Flateyjarbók*. Louis-Jensen's research marks a turning point in *Morkinskinna* scholarship. The earlier conjectures had all been based on the relationships between *Morkinskinna* and other kings' sagas, especially *Ágrip* and *Fagrskinna*. She correctly points out, however, that despite the stu-

---

48 Alfred Jakobsen, 'Om forholdet mellom Fagrskinna og Morkinskinna.'
49 Later Bjarni Einarsson (*Fagrskinna*, pp. ci–cxix) assumed that the author of *Fagrskinna* had often drawn on the narrative in *Morkinskinna*. We will return to his conclusions later.
50 Gimmler, *Die Thættir der Morkinskinna*, pp. 44–66. Gimmler expressed no view as to when individual *þættir* were interpolated into the text.
51 Louis-Jensen, *Kongesagastudier*, pp. 62–108.

dies by Indrebø, Bjarni Aðalbjarnarson and others, 'ÆMsk. [the *Oldest Morkinskinna] is an entity with quite vague contours'.[52] The most detailed previous examination had been Bjarni Aðalbjarnarson's essay about 'the borrowings' from Ágrip, but Louis-Jensen rightly observed that establishing 'any hard and firm delineation of interpolation boundaries is scarcely possible, and that Bjarni Aðalbjarnarson by no means claimed that his list was definitive'.[53] The same uncertainty applies to the þættir, and even Indrebø assumed that some of them were part of the *Oldest Morkinskinna. For Louis-Jensen the chief arguments in favour of regarding the þættir as interpolations were their loose connection to the plot, their 'contradictory' characterisations of kings with respect to the saga as a whole, and possible stylistic differences between þættir and the body of the saga. Although she also pointed out the need for a stylistic study of the differences between þættir and the 'main saga', she accepted these arguments by and large, although they are not based on comparison with other texts.[54]

On the other hand, Louis-Jensen sought to re-examine Finnur Jónsson's important claim that six þættir did not occur in the younger part of Flateyjarbók or had been changed greatly in that version. By comparing Hulda and Hrokkinskinna she showed that these þættir had been included in a common original text, used by GKS 1009 fol and by the younger part of Flateyjarbók, to which she assigned the title '*Msk 2', that is, Morkinskinna with þættir and other 'interpolations'.[55] Louis-Jensen established the following stemma, where MskMs signifies GKS 1009 fol, Yflb Flateyjarbók, *H the forerunner of both Hulda and Hrokkinskinna, and 325 two later manuscript fragments:

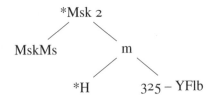

52 Ibid., p. 68.
53 Ibid., p. 68, note 6.
54 Ibid., p. 69, note 12.
55 Ibid., pp. 77–78.

All of the extant versions of the *Morkinskinna* text may be traced back to *Msk 2.[56]

This analysis confirms, in fact, that it is impossible to decide by textual comparison what material in the *Morkinskinna* manuscript was not present in the *Oldest Morkinskinna*. Louis-Jensen, like Indrebø before her, focused closely on the opening of *Morkinskinna* and concluded that in this section there were more 'internal contradictions' in *Msk 2 than Indrebø had assumed, and that the redactor of the younger parts of *Flateyjarbók* or the next primary source had resolved them. Louis-Jensen saw this as 'additional support' for Indrebø's opinion that 'Karls þáttr vesæla' was never part of the *Oldest Morkinskinna*.[57] However, she assumed that the later redactors occasionally resolved contradictions and repetitions, whereas Finnur Jónsson and Indrebø had both seen the contradictions and repetitions as signs of the relative youth of the text. Louis-Jensen agreed with them in regarding the inconsistencies in *Msk 2 as confirmation that 'Karls þáttr' is an interpolation, but nevertheless demonstrated that in a younger version the number of inconsistencies decreased.

Although Louis-Jensen agrees with Indrebø's hypotheses, her views nevertheless appear to undermine their premises in two ways. Firstly, her position challenges the arguments of scholars who claim that the *þættir* absent from or much changed in the later part of *Flateyjarbók* could not have been in the original *Morkinskinna*. Secondly, she shows how the inconsistencies are eliminated as the text developed. It is not possible to consider them as positive evidence in favour of assigning a late date to the text.[58] Louis-Jensen notes that in *Hulda-Hrokkinskinna* there are more changes in the *Morkinskinna* text than in the *Heimskringla* text and wonders whether this could mean that, unlike the *Heimskringla* text, the *Morkinskinna* text was constantly being revised. No clear conclusion emerges, however, as she believes that textual-based evidence is lacking. She also notes that the compiler of *Hulda-Hrokkinskinna* may have regarded the *Heimskringla* text more highly and was thus more inclined to follow it faithfully.[59]

---

56 Ibid., pp. 70–108.
57 Ibid., pp. 78–82.
58 Compare Andersson and Gade, *Morkinskinna*, pp. 13–14 and 24.
59 *Kongesagastudier*, pp. 150–152.

Louis-Jensen's analysis focuses primarily on the later versions of the *Morkinskinna* text, but ultimately adds little to Indrebø's view regarding the development of *Morkinskinna* before the time of 1009. Her main conclusion is that all extant *Morkinskinna* texts derive from the version that she calls '*Msk 2*', texts with 'borrowings' from *Ágrip*, *þættir* and other 'interpolations' in the *Oldest Morkinskinna*. This conclusion is very important for an understanding of the origins of *Morkinskinna*, for it shifts the burden of proof over to those who assume radical changes from the *Oldest Morkinskinna* to the other extant versions of the text.[60]

The argument for interpolations

After the long debate summarised above, all attempts to resolve the inherent difficulties have ended in uncertainty. Scholars have never been in agreement about the extent of the interpolations in *Morkinskinna* and over the years this uncertainty has increased. More recently scholars have quietly begun to turn away from Indrebø's view that the *Oldest Morkinskinna* more closely resembled *Fagrskinna* than *Morkinskinna*. In his 1985 comparison of *Morkinskinna* and *Fagrskinna*, Bjarni Einarsson, although never completely making up his mind about Indrebø's ideas, chose the *Morkinskinna* text in 1009 rather than *Fagrskinna* as the best textual representative of the *Oldest Morkinskinna*. He thus *de facto* rejected the view that *Fagrskinna* is a better representative of the *Oldest Morkinskinna*. Bjarni believed that the author of *Fagrskinna* omitted much from his *Oldest Morkinskinna* source,[61] and assumed that some of the material regarded by others as having been interpolated was already present in the *Oldest Morkinskinna*.[62] He also assumed that *þættir* were a part of this

---

60 See Andersson and Gade, *Morkinskinna*, p. 14.

61 Bjarni Einarsson, *Fagrskinna*, pp. ci–cxix. He maintains that the author of *Fagrskinna* has 'yfirleitt stytt mikið' (in general shortened the work a great deal) (p. cii).

62 Commenting on some *þættir* about Haraldr the Severe, Bjarni remarks: *Þó er þess að gæta að höf. Fagrskinnu hefur víða stytt frásögn fyrirmyndarinnar* (Ibid., p. cvi) 'It must however be noted that the author of *Fagrskinna* has shortened the narrative of his source'. The author of *Fagrskinna* must also have omitted 'Sveinka þáttr' (ibid., p. cxiii). Already in his *To skjaldesagaer: En analyse af Kormáks saga og Hallfreðar saga* (pp. 27, 36–37) Bjarni seemed to assume that there were many *þættir* in the version of *Morkinskinna* that was in existence by 1230.

work. Bjarni's comparison also showed that not only *Morkinskinna* but also *Fagrskinna* are sometimes in agreement with *Ágrip*. Bjarni's conclusions thus contradicted Indrebø's views in many respects, principally by challenging the importance of *Fagrskinna* as a source for the **Oldest Morkinskinna*.

Few ventured to discuss the **Oldest Morkinskinna* until the end of the twentieth century, but then a sceptical movement emerged in which the present author has played his part.[63] Before that, *Morkinskinna* was already examined by scholars who were neutral with regard to the question of its origins. As Marianne Kalinke puts it: 'The purpose of this inquiry is neither to determine the character of the "original" *Morkinskinna* nor to distinguish between the original composition and later accretions and interpolations, but rather to assess the art of *Morkinskinna* in the form

63 Several scholars (for example, Tommy Danielsson, 'Magnús berfættrs sista strid,' p. 68) point out that the arguments of Indrebø (and many others) in favour of interpolations were made in context of problematic notions about the role of an author. Odd Sandaaker has suggested, firstly, that *Morkinskinna* may have already taken its present form by the third decade of the thirteenth century; and, secondly, that this version, with 'interpolations' from *Ágrip,* was used as a source for *Heimskringla* (Odd Sandaaker, 'Ágrip og Morkinskinna: Teksthistoriske randnotar'). Sandaaker develops his theory with reference to a very complex stemma that does not shed much light on the matter. It is worth noting, however, that doubt is cast on the notion that the 'borrowings' from *Ágrip* were not present in the **Oldest Morkinskinna*, especially as these are the 'interpolations' that have attracted most scholarly attention.

   And Andersson and others have suggested that the *þættir* should not be regarded as alien presences within the saga: Andersson, 'The Unity of Morkinskinna'; Andersson and Gade (*Morkinskinna*, p. 13) point out that the idea that *þættir* are interpolations assumes that 'interpolation became epidemic in *Morkinskinna* manuscripts but that this epidemic spared the manuscript traditions of *Fagrskinna* and *Heimskringla* during the same period.' Andersson had previously implied this without being so explicit ('The Politics of Snorri Sturluson,' p. 59, note 9). Prior to *Staður í nýjum heimi*, the present author took a similar position on several occasions: *Í leit að konungi: Konungsmynd íslenskra konungasagna*, pp. 30–34; 'Konge og undersåt i Morkinskinna'; 'King and Subject in Morkinskinna'; 'Rundt om kongen: En genvurdering af Morkinskinna'; 'Royal pretenders and faithful retainers: The Icelandic vision of kingship in transition'; 'The Individual and the Ideal: The Representation of Royalty in Morkinskinna'; 'Kongesagaen som forsvandt: Nyere kongesagastudier med særligt henblik på Morkinskinna'; 'Um uppruna Morkinskinnu: Drög að rannsóknarsögu'; 'Strukturelle Brüche in der Morkinskinna'; 'The Amplified Saga: Structural Disunity in Morkinskinna.'

transmitted to us'.[64] *Morkinskinna*, rather than its *þættir*, is here discussed as an organic whole. Moreover, when *Morkinskinna* is now discussed, attention is directed to the extant text rather than to the putative **Oldest Morkinskinna*.

It is, of course, possible to discuss *Morkinskinna* without taking a position on the origins and age of the text. Those who speak of it as a unified and authored work assume one of two things: that *Morkinskinna* existed in 1220 in more or less its present form or that the **Oldest Morkinskinna* differed substantially from the extant version. In the latter case it would be more reasonable to believe that *Morkinskinna* in its present form is in part the work of one or more author(s), who interpolated the *þættir* and other material between 1220 and 1280, and, also, that it is perhaps a work deriving from the later part of the thirteenth century. Those who engage with *Morkinskinna* need to be clear as to which point of view they are following. It is necessary to identify and evaluate the premises upon which the discussion of the origins of *Morkinskinna* has been based.

The arguments used in the discussion of the origins of *Morkinskinna* have been of several kinds. At first it was considered possible to rely on textual comparison, using *Flateyjarbók* as evidence. The work of Jonna Louis-Jensen, however, has shown that the *Morkinskinna* texts in the younger part of *Flateyjarbók* and in *Hulda-Hrokkinskinna* are insufficiently independent for conclusions to be drawn about the differences between the **Oldest Morkinskinna* and the extant *Morkinskinna*.[65] It was, not least, all of these conclusions that made it necessary to reassess such issues. However, it seems important that such conclusions are extended beyond earlier theoretical parameters rather than merely refining previous conjectures. The burden of proof must be redirected in order to ask: what material in the extant *Morkinskinna* was in all likelihood not included in the **Oldest Morkinskinna*?[66] Otherwise we are constrained by guiding

---

64 Kalinke, 'Sigurðar saga Jórsalafara: The Fictionalization of Fact in Morkinskinna,' pp. 152–153.

65 Louis-Jensen, *Kongesagastudier*, pp. 62–108.

66 As Andersson and Gade put it (*Morkinskinna*, p. 14): 'This observation [that is, Louis-Jensen's conclusions] substantially alters the likelihood of wholesale interpolations in *Morkinskinna* and places the onus of proof on those who hold to the idea of interpolation.'

principles, like those mentioned in the preceding discussion, based upon premises that are no longer valid.

There remains the possibility of comparison between *Morkinskinna* and other kings' sagas, such as *Fagrskinna*. Indrebø built his conjectures about the **Oldest Morkinskinna* on his sense of the aesthetic achievement of these works. Jakobsen later adduced significantly better arguments for believing that *Morkinskinna* was the source of *Fagrskinna* but offered no new support for Indrebø's conjectures about what material in the 1009 text had not been present in the **Oldest Morkinskinna*. Nor did Louis-Jensen provide any such support, concentrating instead on the more recent texts. Bjarni Einarsson compared *Fagrskinna* and *Morkinskinna* and, as noted above, seems to have imagined an **Oldest Morkinskinna* that more closely resembled the text in 1009 than Indrebø had assumed.

The most important aspect of Bjarni Einarsson's position is that it confirms that textual comparison with *Fagrskinna* offers little help in drawing conclusions about the material in the **Oldest Morkinskinna*. *Morkinskinna*, *Fagrskinna* and *Heimskringla* are independent kings' sagas, composed for different reasons and informed by different aesthetic priorities. Thus it is of little or no significance if several episodes of *Morkinskinna* do not occur in *Fagrskinna* and *Heimskringla*, since these omissions may simply be the result of the differing attitudes of three individual authors towards the narrative utility of *exempla*.

Conjectures about the contents of the **Oldest Morkinskinna* have only partly been based on external evidence, that is, textual comparison with other manuscripts. Internal evidence has played a key role, by which we mean the examination of whatever material has seemed best and most logically to blend in with the whole saga and to have a clear purpose. Arguments in support of the notion that particular material has been added later prove most often to be of this nature.

'Borrowings' from *Ágrip* have been the most frequently discussed. It has been assumed that passages in *Morkinskinna* that echo *Ágrip* were interpolated after the composition of *Fagrskinna*, since these passages are rarely to be found in that work. Bjarni Aðalbjarnarson examined these passages.[67] Altogether he identified forty-three places in *Morkinskinna*

---

67 Indrebø, *Fagrskinna*, pp. 22–31 and 34–43; Bjarni Aðalbjarnarson, *Om de norske*

that show clear similarities with *Ágrip*, along with six more questionable instances. Indrebø and Bjarni were not in complete agreement about all of these 'borrowings'; in Indrebø's lengthiest discussion of this matter, his demarcation lines for identifying interpolations are often rather differently drawn.[68]

In order to sense the difficulties faced by those attempting to determine the similarities between *Ágrip* and *Morkinskinna*, it may be useful to examine some of the passages that have been highlighted in the discussion. The following passage is an example of a 'borrowing' from *Ágrip*:

> En þá er guð tók at birta jartegnum um inn helga Óláf, þá réðusk bǫztu menn til at fara ór landi at sœkja Magnús, son ins helga Óláfs, því at menn fundu misræði sín ok iðruðusk ok vildu þá þat bœta á syni hans, er þeir hǫfðu á sjálfum hónum brotit.[69]

> But when God decided to send the signs about the holy Óláfr, then noble men resolved to leave the country to fetch Magnús, the son of Óláfr helgi "the saint", since they realized their mistakes and repented and then wanted to atone to his son for the wrongs they had committed against him.

Morkinskinna reads, on the other hand:

> Í þenna tíma lét guð mjǫk birtask helgi ins heilaga Óláfs konungs, ok sáu þá margir satt mál um sína hagi ok fundu nú misræði sitt ok glœp þann er þeir hǫfðu gǫrt ok þóttusk nú þann veg helzt mega sýna at bœta þat nú á syni hans er þeir hǫfðu á sjálfum honum misgjǫrt (*Msk.* I, 18).

> At that time God revealed the sanctity of the holy King Óláfr, and then many saw the truth about their situation and realized their mistakes and the crimes they had committed

kongers sagaer, pp. 137–151. Andersson and Gade (*Morkinskinna*, pp. 12–13) regard Bjarni's arguments as convincing.

68 Indrebø, 'Aagrip,' 25–40.

69 *Ágrip af Nóregskonunga sǫgum*, ed. Bjarni Einarsson ÍF 29, p. 32.

and now it seemed to them best to atone before his son those
misdeeds they had committed against him.

For all the inevitable differences, the similarities in wording between the
texts are obvious, some of them indeed striking, as with the rare word
misræði. In *Fagrskinna* there is no corresponding text.

Then again, at one point in *Ágrip* we find:

> Ok raufsk þing þat með ⟨þeima⟩ hætti, at konungr bað alla
> menn finnask þar um morgininn. Ok fannsk þá í hans orð-
> um, at guð hafði skipt skapi hans, ok var þá freka snúin til
> miskunnar, hét ǫllum mǫnnum gœzku ok efndi sem hann
> hét eða betr.[70]

> And the assembly broke up in that way, and the king asked
> everyone to assemble there the next morning. And it showed
> then in his words that God had changed his mind, and turned
> then from severity to mercy, promised everyone kindness
> and kept his promises or better.

At this point *Morkinskinna* reads:

> Ok með þessum hætti var slitit þinginu þann dag, ok bað
> konungr þar alla finnask um morgininn eptir. Ok þóttusk
> menn þá finna í orðum konungs at Guð hafði þá mýkt skap
> hans, ok var þá freku snúit til miskunnar. Ok annan dag
> undruðu menn er konungr var þá svá linr, ok váru þá mjúk-
> ar tǫlur til landsmanna og svá til Þrœnda sem annarra. Hét
> konungr þá ǫllum mǫnnum gœzku ok friði ok efndi þat æ
> betr (*Msk.* I, 42).

> And in that way the assembly was broken up for the day,
> and the king asked everyone to assemble the next morn-
> ing. And men seemed to feel in the king's words that God
> had changed his mind, and had turned from severity to
> mercy. And the next day men were astonished then when

70 Ibid., p. 33.

the king was so agreeable, and spoke softly to the people of the country and the *Þrændur* [those from *Þrændalǫg*, now *Trøndelag*] as others. The king then promised everyone kindness and freedom and kept it or better.

Here the wording is very similar, even though the *Morkinskinna* passage is much longer. In addition, in *Ágrip* the corresponding phrases are juxtaposed, whereas in *Morkinskinna* there are longer clauses between them.

In the vast majority of instances the resemblances between *Ágrip* and *Morkinskinna* amount to not more than a sentence (or less), but in a few other instances the similarities extend over longer stretches. In all, this material represents about ten pages in the Íslenzk fornrit edition of *Morkinskinna*. One of the longest texts is the account of the origins of the kingdom of Magnús berfœttr 'Barelegs' and Hákon Magnússon. Here the *Morkinskinna* text recalls that of *Ágrip* in parts, even if the wording differs: for example, the same adjectives and verbs are not always employed.[71] The same applies to the account of the reign of Óláfr kyrri 'the Quiet', to be discussed later; there Óláfr helgi 'the Saint' is variously said to be 'a kinsman' of Óláfr the Quiet or his 'father's brother'.[72] This 'borrowing' is worded differently.

Although there is little doubt that *Ágrip* and *Morkinskinna* are textually related, it remains unresolved as to why this might be so. Indrebø sensed a 'remarkable consistency' in the absence in *Fagrskinna* of material from the other two texts.[73] This does not in itself prove that they are interpolations or that they were not in the **Oldest Morkinskinna*, since Indrebø thought that both sagas were used by the author of *Fagrskinna*.[74] *Fagrskinna* is so much shorter than *Morkinskinna* that its textual omissions should come as no surprise, as Bjarni Einarsson's comparison of the two works shows.[75] Thus it can hardly be surprising that the quotations cited

71 Ibid., pp. 42–43; *Msk.* II, 16–17.
72 *Ágrip*, ed. Bjarni Einarsson, 40–41; *Msk.* II, 10.
73 Indrebø, *Fagrskinna*, 22.
74 Indrebø, *Fagrskinna*, 28, 34–43.
75 Bjarni Einarsson, *Fagrskinna*, pp. ci–cxix. Compare the appendix in Andersson and Gade's *Morkinskinna* edition (pp. 497–511). We may note that all the material from *Morkinskinna* (569 pages in the Íslenzk fornrit edition) is contained in 166 pages in the same edition of *Fagrskinna*.

above are also omitted in *Fagrskinna*. We should note that there is considerable uncertainty as to which phrases are 'borrowings' from *Ágrip* or how they should be identified and demarcated.[76] There has never been any scholarly agreement on this point.

Comparison with *Fagrskinna* thus plays a significant role in the conclusion that these 'borrowings' were not in the **Oldest Morkinskinna*. But Bjarni Aðalbjarnarson also thought it important that this same material created contradictions and clumsiness.[77] We may ask, however, what evidence suggests such clumsiness. Authors may have been no less prone to mistakes than scribes, and clumsiness of this kind – if that is what it is – is not the same thing as scribal error. It seems problematic to base conjectures about origins on alleged clumsiness alone, because of the subjective nature of the judgements involved. For example, among other elements identified as clumsy, is the introduction of the *Bersǫglisvísur* into the *Morkinskinna* narrative. In *Ágrip*, at a meeting in Niðarós, the king behaves somewhat unyieldingly to the Þrændur until a man named Atli stands up and says, *Svá skorpnar skór at fœti mér, at ek má eigi ór stað komask;*[78] 'So tight are the shoes on my feet that I cannot move from this place'. Sigvatr then recites the verses, the *Bersǫglisvísur*. In *Morkinskinna*, on the other hand, Sigvatr's recitation occurs earlier, in response to which the king keeps himself under control despite having *mikit í skapi* (*Msk.* I, 42) 'strong feelings'. He then holds the assembly, and Atli makes his famous remarks. Several though by no means all scholars have found this version of events awkwardly recounted.

We can thus say that considerable uncertainty remains as to whether these *Morkinskinna* 'borrowings' from *Ágrip* are scribal interpolations or authorial augmentations. A comparison with *Fagrskinna* is of limited evidential value; it reveals that the author of *Morkinskinna* has sometimes retained the *Ágrip* wording whereas the *Fagrskinna* author has changed it. Thereafter all that remains is the internal evidence and that is not robust enough to sustain conjectures. And yet these passages from *Ágrip* consti-

---

76 Compare Louis-Jensen, *Kongesagastudier*, p. 68, note 6.
77 Andersson and Gade (*Morkinskinna*, p. 12) agree: 'His analysis shows that the interpolations often produced an awkward text in *Morkinskinna*.'
78 *Ágrip*, ed. Bjarni Einarson, p. 32.

tute the additions that have been most often discussed. This discussion, however, has not resolved the difficulties – rather the reverse.

The arguments relating to clumsiness are important for those scholars who assume that the 'borrowings' from *Ágrip* are interpolations – that is, they were not present in the **Oldest Morkinskinna* – rather than the result of the *Fagrskinna* author having simply omitted them as he did with so much other material from *Morkinskinna*. Bjarni Aðalbjarnarson calls attention to 'compositional mistakes', that is, repetitions, breaches in taste, clumsiness and contradictions. Looking for 'mistakes' of this kind in *Morkinskinna* has been the chief method of determining whether particular material was present in the **Oldest Morkinskinna*, as with 'Karls þáttr' at the beginning, the narrative of the arrival of Haraldr the Severe in Norway, the account of the death of Magnús the Good, the 'Þinga saga' (an account in *Msk.*, LXXVI of a dispute between the brothers King Eysteinn and King Sigurðr Magnússon) or the loans from *Ágrip*. Here, at first sight, the same methodology as that used in textual criticism appears to be employed, in that errors in a particular manuscript can be used by scholars to arrive at an understanding of relationships between manuscripts. But the method is very different in nature.

When a textual contradiction is used as evidence for interpolation, it is clearly necessary to define what we mean by *contradiction*. This can often prove to be difficult. Indrebø selected the account of the arrival of Magnús the Good in Norway as an example in support of his conjectures about the interpolations.[79] Included in this account is the episode about Karl the Luckless, which neither Gimmler nor Bjarni Aðalbjarnarson regarded as an *Íslendinga þáttr*.[80] Although this tale exists in an independent form (in AM 533 4to and AM 557 4to) that is thought to derive from *Morkinskinna*, the two manuscript versions are dissimilar in style.[81] Finnur Jónsson, Indrebø and Jonna Louis-Jensen were all in agreement that this episode was

---

79 Indrebø, 'Nokre merknader til den norröne kongesoga,' 63–71.

80 Bjarni Aðalbjarnarson, *Om de norske kongers sagaer*, p. 158; Gimmler, *Die Thættir der Morkinskinna*, p. 63. Karl is, of course, not an Icelander.

81 Finnur Jónsson (*Morkinskinna*, p. x), Bjarni Aðalbjarnarson (*Om de norske kongers sagaer*, p. 159) and Louis-Jensen (*Kongesagastudier*, p. 80, note 34) all thought that it derived from the episode in *Morkinskinna*.

not present in the **Oldest Morkinskinna*.[82] The argument supporting this
conclusion is that the two episodes differ as to how Magnús the Good
was summoned to Norway. It was first stated that his foster-father King
Jarizleifr sent a message to the Norwegian chieftains urging Magnús' return, but later we are told that the king was reluctant to allow Magnús
to go. This difference has been considered a 'contradiction', and Louis-
Jensen noted its elimination from the more recent part of *Flateyjarbók* or
its immediate source.[83] However, these scribal changes in younger versions of the *Morkinskinna* text prove nothing about interpolations. On the
contrary, they merely show that, for whatever reason, scribes sometimes
make changes in the texts they are copying, something that no textual
scholar has ever doubted. And they are also a reminder that changes in
a text are not always made in order to resolve contradictions; there can be
many other reasons.[84]

In fact, we are not really dealing with a clear contradiction at all.
In the extant *Morkinskinna* text King Jarizleifr sends men to Norway to
build up support for his foster-son Magnús, but when Einarr þambarskelfir
'Paunch-Shaker' and other chieftains come to Jarizleifr's court petitioning
that Magnús should become king in Norway, the reluctant Jarizleifr evades
the question. The king's conduct may be contradictory, but people do not
always behave as might be expected. When the time comes for the young
prince's departure, it is of course difficult for the king and the queen to see
their foster-son leave, even though they themselves have been instrumental
in initiating his departure. It may also be that the couple are simply clever

---

82 While Andersson and Gade (*Morkinskinna*, p. 24) consider the arguments that this
    episode is an interpolation to be reasonably strong, they add that 'even these cases
    may be subject to doubt.' Other possible solutions are then identified (*Morkinskinna*,
    p. 419). Finnur Jónsson ('Indledning,' p. x) regarded 'Karls þáttr' as *romantisk ... og
    mulig er det hele opdigtet* 'romantic [...] and it is possible that it is entirely fictional'.
    And because only that which is factual can be original, 'Karls þáttr' must therefore
    be an interpolation.

83 Louis-Jensen, *Kongesagastudier*, pp. 79–82. Compare Finnur Jónsson, *Morkinskinna*,
    pp. x–xi; Indrebø, *Fagrskinna*, p. 31; Indrebø, 'Nokre merknader til den norröne
    kongesaga,' p. 68.

84 Finnur Jónsson would no doubt have objected to this, since for him the event itself
    was the only true 'original text.' The oldest text usually was closest to the historical
    event and was therefore the 'truest'; see Ármann Jakobsson, 'Den kluntede afskriver.'

politicians, anxious to secure powerful support for their foster-son in Norway. In any event this reluctance causes Einarr Paunch-Shaker, backed by twelve men chosen by the king and queen, to swear allegiance to Magnús, though this had not been his intention.[85] We must thus distinguish between apparent contradictions in the behaviour of a character, which may be explicable in terms of the writer's craft, and real contradictions that impact at the level of plot.

It is in fact unclear what such 'contradictions' prove. It has been assumed that so-called contradictions of this kind, because they are regarded as 'clumsy', are scribal rather than authorial. On the other hand, even scribes sometimes remove such alleged discrepancies from their exemplars. The search for contradictions in the text thus becomes an extension of the search for scribal errors. There is, however, a major difference, and the 'errors' differ in their very nature. Textual scholars have warned against treating factual errors and alleged interpolations as if they were scribal errors, and also against regarding the apparent lack of clear meaning in a scene as an error.[86] We should recall a principle of textual criticism known as the *lectio difficilior* 'the more difficult reading', whereby, given the choice of two readings, the more difficult one is often the more trustworthy.[87] It is by no means certain that a thirteenth-century mindset will always agree with scholarly perspectives from the nineteenth, twentieth and twenty-first centuries. For all of these reasons analysis of substantive contradictions can be highly problematic with regard to the discussion of textual relationships.

Indrebø also mentions that the style of *Morkinskinna* is far from uniform. He seems to be referring, firstly, to the more limited use of the historic present in the younger part of the work and, secondly, to the narrator's use of first person plural pronouns in the older part and first person

---

85 Einarr Paunch-Shaker's claim (*Msk.* I, 20) that it ill befits a king to change his mind points to the recognition on the part of the *Morkinskinna* author that the king's behaviour is inconsistent. This is very different to inconsistencies created by scribal clumsiness.

86 Winfried Woesler, 'Hvordan tekstfejl opstår og udbedres,' pp. 10 and 28.

87 Compare the readings of Ólafur Halldórsson ('Morgunverk Guðrúnar Ósvífursdóttur,' pp. 125–128, and Louis-Jensen ('A Good Day's Work: *Laxdæla saga*, ch. 49,' pp. 267–281) of Guðrún Ósvífursdóttir's famous words concerning her morning tasks.

singular pronouns in the younger when offering personal observations. Indrebø also suggests that the use of particles, or uninflected words, in the older part of the work differs from their use in the younger part.[88] Most of these are small matters, whose applicability is uncertain, and other scholars have made no attempt to determine whether they are correct.

Nevertheless, other scholars have also sought to examine stylistic evidence. Jón Helgason suggests that 'Hreiðars þáttr' exhibits a highly distinctive style, but that is no reason to believe that it was not present in the *Oldest Morkinskinna*. Peter Hallberg points out that use of the historic present occurs least in the section of the work based on *Hryggjarstykki – a now lost kings' saga that is actually cited in the work.[89] This seems to indicate that sometimes the style of *Morkinskinna* is influenced by its sources, but it says little about the development of the saga after 1220, though ultimately, as Louis-Jensen notes, a fully satisfactory stylistic analysis of the overall text is still lacking.[90] Though it might be possible to define variations in style between individual episodes in the work, such variations reveal relatively little about the differences between the authors or about whether the episodes are interpolations.

The main goal in any such stylistic analysis is to decide which features are important. It has been noted that different kinds of narrative by the same author may create more stylistic differences than may be evident in two texts by separate authors. It is, for example, difficult to draw secure conclusions from the use of the historic present, since the subject matters of the texts may exert more influence on style than the identity of the author. It also seems unwise to divide a text like *Morkinskinna* into parts and

---

88 Indrebø, *Fagrskinna*, pp. 16–17.

89 Peter Hallberg, 'Hryggjarstykki: Några anteckningar,' pp. 113–121.

90 Louis-Jensen, *Kongesagastudier*, p. 69, note 12. Concerning the *þættir,* she notes: 'endelig er det ikke udelukket at der kan påvises stilistiske forskelle mellem de enkelte *þættir* og grundstammen in værket' ('finally it is not impossible that stylistic differences between the individual *þættir* and the nucleus of the work can be demonstrated'). Research of this kind has not yet been undertaken. Jakobsen ('Om Fagrskinna-forfatteren,' p. 120, note 41) regarded the *þættir* as archaic in style: 'Mange av tættene i Mork. viser alderdommelige språkdrag. De er sannsynligvis avskrifter etter forelegg som stammer fra det 12. århundrede' ('Many of the *þættir* in *Morkinskinna* show archaic linguistic features. They are probably copied from a source dating from the twelfth century').

then to compare stylistic features in those individual sections since there can be significant differences between the beginning, middle and end of the same work by the same author.[91] No convincing arguments based on style have yet been identified that help illuminate the origins of *Morkinskinna*, and it must be considered doubtful that they will emerge in the future.[92]

While scholars were working hard to determine the core and additional elements of *Morkinskinna*, it was also the fashion in Old Icelandic research to search for early sagas that were no longer extant. Scholars of Finnur Jónsson's vintage regarded the texts they investigated as vital linguistic and historical documents rather than as works of art.[93] At the beginning of the twentieth century textual scholars tended to concentrate more on the sources of sagas than on the works themselves. Other texts were postulated – 'older versions' of which the extant texts were thought to be mere reflections. It was not until around 1960 that this approach was challenged by scholars following in the wake of C. S. Lewis and Eugène Vinaver.[94] Although the literary 'partitionist movement'[95] (whose analysis of lengthy works involved breaking them down into their allegedly constituent elements) has the great merit of helping to address questions that had been posed by an earlier generation – and those questions were by no means unimportant – it can become an obstacle to engaging with sagas on their own terms. The present study will suggest that these tendencies were also applied to the study of *Morkinskinna*. At the beginning of the

91 Andrew Queen Morton, *Literary Detection: How to Prove Authorship and Fraud in Literature and Documents*, pp. 95–107. Morton's method has not been applied, so far as I know, in research on Old Icelandic-Norse literature.

92 Andersson and Gade (*Morkinskinna*, pp. 72–74) point to a few examples that may allow us to speak about a single author of *Morkinskinna*, although their evidential value is slight. One of the most striking instances is when twice in the saga (*Msk.* I, 312 and *Msk.* II, 30) a company of men is likened to 'glistening ice,' once in a *þáttr*.

93 Compare Katherine O'Brien O'Keeffe, 'Introduction' in *Reading Old English Texts*, pp. 3–4; Ármann Jakobsson, 'Den kluntede afskriver.'

94 C. S. Lewis, 'The Anthropological Approach,' pp. 219–230; Eugène Vinaver, *The Rise of Romance*, pp. 53–67.

95 The name is of my own invention and is indicative of the philological trends in Old Norse studies during the latter part of the nineteenth century until the rise of the 'Icelandic school' (see note 98). Similar tendencies are apparent in philology pertaining to other cultures during the same period.

twentieth century the application of textual and editorial methodology to the relationship between sagas seemed self-evident. More recently, however, philologists have concentrated in increasing measure on comparing manuscripts rather than the literary texts that they contain.

The search for supposed contradictions in *Morkinskinna* was seen as another method that could separate the textual wheat from the chaff, the original from the subsequent. On the other hand, such analysis has yielded relatively little in terms of identifying the core and additional elements in *Morkinskinna*. Not even the detailed discussions on the Karl the Luckless episode undertaken by Indrebø, Finnur Jónsson and Louis-Jensen have demonstrated unambiguously that it is an interpolation. The same may be said of the 'clumsy' elements from *Ágrip*.

There remains the question of the *Íslendinga þættir*, most of which have been considered interpolations in *Morkinskinna*. Indrebø also thought that many verses had been interpolated into the **Oldest Morkinskinna*, though more recently Andersson and Gade have argued that this notion is unsustainable.[96] Though the verses in *Morkinskinna* have never received much attention in the discussion of interpolations, the *þættir* in *Morkinskinna* have been widely regarded as interpolations, although many scholars have also believed that some *þættir* were present in the **Oldest Morkinskinna*. It is worth recalling that when Finnur Jónsson and Indrebø first advanced their ideas, it had for some time been the fashion to edit *þættir* about Icelanders as separate texts and thus to regard them as independent narratives. This was tantamount to separating them from the 'main saga' and was very much in the spirit of the aforementioned 'literary partitionists'.

It became fashionable in the nineteenth century to deconstruct the Sagas of Icelanders into what were perceived as being their constituent

---

96 Andersson and Gade (*Morkinskinna*, p. 56) say: 'Although it is clear that some stanzas must have been added in Msk2, there is no evidence that *Msk* at any point in its transmission was subject to a large-scale interpolation of skaldic stanzas.' They nevertheless suggest, for example, that the 'comical poems' of Haraldr the Severe were interpolated (pp. 29–30), but this conclusion is based entirely upon internal arguments.

elements – to divide *Brennu-Njáls Saga*, for example, into two parts.[97] That changed under the influence of scholars from the so-called 'Icelandic school' in the early twentieth century.[98] During this period Guðni Jónsson argued that *Grettis saga* was an organic whole, pointing out that theories about additions to *Grettis saga* were based 'on definite literary premises' rather than on arguments based on textual comparison.[99] Because Guðni's arguments were considered quite convincing, theories of interpolation began to loom less large in discussion about Sagas of Icelanders. That said, interpolations were still assumed to be a part of *Morkinskinna*, and the *Íslendinga þættir* were the key to that view. Thus, the nature of *Morkinskinna* was considered to differ from that of the Sagas of Icelanders.

In the last fifty years the inclination to search for interpolations has more or less disappeared from discussions about the Sagas of Icelanders. During the same period, however, the narrative art of the kings' sagas has not received the same kind of attention.[100] The search for *þættir* in the Sagas of Icelanders was not so much called off as transferred in full to the kings' sagas. And most of the kings' saga *þættir* are to be found in works that have not attracted much scholarly attention, notably *Morkinskinna*. The arguments against partitioning Sagas of Icelanders were duly forgotten, and scholars of the Icelandic school now began to regard *þættir* in the kings' sagas as independent narratives while regarding *þættir* in the Sagas of Icelanders as inseparable parts of the saga. This discrepancy can doubtlessly be linked in part to the nationalist perspectives then prominent in Icelandic studies in Iceland.

97 See Lars Lönnroth, *Njáls Saga: A Critical Introduction*, pp. 1–24. On the structure of *Njáls saga*, see I. R. Maxwell, 'Pattern in Njáls Saga'; Carol Clover, *The Medieval Saga*, pp. 46–49.

98 The 'Icelandic School', formed under the influence of Björn M. Ólsen and led by cultural juggernaut Sigurður Nordal, were the most prominent group of scholars to champion what had become known as the 'book prose' theory, that the origins of medieval Icelandic literature were to be found in a late literary movement rather than long-standing oral tradition. For further reading on the history and legacy of the 'Icelandic school', see Jón Hnefill Aðalsteinsson, 'Íslenski skólinn,' pp. 103–129.

99 Guðni Jónsson, ed. *Grettis saga*, ÍF 7, pp. v–xvi. By recognising changing ideas about medieval literary form, Kathryn Hume ('The Thematic Design of Grettis saga') and Robert Cook ('The Reader in Grettis saga') reawakened interest in the structure of *Grettis saga*.

100 See Ármann Jakobsson, *Í leit að konungi*, pp. 41–42.

Scholars have paid little attention to those episodes in the kings' sagas that resemble *þættir* but are not about Icelanders. Bjarni Aðalbjarnarson and Gimmler, the scholars who worked hardest to evaluate which *þættir* have been interpolated into *Morkinskinna*, cited such episodes, but clearly believed that only scenes dealing with Icelanders can be regarded as real *þættir*.[101] On the other hand, Tor Ulset considered the nationality of *þættir* characters as an unnecessary element in the definition. For him a *þáttr* is 'a short, complete narrative irrespective of whether the main character is an Icelander or not'.[102] But nationality is not so easily removed from the discussion of *þættir*. In fact the tales were originally published separately, and this was precisely because of the nationality of the main characters. This is also the premise for considering *þættir* about Icelanders in Norway as Sagas of Icelanders of some kind. At the same time, in the Sagas of Icelanders, the episodic nature of certain accounts of Icelanders' trips abroad to meet with kings is not regarded as a sign of interpolation since these sagas are considered organic literary structures and not anthologies of short stories.

There are two separate issues concerning the *þættir* in *Morkinskinna*: how many of them were textually independent from their inception, and how many were originally present in *Morkinskinna*. In recent years scholars have assumed that independent *þættir* were present in the **Oldest Morkinskinna*.[103] Indrebø's main argument when identifying several *Morkinskinna þættir* as interpolations was that the narrator states that such

---

101 Bjarni Aðalbjarnarson, *Om de norske kongers sagaer*, pp. 154–159; Gimmler, *Die Thættir der Morkinskinna*, pp. 50–61.

102 'ei kort, avslutta fortelling uten hensyn til om hovedpersonene er islendinger eller ikke.' Tor Ulset, ed. *Utvalgte þættir fra Morkinskinna*, p. ii.

103 Guðni Jónsson (*Fóstbræðra saga*, ed. Björn K. Þórólfsson and Guðni Jónsson, ÍF 6, pp. cix) puts it this way: 'Því miður er margt óljóst um upphaf Morkinskinnu, svo sem um það, hverjir af þáttunum séu upphaflegir í henni og hverjum bætt inn í hana síðar, en hitt virðist ljóst, að þeir séu flestir eða allir samdir sem sjálfstæð rit' ('Unfortunately, much is uncertain about the origins of *Morkinskinna*, such as which of the *þættir* are original to it and which were added to it later, but it appears clear that most or all of them were written as independent creations'). Jakobsen ('Om Fagrskinna-forfatteren,' p. 100, note 21) states: 'Mange af tættene i Mork. slik den foreligger i dag, er sikkert senere interpolasjoner, men mange har også uten tvil tilhørt ur-Morkinskinna.' (Many of the *þættir* in the extant Morkinskinna are surely later interpolations, but many also were without doubt included in the **Oldest Morkin-*

an episode is not historical: *Þetta er gamans frásǫgn ok eigi sǫguligt eins kostar (Msk.* I, 252) 'This is a story told for pleasure and not particularly historical'. Indrebø took this statement to mean that the author of the *Oldest Morkinskinna* did not believe that *þættir* had any place in a kings' saga.[104] The obvious weakness of this argument is that the author of *Morkinskinna* saw fit to include this 'unhistorical' narrative in his work, and it also occurs in *Fagrskinna* and *Heimskringla*.[105] Another argument involves the alleged contradictions between the *þættir* and the 'main saga' in the characterisation of Haraldr the Severe.[106] But, as already suggested, contradictions (if they are in fact such) need not be the result of interpolations. The frequently discussed example of the contradictory accounts of the return of Magnús the Good to Norway has failed to convince sceptics in the discussion of interpolations.[107]

A word or two needs to be devoted to the question of literary structure. Jonna Louis-Jensen claimed that *þættir* 'often have a very loose connection to the main plot, which in many cases they interrupt in a clumsy way'.[108] As noted above, clumsiness is a dubious determiner of age, especially when its identification is so problematic, and whether *þættir* are more digressive than the rest of the saga is also a matter of opinion. We should also recall that most of Indrebø's followers assumed that some *þættir* were present in *Morkinskinna* from the outset; among them were Bjarni Aðalbjarnarson and Gimmler, both of whom have written extensively about this matter. Those *þættir* regarded as interpolations by Bjarni and Gimmler deal with Icelanders and were considered most likely to have

skinna.) Bjarni Einarsson (*Fagrskinna*, ÍF 29, p. cxiii) seems to be in agreement. Compare also Andersson and Gade, *Morkinskinna*, pp. 22–24.

104 Indrebø, *Fagrskinna*, pp. 32–33.

105 *Fagrskinna*, ed. Bjarni Einarsson, p. 270; *Heimskringla* III, pp. 152–154.

106 Indrebø, 'Harald Hardraade i *Morkinskinna*.' They will be discussed in part IV, chapter 2.

107 Another *þáttr* considered an interpolation was the episode about the knight Giffarðr but Gade ('*Morkinskinna*'s Giffarðsþáttr: Literary fiction or historical fact?') has challenged this view. She agrees with Sigurður Nordal (*Snorri Sturluson*, p. 166), who considered that in his remarks about derision and praise in the preface to *Heimskringla*, Snorri Sturluson was taking his cue from *Morkinskinna*.

108 'ofte en meget løs forbindelse med hovedhandlingen, som de i flere tilfælde afbryder på en klodset måde.' Louis-Jensen, *Kongesagastudier*, p. 69.

had an independent existence. While the independence of *þættir* is one thing, their incorporation in *Morkinskinna* is quite another. Although a *þáttr* may once have stood on its own, there is nothing to prove that a scribe interpolated it. On the contrary, the episode could have been an integral part of *Morkinskinna* from the beginning.

The *Íslendingaþættir* from *Morkinskinna* had begun to appear in independent editions before scholars started to discuss the overall work in detail. It may even be the case that these volumes held a degree of influence over scholarly opinions. *Þættir* were thought of as independent narratives about Icelanders and were treated as individual elements rather than parts of longer sagas. It was not much of a stretch to call them interpolations. The arguments in support of *þættir* as interpolations were based on the real or imagined clumsiness or contradictions that were attributed to scribes rather than to authors. Scholars paid insufficient attention to the role of *þættir* within the structure of sagas and to their aesthetic qualities. These issues will be examined later (see part II, chapter 2).

Two versions of *Morkinskinna* or one?

If we ask what is certain about the origins of *Morkinskinna*, we are compelled to answer that we can be certain about very little. The GKS 1009 fol manuscript version of *Morkinskinna* is not the original saga. On the other hand, we need not doubt that the origins of the work may be traced to some extent to the events narrated. Medieval narratives were not original creations in any modern sense. There is no way of knowing the extent to which oral or written sources were relied upon; doubtless both played their part. For a lengthy period after the age of writing in Iceland began, we may assume the existence of written narratives about historical matters – no doubt there was more material than survives in *Ágrip* and **Hryggjarstykki*. Equally, the events narrated (not least those at the conclusion of the saga) were sufficiently close in time as to permit some reliance on oral narratives. The stories are duly recorded in book form, and *Morkinskinna*, as are all other lengthy sagas, is definitely a narrative compilation, and – according to one of the central tenants of this study – one that was composed with a certain cohesion in mind. There is, however, no need to treat the work as a special case, any more than is this case with *Heims-*

kringla or the Sagas of Icelanders. Additional arguments must be adduced if *Morkinskinna* is to be regarded as merely a loosely structured compilation of sagas.

Louis-Jensen's work has revealed that it is impossible to use textual comparison to prove that material in *Morkinskinna* did not occur in the **Oldest Morkinskinna*. All the extant *Morkinskinna* texts may be traced to the same original, in which the supposed 'interpolations' are already present. Depending on *Fagrskinna* is questionable since it is considerably shorter than *Morkinskinna*. The so-called 'borrowings' from *Ágrip* could also have been included in the **Oldest Morkinskinna,* even though they are considered maladroit. In fact in terms of the overall text they do not bulk particularly large. When all is said and done, the evidence available for identifying particular interpolations amounts to little more than using contradictions and awkwardnesses, real or imagined, as proof equivalent to the evidence that can be derived from scribal errors. But, as we have noted, the evidential value of those latter errors is of a wholly different and more substantive nature, whereas it is a matter of opinion as to whether the identified contradictions are really contradictory.

Most evidence suggests that the **Oldest Morkinskinna* was in existence around 1220 and that it was the source for *Fagrskinna* and *Heimskringla*. Its linguistic profile is archaic, and when the work's relationships with *Fagrskinna* and *Heimskringla* are assessed, it seems very likely that it took its present form around 1220. There is no decisive evidence that material has been interpolated into the **Oldest Morkinskinna*. Though scholars have long assumed that such interpolations are certain to have been present, they have disagreed about most of the details. Despite some discussion, little progress has been made in distinguishing the 'core' of *Morkinskinna* from the 'interpolations'. Scholars have gradually abandoned the problem rather than engaging in any sustained critical re-examination of it.

What is then to be done? It is impossible not to take some position as to the date of the text. It is in the nature of things that no proof will ever emerge to confirm that all the matter in the extant version of *Morkinskinna* was also present from the beginning. There is no clear evidence, on the other hand, that *Morkinskinna* has changed all that much from its origins. As matters now stand, the evidence may allow us to suppose that the text in

1009 represents reasonably well the *Morkinskinna* that was in existence by around 1220. Thus, it is this text that provides the basis for the analysis that follows, together with the text of *Flateyjarbók* and *Hulda* in order to cover the 1009 lacunae. For better or for worse, there is no other *Morkinskinna* text available.

Part II.

STRUCTURE

1. Medieval Structure

In the shadow of Snorri

The fact that *Heimskringla*, a *tour de force* of the Icelandic Middle Ages, is ascribed to Snorri Sturluson[1] may account, at least in part, for the propensity of other kings' sagas to fall under its shadow.[2] Bjarni Aðalbjarnarson's remarks are representative of this phenomenon:

> The sagas of the Norwegian kings were in some respects rather pitiful literature before Snorri took up their cause; many were badly put together, stylistically poor and full of unremarkable material.[3]

Whether or not the priority enjoyed by *Heimskringla* actually depends upon its stylistic superiority to other kings' sagas, most scholars of both the distant and the recent past have largely ignored *Morkinskinna*,[4] and

---

1   But the authorship has been contested: see Louis-Jensen, 'Heimskringla – Et værk af Snorri Sturluson?' and Margaret Cormack, '*Heimskringla, Egilssaga*, and the Daughter of Eiríkr blóðöx.' Snorri's present literary reputation owes a great debt to Sigurður Nordal, who praises the author, not uncharacteristically, in the following vein: *Hann sér víðar en aðrir menn, meira samhengi, dýpra skyldleika viðburðanna (Snorri Sturluson*, p. 261) ('He sees further than other men, deeper into the relationship between events, and more contexts').

2   In a survey of literature of the Middle Ages (*Íslensk bókmenntasaga* 1, ed. Vésteinn Ólason *et al.*, pp. 364–383) it receives more than seventeen pages and *Fagrskinna* two, and such proportions are not unique. In addition, *Heimskringla* has received excellent scholarly treatment on a regular basis.

3   *Noregskonunga sögur voru að sumu leyti heldur ömurlegar bókmenntir, áður en Snorri tók að fást við þær, margar illa saman settar, illa stílaðar og fullar af ómerkilegu efni.* Bjarni Aðalbjarnarson, ed. *Heimskringla* I, ÍF 26, p. xxxi.

4   In a recent history of Norway (Jón Viðar Sigurðsson, *Norsk historie 800–1300: Frå høvdingmakt til konge – og kyrkjemakt*), though the kings' sagas are much used as sources, as is common nowadays, *Morkinskinna* is never mentioned. An even better example is the fine article by Sverre Bagge on Haraldr the Severe's youth ('Harald

STRUCTURE

when they do express an opinion it is usually pejorative.⁵ Gustav Indrebø,
for example, dismissed the saga with the following words:

> *Morkinskinna* is a strange, rich book. Rich not in its ex-
> cellence of composition or literary structure, nor in its per-
> sonal descriptions and characterisation. In this respect in its
> present form it is in a sad state.⁶

The saga's unattractive title may have contributed to the low esteem it
enjoys; the uncertainty about its origins has also no doubt had an influence; the difficulty of its text, and the fact that until recently it had not
been translated into any modern European language, has also made it
less accessible than *Heimskringla*. But several major scholars have come
to *Morkinskinna*'s rescue, among others Sigurður Nordal,⁷ Jón Helga-

---

Hardråde i Bysants: To fortellinger, to kulturer,' pp. 169–192). Though conceding
that *Heimskringla* is neither the earliest nor the most detailed source, Bagge concentrates on it on the grounds that it is 'den mest gjennomarbeidede og gjennomtenkte
og dermed best egnet når hovedformålet er å undersøke synet på Harald mer enn hva
Harald faktisk gjorde' ('Harald Hardråde i Bysants', p. 175) ('the most worked over,
the most consistently thought through and thereby the best suited [source] whenever
the main objective is to investigate the characterisation of Haraldr rather than what he
actually did'). There is no explanation offered for believing that more work or thought
lies behind *Heimskringla* than *Morkinskinna*.

5   It is customary to dismiss the *Morkinskinna* version of the *mannjafnaðr* between Eysteinn and Sigurðr in favour of the similar account in *Heimskringla*. Lars Lönnroth
(*Den dubbla scenen: Muntlig diktning från Eddan till ABBA*, p. 70) has also judged the
narrative in *Heimskringla* to be superior, following the examples of Sigurður Nordal
(*Snorri Sturluson*, pp. 228–233) and Hallvard Lie (*Studier i Heimskringlas stil: Dialogene og talene*, pp. 66–68). Marianne Kalinke ('Sigurðar Saga Jórsalafara: The
Fictionalization of Fact in Morkinskinna,' pp. 164–165) disagrees, and even Sigurður
Nordal (*Snorri Sturluson*, p. 244) conceded that sometimes the narrative in *Morkinskinna* surpassed that in *Heimskringla*.
6   *Morkinskinna er ei forunderlig rik bok. Rik ikkje ved framifrå komposisjon og litterær
reisning, og ikkje ved fylgjerett personskildring og karakterteikning. I desse leider
stend det tvertimot syrgjeleg ille til med henne, soleis som ho ligg fyre no.* Indrebø,
'*Nokre merknader til den norröne kongesoga*,' p. 62.
7   'Snorri Sturluson: Nokkurar hugleiðingar á 700. ártíð hans,' p. 21. See also Sigurður
Nordal, *Snorri Sturluson*, p. 170ff.).

74

son,[8] Gabriel Turville-Petre,[9] and Sverrir Tómasson.[10] And Eivind Kvalén (1925) wrote a book about *Morkinskinna* more than eighty years ago. He was for a long time the only scholar to show *Morkinskinna* such respect.

In recent decades an increasing number of scholars have regarded *Morkinskinna* as well worthy of study,[11] along with other texts previously consigned to the outer margins of literary discussion. Postmodernism may have helped to change the climate of opinion,[12] for *Morkinskinna* had little appeal for scholars in the nineteenth – or indeed for much of the twentieth century. The history of the reception of the manuscript is typical of traditional responses to other aspects of a murky and misunderstood medieval world that still remained somewhat familiar.[13] Yet at the end of the twentieth century scholarly interest in the Middle Ages developed more appropriate stylistic yardsticks for assessing medieval literary achievement.[14]

8   *Morkinskinna: MS. No. 1009 fol. in the Old Royal collection of The Royal Library* (Copenhagen, 1934), pp. 13–14. Jón believes that although the *þættir* often break the flow of the saga, they 'reach great heights' in the art of storytelling (p. 13).
9   *Origins of Icelandic Literature*, p. 219. Guðni Jónsson, the editor of *Konungasögur 1: Ólafs saga Tryggvasonar eftir Odd munk. Helgisaga Ólafs Haraldssonar. Brot úr Elztu sögu*, p. xix, regarded *Sverris saga* and *sögur Morkinskinnu bera af öðrum konungasögum, sem eldri eru en Heimskringla* 'the sagas in Morkinskinna [as] superior to other kings' sagas that were older than Heimskringla'.
10 'Vinveitt skemmtan og óvinveitt,' p. 68.
11 Theodore M. Andersson, 'The Politics of Snorri Sturluson'; 'Composition and Literary Culture in Þiðreks saga'; Kari Ellen Gade, 'Northern Lights on the Battle of Hastings'; 'Kaupangr – Þrándheimr – Niðaróss: On the dating of the Old Norse kings' sagas'; Marianne E. Kalinke, 'Sigurðar Saga Jórsalafara: The Fictionalization of Fact in Morkinskinna'; Lars Lönnroth, *Den dubbla scenen: Muntlig diktning från Eddan till ABBA*, pp. 68–70; Lars Lönnroth, 'The Man-Eating Mama of Miklagard: Empress Zoe in Old Norse Saga Tradition,' pp. 37–49.
12 See Lee Patterson, 'On the Margin: Postmodernism, Ironic History, and Medieval Studies,' pp. 87–108.
13 Hans Robert Jauss, *Alterität und Modernität der mittelalterlichen Litteratur: Gesammelte Aufsätze 1956–1976*, pp. 9–47; Robert Darnton, 'History of Reading,' pp. 140–141. Some have pointed out (Patterson 'On the Margin,' p. 92; Gabrielle M. Spiegel, *Romancing the Past: The Rise of Vernacular Prose Historiography in Thirteenth-Century France*, p. 58) that this 'otherness' has been a feature of research on the Middle Ages from the beginning. Spiegel (pp. 71–80) claims that this sense of alterity has encouraged postmodernist approaches to the Middle Ages.
14 Norman F. Cantor, *Inventing the Middle Ages: The Lives, Works, and Ideas of the Great Medievalists of the Twentieth Century*; Umberto Eco, 'The Return of the Middle Ages,' pp. 61–85.

In particular, postmodernist evaluations of *Morkinskinna* have been less harsh than those modernist creeds that tended to dictate the aesthetic rules by which a work's structure would be judged.[15] Many scholars have come to recognise that notions of consistency and homogeneity need not apply to this saga any more than they should to other medieval texts. It is hardly a coincidence that the attention now being directed towards *Morkinskinna* follows hard on the heels of the recognition that Old Icelandic literature is also medieval European literature – this change of mindset has led to a growing interest in the international element in medieval Icelandic literature, notably saints' lives and the romances.

The structure of *Morkinskinna*, as we have noted, has long been considered deficient. The extant saga has tended to be viewed as a kind of narrative gruel – a shapeless narrative mass – for which, of course, no author was responsible but rather a committee of scribes, each of whom had fiddled haphazardly and unsuccessfully with the text. Finnur Jónsson thought *Morkinskinna* lacked organic coherence, and Indrebø considered its narrative form simply tragic.[16]

The *þættir* have been seen as especially detrimental to the saga's structure, since, as we have seen, they were held to have introduced contradictions into the historical record. The chief argument that Louis-Jensen deploys to prove that the *þættir* are interpolations is that they were poorly integrated into the fabric of the work.[17] The structure of *Morkinskinna* played a key role in all conjectures about the interpolations, with the text in 1009 judged to be thoroughly disjointed. One way of addressing such structures was to claim that the elements that most compromised the narrative structure are scribal interpolations. But in order to understand the structure of *Morkinskinna* we need to examine the medieval European aesthetics – notably concepts of structure – that informed the text. Much has been written about these notions in recent years, and the discussion that follows seeks to develop our understanding of the structure of *Morkinskinna*, not least of the role of the *þættir* in the work.

15 Lars Lönnroth, 'Saga and Jartegn: The appeal of mystery in saga texts,' p. 123.
16 Gustav Indrebø, 'Nokre merknader til den norröne kongesoga,' p. 62.
17 Louis-Jensen, *Kongesagastudier*, p. 69.

2. The Quest for Medieval Narrative Structure

The order in which narrative events are presented has been a major concern of literary theorists from Aristotle to Seymour Chatman and beyond.[1] In some branches of literature clear principles regulate this order; in others – including Old Icelandic-Norse literature – they are difficult to identify. The ancient classical tradition, still well known in the Middle Ages, involved choosing between two means of narrating events – the natural (that is, chronological) order (*ordo naturalis*) or an unnatural order (*ordo artificialis*), with the latter regarded as more artistic. Homer began his narrative *in medias res*, and then traced those events back to their origins. This method, which draws the listener immediately into the story, was also popular in romance writing. Medieval Icelandic sagas, on the other hand, by and large favour the natural order, albeit with some variations.[2] Thus the saga often begins not with the main characters but with their ancestors, and suspense is created by means of retardation or prolepsis. The authors of Icelandic medieval sagas definitely had an artistic choice as to how a saga should be laid out.

In the 1960s interest in the structure of Old Norse-Icelandic sagas (primarily the Sagas of Icelanders) generated new applications of narrative theory, and ambitious attempts were made to understand the structural rules governing the medieval sagas. Theodore M. Andersson, the progenitor of such approaches in Old Norse scholarship, adopted Aristotelean concepts into his stylistic model.[3] Later, different principles of structure

---

1 Chatman, *Story and Discourse: Narrative Structure in Fiction and Film* (Ithaca, 1978).
2 Kathryn Hume, 'Beginnings and Endings in the Icelandic Family Sagas,' pp. 593–606; Vésteinn Ólason, *Dialogues with the Viking Age: Narration and Representation in the Sagas of Icelander*, pp. 84–89; Alastair Fowler, *Kinds of Literature: An Introduction to the Theory of Genres and Modes*, pp. 98–105.
3 *The Icelandic Family Saga: An Analytic Reading*, pp. 3–30; Joseph Harris, 'Genre and Narrative Structure in Some Íslendinga þættir.'

were invoked, among them genealogical lists.[4] Some kings' sagas relate events from one king's life to another, with each monarch receiving his own chapter (for example, in *Ynglinga saga*).[5]

The way in which the *þættir* are incorporated within the saga by no means agrees with Aristotle's ideas about the unity of historical context in a poetic work. Digressions (*digressiones*), however, were known from classical rhetoric as well as medieval poetics.[6] Herodotus and Thucydides were among the ancient historians who made use of them.[7] Digressions serve as a dramatic and distilled representation of the substance and spirit of the saga. They have legitimacy, both as individual *exempla*, a narrative used to illustrate a certain general principle or moral point, and as elements that contribute to the overall meaning of the saga.[8] But use of the term *digressions* fails to describe the structure of *Morkinskinna* adequately, for virtually the whole work can be seen as an assemblage of digressions. Thus they do not augment the core of *Morkinskinna*: they *are* the core of the saga.

As such the saga represents an interpretative challenge. Since the Renaissance, Aristotle has exercised a profound influence on literary theory in the western world. In the thirteenth century, however, his ideas were known only via a 1256 Latin translation from Arabic sources. This translation, dating from several decades after the creation of *Morkin-*

---

4   Margaret Clunies Ross, 'The Development of Old Norse Textual Worlds: Genealogy as a Principle of Literary Organisation in Early Iceland,' pp. 372–385.

5   In the same way, various *Íslendingasögur* may be regarded as family chronicles, as with *Laxdæla saga* and *Vatnsdæla saga*. In both cases this form reflects the content of the saga; see Ármann Jakobsson, 'Konungasagan Laxdæla'; 'Royal Pretenders and Faithful Retainers: The Icelandic vision of Kingship in Transition.'

6   See, among others, Ernst Robert Curtius, *European Literature and the Latin Middle Ages*, pp. 71, 501; Eugène Vinaver, *The Rise of Romance*, pp. 74–76. Among those who favoured narrative digressions was Geoffrey of Vinsauf. See *Medieval Literary Criticism*, ed. O.B. Hardison, Jr., *et al.*, pp. 123–144.

7   Klaus Meister, 'Herodotos,' *Der Neue Pauly* 5 p. 471; Roland Barthes, 'The Discourse of History,' p. 129. Andersson and Gade (*Morkinskinna*, p. 83) actually compare the author of *Morkinskinna* with Herodotus.

8   Joel Fineman, 'The History of the Anecdote: Fiction and Fiction,' pp. 49–76. Kurt Johannesson (*Saxo Grammaticus: Komposition och världsbild i Gesta Danorum*, pp. 19–23) has discussed the *exemplum* in antiquity and the Middle Ages in connection with Saxo Grammaticus.

skinna, seems not to have influenced European literary aesthetics. It was not until the sixteenth century that Aristotle's views on poetics were rediscovered and soon became almost universally accepted.[9] As Renaissance scholars embraced Aristotelean aesthetics, they tended to repudiate medieval literature and the medieval aesthetics that underpinned it.[10] They saw the Middle Ages as a period of decline, a valley between the classical and renaissance peaks. Even when, during the eighteenth century, interest in the Middle Ages was somewhat revived, responses to medieval literary texts remained considerably constricted by the aesthetic parameters and injunctions of the Aristotelian system. Literary scholarship tended to revolve around the search for the pre-medieval texts that had been (it was thought) ineptly reshaped during the Middle Ages. It was not until the work of Joseph Bédier on *Tristrams saga*[11] at the beginning of the twentieth century that scholars began to regard medieval narratives as unified and skilfully crafted works created by an author.[12]

In 1918 Ferdinand Lot pointed the way by suggesting that the Prose *Lancelot* obeyed narrative laws that differed from those valorised by Aristotelian poetics. He compared the episodes in the romance with a finely woven tapestry rather than a collection of individual narratives, any of which could be omitted without compromising the overall unity of the work.[13] In 1936 scholars identified a binary structure in three medieval works. J.R.R. Tolkien concluded that the structure of *Beowulf* was designed to dramatise the two sides of the eponymous hero's life,[14] while

---

9   J.A. Burrow, *Medieval Writers and their Work: Middle English Literature and its Background 1100–1500* (Oxford, 1982), p. 14; Clover, *The Medieval Saga*, p. 13.

10   The negative view of medieval aesthetics culminated in Torquato Tasso's stern critique of Ariosto's *Orlando furioso* (William W. Ryding, *Structure in Medieval Narrative*, pp. 9–19).

11   Joseph Bédier, *Le Roman de Tristan et Iseut*.

12   Ryding, *Structure in Medieval Narrative*, pp. 9–37; Vinaver, *The Rise of Romance*, pp. 71–74.

13   Ferdinand Lot, *Étude sur le Lancelot en prose*, pp. 17–28.

14   J.R.R. Tolkien, '*Beowulf*: the Monsters and the Critics,' pp. 271–275. John Leyerle ('The Interlace Structure of *Beowulf*') develops still more detailed ideas about the interlace structure of the poem.

Ernst Robert Curtius and Wilhelm Kellermann identified a comparable construction in other medieval narratives.[15]

Some three decades later Eugène Vinaver and William W. Ryding further refined our understanding of medieval literary structure.[16] They highlighted the fundamental differences separating medieval and modern literary aesthetics, and emphasised that any reader who seeks neoclassical narrative unity in a medieval work will be sorely disappointed.[17] Aristotelean notions about logical links between episodes,[18] and an overall clear sequence uniting the beginning, middle and end of a work are rarely applicable to medieval romances, with their many-stranded narrative textures.[19] Medieval authors sometimes composed complete and individual works, but at other times they added to an older work a sequel or prelude that were by their nature a beginning or an end to other works.[20] It seems to have been popular to divide a single work into two completely independent parts, each of which had its beginning, middle and end, but taken together offered an overall meaning, like the panels on a diptych altarpiece. In a modern narrative the logical escalation often occurs as the climax in the middle of the work, but in a bipartite work the middle is, in effect, the space between two causal chains. At times this can appear clumsy, but it embodies the aesthetics of its time.[21]

In classical rhetoric, though compression was a stylistic virtue, digressions could have stylistic value. Stylistic amplification was considered an

---

15 Curtius, 'Zur interpretation des Alexiusliedes'; Wilhelm Kellermann, *Aufbaustil und Weltbild Chrestiens von Troyes im Percevalroman.*

16 Vinaver, *The Rise of Romance*; Ryding, *Structure in Medieval Narrative.*

17 Aristotle, *Poetics*, pp. 115–119.

18 Aristotle, *Poetics*, pp. 55–57.

19 Vinaver, *The Rise of Romance*, pp. 68–74; Vinaver, *A la recherche d'une poétique médiévale*, pp. 105–128; C. S. Lewis, *The Discarded Image: An Introduction to Medieval and Renaissance Literature*, p. 194.

20 Ryding, *Structure in Medieval Narrative* p. 12. Such devices are now commonplace in narratology; sequels and, in some cases, preludes of popular movies are offered up on a regular basis. The legendary sagas about the Hrafnista family are medieval Icelandic examples of such serialised work.

21 Ryding, *Structure in Medieval Narrative*, pp. 38–43. The bipartite structure was so dominant that attempts to 'correct' earlier works in this direction can be found. Thus one translator of the *Aeneid* appears to have understood its *in medias res* beginning as an attempt to achieve a binary structure.

appropriate embellishment for writing in an elevated style. This device became one of the principal medieval figures of speech.[22] Ryding argues that the importance of amplification derived from medieval writers' belief that it was their role to discover (compare the French word *trouvère* or troubadour from the Old Provençal *trobar* 'to find') rather than to create. A poet who left a story the same length as he found it was simply breaking faith with his responsibilities as a writer. Literary creativity often involved taking a brief and bare narrative of historical events and amplifying it into a lengthy romance.[23] The art of amplification involved connection, repetition and explanation. A new event in the saga can serve to recall some earlier parallel incident; the repetition of incidents can increase their relative importance; and an event can invoke an interpretation or an explanation.[24] Medieval texts favour artful narrative interlace over the Aristotelian ideal of a single structural strand.[25] Vinaver sees parallels to such interlace in the decorated initial letters in manuscripts, in Gothic arches and in the elaborate vaulting in royal palaces. In all such decoration there is no discernible beginning, middle or end. He notes the structural parallels between Norman architecture and narrative romances, with both seeking to represent aspects of eternity.[26]

Ryding identifies a circular pattern in medieval structural aesthetics, as the simple gives way to the compound, the compound to the complex and finally simplicity is restored, as 'the wheel has come full circle'.[27] It may be said that during the twentieth century the structure of literary works steadily embraced complexity anew.

---

22 Curtius, *European Literature and the Latin Middle Ages*, pp. 487–494; Vinaver, *The Rise of Romance*, pp. 74–76, 85–96; Ryding, *Structure in Medieval Narrative*, pp. 66–82.

23 Ryding, *Structure in Medieval Narrative*, pp. 62–66.

24 Ibid., pp. 82–114.

25 Ibid., pp. 115–161. Vinaver (*The Rise of Romance*, pp. 90–91) discusses the connection between structure and causation in the saga of Morgan le Fay in Arthurian tales and compilations.

26 Vinaver, *The Rise of Romance*, pp. 7–85; Vinaver, *A la recherche d'une poétique médiévale*, pp. 129–149.

27 Ryding, *Structure in Medieval Narrative*, pp. 162–168.

Narrative stranding in medieval sagas

Bédier's resurrected version of the Tristan and Isold myth, his *Le roman de Tristan et Iseut*, stimulated other scholars to reconsider medieval texts as imaginative authorial works.[28] Several of Bédier's contemporaries regarded medieval Icelandic sagas in this way (for example, scholars of the aforementioned Icelandic school who considered the Sagas of Icelanders as authored works). On the other hand, an understanding of the structure of these works did not begin to develop until later.

In 1982 Carol Clover revealed the clear relationship between medieval Icelandic literature and its English and French counterparts. She considered that the difficulties scholars had encountered in attempting to define the form of the Sagas of Icelanders derived from their searching for Aristotelian unity, whereas the sagas were more like romances – in their form, expansiveness and sense of *Stoffreude* 'joy in the material'.[29] Each was a unified work, but the unities were often difficult to perceive at first. For Clover, *Brennu-Njáls saga*, for example, is bipartite whereas *Grettis saga* is more reminiscent of a *roman à tiroirs*, an episodic novel. Thus there were several saga forms rather than a single one. In all sagas we find parallel strands and episodes that can be connected to the main narrative thread, but at the same time these may be seen as a kind of digression. Clover considered the differences between *Brennu-Njáls saga* and *Óláfs saga Tryggvasonar* in *Flateyjarbók* to be a matter of degree rather than of kind, with three-fifths of the latter work consisting of *þættir*, some of them as lengthy as whole sagas.[30]

Clover discusses the notion of stranding at some length. Most Sagas of Icelanders are multi-stranded, and some are works of great complexity, such as *Brennu-Njáls saga*, *Grettis saga* and *Eyrbyggja saga*. Clover uses the notion of a saga *þáttr* 'strand' in a broad sense, applying it to a smal-

---

28 See Vinaver (*The Rise of Romance*, pp. 15–30) on Bédier and his scholarly methods.

29 This term was used by Andreas Heusler to explain the *Brennu-Njáls saga* author's seemingly unwarranted inclusions of apparently superfluous material into the text (*Die Geschichte vom weisen Njal*, p. 5).

30 Clover, *The Medieval Saga*, pp. 54–60. These notions of saga structure were developed in response to those influentially outlined by Andersson in *The Icelandic Family Saga*, pp. 3–30.

ler saga within a larger one (as with *Hallfreðar saga* within *Óláfs saga* in *Flateyjarbók*), and to leitmotifs (Skarphéðinn's sneer or Hallgerðr's hair in *Brennu-Njáls saga*, the sword Grásíða in *Gísla saga*). The art of the Icelandic *þáttr* has a special language, which Clover focuses on. The sagas themselves use words that refer to weaving (*snúa*, 'turn, twist', *snara*, 'turn', *þáttr*, 'a strand') in a way similar to Latin usage (the verb *texere* 'to weave', from which the word 'text' derives). Clover thinks that sagas were regarded as complex narrative fabrics, woven and interlaced like medieval romances. They may be likened to the art of decoration which Vinaver associates with romance.[31] Clover also discusses scene shifts in sagas and concludes that sagas, like French romances, were works of art in which aesthetic order (*ordo artificialis*) rather than just natural order (*ordo naturalis*) is widely discernible.[32]

Clover discusses *Brennu-Njáls saga* at some length, following in the footsteps of I.R. Maxwell, who stated that *Brennu-Njáls saga* was not so much one saga but several, each one following its own laws of composition.[33] Like *Beowulf* the saga was symmetrical but also many-stranded. *Brennu-Njáls saga* included episodes (for example, the sequence of journeys abroad) that were not just constituent elements in a larger narrative unit but also independent and intriguing episodes in their own right. He also drew attention to the middle of the saga, which served to divide the work into two parts, to connect those parts and to create variety.

Maxwell further argues that other well-known Sagas of Icelanders are as multi-stranded narratives as is *Brennu-Njáls saga*, and they are also

31 Ibid., pp. 61–108. On the language of stranding, see Clover 'The Language of Interlace: Notes on Composition in Saga and Romance.' Sverrir Tómasson ('Skorið í fornsögu: Þankar um byggingu Hrafnkels sögu,' p. 791) provides examples of how narrative construction can be compared to the structure of a building. Anne Heinrichs ('"Intertexture" and its Functions in Early Written Sagas: a Stylistic Observation of Heiðarvíga saga, Reykdæla saga and the Legendary Olafssaga,' pp. 127–128) points to parallels with the Bayeux tapestry and similar works.

32 Clover, *The Medieval Saga*, pp. 109–147.

33 I.R. Maxwell, 'Pattern in Njáls Saga,' pp. 17–47. A similar method may be seen in A.C. Bouman, *Patterns in Old English and Old Icelandic Literature*. Lars Lönnroth (*Njáls Saga: A critical introduction*, pp. 23–55, 68–82, 215–248) divided *Njála* more precisely into episodes. He emphasised the independence of each episode but also its importance for the whole. His work on *Njáls saga* is the most detailed interpretation of an Icelandic saga that is informed by new understandings of saga structure.

held together by a deep structural unity.[34] Following Clover's example many scholars have referred to the interlace structure of Old Icelandic sagas in recent years, while others have discussed amplification and bipartition.[35] The structure of the kings' sagas has been discussed less than that of the Sagas of Icelanders and legendary sagas, though the form of *Flateyjarbók* has received some attention, notably the part played by *þættir*.[36] Stefanie Würth, for example, suggests that the *þættir* in *Flateyjarbók* add new emphases to the saga.[37] In kings' sagas from the twelfth century there are also examples of bipartite constructions and stranding. Inge Skovgaard-Petersen has noted that Saxo Grammaticus's *Gesta Danorum* is bipartite, and Saxo is probably little older than the author of *Morkinskinna*.[38] Moreover, the Norwegian historian Theodoricus used digressions in the *Historia de antiquitate regum Norwagiensium*, a work that predates *Morkinskinna* by nearly forty years. In that instance Theodoricus is following the traditions of Latin historiography, and seeking simply, in his own phrase, to amuse the reader.[39] Theodoricus helps to introduce these learned traditions into the Icelandic kings' sagas, and digressions are an important part of those traditions.[40] Thus Clover points out that digression is an important element in many early kings' sagas, for example, in *Óláfs saga Tryggvasonar* by the monk Oddr Snorrason.[41] In this way Norse literature was influenced by general principles not unlike those

34 Maxwell, 'Pattern in Njáls Saga,' pp. 20–21.
35 See some of the examples mentioned in *Staður í nýjum heimi*, p. 67.
36 Rowe, 'Cultural Paternity'; Julia Zernack, 'Hyndlulioð, Flateyjarbók und die Vorge-schichte der Kalmarer Union.'
37 Würth, *Elemente des Erzählens: Die Þættir der Flateyjarbók*, pp. 60–159.
38 Skovgaard-Petersen, *Da Tidernes Herre var nær: Studier i Saxos historiesyn*, pp. 61–178.
39 *Digressiones etiam more antiquorum chronographorum non inutiles, ut arbitramur, ad delectandum animum lectoris locis competentibus adjunximus* (*Monumenta Historica Norvegiae* 1889, p. 2) 'In keeping with the custom of earlier history writers we have added digressions in the appropriate places; in our opinion these are not useless since they are for the delectation of the mind of the reader'.
40 Clover, *The Medieval Saga*, pp. 154–159; Bagge, 'Theodoricus Monachus – Clerical Historiography in Twelfth-Century Norway,' pp. 117–123.
41 Clover, *The Medieval Saga*, p. 168.

dominant in romances long before 1226, when *Tristrams saga* was translated into Old Norse.[42]

How does this change how we might approach the *þættir* in *Morkinskinna*? We must first refine our method. The *þættir* genre was invented before scholars began to examine the function of these narratives in *Morkinskinna*, and those explorations have certainly had a considerable influence upon our understanding of the structure of the saga.

The notion of the *þættir*

As *þættir* often tend now to be regarded as a separate literary genre[43] and as the *þættir* in *Morkinskinna* have been viewed by some scholars as interpolations – a view that necessarily assumes that they had previously existed as entities independent of their extant context – the nature of this short narrative form merits some discussion.[44] Though critical tradition encourages us to retain the term *þættir*, it is misleading to confine its use to those episodes that have been identified as *þættir* in studies of Old Norse-Icelandic narrative. The term *þáttr* needs to be used carefully, with due regard to context in each instance. Although most of the narratives now known as *þættir* occur in kings' sagas, as a saga genre they are more often associated with the Sagas of Icelanders. The word *þáttr* did not exist as a generic marker in the Middle Ages, but served simply to designate 'part of a text'.[45] Very few narratives now called *þættir* were so named in the Middle Ages, and the term is now used to identify various other medieval narrative forms.[46]

42 Clover, *The Medieval Saga*, pp. 148–184.
43 Jónas Kristjánsson, 'Bókmenntasaga,' *Saga Íslands*, pp. 261–350 (343–349); Vésteinn Ólason, 'Íslendingasögur og þættir,' pp. 29–38.
44 I discuss the issue of the *þættir* more extensively in: 'The Life and Death of the Medieval Icelandic Short Story.'
45 Lindow, 'Þáttr,' p. 661.
46 Lindow, '"Hreiðars þáttr heimska" and AT 326: An Old Icelandic Novella and an International Folktale'; Lönnroth, 'Tesen om de två kulturerna: Kritiska studier i den isländska sagaskrivningens sociala föruttsättningar,' pp. 10, 19–21; Lönnroth, 'The Concept of Genre in Saga Literature,' pp. 419–426. Heinrich Gimmler (*Die Thættir der Morkinskinna: Ein Beitrag zur Überlieferungsproblematik und zur Typologie der*

STRUCTURE

In 1855 Jón Þorkelsson edited a collection of *þættir* (*Sex sögu-þættir*) and may be regarded as the father of this literary form, although some early nineteenth-century manuscript redactors preceded him. Some fifty years later Reverend Þorleifur Jónsson's *Fjörutíu Íslendinga-þættir* (1904) was included as a volume in Sigurður Kristjánsson's edition of Sagas of Icelanders. While Þorleifur does not explain his choice of *þættir* in the preface, the main focus of the edition seems to have been to collect short narratives about Icelanders, several from kings' sagas or shorter Sagas of Icelanders such as *Ǫlkofra þáttr*. In order to justify its inclusion in the anthology, it appears that a text's principal character needed above all to be an Icelander.

The narratives in Þorleifur's edition have represented the core of the *þáttr* genre ever since. When Guðni Jónsson edited his own *þættir* collection in 1935, he sought to explain the criteria that governed his selection of texts. He regarded *þættir* as independent narratives that at an early stage had been absorbed into the kings' sagas;[47] as literature they were 'the most closely related to the Sagas of Icelanders and represent in fact a branch of them',[48] a view similar to that of Þorleifur Jónsson. Since then it has been customary for *Íslendingaþættir* to be edited as separate short stories alongside Sagas of Icelanders.[49]

In 1885 the Swedish poet Albert Ulrik Bååth suggested that *þættir* may have been the precursors of Sagas of Icelanders, with the latter genre having developed out of the former.[50] This theory was immediately challenged,[51] and by the time Guðni Jónsson's edition appeared half a century

altnordischen Kurzerzählung pp. 30–34) discusses issues of terminology, but regards the *þáttr* as a unique literary genre.
47 Guðni Jónsson, ed. *Íslendinga þættir*, pp. v–vi.
48 Guðni Jónsson, ed. *Grettis saga*, ÍF 7, p. xcix.
49 As with, for example, *Íslendinga sögur* 1–9, 1968–1976, and *Íslendinga sögur og þættir* 1–2, 1985–1986.
50 Bååth, *Studier öfver kompositionen i några isländska ättsagor*.
51 Andreas Heusler ('Die Anfänge der isländischen Saga,' pp. 74–80) more or less repudiated Bååth's view on *þættir*. Among those who have adopted his theories, albeit with variations, are Walther Heinrich Vogt, 'Die frásagnir der Landnámabók,' and Wolfgang Lange, 'Einige Bemerkungen zur altnordischen Novelle.' On this debate, see Andersson, 'The Doctrine of Oral Tradition in The Chanson de geste and Saga,' pp. 231–32; *The Problems of Icelandic Saga Origins: A Historical Survey*, pp. 61–64;

later, most scholars had come to regard *þættir* as a short-story genre rather than as the narrative seeds out of which sagas had grown. The stories were, however, still considered to be older than the sagas.[52] This position was connected with book prose theory, the foundations upon which the afore-mentioned 'Icelandic school' was built, under which *þættir*, no less than sagas, were regarded as authored works of literature.[53]

Throughout the twentieth century the *Íslendingaþættir* were generally thought of as an early literary genre, related to the Sagas of Icelanders. It was not, however, until 1970 that a literary-theoretical basis for this view was developed. Joseph Harris sought to characterise the literary and thematic nature of the *þættir*, with his analysis much influenced by structuralist and narratological theory.[54] He directed particular attention to those *þættir* that told of the dealings between Icelanders and kings in the kings' sagas. Harris, like scholars of the 'Icelandic school', suggested that *þættir* had originally been independent narratives, which had eventually been introduced into the kings' sagas. He argued that the narratological

Gimmler, *Die Thættir der Morkinskinna*, pp. 1–8); Clover, 'Maiden Warriors and Other Sons,' pp. 31–39).

52 Discussion of this issue can be found in every *Íslenzk fornrit* volume containing a *þáttr*. Björn M. Ólsen may be called the father of this notion as well as of many other views associated with the 'Icelandic school'; see, for example, his edition of *Stúfs saga: Gefin út í firsta sinn eftir handritunum*; *Um Íslendingasögur: Kaflar úr háskóla-fyrirlestrum*, ed. Sigfús Blöndal and Einar Ól. Sveinsson, pp. 117, 177, 414. The idea is subsequently adopted by Sigurður Nordal, 'Sagalitteraturen,' pp. 191, 243–244, and by most other Icelandic scholars; many foreign scholars also adopted this view (including Turville-Petre, *Origins of Icelandic Literature*, p. 218; Dag Strömbäck, 'The Dawn of West Norse Literature,' pp. 7–24; Gimmler *Die Thættir der Morkinskinna*, pp. 8–14).

53 Anthony Faulkes phrases it well in his edition, *Two Icelandic Stories: Hreiðars þáttr, Orms þáttr*, p. 4: 'the *þættir* as we have them are literary works, bearing all the marks of careful composition and deliberate artistry.' Much of this theoretical speculation was based upon notions common to their time: the analogy between biological evolu-tion and literary development, on the one hand, and the controversy between adherents of the freeprose versus bookprose theories. For a useful summary of these issues, see Andersson, *The Problems of Icelandic Saga Origins*, pp. 65–81.

54 Andersson's book on the structure of the sagas (*The Icelandic Family Saga*) has been particularly influential. Harris also draws on Vladimir I. Propp, *Morphology of the Folktale*, and Alan Dundes, *The Morphology of North American Indian Folktales*, scholars whose work was very much in vogue at this time.

characteristics of the *þættir* indicated that they represented an independent literary genre.[55] Most scholars who have subsequently discussed *þættir* have accepted Harris's arguments, emphasising the independence of the narratives and analysing their principal features.[56] However, the idea of *þættir* as a separate literary genre has been called into question by Lars Lönnroth,[57] and by Sverrir Tómasson, who points out that there is no theoretical reason to encourage belief in their independence before they became part of a saga.[58]

Scholars seeking to understand *þættir* as a literary genre have several problems to wrestle with. To begin with, no one has ever identified the exact number of texts that comprise the genre. Lindow states that 'the number of such *þættir* probably exceeds 100, but they vary greatly, and one cannot speak of a single genre'.[59] Þorleifur Jónsson's *þættir* edition includes forty texts, whereas the edition of Guðni Jónsson has forty-two. Harris considered the lines of demarcation established by both scholars to be arbitrary, claiming that there were more *þættir* than either had suggested. He in turn identified thirty-one *þættir* that treated dealings between Icelanders and kings, viewing this narrative template as a sub-category of a larger literary genre. He identified the narrative characteristics of these tales but made no attempt to distinguish them from many other narratives of similar structure and plot in the Sagas of Icelanders. Following Harris's

---

55 Harris, 'Genre and Narrative Structure in Some Íslendinga þættir'; 'Theme and Genre in some *Íslendinga þættir*'; 'Þættir,' p. 3; 'Gender and genre: short and long forms in the saga literature,' pp. 49–52; 1969. Since then, Danielsson (*Om den isländska släktsagans uppbyggnad*, pp. 62–81) has discussed the *þættir* in *Morkinskinna* in light of narratological theory without, however, concluding that they are a unique literary genre.

56 Among those who have designated the *þættir* as an independent literary genre are: Bjarni Guðnason, 'Þættir,' pp. 405–410; Sigurður Svavarsson, 'Athugun á þáttum sem bókmenntagrein með dæmi af Auðunar þætti vestfirska,' pp. 20–37; and Vésteinn Ólason, 'Íslendingaþættir,' pp. 60–62. Studies of the *þættir* in *Morkinskinna* as independent narratives have far outnumbered those examining the saga as an organic whole.

57 Lönnroth, *Njáls Saga*, pp. 53–54.

58 *Íslensk bókmenntasaga* 1, p. 384.

59 Lindow, 'Þáttr,' p. 661.

detailed discussion of *þættir* in the kings' sagas, the debate on *þættir* as a genre has been mostly concerned with these tales.[60]

Although Harris sought to identify common structural features and leitmotifs in *þættir*, most scholars have suggested that it is in their origins that *þættir* can be distinguished from short narratives that are not *þættir*. Bjarni Aðalbjarnarson and Gimmler both cite literary, and supposed textual independence as the defining characteristic of the genre. Bjarni pointed out that many similar narratives in *Morkinskinna* cannot be called *þættir* since they never enjoyed an independent existence; in all he identified sixteen *þættir* in *Morkinskinna*.[61] Gimmler also distinguished between *þættir* and '*þáttr*-like' narratives; he identified twelve *þættir* in *Morkinskinna* but twenty-eight *þáttr*-like episodes. He recognised the danger of 'inventing' *þættir* by publishing narratives from *Morkinskinna* as *þættir* regardless of their origins.[62]

The existence of *þættir* outside the kings' sagas and in multiple versions would indeed suggest that they are seen as independent narratives from the fifteenth century onwards. Of the *þættir* in *Morkinskinna*, 'Stúfs þáttr', 'Íslendings þáttr sögufróða', 'Sneglu-Halla þáttr' and 'Ásu-Þórðar þáttr' exist independently in other manuscripts. The tale of Karl the Luckless exists independently in AM 533 4to and AM 557 4to (both fifteenth-century manuscripts), where it is called *Karls þáttr*. Some *þættir* exist in multiple versions, as with 'Auðunar þáttr vestfirska' and 'Sneglu-Halla þáttr', which differ considerably in their *Morkinskinna* and *Flateyjarbók* forms. There are also collections of *þættir*, such as the seventeenth-century AM 426 fol.[63] On the other hand, very few of the *þættir* discussed by Harris exist except as episodes in kings' sagas.

The *þættir* in *Morkinskinna* have generally been regarded as older than the saga. They must have existed, some scholars have argued, in independent versions that were longer than those now extant. *Þættir* were thus shortened before being introduced into the saga.[64] Björn M. Ólsen

---

60 The number of studies of *þættir* whose narratives are set in Iceland is considerably smaller. Discussion of *þættir* is most often about those included in kings' sagas.

61 Bjarni Aðalbjarnarson, *Om de norske kongers sagaer*, pp. 154–159.

62 Gimmler, *Die Thættir der Morkinskinna*, pp. 30–66.

63 *Katalog over den arnamagnæanske håndskriftssamling* 1889–94.

64 Faulkes, *Two Icelandic Stories*, p. 2.

believed that this idea could help to explain the form of 'Stúfs þáttr'.[65] Although very few of the twelve *þættir* identified by Gimmler are extant in independent versions, scholars have nevertheless thought that they could trace their independent existence. But clear proof has been lacking, while comparison of versions of the same *þáttr* is seldom possible.

Another difficulty is the generic categorisation of *þættir*. Lars Lönnroth points out that the term is never used in the Middle Ages in respect of any literary genre. Thus, hardly any of the narratives edited by Þorleifur Jónsson and Guðni Jónsson are identified as *þættir* in any of the manuscripts. More frequently the word was used to denote that which was a part of a whole, as noted above, or as a thread in a woven fabric.[66] Harris saw this as a somewhat circular argument, claiming that the meaning of the word was irrelevant because almost none of the *þættir* were identified as such in the manuscripts. He has argued that the literary characteristics of the works in question should bear more weight than medieval terminology in defining *þættir*.[67]

From the time that *þættir* were first edited as separate literary entities, they have been linked by scholars with the modern literary genre of the short story.[68] In many ways this is a problematic connection. Sverrir Tómasson has noted the implausibility of associating *þættir* with a literary genre that was virtually unknown before the fourteenth century.[69] Even then stories normally appeared in collections, as parts of a larger whole, as with Boccaccio's *Decameron* or Chaucer's *Canterbury Tales* – works in which the individual tales were probably not intended to exist outside their frames. They are not like the short stories from the nineteenth or the twentieth centuries, which establish their own independent fictional world, with each work a self-contained narrative in miniature. The *Íslendingaþættir* would have been a unique medieval genre, but this

---

65 Björn M. Ólsen, *Stúfs saga*, p. xi.
66 Lönnroth, 'Tesen om de två kulturerna,' pp. 19–21; 'The Concept of Genre in Saga Literature.'
67 Harris, 'Genre in Saga Literature: A Squib,' pp. 427–436; Andersson, 'Splitting the Saga,' pp. 437–441.
68 Gimmler, *Die Thættir der Morkinskinna*, pp. 67–70.
69 'Konungasögur,' p. 384; see also Würth, *Elemente des Erzählens*, pp. 11–22.

has not dissuaded some scholars from attributing the invention of the short story to medieval Icelanders.[70]

The invention of the *þættir* as a genre is connected with the partitioning movement that became fashionable in the nineteenth century. Scholars first divided Sagas of Icelanders into narrative episodes (*þættir*) but then the *þættir* in the kings' sagas were gradually considered to be the base from which that genre developed. More recently *þættir* have been increasingly regarded as parts of a whole rather than independent narratives. Discussion of the role of *þættir* in kings' sagas as a whole has been a still more recent development.[71]

A new perspective

The structure of medieval Icelandic sagas is nowadays discussed in a new light, now that long-cherished neo-classical notions have been sidelined. Modern discussion began with an examination of the structural principles of European romance, some of which are also identifiable in Icelandic sagas. Carol Clover's work pays surprisingly little attention to *Morkinskinna*, though she does note that the saga contains many more digressions than had previously been the case with the synoptic kings' sagas.[72] Marianne Kalinke has explored the story of the brothers Eysteinn and Sigurðr the Crusader in the light of new approaches to the structure of medieval narrative, comparing *Morkinskinna* with earlier kings' sagas, notably *Ágrip* and *Historia de antiquitate regum Norwagiensium*.[73] In 1975 Lars Lönnroth remarked of the *Morkinskinna* episodes:

> Several of the stories about travelling Icelanders found in *Morkinskinna*, for example, cannot be fully understood unless we know that they were introduced at a particular point in the biography of some particular Norwegian king, whose

---

70 See the more detailed discussion in Ármann Jakobsson, 'The Life and Death of the Medieval Icelandic Short Story'; *Íslendingaþættir: Saga hugmyndar.*

71 Rowe, *The Development of Flateyjarbók: Iceland and the Norwegian Dynastic Crisis of 1389.*

72 *The Medieval Saga*, pp. 172–173, 177 and 179.

73 Kalinke, 'Sigurðar Saga Jórsalafara,' p. 155.

vices or virtues are illustrated in the stories by showing
the king's relationship to some particular type of visiting
Icelander (the fool, the impetuous warrior, the skald, etc.).
Merely studying the internal structure of these stories thus
cannot give us a clear understanding of the genre to which
they belong.[74]

These remarks encourage us to explore the larger picture, the sagas that
frame the episodes,[75] thus setting the stage for the present investigation
upon the structure and the aesthetics of *Morkinskinna* within the context
of new understandings about medieval aesthetics.

---

74 Lönnroth, 'The Concept of Genre in Saga Literature,' p. 423.
75 Sverrir Tómasson accepts this point (*Íslensk bókmenntasaga* 1, p. 384). Kalinke's approach ('Sigurðar Saga Jórsalafara') was a first step in this direction; Stefanie Würth
(*Elemente des Erzählens*) examines *Flateyjarbók*, as does Andersson in his articles
on *Morkinskinna* (among others, 'The Politics of Snorri Sturluson').

3. Strands in the Saga Web

Sad clowns and sympathy

The dispute over the structure of *Morkinskinna* – particularly the suggestion that the *þættir* did not belong in the saga – was an important factor in
the debate about the saga's origins. These episodic narratives were considered interpolations, regarded as extraneous to the (supposedly) main
strands of the saga, their purpose unclear and their relevance for the whole
work minimal. And yet, as several examples below will attest, it emerges
that *þættir* could work effectively within the aesthetic of amplification
(*amplificatio*) that Icelandic saga writers knew from other medieval works.
But whereas rhetorical amplification in these works always appeared to
have had a demonstrable purpose, the functions of the *þættir* in *Morkinskinna* are far from clear. It is thus necessary to examine some individual
episodes from the saga, particularly with regard to their narrative contexts,
in order to be able to say something about their function and role in the
overall work, and to explore the notion that they are more than just well-
told stories designed to entertain readers.

Morkinskinna contains a short narrative, unique to the saga and often
known as 'Ívars þáttr Ingimundarsonar'.[1] As a fragment, it appears to be
concerned with an Icelander's trials and tribulations in love – a short tale
about one Ívarr Ingimundarson. Its *Morkinskinna* title, however, is *Fra
Eysteini konvngi oc Ivari* 'Concerning King Eysteinn and Ívarr',[2] which
indicates that since the sovereign is mentioned first, the story is not only
about Ívarr but might even be principally about King Eysteinn. Ívarr's
story is, to be sure, a love story, but it is only the introduction to this story
that really matters. The Ívarr episode takes up seventy-two lines in the

---

1 It has appeared several times under this name, as edited, for instance, by Bragi Halldórsson *et al.* (*Íslendinga sögur og þættir*) and twice by Guðni Jónsson (*Íslendinga
þættir*; *Íslendinga sögur*, Vol. 12).
2 *Morkinskinna*, ed. Finnur Jónsson, p. 354.

93

Íslenzk fornrit edition of *Morkinskinna*, of which the love-triangle element occupies only fifteen lines. Ívarr is a fine poet, but his brother Þorfinnr does not seem to be his equal among the retinue surrounding the Norwegian king. For this reason the brother returns home, carrying Ívarr's request that Oddný Jónsdóttir should await his return; instead Þorfinnr himself successfully woos and wins Oddný, and *Ívarr tekr nú ógleði mikla* (*Msk*. II, 103) 'Ívarr now becomes very unhappy'. Ívarr's unhappiness, then, is the issue with which the tale is concerned. He is a poet in the king's court, one of the main entertainers in a retinue whose functions include the spreading of good cheer. The story is constructed around contrasting elements of joy and sadness. Ívarr's individual story is a tale concerned with character psychology, while the story within *Morkinskinna* can also be read on a socio-political level, as it relates to the social order of which King Eysteinn is the custodian.

Central to the episode are the king's questions about what is wrong with Ívarr. The king mentions five possible causes for his unhappiness and proposes five solutions. The last is that every day Ívarr should seek

> 'á fund minn ok ek sitk eigi um nauðsynja málum, ok mun ek hjala við þik. Skulum vit rœða um konu þessa alla vega, þess er ⟨þú vilt⟩ ok má í hug koma, ok mun ek gefa mér tóm til þessa, því at þat verðr stundum at mǫnnum verðr harms síns at léttara er um er rœtt (*Msk*. II, 104).'

> 'my company, and if I am not occupied with important business, I will chat with you. Let us talk about this woman in every way that occurs to you, and I will make time for this, for it is sometimes the case that one's troubles are lighter when they are talked about'.

The modern reader doubtlessly detects shades of Freud here as the King suggests that Ívarr take to the metaphorical 'couch' to talk out his troubles. And, with this,

> þetta hlýddi bragðit, ok bœttisk nú Ívari harms síns vánum bráðara [ok] gladdisk hann eptir þetta, ok kømr í samt lag sem fyrr hafði verit um skemmtun hans ok gleði (*Msk*. II, 103–105, at 104 and 105, repectively).

the strategy worked and Ívarr was relieved of his problems
sooner than was expected ... He was happy afterwards and
his sense of fun and happiness were now as before.

By the end of the episode joy is restored.

If the tale is examined in isolation, without interpreting it as a *þáttr*,
then the king appears to be the main character. He speaks more often than
Ívarr and has much to say. It is he who solves the problem, and in so doing
the episode helps to characterise him. Ívarr is the stereotypical lovesick
poet. His kind of story is well known in the sagas: someone trusts a brother
or friend with a mission to a betrothed woman, but the emissary breaks
faith and acquires the woman for himself.[3] This motif is, on the other
hand, secondary in the tale, whose main concern is not the love triangle but
rather Ívarr's unhappiness. What matters is the king's search for a solution,
which is that Ívarr should forget the woman, recover his lost happiness, and
remain with the king.

If this isolated examination helps to identify the tale's main theme, its
meaning becomes even clearer when it is set within its wider context. The
episode begins thus:

> Í þeima hlut má marka, er nú mun ek segja, hverr dýrðar-
> maðr Eysteinn konungr var, eða hvé mjǫk hann var vinhollr
> ok hugkvæmr eptir at leita við sína ástmenn hvat þeim væri
> at harmi (*Msk.* II, 102).

> In what I am about to tell it may be noticed what an excellent
> friend King Eysteinn was and how devoted and dedicated he
> was in taking care of the men closest to him when they were
> in trouble.

The 'I' who speaks says explicitly that what follows is an example of just
how devoted a friend King Eysteinn really was, and only then is Ívarr
introduced into the saga. Prior to this segment of the story we have an
account of Eysteinn's reign in Norway that concludes with a description
of the king:

3   This narrative pattern is repeated in *Laxdæla saga*, *Gunnlaugs saga* and *Bjarnar saga*.
    See Andersson 'Skald Sagas in their Literary Context 3: The Love Triangle Theme,'
    p. 273.

Hann var spekingr mikill at viti, ok allra manna var hann
fríðastr sjónum, hvítr á hár, meðalmaðr á vǫxt, snjallr í máli
ok inn mildasti af fé, ok allra konunga hefir hann verit ástsælastr við sína menn, glaðr ok lítillátr í máli (Msk. II, 102).

He was a man of great intelligence and of all men the
most handsome, white haired, of medium build, articulate
in speech and most generous with money and of all kings the
most beloved by his men, cheerful and humble in speech.

The king's popularity among his subjects is emphasised, and the episode
that follows provides evidence of this quality.[4]

The episode thus is important within the saga as part of the characterisation of Eysteinn. It is also an example of how the king exercises
his responsibility for looking after his thanes. Eysteinn is an affectionate
and wise counsellor. As such he is the opposite of his brother Sigurðr,
and the episode, along with other material in the saga, for example, the
mannjafnaðr 'flyting' between the brothers, highlights this feature of his
character.[5] Though Ívarr's problem and Eysteinn's solution might seem
insufficiently striking to justify their inclusion in a kings' saga, as an exemplary narrative about royal power and Eysteinn's virtues, the episode
makes a significant contribution to Morkinskinna.[6]

'An honour for a noble man'

The Ívarr episode is a dialogue between two men, a story with a simple
structure about one man's problem and its resolution.[7] More complicated
in structure is the episode concerning Auðun of the Westfjords, a popular

4 Hermann Pálsson, 'Mannfræði, dæmi, fornsögur,' pp. 307–309.
5   In this scene Sigurðr says about Eysteinn: 'margir sœkja til ráða á þinn fund. En heyri
    ek suma þat mæla at þú heitir stundum því er þú endir ekki af' (Msk. II, 132) ('many
    come to you for advice. But I hear that some say that you sometimes make promises
    that you do not keep'). See Ármann Jakobsson, Í leit að konungi, p. 194.
6   Marianne E. Kalinke, 'Sigurðar Saga Jórsalafara: The Fictionalization of Fact in
    Morkinskinna,' pp. 159–161.
7   Gimmler (Die Thœttir der Morkinskinna, pp. 81–82) believes six of twelve þœttir
    in Morkinskinna were of the same type as 'Ívars þáttr,' that is, one-stranded (ein-
    strängig).

tale in which Auðun is the principal figure from beginning to end, but, unlike Ívarr, the eponymous hero's role does not require him to remain with
a king.[8] The story begins like many an *Íslendingasaga*: *Maðr hét Auðun*
'A man was named Auðun', (*Msk.* I, 217), while, at the end, a descendant
of Auðun is named, one Þorsteinn Gyðuson (*Msk.* I, 223).[9] Nevertheless,
in the 1009 manuscript, the story is not simply named after Auðun alone:
its introductory title is *Fra þvi er A/þvn enn vestfirðzki førþi Sveini konvngi biarndyri* 'Concerning how Auðun from the Westfjords brought King
Sveinn a bear'.[10]

The episode tells of how a poor man endures privation and faces danger
in order to present a gift to the King of Denmark. He breaks his journey in
Norway and is summoned to meet with King Haraldr, who seeks either to
buy the animal or have it presented as a gift. Auðun rejects both possibilities and states his intention of giving the bear to King Sveinn of Denmark.
Taking leave of King Haraldr, Auðun duly arrives in Denmark, presents
the animal to King Sveinn, receives royal gifts and then embarks on a pilgrimage. On the way home he again stops at the Danish court and receives
additional tokens of Sveinn's esteem. In all he receives six gifts from the
King of Denmark: the King agrees to accept the animal,[11] provides Auðun
with silver for his pilgrimage, makes him his retainer and, at their final
parting, presents him with a ship, some silver, and a ring. He requests that
Auðun should only give the ring to a noble man to whom he owes something important, 'for it would be an honour for a noble man to accept it'
(*Msk.* I, 222). When Auðun once again stops at King Haraldr's court, he

8   'Auðunar þáttr' has always been considered an excellent 'short story', which Gwyn
     Jones (*Eirik the Red and Other Icelandic Sagas*, p. xv) called 'one of the most flawless
     short stories ever written,' and Guðni Jónsson ascribed to Snorri Sturluson (*Vest-
     firðinga sögur*, ÍF 6, p. cvii). Guðni, a scholar belonging to the Icelandic school, could
     hardly pay any narrative a greater compliment than to ascribe it to the great master of
     saga narrative.

9   Guðni Jónsson (*Vestfirðinga sögur*, ÍF 6, p. cvi) thought the wording indicated that
     the *þáttr* was composed after the death of Þorsteinn – that is, about 1200. Hermann
     Pálsson (*Sagnaskemmtun Íslendinga*, p. 139) disagreed.

10   *Morkinskinna*, ed. Finnur Jónsson, p. 180.

11   Auðun specifically mentions that he considers this a gift, and the king certainly be-
     stows a great honour upon a poor man by accepting the gift from him. Cf. William
     Ian Miller, *Audun and the Polar Bear: Luck, Law, and Largesse in a Medieval Tale
     of Risky Business,* pp. 114–20.

presents King Haraldr with the ring[12] in return for the king's generosity, 'for you had the chance of depriving me of both things, the animal and, in addition, my life, and you gave me safe conduct, which others did not obtain' (*Msk.* I, 223).

These two episodes share the feature that, when read in isolation, their narrative themes differ in important respects from their significance within the saga. The Auðun episode as an independent narrative seems, on its surface, at first to focus almost exclusively on the eccentric eponymous hero whose acts of buying the bear, withholding it from one king and presenting it to another appear considerably unmotivated. Why he chooses to bestow his generosity upon the King of Denmark rather than the King of Norway, for example, is a question the tale does not ask, let alone answer. This is one of many such queries for which we cannot find answers in a tale that seems only to operate on the level of plot, and we are left to conclude simplistically that if the story has a wider significance beyond being a well-told story, it might be that Icelanders are remarkable people who have a knack for getting along with difficult kings.

However, when read within the context of *Morkinskinna* the themes of this episode, overlapping with those from the Ívarr episode, include a deep-seated concern with the role of a king in relation to his retainers as well as an interest in the nature of kingship. Let us look briefly at this content and how it affects a reading of the episode. After the death of King Magnús the Good, the main part of the narrative involves the constant antagonism between his successors, King Sveinn of Denmark and King Haraldr of Norway, who also claims the Danish throne as well. (*Msk.* I, 188–204). Prior to the episode there has been a hiatus in their disputes, and the disagreement between King Haraldr and Einarr Paunch-Shaker is touched upon briefly (*Msk.* I, 207–216). But just before the episode appears, a tendency among the Norwegian magnates is mentioned:

> þegar er þeim líkaði nǫkkut illa við konung þá hlaupu þeir ór landi suðr til Danmerkr til Sveins konungs (*Msk.* I, 216).

> When they were displeased with the king, they fled the country south to Denmark to King Sveinn.

12 It is, of course, possible that Sveinn intended the gift for him (see Njörður P. Njarðvík, 'Maður hét Auðun,' p. 615.)

In this *Morkinskinna* context we are, of course, meant to recognise the courage – if not downright foolhardiness – required of Auðun to stand before King Haraldr the Severe and refuse to give him the bear that he rashly confesses is intended as a gift for the King's worst enemy, a man Haraldr considers to be a usurper. (Auðun is not merely eccentric; he seems to harbour a death wish!) The context, more importantly, also helps us to see that the absence of any stated motivation for Auðun's conduct points to the use of the tale in the saga as an *exemplum*. The author's interests seem to be focused on something outside of Auðun, on themes and issues that recur in the saga. Auðun's part in his own tale is merely to serve the author's larger interests in the saga and this is probably one reason why he is only viewed from the outside.

One of the author's interests is the often fractious relationship between kings. When Haraldr decides to allow Auðun to give his rival a precious gift, his act becomes understood by his enemy as a peace offering and shows Haraldr's generosity and willingness to be reconciled. On the other hand, Sveinn succeeds, by proxy, in giving Haraldr a ring as a token of thanks, and this gift appears to be understood by Haraldr, reciprocally, as expressing Sveinn's esteem for his Norwegian adversary. Each king is thus able to use Auðun as a diplomatic forerunner to test the political waters without making a personal commitment ('Sveinn, here is a bear ...'; 'I'm sending you, Haraldr, this ring ...') that would carry the danger of losing face should the offer be rejected. This is a significant stage in their feud, from which, although it continues, most of the venom has disappeared and it finally enables the kings to make peace. In the narrative of Auðun and the bear both kings are prominent in their own countries as generous men of honour rather than, as in the case of King Haraldr, a king insulted because his rival King Sveinn is made the recipient of a trophy Haraldr had set his eye upon. The episode presages the conclusion of their strife. Far from being a precious story about another Icelander who goes abroad and does well, this tale develops themes central to the saga author's concerns in the narrative as a whole.

Both the Ívarr episode and the Auðun episode are thus important in the context of *Morkinskinna*. Scholars' assertions that they retard the flow of the saga and detract from its logical dramatic or thematic development or are clumsily handled hardly seem justified – but all of these are indeed arguments that have been mounted to prove that the *þættir* originally did not occur in *Morkinskinna*. To be sure, the *Flateyjarbók* version of the Auðun episode contains additions and changes from the version in *Morkinskinna*.[13] The episode is also a perfectly organic narrative, and scholars have been eager to interpret it independently.[14] But although the episode could have existed before its inclusion in *Morkinskinna* and has had an independent existence afterwards, these factors do not alter its importance within the saga. Nothing in the structure of the episode indicates that it was not present in *Morkinskinna* from the beginning. In fact the episode has an 'introduction' (eighteen lines in the Íslenzk fornrit edition) in which Auðun's history is recounted before he faces King Haraldr and states that he intends to give the king's arch-enemy the precious gift. But the story is brief and indicates that Auðun is more a type than an individual. His family is not traced and he is not given a place of origin more specific than the west of Iceland. Auðun is a stock male character, like Ívarr the poet: the former a poor, honest but eccentric Icelander, the latter a good poet and prominent member of a king's court. But their tales contribute as much to the thematic density and unity of the text as to its dramatic development.

The warp and the weft

Occurring very early in *Morkinskinna*, the episode of Karl the Luckless has been considered a definite interpolation because of the alleged contradictions it introduces. In fact, as discussed above, whether any actual contradiction is involved is a matter of interpretation, and in this instance there seems no need to excise the episode from *Morkinskinna* for introducing elements into the saga that clash with the 'main' text. Karl himself

---

13   'Auðunar þáttr' is one of six *þættir* that Finnur Jónsson (*Morkinskinna*, p. ix) used as evidence for *Morkinskinna*'s being full of interpolations.

14   Among others, Guðni Jónsson, ed. *Vestfirðinga sögur*, p. c–cviiii; Arnold R. Taylor, 'Auðun and the Bear'; Stig Wikander, 'Från indisk djurfabel till isländsk saga'; Edward G. Fichtner, 'Gift Exchange and Initiation in the "Auðunar þáttr vestfirzka"'; Sigurður Svavarsson, 'Athugun á þáttum sem bókmenntagrein'; Njörður P. Njarðvík, 'Maður hét Auðun'; William Ian Miller, *Audun and the Polar Bear: Luck, Law, and Largesse in a Medieval Tale of Risky Business*.

is from an insignificant family, but proves, in ways parallel to the case of Auðun from the Westfjords, to be a character of a degree of complexity beyond the dimensions that his modest family connections promise. His story has a major impact on the history of Norway, in that Kálfr Árnason saves Karl from King Sveinn's men, refuses to hand him over to the king and transfers his allegiance to Magnús the Good (*Msk.* I, 15–18). The episode begins when Karl, on a trading voyage to the east, appears in the court of the Russian King Jarizleifr, Magnús the Good's foster-father, ostensibly to obtain permission to trade in the country, and ends when Karl brings Kálfr to Magnús and accomplishes his mission:

> Þeir Kálfr Árnason ok Karl váru þá austan farnir, ok hafði Karl þegit margar góðar gjafir af Jarizleifi konungi ok Magnúsi ok mikla sœmð aðra (*Msk.* I, 19).

> Kálfr Árnason and Karl had by then left the east and Karl had received many good gifts from King Jarizleifr and Magnús and many other honours.

Since Einarr Paunch-Shaker had previously pledged his support for Magnús, it may be claimed that the episode is part of the large narrative of how Norway slips away from King Sveinn, in part with the help of the machinations of King Jarizleifr's agents.

Shortly thereafter (*Msk.* I, 29–30) Kálfr Árnason and Magnús gladly take leave of each other. There are two tales that require interpretation here, but Finnur Jónsson never thought that they were interpolations.[15] The first is an amusing little tale about a spat between Kálfr and Einarr as to which of them will sit next to the king. This matter could seem too unremarkable to merit inclusion in the *Older Morkinskinna* were it not for the fact that such important people are involved in the story. The stories end with a statement that is typical of the episodes in *Morkinskinna*: *Ok fór Kálfr með þessum hætti ór landi, sem nú var sagt, ok fyrir reiði konungs* 'And Kálfr left the country in the way that was now said and because of the king's anger' (*Msk.* I, 30).

---

15 *Morkinskinna*, p. xii. Finnur does however consider another story about Kálfr later in the saga to be an interpolation (p. xiii).

A central thesis of the present book is that all episodes in *Morkin-skinna* have a thematic function within that saga. We may additionally observe how these episodes are used in a similar way in the story of Sigurðr the Crusader, in which a sequence of five narrative incidents highlight Sigurðr's madness during the later years of his reign. (Gimmler regarded them as '*þáttr*-like' narratives rather than proper *þættir*).[16] This madness is also mentioned in *Ágrip*, *Fagrskinna* and *Heimskringla*, but only in *Heimskringla* (one example) and *Morkinskinna* (where there are five) is it dramatised through *exempla*.[17] It could be that the author of *Heimskringla* considered the number of *exempla* in *Morkinskinna* to be excessive, but they do in fact add important character nuances to the figure of King Sigurðr. The five episodes have one object, which may be thought of as typical of *Morkinskinna*: several of its episodes gain added meaning as links in a chain. This same chainlike function applies also to some ten narratives that relate to the joint reigns of Magnús the Good and Haraldr the Severe. Many of the tales revolve around disagreements between the kings. These tales enable the author to compare and contrast kings, which is a main preoccupation in the saga.

Another category of these episodes involves narratives about poets and Icelanders in the service of Haraldr the Severe, including the Sneglu-Halli episode and the Stúfr episode, together with the episode about Þorgils the fisherman and the tale about an Icelandic storyteller (*Msk.* I, 235–237, 270–293). As stories about the relations between King Haraldr and Icelanders (especially Icelandic poets), they deal with an important aspect of the characterisation of the king, but also offer a statement about the position of Icelanders and poets in the retinue of the king and in the world.

16 Gimmler, *Die Thættir der Morkinskinna*, p. 64.
17 For a characterisation of these narratives, see Ármann Jakobsson, *Í leit að konungi*, pp. 226–227. Of the exemplary character of the *þættir*, Hermann Pálsson says: *Íslendinga þætti lesum vér ... einkum til að glæða skilning vorn á mannlegum verðmætum yfirleitt, hvenær og hvar sem vera skal á kringlu þessa heims* ('Brands þáttur örva,' p. 117) 'We read *Íslendinga þættir* ... especially to quicken our understanding of human values in general, when and where they occur in the realm of this world'. See *Heimskringla* III, ÍF 28, pp. 269–270.

As indicated above, the key structural principle that the author of *Morkinskinna* follows throughout the saga is amplification (*amplificatio*), the regular augmentation and amplification of the narrative. To register this point we may compare *Morkinskinna* with *Ágrip af Nóregskonunga sǫgum*, a work that the author of the former knew and used. *Ágrip* is a truncated narrative, written partly in the spirit of Ari fróði 'the learned'.[18] Out of this material the author of *Morkinskinna* creates a lengthy saga in which the *þættir* comprise one of his key building blocks. Their presence within the saga does not bear witness to structural deficiencies or scribal clumsiness, but rather to thirteenth-century literary aesthetics. The order of narrative events remains the same as in other kings' sagas, but many of the new episodes are chronologically vague, and are positioned within *Morkinskinna* in accordance with their narrative significance.

Among the items added are *exempla* such as the tale of Ívarr. In *Heimskringla* Eysteinn is said to be *manna glaðastr ok lítillátastr, hugþekkr ok ástsæll allri alþýðu* (*Heimskringla* III, 256) 'the most cheerful and humble of men, accommodating towards and popular among all the people'. In *Morkinskinna* these attributes are dramatised, rather than bluntly stated, through his dealings with Ívarr. *Fagrskinna* and *Heimskringla* report on the peace negotiations between Haraldr the Severe and King Sveinn.[19] The author of *Morkinskinna*, on the other hand, uses the Auðun episode to enrich the story and provide it with an ethical and political dimension. Its position in the saga is dictated by thematic context, rather late in the saga of Haraldr the Severe, after the tensions between Haraldr and King Sveinn of Denmark have reached their peak. As we have seen above, it adds to the theme of the nature of kingship.

It is clear from comments included in the saga that the author of *Morkinskinna* had expected to be accused of saying too little rather than too much:

---

18 'Ágrip er lítil bók um langa sögu' (Bjarni Einarsson, *Ágrip af Nóregskonunga sǫgum, Fagrskinna, Nóregs konunga tal*, ÍF 29, p. xvii) ('*Ágrip* is a short book about a long history'). In *Ágrip* Norwegian history from 1030 to close to 1150 is recounted in twenty-three pages in the *ÍF* edition, whereas the Íslenzk fornrit edition of *Morkinskinna* is 569 pages.

19 *Fagrskinna*, p. 273; *Heimskringla* III, p. 161.

liggja þó niðri ósagðir miklu fleiri hlutir, þeir sem ósagðir
eru af hans afreksverkum, ok kemr mest til þess ófróðleikr
várr ok þat með at vér viljum eigi rita vitnisburðarlausar
sǫgur, þótt vér hǫfum heyrt þær frásagnir, því at oss þykkir
betra at heðan af sé við aukit heldr en þetta sama þurfi aptr
at taka (*Msk.* I, 204–205).

yet many more things remain unsaid, those of his great
deeds that are untold, which is because of lack of reliable
information, and in addition we do not wish to write down
unsubstantiated stories, although we have heard such tales,
because it seems better to add something in the future than
to have to retract it.

It would probably have surprised the author of *Morkinskinna* that readers have so often regarded some material in his saga as unnecessary. It is
true that he presents five *exempla* about the deteriorating mental health
of Sigurðr the Crusader, whereas one such story is enough for the author
of *Heimskringla*. In this respect, the author of *Morkinskinna* resembles
an author of medieval romance, who regarded an amplified narrative as
preferable to one that presented the bare bones of an account.

One aesthetic principle discernible in the work of the *Morkinskinna*
author is the staging of events. It is not enough for him to report the dissension and difficulties of the dealings between Haraldr the Severe and
Magnús the Good, but rather he provides *exempla* that dramatise these
matters. Like the author of *Heimskringla* later, the author of *Morkinskinna*
describes Haraldr the Severe as a great friend of Icelanders.[20] But it is not
enough simply to make this observation in expository form; he chooses
to show it in many episodes. Dramatised narratives – for those who love
storytelling – carry a greater ability to explain the nature of reality than
adjectival description – showing rather than telling – and the skill is extensively used in *Morkinskinna*. At the same time this is not to say that the
saga may be added to endlessly. It could well have been the case that the
author of *Morkinskinna* knew still more sagas about the insanity of King
Sigurðr, and it is a measure of his attitude towards psychological matters

20 *Heimskringla* III, p. 119.

that he chose to include so many stories about this affair within his saga. It is also no coincidence that many episodes treat the single year in which Magnús and Haraldr reigned jointly. The two kings' disagreements help to define the theme that trouble always ensues when there is more than one king at a time in a given country.

The structure of *Heimskringla* in some respects conforms somewhat more closely to Aristotle's poetics than does *Morkinskinna*, even if Snorri was not familiar with them. Accordingly nineteenth-century disapproval of medieval aesthetic values tended to pass *Heimskringla* by, whereas *Morkinskinna* felt the full force of that scepticism. If the last third of *Heimskringla* is compared to *Morkinskinna*, it is obvious that the author of the *Heimskringla* text often omits much of the *Morkinskinna* material and adds little.[21] In this part of *Heimskringla* there are no *þættir* except those recounting the miracles of Óláfr the Saint, which are periodically woven into the saga.[22] On the other hand, there are quite a few episodes in *Óláfs saga helga* that resemble those in *Morkinskinna*.[23] Snorri's methods in *Óláfs saga helga* and the third part of *Heimskringla* are thus different. Even though Snorri – if Snorri it is – omits many of the *Morkinskinna* episodes, the intentions of these two authors were much the same – they wished to make the saga more complete and dramatic. Snorri's narrative strategy clearly resembles that often to be found in the Sagas of Icelanders,

---

21 Among other things he omits many episodes but not all of the episodic material in *Morkinskinna*. This comparison assumes that *Morkinskinna* did not change much from 1220 to 1280. We should also note that it is not certain that Snorri is the author of all of *Heimskringla* (see Jonna Louis-Jensen, 'Heimskringla – Et værk af Snorri Sturluson?' pp. 230–245).

22 Óláfr the Saint is omnipresent in *Heimskringla*, in the works that both precede and follow his saga. The *Morkinskinna* material added to *Heimskringla* deals mostly with Óláfr the Saint. This can easily be seen in 'Óláfs saga kyrra' where Snorri actually abbreviates the *Morkinskinna* narrative but adds material concerning Óláfr the Saint. See Ármann Jakobsson, 'The Individual and the Ideal: The Representation of Royalty in *Morkinskinna*,' p. 81. The emphasis in *Heimskringla* on Óláfr the Saint after his death shows that Snorri Sturluson is far from being a 'secular' historiographer who places little emphasis on the sanctity of Óláfr. See Sverrir Tómasson, 'Snorri Sturluson als Hagiograph,' pp. 275–286.

23 Sigurður Nordal discusses the purpose of these *þættir* in *Heimskringla* (*Snorri Sturluson*, p. 247).

whereby tension is increased by focussing on feud-patterns rather than by making use of episodes in the manner of *Morkinskinna*.

We need not restrict ourselves to those narratives that are usually called *þættir*. The narrative web is intricate, and the episodes in the narrative are actually more numerous than those tales specifically identified as such. Before the battle at *Hlýrskógsheiði* 'Lyrskov Heath', leave is taken of Magnús the Good just before the battle:

> verðr hér frásǫgn at hvílask fyrst, því at eigi má allt senn segja. Magnús konungr er nú áhyggjufullr, því at liðsmunr er mikill, svá at menn segja sannliga at eigi sé færi en sex tigir um einn, en konungr vill þó fyrir ǫngvan mun flýja, en allillr kvittr er í þeim Dǫnunum ok þykkir þeim sér stýrt til váða.
>
> Nú er hér til at taka í ǫðrum stað at ... (*Msk.* I, 55).

> here the story must rest for now, because it is not possible to say everything at once. King Magnus is worried because his men are outnumbered, so that men truthfully say there were sixty to every one of them, and yet the king refuses to flee, but the troubling report has the Danes thinking they are being led to a certain death.
>
> Now we turn to another place where ...

Here two narratives run parallel to each other, as the narrative voice tells us. Thus Magnús is left on his own for a while, the past briefly invoked and his sister's story told up to the point where Óláfr the Saint appears before her and her new husband to call for their assistance with Magnús (*Msk.* I, 55–59).

Another web is spun when King Haraldr the Severe sails into the saga to meet King Magnús the Good. His tale, like a Homeric epic, begins *in medias res*, followed by a long flashback that is framed by the first meeting between Magnús and Haraldr. The tale of Haraldr from the time he parted from Óláfr the Saint at Stiklastaðir is woven into the tale of Magnús at this point. The episode begins thus:

> Nú hvílisk fyrst at segja frá Magnúsi konungi, ok skal fyrst segja frá ferðum Haralds (*Msk.* I, 82).

Now the story of King Magnús must rest while the story of
Haraldr's journey is told.

It ends thus:

> Nú er þar til sǫgu at taka er fyrr var frá horfit, er þeir finnask
> í Danmǫrk, Magnús konungr ok Haraldr fǫðurbróðir hans
> (*Msk.* I, 120).

> Now we get back to the narrative where we left it, as they
> meet in Denmark, King Magnús and his uncle Haraldr.

The whole of the intervening chapter is the tale of Haraldr, perhaps the one
that Haraldr tells Magnús when they meet in Norway. It is well integrated
here in that its inclusion fully satisfies artistic criteria (*ordo artificialis*),
but its failure to reflect the natural order of events meant that it met with
Finnur Jónsson's disapproval.[24] Along with the other instances discussed
in this section, it represents one of many examples of the distinctive forms
of structural amplification identifiable in *Morkinskinna*.

As yet unmentioned are the many poems that form an important element in *Morkinskinna*. By including poems in his saga, the *Morkinskinna*
author connects his new-fangled saga to the old poetic tradition, but the
use of poetry by Icelandic kings' saga writers is also evidence of aesthetic amplification.[25] The poems provide a direct connection to a past
that comes to life and speaks in the middle of the historical narrative.[26]
Of course, they are often cited in the saga as authoritative references for
the substance of the narrative that has just been presented.[27] But some

24 'Dette er en højst mærkelig anordning af begivenhederne.' (This is a most unusual
 ordering of events) *Morkinskinna*, p. xv. See Ármann Jakobsson, 'Den kluntede afskriver: Finnur Jónsson og *Morkinskinna*.'
25 Skaldic poetry was not an inseparable part of kings' sagas from the beginning. Very
 few verses are to be found in *Ágrip* and *Sverris saga* (Preben Meulengracht Sørensen,
 'The Prosimetrum Form 1: Verses as the Voice of the Past,' pp. 182–183). Here the
 author of *Morkinskinna* seems to be following in the footsteps of the author of the
 *Oldest Saga of St. Óláfr (see Kari Ellen Gade, 'Poetry and its changing importance
 in medieval Icelandic culture,' pp. 69–70). The author of *Heimskringla* is also an
 amplifier through his use of skaldic verse.
26 Meulengracht Sørensen, 'The Prosimetrum Form 1,' p. 182.
27 Bjarni Einarsson, 'On the rôle of verse in saga-literature.'

verses come closer to being independent sections, notably *Bersǫglisvísur*, which is really an episode about the poet Sigvatr, a tale with a happy end and an unmistakable hero.[28]

The referential role of verses recalls the time-honoured debate as to whether medieval Icelandic sagas are historical or literary. In terms of structure kings' sagas and Sagas of Icelanders resemble works of history. Their authors feel free to turn aside from the main narrative thread in order to add genealogies, place names and all kinds of information about additional characters and extraneous matters.[29] In this respect these saga narratives resemble Aristotle's description of history, as not just the narration of a single action but rather an account of all related events, where much of the action depicted was of little importance for the main matter.[30]

The author of *Morkinskinna* presents himself as an historian. But his history is unlike that to be found in *Íslendingabók* or *Ágrip*. His usage of available sources suggests that he regarded such writing as a skeleton that needed to be fleshed out. As a text *Morkinskinna* resembles a patch-work quilt. Such quilts are works of art in themselves, but they consist of separable units, just as the Auðun episode functions as a unit within the whole of *Morkinskinna*. The text lacks organic unity and has no obvious singular narrative thread. On the other hand, no material can be regarded as extraneous – all the tales and other anecdotes are of equal importance. Many stories and poems are woven together all at once, and yet they all remain in the mind of the author and his audience.[31] As C.S. Lewis puts

28 Heather O'Donoghue (*The Genesis of a Saga Narrative*, pp. 175–177) calls some of the verses in *Kormáks saga* 'anecdotes,' but the same word also applies to the *þættir*. Edith Marold ('The Relation Between Verses and Prose in *Bjarnar saga Hítdœlakappa*,' p. 124) notes that the verses in *Bjarnar saga* are woven into the overall narrative texture (*entrelacement*) in a way that is reminiscent of the structure of romances.

29 See, for example, I. R. Maxwell, 'Pattern in Njáls Saga,' pp. 18–23; Meulengracht Sørensen, 'The Prosimetrum Form 1,' p. 172. For further discussion, see Ármann Jakobsson, 'History of the Trolls?: *Bárðar saga* as an historical narrative,' pp. 53–60.

30 *Poetics*, pp. 115–119. Clover (*The Medieval Saga*, p. 41) calls attention to this.

31 Compare Eugène Vinaver, *The Rise of Romance*, p. 76: 'The next and possibly the decisive step towards a proper understanding of cyclic romance is the realization that since it is always possible, and often even necessary, for several themes to be pursued simultaneously, they have to alternate like threads in a woven fabric, one theme interrupting another and again another, and yet all remaining constantly present in the author's and the reader's mind.'

it: 'Everything leads to everything else, but by very intricate paths'.[32] If something is excised from a narrative web of this type, the overall artefact is damaged. Nothing is redundant, and the work does not proceed in a straight line. The author is aware of this and describes his method by means of an additional explicatory image, which is dramatised in a particular *þáttr*, the final one to be discussed in this chapter.

Circumspecting the King

As mentioned above, Indrebø drew attention to a chapter in *Morkinskinna* in which the comic tale concerning King Sveinn and a certain woman is said by the narrator to be unhistorical (*Msk.* I. 251–252). He thought this bore witness to the methods and mindset of the author of *Morkinskinna*.[33] Indrebø was right to look within the saga for arguments that clarified the work's structure. But in this regard another narrative to which he paid no attention plays a more important role.

Like many writers, the author of *Morkinskinna* provides an internal key to understanding the structure of his work. Since *þættir* are essential in the saga, his methodology is indeed revealed in a particular *þáttr*; and a pair of characters who fulfil those most prominent roles within *Morkinskinna*, that of king and Icelander, also feature in this tale. The Icelander Hreiðarr the Simple meets King Magnús the Good and starts behaving in a strange manner:

> 'Ek vilda sjá þik, konungr.' 'Þykki þér nú vel þá,' segir konungr, 'er þú sér mig?' 'Vel víst,' svarar Hreiðarr, 'en eigi þykjumk ek enn til gǫrla sjá þik.' 'Hvernug skulu vit nú þá?' spyrr konungr, 'vildir þú at ek stœða upp?' Hreiðarr svarar: 'Þat vilda ek,' segir hann. Konungr mælti er hann var upp staðinn: 'Nú muntu þykkjask gǫrla sjá mik mega.' 'Eigi enn til gǫrla,' svarar Hreiðarr, 'ok er nú þó nær hófi.' 'Viltu þá,' spyrr konungr, 'at ek leggja af mér skikkjuna?' 'Þat vilda ek víst,' svarar Hreiðarr. Konungr mælti: 'Vit skulum þar

32 C.S. Lewis, *The Discarded Image: An Introduction to Medieval and Renaissance Literature*, p. 194.

33 Gustav Indrebø, *Fagrskinna*, pp. 31–33.

þó nǫkkut innask til áðr um þat málit. Þér eruð hugkvæmir margir, Íslendingar, ok veit ek eigi nema þú virðir þetta
til ginningar. Nú vil ek þat undan skilja.' Hreiðarr svarar:
'Engi er til þess fœrr, konungr, at ginna þik eða ljúga at
þér.' Konungr leggr nú af sér skikkjuna ok mælti: 'Hyggðu
nú at mér svá vandliga sem þik tíðir.' 'Svo skal vera,' segir
Hreiðarr. Hann gengr í hring um konunginn ok mælti opt
it sama fyr munni sér: 'Allvel, allvel,' segir hann. Konungr
mælti: 'Hefir þú nú sét mik sem þú vilt?' 'At vísu,' svarar
hann. (*Msk.* I, 155–156).

'I wanted to see you, king.' 'And are you happy now,' said
the king, 'now that you see me?' 'I am indeed,' said Hreiðarr,
'but I do not think I see you well enough.' 'What shall we
do about that?' said the king. 'Would you like me to stand
up?' Hreiðarr said: 'Yes, I would like that.' The king said,
when he had stood up: 'Now you must think you see me
well enough.' 'Not well enough yet,' said Hreiðarr, 'but we
are getting there,' 'Would you like me,' said the king, 'to
take off my cloak.' 'Indeed I would,' said Hreiðarr. The king
said: 'We would like to think about that. You are a creative
lot, you Icelanders, and for all I know you are trying to trick
me. I think I will pass on this one.' Hreiðarr said: 'Nobody
can trick you, king, or lie to you.' Now the king takes off his
cloak and said: 'Now you can look as much as you like.' 'I
shall,' said Hreiðarr. He now walked around the king, and
repeated the same thing again and again: 'Good, good,' he
said. The king said: 'Have you then looked at me as much
as you please?' 'I have indeed,' he said.

The circumstances described here border on the absurd. The king himself
is asked to stand up by an Icelander, a stranger at court, who then proceeds
to walk around the king as if he were a prize bull at a stock show. This is
by no means the only occasion on which an event in *Morkinskinna* seems
highly peculiar. But one of *Morkinskinna*'s idiosyncratic narrative laws
seems to be that the more bizarre or comic an event may seem, the more
significant it may be.

This peculiar narrative is a prime example of the distinctive role of amplification that finds expression throughout *Morkinskinna*. It also embodies the role of the episodic narrative, the *þáttr* in the saga, in that such episodes are often a way of examining a king from all sides. The king's subordinate in such episodes is often some innocent abroad who arrives unknown in the country of the king, 'unblinded', as it were, by knowledge.[34] But this figure proves to be a vital lens in this narrative. He takes the place of the child who sees everything directly and describes what he sees, the ingénue who perceives more than others and gives the game away by stating what all others are afraid to say. Hreiðarr alone – with the exception of Haraldr the Severe – sees a flaw in Magnús: the king's eyes are not perfectly aligned (*Msk.* I, 156). The least of the king's subjects, along with another king, is the one permitted to describe the king as he actually is. Thus the episode about the simple Icelander introduces a defamiliarising effect into the kings' saga: when the known becomes strange, it then becomes much clearer.

Each of the episodic narratives in *Morkinskinna* centres upon, and circles around, the king that features within it. It might even be said that Hreiðarr the Simple represents the saga author, who views his kings from all sides in order to see them better, warts and all. In the Ívarr episode King Eysteinn is presented from a new perspective and becomes a multi-facetted, three-dimensional figure. The Auðun episode traces the hostile relationship of two kings, Haraldr the Severe and Sveinn Úlfsson. The episodes about the differences between Magnús and Haraldr offer careful and varied scrutiny of the joint regency of the two monarchs. And, finally, the episodes about Haraldr the Severe and visiting Icelanders reveal sides of his character that other sagas fail to represent.

That circles, like webs, symbolize eternity and the universe, was a medieval truism. King Arthur and his knights sat at a round table, and the stories of those knights form a cycle that is the story of the king. In much the same way the Sagas of Icelanders and the retainers in *Morkinskinna* circle around both the kings and the social and cultural institutions of king-

---

34 The adjectives *heimskur, heimski* means here something resembling *heimaalinn* (literally, 'raised at home'), 'provincial' or inexperienced', but does not have to be perjorative or imply stupidity.

ship. In this episode we witness a pair of concentric circles. As Hreiðarr circles the king, the king scrutinises his scrutineer, likewise rounding him into shape, representative of the wider wary reciprocal examination that takes place between the Icelanders and each of the tales in the saga.

The circular route followed by Hreiðarr the Simple symbolises the aesthetics of the saga. Although the saga follows the course of linear time, it also describes a circle. The life of each king consists of many circles. And in the circles of the story the Icelanders and the kings look each other in the eye as they so often do in medieval Icelandic literature. Such eye contact reminds us that manipulation of narrative viewpoint is yet another key structural feature of *Morkinskinna*.

4. Dramatic Narrative

The function of the episode

In a stranded saga each narrative thread has its own internal structure, as does the whole work. Each episode must be a complete unit in order to fulfil its role in the larger saga without detracting from the integrity of the overall work.[1] In order to understand the larger form, it is appropriate to examine these smaller structures and to consider elements such as narrative style, point of view and staging, the construction of the elements of a particular scene.

The Ívarr episode alludes to many narrative events: the love of a man for a woman, the unhappy experiences of a man's brother in a Norwegian court, his return home, his promise to his brother, deception and marriage. All of this information is conveyed in a short introductory summary, but the core of the episode lies in a verbal exchange between Ívarr and the king. The pace of the narrative slows, and the exchange is presented in some detail. The king first asks Ívarr why he is so downcast *'ok fyrr er þér váruð með oss var margs konar skemmtan at yðrum orðum'* (*Msk.* II, 103) '"for, when you were with us earlier, there was much delight at your words"'. Ívarr shows no wish to explain, and the king then begins to speculate. The first surmise is that Ívarr has developed an antipathy towards someone at court, the second is that Ívarr believes he is receiving less honour than is his due, the third is that Ívarr is unhappy with something in Norwegian society, and the fourth is that he wishes to assume control over some property or possessions. Finally, the king determines that a woman is the cause of the problem. He first offers to obtain the woman for Ívarr even if she is married to someone else. The next suggestion is that Ívarr accompany him as he attends a number of feasts after Christmas where he will see

---

1   I.R. Maxwell ('Pattern in Njáls Saga,' p. 25) calls this 'the principle of the integrity of episodes.'

'margar kurteisar konur; ok ef eigi eru konungbornar þá
mun ek fá þér einhverja.'[2]

'many courteous women, and if they are not of royal birth
then I will find one for you'.

In reply Ívarr claims that *'jafnan er ek sék fagrar konur þá minnir mik
þessar konu'* (*Msk.* II, 104). '"whenever I see beautiful women, they remind me of this woman"'. Accordingly, such visits would only cause
his grief to increase. Then the king offers him authority and wealth, *'ok
skemmtir þú þér við þat'* 'with which you can entertain yourself' and, finally, money for trading voyages. Ívarr refuses all of these blandishments,
so that only one choice remains, *'ok er sá alllítils verðr hjá þessum er ek
hefi boðit þér'* (*Msk.* II, 104) '"and this is very little compared to what I
have offered you"'. The suggestion is that Ívarr speak about the woman to
the king, who promises to listen carefully.

The dialogue between the king and Ívarr is the most important part
of the episode, not because of its significance in relation to other events
but rather because of its own narrative energy. On the surface, the story
exists for the sake of the story and its distinctiveness sets its stamp on
Morkinskinna. The individuality of the saga narrator is immediately apparent, through the use of the first person at the beginning of the episode
– *Í þeima hlut má marka, er nú mun ek segja* (*Msk.* II, 102) 'In this part it
is noted, as I am about to tell' – and the structure of the scene is also unusually clear, with five questions followed by five suggestions. Each new
conjecture is met with a negative response from Ívarr and an aesthetically
satisfying rhythm is established. The king's conjectures escalate until a
solution finally emerges. The king's remarks, occasionally ironic, help to
increase the narrative tension, as when he stops to ponder the course of
the exchanges: *'Vandask oss nú getan,' segir konungr* (*Msk.* II, 103) '"The
guessing is getting more difficult" says the king'.

The loquacious king and his reticent retainer are opposites who inter-
act through language. The one asks, the other answers. It says something

2 Translator's note: In English two words for translating *kurteisi* are available, *courtesy*
and *courteousness*, both related etymologically. The *OED* notes that someone behaving courteously has the manners of a prince, someone who is *courtly*. I use the word
'courtesy' since it is closer graphemically to *kurteisi*.

about the fondness of the author of *Morkinskinna* for this form that we find it repeated more succinctly later in the saga, with Eysteinn playing the same role.[3] The king is persistent, and his repeated questions serve to identify the necessary conditions for an ideal life: money, fame, love, harmony and justice. An element of urbane teasing, combined with an underlying seriousness in respect of matters of love, invests the overall dialogue with a pleasing complexity. From the outset Ívarr is a reluctant interlocutor, and considerable tension exists between his few words and his underlying emotional distress. Perhaps inadvertently Ívarr also makes an astute observation about love that introduces a profound note into the gentle bantering of the episode: beautiful women offer him no solace, since they remind him of his irrecoverable loss.

This use of dialogue between two or more characters in a single setting is a narrative strategy that helps to create a sense of the broader society. In this instance, the characters are the king and the retainer, and the scene is the king's court and his hall. Although no one except the king and Ívarr speak, other characters hover in the background. The court is mentioned and so are its values that help determine lesser and greater honour among its members – this was the society that had granted Ívarr's brother so little regard and esteem. The king's questions refer to the men with whom Ívarr is perhaps at odds, as well as to courtly ladies and feasts, and finally he tells Ívarr to appear when the tables have been cleared and removed, and again eating and festivities are mentioned, but also the role of the king in granting an audience to his subjects. Although the dialogue needs only two individuals, other characters form a backdrop subtly introduced into the narrative.

The Ívarr episode represents a performance. The saga author, not content merely to describe the dealings between the king and Ívarr, prefers to dramatise them; the scene, and others like it, illustrate the importance of dramatic elements in the art of amplification in *Morkinskinna*. Characters from earlier historical writings are set upon something of a stage and are interpreted as the drama unfolds.[4] Here *Morkinskinna* departs from

3   King Sigurðr the Crusader becomes unhappy and Eysteinn seeks an explanation and makes a number of suggestions, in a way similar to that in the Ívarr episode.
4   Marianne E. Kalinke, 'Sigurðar Saga Jórsalafara,' pp. 153, 155–56. Lars Lönnroth (*Den dubbla scenen: Muntlig diktning från Eddan till ABBA*) has discussed the dra-

the narrative discourse of older synoptic kings' sagas. The saga is no dry enumeration of facts concerning the kings, but rather a romantically and dramatically fleshed out narrative. In this respect it resembles those Sagas of Icelanders in which direct speech plays such a prominent role, such as *Brennu-Njáls saga* and *Laxdæla saga*.[5] In *Morkinskinna* we learn first in general terms of the disagreement between King Haraldr and Einarr Paunch-shaker, and then the conflict is dramatised. First there are two episodes in which, though they are not the principal characters, Haraldr and Einarr are part of the mix. Then there is a scene at King Haraldr's feast in which Einarr falls asleep, a misfortune that would eventually lead to his death. Thus, in *Morkinskinna* three unique episodes dramatise the downfall of Einarr. Some readers may regard them as unnecessary in context, but the author of *Morkinskinna* favours this narrative method, both because of his fondness for drama, but also because it adds something that cannot be found in other sagas.

Another example of dramatic amplification is the dispute between Magnús the Good and Kálfr Árnason, which begins with two episodes concerning the feud between Kálfr and Einarr Paunch-Shaker (*Msk.* I, 28). Then we are told about Magnús's attitude towards slander and about King Magnús's request that Einarr describe to him the events surrounding the killing of his father, King Óláfr, at the battle of Stiklastaðir (*Msk.* I, 29–30). Einarr becomes evasive at this point and points to Kálfr. Subsequently the three men visit Stiklastaðir where Magnús accuses Kálfr of treachery against Saint Óláfr; Kálfr, anticipating this turn of events, had already prepared his departure and flees the country.[6] This course of events becomes a dramatic episode with three actors. One of them (Einarr)

matic element in the flyting between Ívarr and Sigurðr. See also Clover, *The Medieval Saga*, pp. 177, 179.

5   See Irmgard Netter, *Die direkte Rede in den Isländersagas*, on direct speech in the Old Icelandic sagas, where she mentions the Ívarr episode (p. 223). See also Werner Ludwig, *Untersuchungen über den Entwicklungsgang und die Funktion des Dialogs in der isländischen Saga*. Björn M. Ólsen (*Um Íslendingasögur: Kaflar úr háskóla-fyrirlestrum*, p. 46) notes: 'Höfundur vill láta viðburðina sjálfa tala til lesendanna eða áheirandanna og eftirláta þeim dóminn' ('An author wishes to allow the events themselves to speak to readers or listeners and have them decide matters').

6   This event is also covered in *Heimskringla III*, pp. 23–25, and the narrative was certainly part of the *Morkinskinna* known to the *Heimskringla* author.

has just a single line in the final stages of the episode, but it is a significant one, as it serves to direct Magnús's suspicions towards Kálfr. The result is that Magnús stages a 'play within a play' at Stiklastaðir that concludes with his implicit indictment of Kálfr for having killed King Óláfr. At this point, Magnús, in the only reference to a character's appearance in the episode, becomes *dreyrrauðan yfirlits* (*Msk.* I, 30) 'blood-red in the face'. This image of the king's face, flushed with barely suppressed rage, accomplishes what saga rhetoric only rarely manages to convey – it offers us a vivid sense of a character's emotional state. It is a saga picture worth a thousand words.

The episode of Arnórr the Earls' Poet is a prose narrative, reading almost as a synopsis of a short drama, that frames four stanzas from Arnórr's *Magnússdrápa* (*Msk.*, XXIII). It begins in this way:

> Nú er getit eitthvert sinn, er konungar báðir sátu í einni hǫll yfir matborðum, at þar var þá kominn Arnórr jarlaskáld ok hefir ort sitt kvæði um hvárn þeira (*Msk.* I, 143)

> Now it is told that once both kings were at table in a hall when Arnórr jarlaskáld ('Earls' poet') arrived; he had composed a poem about each of them.

The scene is set in a hall where the principal characters, two kings (Magnús and Haraldr), are dining. Arnórr is summoned to court to recite his poems to them. He sets out in great haste since we are told that he does not even wash the tar off his hands (he had been working on his ship when he received the summons). He arrives at the hall where two or more additional figures are guarding the door. He says to them: '*Gefið rúm skáldi konunga!*' (*Msk.* I, 143) '"make way for the kings' poet!"'. These are the first spoken words in the episode, and seem completely unnecessary for its development, since no one had challenged Arnórr. On the other hand, they reveal much about Arnórr's attitude as a poet or perhaps Icelandic court poets' conception of themselves.

Arnórr approaches and greets the kings. Haraldr seizes the initiative and asks him whose poem is to be recited first, and in this way is presented as the more dominant party in this verbal exchange. Arnórr defends himself adroitly, indicating that he will first recite his poem in praise of

Magnús since he is the younger monarch and '*bráðgeð verða ungmenni*' (*Msk.* I, 143) '"bears the impetuousness of youth"'. Even in the limited context of this episode the irony in this answer is obvious, since Haraldr has already demonstrated his impatience and headstrong nature in speaking first. As the saga develops, and his impulsive lack of self-control becomes a *leitmotif*, this irony becomes all the more apparent (compare part IV, chapter 2). The narrator, however, makes sure that his intentions will be understood by adding: *En þat þótti hvárumtveggja virðiligra er fyrr var kvæðit fært* (*Msk.* I, 143) 'But both thought it more honourable to be addressed in verse first'. The episode clearly concerns the rivalry between the kings and is one of many scenes in the saga that dramatises the tensions between them during the one year in which they ruled Norway jointly. On this occasion Arnórr acts as referee, but it is the honour represented through his poetry that presently lies at the heart of the dispute.

The poem begins (we are told in indirect speech) with the Orkney Earls' travels and those of the poet. Then Haraldr interrupts Arnórr for the first but not the last time and faults Magnús for listening to a poem about the Earls of Orkney. King Magnús requests his patience, claiming that before the poem is finished Haraldr will think Magnús's honour sufficiently celebrated. A verse then follows in which Magnús is highly praised: '*hverr gramr es þér stóru verri*' (*Msk.* I, 144) '"every king is much inferior to you"'. Haraldr, unable to restrain himself, again interrupts the poem and cautions Arnórr: '*Lofa konung þenna sem þú vill ... en lasta eigi aðra konunga*' (*Msk.* I, 144) '"Praise this king as you wish ... but do not find fault with other kings"'. Haraldr, the cleverest of men and an aficionado of skaldic verse, does not like the way things are going. Arnórr continues and for the third time Haraldr interrupts: '*Allákaflega yrkir sjá maðr, ok eigi veit ek hvar kømr*' (*Msk.* I, 145) '"The man composes with great relish, and I cannot see where this is going to end"'. In this unusual narrative conversation one man speaks in the *hrynhent* metre and the other interjects comments that resemble either literary criticism or the commentary of a modern sports broadcaster. The scene ends with an account of the poet's recitation of a second poem, this time in praise of Haraldr, though the poem itself is not included in the text. Asked by another (anonymous) character how he likes the poem, Haraldr replies in direct speech to the effect that whereas his poem will be forgotten, the one about Magnús will be recited as long as Scandinavia is inhabited. It is tempting to conclude that *Blágagladrápa* – the poem composed about Haraldr – had already been forgotten when *Morkinskinna* was written, in about 1220. In that case, the narrative takes on an additional irony, for in having Haraldr predict the truth, the author uses historical distance (of some 175 years) to enter into a conspiracy with the saga audience against the characters in the episode.[7] Following his uncompromising comparison of the kings, the poet now chooses to reconcile them. He brings their gifts together by drawing his gold ring, a gift from Magnús, over the point of the gold-inlaid spear that Haraldr had given him, saying: '*Hátt skal bera hváratveggju konungs-gjǫfna!*' (*Msk.* I, 146) "'each gift from a king shall be borne on high!'". In this way Haraldr is mollified. He, of course, has the last word: '*Kom sjá til nakkvars lǫngumorðinn*' (*Msk.* I, 146) "'He was certainly a wind-bag'", but in conclusion we are told that Arnórr promised to compose a memorial poem for Haraldr, and that the skald and Magnús became close friends thereafter.

The fondness that the author of *Morkinskinna* has for poetry and narrative drama is evident in the way he weaves together the recitation of famous poems and near theatrical comedy. The Arnórr episode is more or less related through direct speech throughout and takes place in a single setting and time. In the brief period depicted in the episode, more than one narrative is at work. The comparison between the kings not only depicts the monarchs themselves but reveals the author's ideas about royal power. The episode also refers to eternity. Haraldr asserts that the poem about Magnús will exist for as long as Scandinavia remains settled. In this way a brief narrative about an afternoon's entertainment can become very meaningful as long as it has general value and is maintained in the historical memory of ordinary people.

Many of the episodes in *Morkinskinna* bear characteristics reminiscent of dramatic performances. In the Arnórr episode the 'stage' is clearly described as a space consisting of dining tables in a hall. There are three characters, two kings seated and the unwashed Arnórr standing. Hovering in the background are additional figures that provide the chief characters with the opportunity to see themselves better. The text is both sonorous

---

7   On this episode, see Ármann Jakobsson, 'Um hvað fjallaði Blágagladrápa?'.

and dramatic, both poetry and prose. Thus, in the middle of an epic narrative about battles and other royal activities, we find dramatic sketches that
endow the narrative with additional energy. By means of such additional
material the nature of kings' sagas was changed almost beyond recognition. A work emerged that is difficult to understand merely with the tools
provided by Aristotelian theory.

The multifaceted episode

Although the episodes in *Morkinskinna* are dramatic, they can scarcely be
said to satisfy the neo-classical unities of time, place, and action. Some
episodes consist of a string of minor events having in common only their
association with one man. They may be said to constitute a model of
Morkinskinna as a whole. A brief example is provided in the Sneglu-Halli
episode, an anthology of interwoven comic episodes about Halli and his
period of residence at the Norwegian court.[8]

The episode (*Msk.* I, 270–284) can be divided into ten smaller episodes. The episode begins with Halli's arrival at the Norwegian court and
his initial brief and brisk exchanges with King Haraldr whose disguised
figure Halli fails to recognise. The second part consists of what might be
called a play within an episode: the king commissions the poet Þjóðólfr
Arnórsson to compose a poem about a quarrel between a tanner and a
blacksmith, making use of mythological imagery. In the third part we hear
it said that Halli would not be able to compose as well as Þjóðólfr, before
the saga moves to a different setting, a feast in the king's hall. There Halli
composes a poem about Túta, the king's dwarf, and receives a splendid
reward from the king. The brief fourth segment takes place back on the
streets of Niðaróss, where Halli finds himself in disgrace because of his

8 In *Morkinskinna* the episode is called 'Frá Sneglu-Halla.' Its *Flateyjarbók* version is
   longer and has been thought of as exaggerated. Some, among others, Finnur Jónsson
   ('Flateyjarbók,' pp. 187) and Bjarni Aðalbjarnarson (*Om de norske kongers sagaer*,
   p. 156) have considered the *Morkinskinna* analogue to be a shortened version, possibly
   ad interim, between the *Older Morkinskinna* and the extant version. The *Morkinskinna* version, however, is early, as can be seen by the extensive use of the preposition
   of (see Peter Foote, 'Notes on the Prepositions OF and UM(B) in Old Icelandic and
   Old Norwegian Prose,' p. 67).

'gruel greed', that is, his excessive consumption of gruel. In the fifth section the king requires Halli to compose a verse quickly and deftly, with a death penalty hanging over his head in the event of failure. As a reward for his excellent poem his transgression with the gruel is forgiven. As with the second and third episodes of the Halli tale, these two brief sections form a narrative pair.[9] There follows a longer scene, set in the king's hall on Christmas Eve, in which Halli and Þjóðólfr quarrel. Though the scene observes the unities of place and time, the poets' quarrel is nevertheless bifurcated: first they abuse each other over what was the worst poem each has ever composed, and then they quarrel about the relative merits of avenging one's father too much or too little. Shortly thereafter Þjóðólfr 'is out of the saga' for the time being. 'Sneglu-Halla þáttr' is thus divided into two: Þjóðólfr is Halli's chief adversary in the first part, and then he disappears.

The seventh scene in the play concerns Einarr fluga 'the Fly', a typical *ójafnaðarmaðr* (an 'uneven' or 'unfair man'), a killer who never pays compensation to the relatives of his victims.[10] Halli wagers with another retainer that he will persuade Einarr to act differently in such matters. He then dupes Einarr into paying compensation for a man whom Halli untruthfully claims as a relative. This is a long episode whose constituent elements take place at the same location but with intervals between them. Finally there are three short interludes that deal with how Halli silences a *þing*-meeting in Denmark, dupes the king into rewarding him for an inferior poem, and secures a passage to Norway. The episode concludes with these words: *ferr Halli síðan á fund konungs, ok var hann nú þar of hríð með konungi (Msk. I, 284)* 'then Halli went to see the king and was with him there for a while'.

---

9   I have written about this narrative at greater length elsewhere: Ármann Jakobsson, 'Munnur skáldsins: Um vanda þess og vegsemd að vera listrænn og framgjarn Íslendingur í útlöndum'; Ármann Jakobsson, 'Food and the North-Icelandic Identity in 13th century Iceland and Norway.'

10   William Ian Miller considers the *ójafnaðrmaðr*, a figure featured throughout much of Old Norse literature, a kind of 'bully, a man who shows no justice or equity in his dealings,' in contrast to the *jafnaðrmaðr*, who 'is even, of even temper and fair in his dealings' (*Eye for an Eye*, p. 8).

STRUCTURE

The structure of this episode is comparable to *Morkinskinna* as a whole, and thus it may be said that the Halli episode is a sort of *Morkinskinna* writ small. The person of Halli lends cohesion to the units as a whole, and the dramatic narrative provides character description rather than a chain of events.[11]

Saga heroes on display

As he walks around the king Hreiðarr the Simple studies him closely, and his perambulation, as suggested above (part II, chapter 3), reflects the overall circular structure of *Morkinskinna*. Similarly, Hreiðarr's well-focused gaze directed at the king could well stand for the importance of narrative point of view throughout the saga. In setting a stage for its events, as a kings' saga, it differs from older historical writings that are primarily assemblages of facts, and those differences align it more with the Sagas of Icelanders than with other members of its text-type. *Morkinskinna* and *Heimskringla* are similar in this respect.[12] Everywhere in the narrative the vision of an artist with a tale to tell can be perceived. Sometimes we are told how a set is bathed in light and hidden in shadows: *Myrkt var í húsinu, ok stóð Benteinn við dyrnar* (*Msk.* II, 191) 'It was dark in the house, and Benteinn stood at the door'. The saga offers occasional descriptions of the weather, some of them quite colourful: *Ok þegar um morguninn í sólarroð vakna þeir ok sjá at mjǫrkvi lá mikill allt um eyna. En litlu síðarr sjá þeir annan veg í hafit frá sér, sem eldar nǫkkurir væri* (*Msk.* I, 201) 'And when morning arrived with sunrise they awoke and saw a dense fog lay over the whole island. But a little later they saw another way out to sea where some fires were'. The weather, though, is never described superfluously, but only when it exerts an influence over the course of events.[13]

---

11 We might note that 'Sneglu-Halla *þáttr*' exists as as a play in an Icelandic children's book (*Samlestrarbókin*, pp. 144–147).

12 On staging in the *Íslendingasögur*, see among others Carol Clover, 'Scene in Saga Composition.'

13 The terrain around Ulster where Magnús Barelegs falls is described in order not only to help explain the course of events but also to provide a venue for the major event that follows: *En þar var svá landsleg sem þeir fóru at í stǫðum voru hrískjǫrr þau ok mýrar nǫkkurar ok sumum stǫðum fen djúp milli hrísanna, ok váru klappir yfir fenin*

122

The manipulation of narrative perspective is an important element in the art of *Morkinskinna*. Haraldr the Severe's entrance into the saga is unique. He does not announce his arrival; it is the calm before the storm. King Magnús and his men observe *at skip sigldi austan fyrir land* (*Msk.* I, 80) 'a ship sailing west along the coast', arousing the curiosity of King Magnús and prompting a detailed description of the ship. The captain then engages in *rœðu við ráðgjafa Magnúss konungs, Úlf stallara* (*Msk.* I, 80–81) 'a conversation with Magnús's counsellor Úlfr the marshal'. The captain is described, from Úlfr's vantage point, as

> mikill vexti ok með tíguligu yfirbragði, þat er hann mátti á
> sjá, en ávallt var nǫkkur hulða á dregin (*Msk.* I, 81);

> tall and of noble appearance as far as he could see, but some
> sort of veil was always drawn over him.

Then the man meets Magnús and it turns out to be King Haraldr himself. The veil that was drawn over him could be almost any natural (or unnatural) phenomenon, a hat or fog or even some kind of magic helmet that makes the wearer invisible. Whatever it is, it serves to limit the viewpoint of the observer, the one who looks on. In this respect it symbolises the nature of the narrative discourse in that, just as Úlfr the Marshall sees Haraldr in a fog, the narrative focus of the text is itself fragmented and the knowledge of the saga listener or reader is partial. But shortly thereafter when Haraldr emerges from the fog, the counsellor clearly recognises him *ok fleiri menn kenndu hann nú* (*Msk.* I, 82) 'and more men recognised him then'. Here the limited focus of the narrative discourse results in increased awareness. Úlfr and the saga audience have been turned into the ignorant observer circling the king in order to recognise him, much like Hreiðarr the Simple later in the saga. Ignorance leads the way to a clearer vision, a deeper understanding. Because Úlfr and the saga audience at first had seen Haraldr 'through a glass darkly', their later insight is all the more powerful.

(*Msk.* II, 67) 'But on the terrain where they crossed brush wood could be found here and there, and some swamps, and in places deep pools between the bushes over which stepping stones made a path'.

STRUCTURE

Old Icelandic sagas have repeatedly been characterised as possessing an objective narrative style in which individuals are described externally. Usually, though, it is clear who the people in a particular scene actually are. Although Hrútr does not know the identity of Gunnarr of Hlíðarendi the first time they meet in *Brennu-Njáls saga*, the audience is in on the secret. Another device is reminiscent of scenes in modern crime novels where a limited point of view is required – where the reader stands beside one character and looks through his eyes at all the others. This narrative strategy is known from *Færeyinga saga* where Þrándr of Gata appears to the king as a stranger even though he has been introduced into the saga in a manner that would make him known to the audience.[14] This narrative mode is a kind of defamiliarisation, a way of scrutinising saga heroes anew in a way that recalls Hreiðarr the Simple's circumspection of King Magnús in order to see him better. As in Brechtian drama this alienation effect (German: *Verfremdungseffekt*) is intended as a way of seeing reality more clearly. By examining the known as if it were unknown, a new understanding may be reached.

The key figures in the saga are on display, such as King Magnús in the Hreiðarr the Simple episode. They are examined from the outside in order to help the saga audience develop a better feel for them. This narrative technique is used when Hákon Ívarsson runs out of the woods unrecognised, like an old northern Robin Hood (*Msk.* I, 267). Shortly thereafter the Sneglu-Halli tale begins with the acrimonious (and scurrilous) exchange between Halli and an unknown man who turns out to be the king, although at first we learn only that *stóð maðr upp á drekanum, er fyrir fór, í rauðum kyrtli* (*Msk.* I, 270) 'a man in a red tunic stood up in the leading longship'. Because neither Halli nor Hreiðarr the Simple knows the king at the beginning of their stories, they become counterparts. The foreigner is like an untutored child who has much to learn, and the narrative technique is designed to show this. The limited point of view is important when Icelanders are in the main role. Inexperienced Icelanders sometimes

---

14 On narrative irony in *Færeyinga saga*, see Peter Foote, *On the Saga of the Faroe Islanders: An Inaugural Lecture delivered at University College London*, pp. 14–17, 20–21; Ólafur Halldórsson, ed. *Færeyinga saga*, pp. 32–45. The complex character description of Þrándr of Gata in several respects resembles that of Haraldr the Severe (see part IV, chapter 2).

encounter difficulties while they are in foreign lands. Their limited awareness is reflected in the narrative point of view. That same narrative focus
also reflects the understanding of an Icelandic audience as it comes into
contact with the foreign world through *Morkinskinna*.[15]

The Halli episode consists, as we have seen above, of several scene
changes. Halli can appear as an unknown man when he has been forgotten
for a while at a feast: *Þá kvað maðr vísu á bekkinn, ok var þar Halli* (*Msk.* I,
273) 'Then a man recited a verse to the bench and it was Halli'. The scene-
changes within the tale resemble those created by the episodes themselves
in the overall structure of the saga. The scene-changes in the episodes are
echoed in Hreiðarr's circuit around the king. The point of view becomes
that of the retainer in order better to examine the king.

The Stúfr tale begins with Stúfr's arrival in Norway and his finding
lodgings with a prosperous farmer. One day guests arrive unexpectedly at
the farm:

> Ok einn dag er menn váru úti staddir þá sá þeir menn fara
> at bœnum marga ok riðu ok váru búnir skrautliga (*Msk.* I,
> 290);
>
> one day when people were standing outside, they saw many
> splendidly-dressed men approaching the farm on horseback.

As readers we observe the king approaching with his retinue – our vantage point is the same as Stúfr's (who is, in fact, blind). In this passage
the king remains unidentified, and thus 'unrecognised', although we have
been following him – in the *Íslenzk fornrit* edition of the saga – for the
last 211 pages. We then accompany the king inside, taking in the farm-
house through his eyes, which immediately focus upon *maðr einn mikill
sat útarr á bekkinn* (*Msk.* I, 291) 'a large man sitting on the end of the
bench towards the door'. This is, of course, Stúfr, and we have now observed both characters. It is as if the episode is partly designed to teach
the reader something about manipulation of narrative perspective.

15 It is not uncommon in medieval Icelandic sagas for the narrative point of view to
   be clearly defined, and for an Icelander in a foreign country to receive special attention. There are well known examples in *Laxdæla saga* (ed. Einar Ól. Sveinsson, *ÍF* 5,
   pp. 54–56).

In the tale of Sveinki Steinarsson (*Msk.* II, 29–38) we accompany King Magnús's envoy to Vík in order to meet with Sveinki. At a meeting the envoy has an exchange with an extraordinary man, whose physical appearance is described thus:

> Þá stendr maðr upp í flokki þeira Elfargrímanna, mikill vexti ok þrekligr. Sá var í loðkápu ok hafði refði um ǫxl. Danskan hǫtt mikinn hafði hann á hǫfði (*Msk.* II, 31)

> Then a tall and powerfully built man stood up in the midst of the *Elfargrímar* [those who live alongside the *Gautelfr* River in Sweden]; he was wearing a woollen coat and had a cudgel on his shoulder and a large Danish hat on his head.

Afterwards we are told that this is Sveinki Steinarsson himself. First we have a picture of the man; when the audience has seen him, then it is possible to identify him. At the same time, however, a definite irony is created where it may be assumed that quite a few of the audience are aware that the character is indeed Sveinki even before he is identified. This narrative method works through indeterminacy and hunches.

The last journey undertaken by King Haraldr the Severe is the invasion of England. The discussion of the army's preparations in Norway creates dramatic tension and expectations:

> Segja svá allir þeir er nǫkkur frásǫgn er kunnig hér um at eigi hafi betra mannval búizk af Nóregi til einnar ferðar en þetta. Er sjá nýjung rœdd í hvers manns húsi ok þó optast í konungs hirð, hversu Haraldi konungi myni farask til Englands. Telja það sumir upp hversu mǫrg stórvirki Haraldr konungr hefir unnit víða um lǫnd; kalla þat at ǫngan hlut muni hann finna ófœran fyri sér. Sumir mæla þat at England er ríkt ok fjǫlmennt, ok þar er ok þat lið er kallaðirru þingamenn ok valizk hǫfðu saman af ýmsum lǫndum ok mest af danskri tungu (*Msk.* I, 302).

> All those who know anything about the story told here say that never has a finer selection of men from Norway been prepared for a military expedition than this. This news was

spoken of in every house, but most of all among the king's retinue, how King Haraldr would succeed in England. Some spoke of the great deeds that King Haraldr had accomplished in many lands, and said that he would find nothing that would stand in his way. Some said that England was powerful and densely populated, and that there was also a fighting force called the 'þingamenn', selected from various lands, and most of them speakers of Norse.

Haraldr's successful campaigns are recalled, suggesting that nothing is beyond him, but such optimism is immediately followed with counter-arguments. The audience thus soon comes to realise that this invasion is a risky and even ill-advised venture. This same realisation hits Haraldr and his army much later, and it is from their perspective that we see this increasing awareness developing.

We observe a buoyant army of Norsemen who anticipate nothing unfavourable. Then in the distance they see a cloud of dust. Such a cloud is a classic example of synecdoche. The symbol occurs first; they then see shield and armour and finally an army that increases in size the closer it comes:

Veðrit var heitt mjǫk af skini, ok lǫgðu þeir eptir brynjur sínar, en gengu upp með skjǫldum ok hjálmum ok kesjum ok váru gyrðir sverðum, ok margir hǫfðu skot ok boga. Þeir váru kátir mjǫk ok hugðu nú til enskis ófriðar. Ok er þeir sœkja í nánd borginni sjá þeir jóreyki mikla ok þar undir því næst fagra skjǫldu ok hvítar brynjur, sjá þar ríðr í móti þeim mikit lið. Ok þegar stǫðvaði Haraldr konungr herinn, lét kalla til sín Tósta jarl ok spyrr hann hvat liði þetta mun vera er í móti þeim fer (…) er liðit æ því meira sem meirr nálgaðisk ok þeir sá gørr, ok allt var á at sjá sem ísmǫl væri (*Msk.* I, 311–312).

The weather was hot, the sun shone brightly, and they took off their armour and advanced with shields, helmets, pikes and girded swords, and many had bows and arrows. They were very merry and anticipated no resistance, and when

> they came near to the city they saw a great cloud of dust and then beneath it bright shields and white coats of armour; they saw riding towards them a great fighting force, and Haraldr immediately halted his army, had Tósti jarl [Tostig Godwinson] summoned and asked him what army this could be that was approaching them … the army became ever larger the closer it came, and they saw it clearly, and it looked to them like gleaming ice.

As usual King Haraldr reacts quickly, but we sense from his behaviour that he is shocked by what he has seen. The author's use of figurative language is clear in the last simile where the white shields of the English invoke for the Norse eye shining ice (a comparison used elsewhere in *Morkinskinna*: for example, *Msk.* II, 30). And because we view the scene through Haraldr's eyes we feel the same impotence in the face of this great army. The king is in the position of the simpletons and the powerless who ventured too far. Now he is a foreigner in a strange land.[16]

Here point of view serves not simply as an aesthetic device but as a means of promoting meaning. Its use is a major element in the narrative artistry of *Morkinskinna*, as in several other medieval Icelandic sagas. The moment when Hreiðarr the Simple walks round Magnús the Good reminds the audience of this. His circuit is a key to the interpretation of the saga.

Ironies

In all interpretations of *Morkinskinna* form and content are virtually indivisible. In the discussion so far, while questions of structure have been highlighted, matters of content have repeatedly been noted. Both elements are equally complex. In the weave of *Morkinskinna* there is both warp and weft, yet these are impossible to separate. Both sides of the saga page must be read – recto and verso.[17] Events have a literal meaning, but can

16 Ludvig Holm-Olsen ('En replikk i Harald Hardrådes saga,' pp. 35–41) has discussed the use of figures of speech in this description and emphasised the saga's incisive narrative art.

17 I derive the image from Svava Jakobsdóttir (*Skyggnst á bak við ský*, p. 146).

also bear a variety of interpretations. Just as Hreiðarr the Simple did not see King Magnús in full before he walked around him, the numerous and inextricably linked levels of meaning in *Morkinskinna* must be observed from all sides. At the heart of the saga is the key theme of the relationship between individuals and their society, and the saga's characters emerge at the interface of those two levels of meaning.

Belonging to the society of the Ívarr episode are a king, his retainers, entertainments, polite dining and elegant women. Portrayed is a courtly community in which everyone has a role to play. The retainer and the poet, for instance, must be of good cheer and must also make others cheerful. For a while Ívarr fails in this duty. King Eysteinn, on the other hand, is ever ready to support his retainers in times of need. He demonstrates his affection and friendship, is moderate in his dealings with others and does not take a hard line with problems such as Ívarr's temporary bout of low spirits. He is generous, with both his goods and his time, and Ívarr is comforted. The time that Eysteinn makes available from his *nauðsynja málum* (*Msk*. II, 104) 'necessary business' is the greatest gift that he can give to his retainer and friend, Ívarr the Icelander. The episode reveals that the king attaches great importance to the welfare of his friends. Moreover, Eysteinn's remarks show him to be a playful and ironic man with a sharp sense of character and a social conscience. He has a way with words and uses language to further his understanding of life. He is obstinate, and will not give up until he has the right answer. Above all, he is an excellent counsellor and will not rest until he has solved any problem with which he is wrestling.

The importance of this episode is highlighted in the subsequent *flyting*, or exchange of insults, between the brothers Sigurðr the Crusader and Eysteinn. Shortly after the Ívarr episode the brothers enter upon a comparison between themselves with respect to their individual achievements (*Msk*., LXXVIII), but in addition they have previously locked horns in the so-called 'Þinga saga' (*Msk*., LXXVII, the legal dispute between the brothers) where they likewise put their different character traits to the test. Because the Ívarr episode shows Eysteinn in a positive light, performing important royal duties and serving as a mainstay to his retainers, the story is important in relation to this comparison of the two kings. For this reason the *flyting* episode comes soon after the Ívarr episode. Sigurðr has embarked upon a crusade to the Holy Land and is everywhere regarded as a hero. It is thus important for Eysteinn to do well on the home front. The Ívarr episode confirms that, in this respect, he has the advantage over King Sigurðr.

The Ívarr episode is an *exemplum* about how one role of the king is best fulfilled. Like many *exempla* this episode describes a humdrum activity of little significance that takes place on the stage usually reserved for affairs of state. The story in isolation could be understood in several ways, but it is also more abstract and more universal than the saga narrative that provides its framework.[18] Such is the nature of these episodes, and of other similar *exempla*.[19] Moreover, this episode provides a description of society, and by dramatising the king's admirable treatment of his retainers, the story of Ívarr and Eysteinn teaches the audience about exemplary courtly behaviour, as *exempla* are by definition teaching devices.

This story depicts love, friendship and the conduct of men in the daily routine of court life. It deals with feelings: gaiety and depression. It can thus certainly be thought of as a 'foreign body' in a 'kings' biography', as Finnur Jónsson designates such works.[20] The story of Ívarr concerns love. Although the poet and retainer fails for a while in his duty to be joyful and to be the cause of joy in others, he carries out his duty to love and appears to behave properly according to the rules of romantic engagement.[21] On the other hand, the *þáttr* focuses upon the solution of a problem rather than on the problem itself. It is not Ívarr's love for the woman that is the main issue, but rather the reciprocal affection between the king and his

18 See Stephen Greenblatt, *Marvelous Possessions:The Wonder of the New World*, p. 3: 'If anecdotes are registers of the singularity of the contingent ... they are at the same time recorded as representative anecdotes, that is, as significant in terms of a larger process or pattern that is the proper subject of history.'

19 See Sverre Bagge, 'Icelandic Uniqueness or a Common European Culture? The Case of the Kings' Sagas,' p. 421: 'This ... form of exemplarism largely serves to explain the episodic structure of medieval historiography.'

20 See Ármann Jakobsson, 'Den kluntede afskriver: Finnur Jónsson og Morkinskinna'; Kalinke ('Sigurðar Saga Jórsalafara,' 153, 160–162) disagrees, arguing that the *þættir*, 'Ívars þáttr' among them, have wider implications for the saga as a whole.

21 Here the word *romantic* is used with reference to its original association with romance (that is, Roman or Latin derived) vernaculars and their secular literatures. The love between Ívarr and Oddný is thus 'romantic' in this sense, that is, in the spirit of French courtly love poetry of the twelfth and thirteenth centuries.

retainers and the spirit of friendship that moves Eysteinn to become Ívarr's therapist.

The narrative focuses on society and the individual but also on the lands from which they come. The characters speak the same language but come from different places; the king is Norwegian whereas Ívarr is an Icelander. His saga is a tale within a larger tale called *Morkinskinna*, itself largely a saga about Icelanders and kings. The king treats the Icelander well, showing him respect and helping him work through his problem. But the king's behaviour has a more general import; the affection he shows towards Ívarr signifies that the presence of this Icelandic retainer is important in the Norwegian court. His happiness is uppermost in the king's mind, a fact that is significant in *Morkinskinna*'s overall message about relations between the Norwegian monarch and the people of Iceland, herein represented by their compatriots at the Norwegian court.

The main sociological message in the Auðun episode lies in the dealings of King Haraldr and Sveinn and the influence of Auðun upon them. A grim courtly society is depicted, in which envious retainers attempt to come between the king and Auðun the Icelander. He is the child, the 'simpleton' in the story. Auðun is a fortunate man, and the narrative focuses upon his luck and salvation. At the same time the saga seeks to characterise both kings, particularly Haraldr. Auðun travels all the way to Jerusalem. Journeys such as this one to foreign lands are an important part of *Morkinskinna*. An overall interpretation of the episode must involve the concept of fortune and the gift that energises the whole tale. Such a reading would refer to society, the individual and the universal. The tale of Auðun, like the Ívarr tale, is also a dramatic narrative. It reveals a delight in storytelling and reminds us that words can also be deeds.

In essence every story is about itself and its language. But a story cannot exist independently of human beings who are at one and the same time the audience, authors and subject matter of all narratives. The tales in *Morkinskinna* are basically two-sided. They are narratives that have validity in themselves, and they are also *exempla* with a clear and general message. Like all stories, their role involves human character building. They are intended to help mould human beings.[22] Once again we return to

---

22 Davíð Erlingsson, 'Saga gerir mann.'

Hreiðarr the Simple. When he walks around the king a double perspective emerges – that of Hreiðarr himself and that of the text.[23] Within the text is the child's view, innocent or (even) foolish, but the adult author's point of view provides meaning. This generates an irony of discrepant awareness between characters. *Morkinskinna* is an opaque text in which many forms of irony coexist.

One of the most frequent forms of irony is the complicity that is formed between the author/narrator and the audience against one or all of the characters in the saga. A good example is when both Haraldr the Severe, disguised as Norðbrikt (Norbert), and Gyrgir, the kinsman of Queen Zóe in ríka 'the Powerful' of Constantinople (*Miklagarðr*), desire, during one of their military campaigns, to make camp at the upper end of a valley. Neither is prepared to give in and they agree to draw lots:

> Nú eru hlutir gørðir, ok markar hvárr þeira sinn hlut, ok kǫstuðu síðan báðir hlutunum í skikkjuskaut Gyrgis, en Norðbrikt skyldi taka til hlutanna. Þá mælti Norðbrikt til Gyrgis: 'Lát mik sjá hvert mark er þú hefir, til þess at vit mǫrkum eigi á einn veg báðir.' Gyrgir sendir honum hlutinn, ok réð hann ekki í at hér myndi nǫkkut annat undir búa en Norðbrikt segir. Ok Norðbrikt merkir nú sinn hlut ok beint á einn veg ok Gyrgir hafði áðr gǫrt ok kastar síðan í kné hertoganum Gyrgi. Ok síðan tekr Norðbrikt til hlutanna. Ok er hann hafði upp tekit hlutinn annan mælti hann til Gyrgis: 'Þessir skulu fyrri tjalda ok fyrri róa ok fyrri ríða, fyrri til hafnar leggja ok hafa kjósanda hlut af ǫllu.' Leit síðan á hlutinn ok helt upp hátt ok mælti: 'Þetta er hlutr várr,' – ok fleygir síðan í brot ok langt á sjó út. Þá mælti Gyrgir: 'Hví léztu mik eigi sjá hlutinn?' Hann segir: 'Ef þú sátt eigi þann er ek tók upp þá sjá nú þann er eptir liggr, ok væntir ek at þú kennir þitt mark á.' Ok var þá hlutrinn upp tekinn ok kenndr, ok var þar á mark Gyrgis (*Msk.* I, 92).

Lots were now produced, and each marked his own and threw them into Gyrgir's cloak, with Norðbrikt the first

23   Svava Jakobsdóttir, *Skyggnst á bak við ský*, p. 263

to draw. Then Norðbrikt said to Gyrgir, 'Let me see how you've made your mark so that we both do not put the same mark on our lots'. Gyrgir gave him his mark, not suspecting that things were otherwise than Norðbrikt had said. And then Norðbrikt marked his lot in the same way that Gyrgir had done before and tossed it back upon the commander Gyrgir's lap. And then Norðbrikt drew a lot. Then after he had drawn, he said to Gyrgir, 'This lot will determine which of us shall pitch his tents first, have precedence in rowing, riding and in anchorage, and who will have the casting vote in all things'. Then he looked at the lot and held it aloft, saying, 'This is our lot' and then threw it far out to sea. Then Gyrgir said, 'Why did you not let me see the lot?' He answered, 'If you did not see the lot I chose, then look at the one remaining, and I expect you will recognise your mark on it'. And the lot was picked up and examined and it bore Gyrgir's mark.

Haraldr's ruse is indeed simple. The modern reader is astonished that Gyrgir allows himself to be cheated so. Here a dramatic irony appears: Haraldr, the author and the audience all understand what has happened, but Gyrgir and his men do not. The sympathy of most readers probably lies with King Haraldr, since we vicariously take part in his sleight-of-hand, but, unlike Gyrgir, are not deceived.

At Haraldr's arrival in Norway Einarr Paunch-Shaker is the first of the ruling class to speak and declares that he wishes to serve only Magnús. The others follow him, but engage in a long debate, like politicians who follow the party line but pretend to cast their votes according to their convictions:

> ok þó at á sína lund hœfi hverr sitt mál þá kom þó í einn stað niðr um annsvǫr (*Msk.* I, 121);

> and although each began his remarks in his own fashion, the answer nevertheless reached the same conclusion.

A similar scene occurs later in the saga when Óttarr birtingr 'the Trout' seizes power from the other retainers of Ingi Haraldsson:

> Síðan mælti hverr þeira í orða stað annars, sem vanði þeira er til, ok tǫlðu um tǫlur langar, bæði Gyrðr ok Ǫgmundr ok margir aðrir lendir menn, en þó kom í sama stað niðr sem Óttarr hafði mælt fyr ǫndverðu (*Msk.* II, 200).

> Then each of them interrupted the other, as was their custom, and made long speeches, both Gyrðr and Ǫgmundr and many other landed men, but all arrived at the same conclusion that Óttarr had spoken for at the beginning.

Óttarr is called *birtingr* ('the [bright coloured] trout') ironically since he is *døkkr ok svartr* (*Msk.* II, 139) 'of dark complexion and with black hair' and there are other such puerile witticisms. The voice of the text keeps a clear distance and is not shy about referring to itself.[24] Irony is generally directed more towards characters in the saga than at the audience, allowing the latter the chance to take part in the game, and all circumstantial ironies are explained so that they can do so. The author and the audience join together in wryly observing the foibles of human nature.

Irony is a key element in the characterisation of some of the saga's principal characters, as when the cunning of Haraldr the Severe is highlighted.[25] The saga audience can thus engage with the major parts of this saga, no less than in the most subtle of the Sagas of Icelanders.[26] The complexity of meaning to be found in *Morkinskinna*, and other medieval stories, is entirely comparable with that of modern stories. The saga in fact includes an *exemplum* about irony and its function in highlighting cowardice and mendacity – the episode about the Norman Giffarðr (or Giffardus).[27] Giffarðr offers his services to Magnús Barelegs, *ok lézt vera*

---

24 It refers certainly to the former words: *Ok er nú, sem ek gat áður* (*Msk.* I, 162) 'And is now as I mentioned earlier'. See further part V, chapters 1 and 2.

25 Scholars have noted the importance of irony in romance literature: 'without irony there is no courtliness' (Simon Gaunt, *Gender and Genre in medieval French literature*, p. 93); see also Geraldine Barnes, 'Arthurian Chivalry in Old Norse,' pp. 62–66.

26 Cook, 'The Reader in Grettis saga.'

27 Kari Ellen Gade, 'Morkinskinna's Giffarðsþáttr: Literary fiction or historical fact?'

riddari góðr (*Msk.* II, 51) 'saying that he was a good knight', but in battle, he lets the king down by arriving too late. This makes him an unpopular figure and he finds himself mocked in verse by an Icelander. Giffarðr seeks out the borough reeve, an Englishman, and demands his rights. The official requires the Icelander to recite his verse and he does so, but turns it into a poem of praise for Giffarðr. The reeve says:

> 'Lítt em ek skældinn, en heyra kann ek at þetta er ekki níð,
> ok þér er vegr at þessu, Giffarðr, ok lof' (*Msk.* II, 56);

> 'I am little versed in poetry, but I can tell that this is not slander and that you, Giffarðr, are being honoured and praised'.

Where deeds fail to match words, praise becomes mockery. Giffarðr knows *at honum er þetta háð en eigi lof at því sem efni váru til* (*Msk.* II, 56) 'that he is being mocked and not praised, given the circumstances'.

We know few contemporary readers of *Morkinskinna* by name, but in all likelihood one of them was Snorri Sturluson, who says in the preface to *Heimskringla*:

> En þat er háttr skálda at lofa þann mest, er þá eru þeir fyrir, en engi myndi þat þora at segja sjálfum honum þau verk hans, er allir þeir, er heyrði, vissi, at hégómi væri ok skrǫk, ok svá sjálfr hann. Þat væri þá háð, en eigi lof.[28]

> But it is the manner of skalds to praise those most who are present, but no one would dare to tell him of those works of his when all who heard knew that it was nonsense and false, as he also did himself. That would be mockery and not praise.

Could it not have been that Snorri's familiarity with *Morkinskinna* sharpened his awareness of matters such as these?

---

28 *Heimskringla I*, p. 5. Sigurður Nordal (*Snorri Sturluson*, p. 166) noted the connection between these words. He believed that Snorri's general assertion was more important than the dramatic development of the words in the Giffarðr episode.

Part III.

PORTRAITS OF A SOCIETY

1. The Courtly Cosmos

Mise-en-scène and community

Just as provincial town life lies at the heart of George Eliot's *Middlemarch*, and Fårö acts as the common backdrop in several of Ingmar Bergman's most famous films, so also in *Morkinskinna* a sense of place, and of people within that place, is very important. In most of the earlier kings' sagas there are few characters apart from the kings themselves.[1] They seem almost alone in a somewhat undefined environment, but this changes in the later kings' sagas, notably in *Morkinskinna*. Of course, all texts have a social context,[2] but direct concern for social life varies considerably between works. In *Morkinskinna*, however, society is a consistent concern, and deserves careful critical attention. Consideration of the saga as a whole reveals how consistent its portrayal of society is – indeed, we may say that it is its most important unifying element. The Norwegian courtly life depicted does not change even though the events of the saga take place over more than a century.[3]

The saga begins, in fact, in Russia. King Jarizleifr and his queen, Ingigerðr the daughter of Óláfr sænski 'the Swede', live in a lavishly appointed palace, together with many courtiers. In this noble setting a

---

1 However both *Sverris saga* and *Morkinskinna* are full of characters. The two works have this feature, and much else, in common.

2 Fredric Jameson (*The Political Unconscious: Narrative as a Socially Symbolic Act*) notes persuasively: 'there is nothing that is not social and historical' (p. 20).

3 As *Morkinskinna* is a text based on other sources, some of the examples analysed in this part of the book and those ensuing may well derive from these sources which are mostly now lost, apart from *Ágrip* and presumably the poetry (a substantial part of which appears in *Morkinskinna* for the first time but is attributed to poets living in the eleventh and twelfth centuries). Thus it is not safe to say for each example that it is a *Morkinskinna* invention and reflects only the mentality of that text, but the conclusions here are mainly presented as an analysis of the unity known as *Morkinskinna* which, of course, must have been heavily influenced by its sources but that does not mean that the ideas acquired from the sources cannot also be attributable to *Morkinskinna*.

domestic squabble takes place among the nobles that ends with Magnús Óláfsson, later king of Norway, journeying to Constantinople where

> taka þau við honum með sóma, ok fœðisk hann þar upp með hirð ok eigi með minni ást ok elsku en þeira synir (*Msk.* I, 5);

> they received him with honour, and he grew up there in the court with no less love and affection than did their own sons.

The saga is a family saga, but, in some instances, family and society are so closely related that they can hardly be distinguished.

Though the saga begins abroad its narrative focus is essentially Icelandic. It moves repeatedly from Iceland to Norway, from the society of the saga audience to the distant but closely related society of the court. The world of *Morkinskinna* is in many ways somewhat exotic. Whether stone-built halls or stately farms, the settings upon which the events of the saga play out is majestic. There is no shortage of joy and merrymaking. The talk is of play, and men row their boats in a courtly fashion, or ride their horses through the woods. The society is closely knit and culture is elevated. The scene is sometimes a boisterous one, filled with horn-blowing through the forests (*Msk.* I, 171), reminiscent of common elements in romances.[4] Upon these lavishly decorated stages people are received *með miklu liði, með strengleikum ok með alls konar fegrð ok prýði* (*Msk.* I, 45) 'with a large troop, with songs and with all kinds of beauty and pomp'. Events often take place in royal palaces, buildings that probably never existed in Iceland. Stories begin with nobles on high-seats in their halls:

> Þess er við getit eitt kveld at þar gørðisk sá atburðr með hertoganum, þá er hann sat með vinum sínum í hǫllunni, ok Úlfhildr sat hjá honum í hásætinu, at þar sýndisk með þeim hætti at maðr einn gengi í hallardyrin ok hefði danskan hatt á hǫfði (*Msk.* I, 58).

4 Compare Peter Hallberg, 'Some Aspects of the Fornaldarsögur as a Corpus,' pp. 23–27. Several examples of horn-blowing are found in *Morkinskinna* (for example *Msk.* I, pp. 153, 179 and 186) and events sometimes take place in the forest (e. g. *Msk.* I, 167: 'ok lágu þar, er skógr var nær þjokkr').

It is said that one evening the following incident happened
to the Duke when he was sitting with his friends in his hall
and Úlfhildr sat beside him in the high seat: they thought
they saw a man with a Danish hat on his head enter through
the hall doors.

This could be the beginning of an Arthurian tale, but in fact the setting is
in Saxony, at the palace of Duke Otto, who is married to King Magnús the
Good's sister.[5] Though substantial parts of the saga take place in far-off
lands the settings there and in Norway differ little. Magnús requires the
assistance of his brother-in-law. In the opinion of the Duke and Duchess
and their guests, the man with the hat is actually Saint Óláfr. With this, in
realizing the presence of the Saint, the Duke is able to help his kinsman at
the eleventh hour, as in a fairy tale. Other incidents often begin in a similar
way (*Msk.* II, 138), wherein both the high seat and a host of men serve to
render the scene more formal than anything that might happen in Iceland.

In *Morkinskinna* there are frequently many characters present at any
given time. The conflict between Sneglu-Halli and Þjóðólfr begins on a
street in the town:

Ok einn dag er Þjóðólfr gekk at stræti með konungi kómu
þeir fyrir lopt nǫkkur ok heyra deild manna ok því næst
áflog. Þar var skinnari ok járnsmiðr (*Msk.* I, 271)

And one day when Þjóðólfr was walking down the street
with the king they passed an upper room and heard a violent
argument in progress involving a tanner and a blacksmith.

Later in the story the king and his men are out for a stroll in the town
when Halli runs away from the king *í garð einn af strætinu ok þar sem
kona hafði uppi ketil ok var í grautr* (*Msk.* I, 274) 'into a courtyard off the
street where a woman was cooking gruel in a pot'. Halli buys the gruel
and sits down to eat it. Here the scene is a town where there is a need for
craftsmen and where business is transacted. There are houses and yards

5   Various Old Norse-Icelandic Arthurian sagas begin in a similar manner: for example,
    Ívens saga, *Erex saga*, *Möttuls saga* and *Samsonar saga fagra*.

connected by streets through which the king and his retinue stroll.[6] All of these images belong to a time and a place with developing commerce, industry and towns, and new patterns of thought, and such scenes were in all probability unfamiliar to most Icelandic readers and listeners.

Images of this kind of urban life are numerous in *Morkinskinna*.[7] While walking to evening mass Óttarr the Trout is killed while warding off what he thinks is another kind of attack:

> er hann heyrði hvininn af hǫggvinu þá brá hann upp hend-
> inni ok skikkjunni at móti ok hugði at kastat væri snækekki
> at móti honum, sem títt var ungsveinum (*Msk.* II, 212)

> when he heard the sound of the blow, he thrust up his hand
> and cloak to ward off the attack, thinking that a snow ball
> had been thrown at him, as young boys often did.[8]

The picture of boys throwing snowballs at venerable royal counsellors creates an impression of the urban mentality, as does the fact that Óttarr is alone on his walk. The distances involved are clearly short, and, normally, there is little to fear. Some time later Queen Ingiríðr is walking home from vespers and encounters the body of her son Ingi's old retainer, who has been killed. Here we have vespers and violence standing side by side – civilised values alongside the feuding of courtiers.

When King Ingi attacks his brother King Sigurðr, the latter is drinking *í garði Sigríðar sætu* (*Msk.* II, 233) 'in Sigríðr the Grass Widow's courtyard'. Ingi passes the smithy as he approaches while his kinsman comes in from Sandbrú. Sigurðr's courtiers duly break up the ovens to throw bricks

6 Here *garðr* may well mean 'house yard' rather than 'house', and thus Halli does not enter into a house.

7 Of the many other examples, see, for instance, *Msk.* II, pp. 108 and 124. Often a scene is set in a coastal town, as when Sigurðr the Noisy kills Haraldr Gilchrist, and then stands and talks *við þá er stóðu á bryggjunum ... Þangat dreif mart lið ór konungs garði* (*Msk.* II, 178) ('with those who stood on the jetty ... People came in large numbers from the king's court').

8 Theodore Andersson and Kari Ellen Gade (*Morkinskinna* p. 463) point out the rather unusual use of omniscient narration (an 'internal' account that can be thought of as narrating what cannot be known, among other things what a character is thinking); in this instance, the narrator seems to be reading Óttarr's mind.

at the attackers. Once again civilisation and barbarity collide. Furnaces, bridges and gates are representative of civilisation.[9] King Sigurðr himself is with a woman – the intended time for the attack – and the battle disturbs here the private life of the king.

In *Morkinskinna* great pains are taken with the settings. In the disputes between Eysteinn and Sigurðr the Crusader matters come to a head at a meeting, before which the narrative pauses and examines the three kings:

> Eysteinn konungr var fyrir í bœnum, er at sótti þinginu, ok hafði vistir sínar í konungs garði. Óláfr konungr kom fyrri en Sigurðr konungr ok hafði vistir sínar í bœnum skammt frá Óláfskirkju. Sigurðr konungr kom síðarst með skipaliði miklu ok lagði skipin í ána Nið, ok byggja á skipum undir tjǫldum ok hǫfðu allmikit lið. Ok þann dag er þeir skyldu þingit heyja þá var blásit í bœnum ... (*Msk.* II, 125).

> King Eysteinn was in town to attend the *þing*-meeting and was staying in the royal residence. King Óláfr arrived before King Sigurðr and was staying near the Church of Saint Óláfr. King Sigurðr arrived last with a large shipborne retinue and sailed into the river Nið and they lived in tents on board the ships, and they were a large force. And on the day when they were to convene the *þing*-meeting, trumpets sounded in the town ...

We see the kings arrive; the last is Sigurðr, a particular threat to the peace. Then the silence is broken, and trumpets announce the meeting. The suspense is electric.

---

9   Trading centres must have been neutral grounds, generally having less to do with commerce than with peaceful activities. Various examples later show that market squares were protected by law but this context was not attested as such in Norse laws (Lars Wikström and Grethe Authén Blom, 'Torgfrid'). Though civilisation is here associated with towns, this is not to say that urban culture has always been civilised and peaceful. See Jørn Sandnes, *Kniven, ølet og æren: Kriminalitet og samfunn i Norge på 1500- og 1600-tallet*, pp. 65–84) on violence in Bergen in the sixteenth century; also Sverrir Jakobsson's extensive discussion ('Friðarviðleitni kirkjunnar á 13. öld') of the limitations on violence in the thirteenth century.

The purpose of this precise description is first and foremost aesthetic, dramatic and expedient in narrative terms. But the staging is also a part of what the saga seeks to say about the past. More so than with the other kings' sagas, *Morkinskinna* and *Heimskringla* exhibit a real interest in peace and past customs as well as in market places, commerce and the church:

> Sigurðr konungr Jórsalafari setti stól sinn ok hǫfuðstað í Konungahellu, ok efldisk sá kaupstaðr [þá] svá mjǫk at engi var ríkari í Nóregi. Konungr lét gera þar kastala af grjóti ok torfi ok grafa um díki mikit, ok í þeim [kastala] var konungs garðr, ok þar var krossins kirkja, ok þar lét Sigurðr konungr vera krossinn helga, ok fyri altarinu var *tabulum*, gǫrt af gulli ok silfri … (*Msk.* II, 141).

> King Sigurðr the Crusader established his royal seat and capital at Konungahella, and it flourished so well that there was no finer one in Norway. There the king had a castle built of stone and turf and a large moat dug; in this castle was the king's residence and nearby was the Church of the Cross. King Sigurðr had the holy cross placed there, and an altarpiece of gold and silver was made for the altar …

The town itself, the castle, and the church and its altar are thus also important. The author of *Morkinskinna* calls his audience's attention to buildings and architecture and important treasures, both because of the things themselves but also to show that peace, commerce and stately churches are no less important as aspects of a culture, and of a king's reputation, than wars or crusades.

In the saga of Óláfr the Quiet we find a descriptive passage that exemplifies the narrative art of the saga as it moves from the general to the particular in a pictorial fashion:

> Þá prýddisk mikit landit ok gerðisk auðigt ok gnóttafullt. Þá settisk sá kaupstaðr í Nóregi er einn er vegsamligastr þeira er áðr er getit, at fráteknum kaupstað í Niðarósi, ok er sjá kaupbœr kallaðr í Bjǫrgyn. Gerðisk þar brátt mikit setr

auðigra manna. Er þangat mest tilflutning ór ǫðrum lǫnd-
um. Þá hófusk mjǫk drykkjur ok skytningar í kaupstǫðum,
miklu meirr en fyrr hafði verit [...] En þat var forneskjusiðr
í Nóregi, svá ok í Danmǫrk ok Svíþjóðu, þar sem váru stór
konungs bú ok veizlustofur, at konungs hásæti var á lang-
pallinn, þann er vissi í móti sólu. Sat þá dróttning á vinstra
veg frá konungi, ok var þat þá kallat ǫndugi, ok sá sess
vegligastr út í frá hvárntveggja stað til kvenna ok karla er
næst var ǫndugi, en hinn óvegligastr er ýztr var ok næst dyr-
um. Ok inn gǫfgasti maðr, sá er gamall var ok vitr ok væri
konungsráðgjafi kallaðr, sem konungum hafði lengi títt verit, at hafa með sér gamla spekinga til þess at vita forna siðu
ok dœmi forellra sinna; þessi maðr skyldi sitja á inn óœðra
pall gegnt konungi, ok hét þat it óœðra ǫndugi. Var frá honum til hœgra vegs kvenna sæti, en á vinstra veg karla sæti
(*Msk.* II, 7–8).

Then the land grew very beautiful and became wealthy and
abundant. That trading centre was established in Norway
which was the most splendid of those previously mentioned
with the exception of the trading centre in Niðaróss, and that
trading town was called Bjǫrgvin [Bergen]. It soon became
a great centre for wealthy men, and the greatest place of
trade with other countries. Then many drinking festivities
and inns started in the trading centre, to a much greater extent than before [...] It was an ancient custom in Norway,
as in Denmark and Sweden, that wherever there was a large
king's residence and feasting halls the king's high seat was
placed on the long bench facing the sun. The queen sat to
the left of the king and this was called the second seat, and
on both the women's and men's sides the most desirable
seat was the one closest to the second seat, while the least
desirable was that furthest away and the closest to the door.
And the most noble man, the one who was old and wise
and known as the king's counsellor, for it had long been the
custom of many kings to have with them elderly wise men

in order to know about the old customs and habits of their ancestors – this noble man was to sit on the lesser bench opposite the king and this was called the lesser second seat. On his right were the women's seats and to the left were the men's seats.

Having started out by noting the wealth of the country, the author of *Morkinskinna* then focuses more narrowly on the trading centres, before finally turning his attention to the king's rooms and the seating arrangements. Thereafter follows a detailed description of the particular innovations King Óláfr the Quiet introduced in his palace (*Msk.* II, 8–9) The interest in court customs seems inexhaustible, and such small details are deemed essential in creating a sense of the society depicted in the saga.[10]

In *Morkinskinna* the society of the past can be recreated. It was close-knit and civilised, featuring successful commerce and industrial development within a relatively peaceful environment.

Seating order and other details

Nú er þess við getit þá er þeir váru á einni veizlu báðir, Kálfr Árnason ok Einarr þambarskelfir með Magnúsi konungi, en þetta var í Vík austr. Einarr skipaði mǫnnum, en Kálfr settisk í rúm hans á meðan ok þokar at konunginum, því at Einarr sat ávallt á aðra hǫnd konungi. En er Einarr sér þetta snýr hann þá til rúms síns ok sezk á öxlina ⟨Kálfs⟩, er vildi eigi áðr undan þoka, ok mælti: 'Fyrr á gǫmlum oxanum at bæsa en kálfinum,' – ok sígr hann síðan niðr á milli þeira, ok er nú kyrrt (*Msk.* I, 28).

This is now to be told of when both Kálfr Árnason and Einarr Paunch-Shaker were at a feast with King Magnús, and this was to the east in Vík. Einarr arranged the men, but in the meantime Kálfr sat down in Einarr's place and moves slightly towards the King, for Einarr always sat to the right

---

10 I take this discussion up again in: 'En plats i en ny värld: Bilden av riddarsamhället i Morkinskinna.'

of the King. But when Einarr saw this he returned to his place and sat on the shoulder of Kálfr, who refused to give way. Einarr said: 'an old ox should be driven into his stall before the calf'. He then settles down between them and was now content.

This incident may at first glance appear to be of little significance, the point of contention unremarkable and the behaviour of the chieftains even somewhat childish. Einarr squeezes into his seat by force, comparing himself to an ox and Kálfr (of course) to his namesake: a calf. This seems egregiously discourteous, but in the courtly society of *Morkinskinna* seating positions were very important. Kálfr had taken Einarr's seat next to the king, an unacceptably presumptuous move, for Einarr's official position in the seating hierarchy symbolised his powerful position in society.[11]

It is not possible to ignore seating arrangements in this world. Thirteenth-century European society was based on hierarchies, which were by no means mere abstractions but symbolic structures of power that found expression in the physical seating arrangements.[12] Kings sit on thrones in order to confirm that they are raised above others, and from the Sagas of Icelanders we know of the elaborately descriptive passages concerning certain seating arrangements at feasts and such, and thus the importance of who sits where.[13]

In any good drama not only are the characters necessary but also the stage properties. The scenery for a kings' saga must not be drab and the proper tone is struck at the outset. When Haraldr the Severe sails into Magnús the Good's story before becoming the centre of attention, his ship receives initial treatment:

11 Somewhat later we are told that Einarr arrives at the King's residence and sits *it næsta konungi* (*Msk.* I, 142) 'beside the king'. See also *Ljósvetninga saga* (*ÍF* 10, pp. 58–59).

12 See David Crouch, *The Image of the Aristocracy in Britain, 1000–1300*, pp. 27–38; Johan Huizinga, *Homo ludens: A Study of the Play Element in Culture*, pp. 38–48, 54–64; Norbert Elias, *The Court Society*, pp. 78–116.

13 A good example of this is the description of the wedding of Gunnarr and Hallgerðr in *Brennu-Njáls saga* (*ÍF* 12, pp. 88–89). A similar emphasis on seating arrangements can be found in *Konungsskuggsjá*; see Susanne Kramarz-Bein, 'Zur Darstellung und Bedeutung der Höfischen in der Konungs skuggsjá,' p. 70 and Hermann Reichert, 'King Arthur's Round Table: Sociological Implications of its Literary Reception in Scandinavia,' pp. 394–414.

Þat var allt gulli búit fyrir ofan sjó ok váru á drekahǫfuð fǫgr, en seglit var tvefalt pell af inum dýrstum vefjum. Ok er þessi nýlunda hófsk upp þá þótti mǫnnum mikils um vert. En þetta skip var með þess konar farmi at þat var fermt með rauðu purpuragulli, en allir veðrvitar váru svá at sjá sem rautt gull væri, svá ok allir spœnir í, en fyrir borðin innan þá váru vaskir drengir klæddir með dýrum vefjum ok pellum (*Msk.* I, 80).

Everything above the waterline was adorned with gold and there were beautiful dragons' heads too, and the sail was of the most expensive double weave. When this novel ship hove into view, people thought it splendid. And the ship's cargo was loaded with red-purple gold and all the weather vanes glistened as if they were red gold, as did the dragons' heads, and on board were noble men dressed in precious fabric and raiment.

Before reaching Haraldr the gold-adorned ship is described and then, in sequence, the dragons' heads, the sails, the cargo, the weather vanes and the men on the ship and their clothes. The word *gull*, 'gold', occurs here three times and the half-rhyming word *pell* twice. As yet Haraldr has not been seen, only his men who are part of that whole which is the king's retinue (and the king himself embodies the values of the group). The king's men are dashing and represent Haraldr's vitality. The gold in turn signifies how widely travelled the monarch is, for such can only be found in southern countries.[14] As for the symbolism of dragons' heads, we may say that dragons are noble creatures but dangerous. The heads signal fear and grandeur and serve to introduce the king, wherever he goes.

The setting is observed and described in great detail: elegant men in coloured clothing fashioned from costly materials who bear golden

---

14 A similarly ostentatious description of a hall raised by King Jarizleifr and filled with gold and jewels appears at the outset of the saga (*Msk.* I, 3–4). On the importance of gold in Germanic and Old Norse Viking culture, see Aaron J. Gurevich, *Categories of Medieval Culture*, pp. 215–219. Guðrún Nordal (*Tools of Literacy: The Role of Skaldic Verse in Icelandic Textual Culture of the Twelfth and Thirteenth Centuries*, pp. 309–338) discusses gold in skaldic verse.

swords; some items function on the level of plot while others adorn the 'stage' and announce that this is a story about noble men as the small details help to create a decorative mosaic. The aesthetics of the saga involve the creation of a single narrative web from multiple thematic and ornamental threads; if it can be described in theatrical terms, the lavishly decorated *Morkinskinna* 'stage' is a deftly selected collection of meaningful objects.

A man adorned with much gold

A number of cameo performances appear in the saga and seem to function as indications of the broader drama of the saga. One such performance takes place in a forest through which King Haraldr and King Magnús are journeying:

> Þá reið maðr fram ór skóginum með góðum riddarabúnaði ok lét hest sinn fagrliga burdeigja. Þessi maðr var búinn með miklu gulli ok dýrum klæðum. Maðr var inn kurteisasti ok lék marga leika með mikilli list, ok sá menn Magnúss konungs á er hann lék (*Msk.* I, 167).

> Then a man rode out of the woods in the fine clothing of a knight, and had his horse prance around elegantly. He was adorned with much gold and expensively clad; he was the most courteous of men and played many a game with great skill. And King Magnús's men looked on as he performed.

This man performs for the kings and then says at the conclusion that the kings are unequal. He turns out to be the Danish King Sveinn. Magnús the Good appears to be moved and says: '*Gersimi er Sveinn*' (*Msk.* I, 167) '"Sveinn is a treasure"'. He compares Sveinn to a jewel, a characterisation lent credence by the description of his gold decoration, expensive clothes and elegant knightly armour, and by the horse being put through its courtly paces. A series of details – the loan word *burdeigja*, the forest, the clothes, the courtliness and the knightly trappings – are all part and parcel of the

knightly whole.[15] He then delivers his judgement, which is the main point
of the scene, but a secondary point is Sveinn himself and the knightly
accoutrements in which he is arrayed.

Every outfit tells its own tale, and in the battle at Lyrskov Heath
Magnús the Good's silken shirt plays a major role; the king heads into
battle without a coat of mail, and the shirt thus symbolises his courage
(*Msk*. I, 61, 63). And when King Magnús Sigurðarson is stripped of his
power, *tók hann við munkaklæðum* (*Msk*. II, 162) 'he adopted the habit of
a monk'. Sometimes it is as if kings and their noblemen are a function of
the clothes they wear. When Magnús Bareleg's envoy travels in disguise,
he needs only to reveal his scarlet cloak under his costume in order to
become himself again (*Msk*. II, 32).

King Sveinn's penchant for extravagant fashion demonstrates how
chieftains willingly set themselves apart from the crowd by their 'conspicuous consumption' and lavish clothes.[16] In the story of Óláfr the Quiet
there is another example of such a chieftain. In Óláfr's time men wore
drambhosur lerkaðar at beini. Sumir spenntu gullhringum um fótleggi sér
(*Msk*. II, 7) 'fancy-pants laced up their legs; some attached gold rings
around their legs'. Óláfr the Quiet's reign is described as a golden age, not
least one of ostentation, wherein his main achievement was to increase the
number of his courtiers and 'guests' or retainers.[17] Splendour is a social

15 In his edition Finnur Jónsson (*Morkinskinna*, p. viii) refers to *burdeigja* as a loan
word in *Morkinskinnna*. The word may derive from Middle Low German. Noting that
it is also used in *Þiðreks saga*, Andersson and Gade (*Morkinskinna*, p. 433, note 8)
translate the word as 'prance'.

16 The term 'conspicuous consumption' was coined by the Norwegian-American sociologist Thorsten Veblen (*The Theory of the Leisure Class: An Economic Study of
Institutions*, pp. 35–101). Max Weber (*Wirtschaft und Gesellschaft: Grundriss der
Sozialökonomik*,) emphasised the validity of consumption for prestige and social position, and Pierre Bourdieu (*Distinction: a social critique of the judgement of taste*)
brings in ideas such as taste and sets them in a new context. Much of my discussion
on cultural wealth is based on Bourdieu's work. Torfi H. Tulinius ('Snorri og bræður
hans: Framgangur og átök Sturlusona í félagslegu rými þjóðveldisins') has applied
Bourdieu's ideas to thirteenth-century Icelandic society; see also Torfi H. Tulinius,
'Virðing í flóknu samfélagi.'

17 *Óláfr konungr tók með sér hundrað málamann; [þeir] váru hirðmenn hans, en forn
lǫg váru til þess at konungr skyldi hafa sex tigu hirðmanna. Hann hafði ok sex tigu
gesta, en áðr hǫfðu konungar haft þrjá tigu* (*Msk*. II, 9) 'King Óláfr took on one

phenomenon and pregnant with meaning, since visible wealth testifies to the special status of the nobility.[18] In other kings' sagas we learn that King Haraldr Eiríksson started a new fashion in Norway by buying a grey fur cloak.[19] Haraldr the Severe wears a similar cloak in Constantinople, and it performs a similar function protecting him in his attack against a serpent as 'hairy-breeches' had done for King Ragnarr loðbrók long before (*Msk.* I, 110). Sigurðr slembir 'the Noisy'[20] is also seen wearing a grey cloak (*Msk.* II, 191), and Sveinn Úlfsson is wearing just such a garment when he receives the gift of a cloak from King Magnús (*Msk.* I, 51). King Haraldr gráfeldr 'Greycloak' made a grey cloak into a feature of royal apparel, thereby assigning it a new symbolic value, even if we cannot be sure what it looked like or what it was made of. Thus not only can clothes make the man, but, in turn, the man can, on occasion, give clothes a new significance. And kings determine symbols of this kind.

The costumes of lesser noblemen are also a key element in the staging of the saga. Chieftains go around in lavishly decorated clothes. Gregoríus Dagsson goes to the *þing* 'assembly' in a 'red-gold helmet'. This costume

hundred soldiers. They were his courtiers, although it was custom that a king should have sixty courtiers. He also had sixty guests, although kings before him had just thirty'.

18 Attention has been drawn to the significance of ostentation in the lives of the Danish nobility in the late Middle Ages: *adelens liv var ... også gennem ydre omgivelser og handlinger at synliggøre og manifestere den rigdom, man besad. Flotte og prægtige klædedragter, dyre, ødsle og ugelange fester, heste og beredne svende hørte med til den adelige livsstil* (Lars Bisgaard, *Tjenesteideal og fromhedsideal: Studier i adelens tænkemåde i dansk senmiddelalder*, p. 122) 'the life of the aristocracy was [lived] ... also through external surroundings and actions in order to reveal and make visible by the riches one possessed. Stylish and expensive dress; expensive, extravagant and week-long parties; horses and mounted riders all belonged to the aristocratic life style'. See Elias's analysis (*The Court Society*, pp. 37–38 and following) of courtly culture of the Middle Ages and later periods; see also Crouch, *The Image of the Aristocracy in Britain*.

19 *Heimskringla I*, ÍF 26, p. 212. The raiments of a king have considerable political importance: thus, Charlemagne always dressed as a Frank to show that the Frankish kingdom was the core of his kingdom, even though he bore the title Holy Roman Emperor (Gabor Klaniczay, *The Uses of Supernatural Power: The Transformation of Popular Religion in Medieval and Early-Modern Europe*, p. 58).

20 The meaning of Sigurðr's sobriquet *slembir* (or *slembidjákn*) is not entirely clear but could mean 'noisy' (or 'noisy deacon') (*Msk.* II, 114 note 2).

greatly irritates his opponents; King Sigurðr promises that '*steypa skyldi hann hjálminum þeim inum gullroðna*' (*Msk.* II, 232) '"he would bring down the red-gold helmet"'. The gold helmet duly becomes a symbol for Gregorius,[21] revealing what sort of mettle he is made of, but with his penchant for splendour proving a thorn in the side for others.[22]

Dress can be deceptive, as may be seen in the cunning with which Hreiðarr the Simple asks King Magnús to cast off his cloak so that he can see him more clearly. The gaze is no longer directed at the decoration but at the man himself. In the light of the value assigned to costume in the saga, it is no surprise that the king was shocked. A decorative costume is no less important when it is removed and the man examined without it.

Half the kingdom with the sceptre

The lavish clothing Sveinn wears in the forest signifies a great deal. Similarly, when Haraldr Sigurðarson and his men make their initial appearance (*Msk.* I, 80), their costly, gold fabrics are also seen for the first time, making the statement that significant people are approaching. In the thirteenth century it was common to symbolise a king's power in terms of costly objects such as crowns, orbs and royal sceptres.[23] In *Morkinskinna* this can be seen when Magnús the Good accepts his uncle Haraldr the Severe as joint king:

> Ok síðan kømr hann fyrir frænda sinn, Harald konung, ok hafði í hendi sér tvá reyrteina fagra ok mælti: 'Haraldr frændi, hvárn reyrtein vilið ér [þiggja at] oss at gjǫf?' Haraldr segir: 'Þann, herra, er áðr er nærri oss'. Þá mælti Magnús konungr: 'Með þessum reyrsprota gefum vér yðr hálft Nóregs[konungs] veldi með ǫllum skatti ok skuld ok allri eign …' (*Msk.* I, 126).

21 On symbols of men as ornaments, see Ármann Jakobsson, 'Laxdæla dreaming: a saga heroine invents her own life.'

22 One Norwegian in the service of Þorgils Oddason along with Sigurðr the Noisy is described as a *skartsmaðr mikill ok barsk mikit á* (*Msk.* II, 174) 'a great dandy who made quite a show of himself'. In this case the reference could be applied to the man as a form of ridicule.

23 See the discussion in Ármann Jakobsson, *Í leit að konungi*, pp. 108–111.

and then he came before his kinsman, King Haraldr, and had in his hand two beautiful reed stalks, and said: 'Kinsman, Haraldr, which reed stalk do you wish to accept from me as a gift?' Haraldr said, 'The one, sir, that is closer to me'. Then King Magnús said: 'with this stalk I give you half of Norway ... with all its taxes and duties and all properties ...'

The half of the realm is signified by the reed stalk. With the exchange of such an object, the symbolic value of the event remains unstated.[24] Something similar can be seen when Haraldr the Severe has Úlfr inn auðgi 'the Wealthy' put on a slave's cloak:

> 'Tak nú þenna kyrtil er ek bauð þér áðan er frændr ⟨þínir⟩ hafa áttan ok þar með nafn þat ok slíkan sóma með sem þeir hǫfðu' (*Msk.* I, 230)

> 'Take this tunic that I just offered you which your kinsmen have worn and with it the name and such honour as they possessed'.[25]

The dishonour that Haraldr has done Úlfr is represented by the white tunic he must wear for the remainder of his life: once again clothes make the man, since in this case they symbolize the transformation of a free man into a slave.

In *Morkinskinna* there is a chapter in the tale of Hákon Ívarsson concerning the standard owned by King Magnús. Ragnhildr, the king's daughter, hands this standard over to Hákon with these words:

24 Brian Stock, *The Implications of Literacy: Written Language and Models of Interpretation in the Eleventh and Twelfth Centuries*, p. 47. He points out (pp. 47–52) that in an oral culture symbols (such as sprigs) are used to signify the transfer of ownership. Manumission makes use of this concept: see Michael T. Clanchy, *From Memory to Written Record: England, 1066–1307*, pp. 21–28, and Crouch, *The Image of the Aristocracy in Britain*, pp. 177–251.

25 Then King Sigurðr the Crusader dreams that he and his brothers Eysteinn and Óláfr were all sitting on a bench, and Eysteinn interprets the dream in such a way: '*at stóllinn jarteini ríki þetta er vér hǫfum brœðr*' (*Msk.* II, 107) 'that the bench signifies the kingdom that we brothers rule'.

'En merki þessi vil ek gefa þér er faðir minn hefir átt, ok þessi hafði hann þá er hann barðisk við Skotborgará. Ok þessi merki vildi Haraldr konungr gjarnsamliga hafa ok hefir enn eigi nát hingat til.' Þau váru ǫll gullsaumuð (*Msk.* I, 263).

'But this standard, which belonged to my father, I wish to give you; he had it with him when he fought at Skotborg River. And King Haraldr very much wanted to have this standard, but up to now he has never been able to get his hands on it'. It was totally embroidered with gold.

The standard is a precious object that people especially covet because it belonged to Magnús the Good. Later Haraldr appropriates the standard in battle:

Ok nú mælti Hákon, er hann flýði, at konungsdóttir myndi hann laust þykkja á hafa haldit merkinu Magnúss konungs er hon hafði gefit honum (*Msk.* I, 266).

and Hákon now said, as he fled, that the king's daughter would think he had not held very firmly onto Magnús's standard that she had given him.

And finally Hákon risks his life to reclaim the standard:

Ok er þeir riðu skógargǫtu ok þeim var minnst ván hleypr maðr of þvera gǫtuna ór skóginum fram ok þrífr merkit annarri hendi af þeim er bar, en annarri hendi leggr hann þann með spjóti. Hleypr þegar í skóginn ǫðrum megin gǫtunnar, ok hafa þeir ekki hans, en hinn deyr er lagðr var (*Msk.* I, 267).

And when they were riding along a path in the woods and were least expecting it, a man ran into their path from out of the forest and with one hand grabbed the standard away from the man holding it and with the other hand stabbed him with a spear; he then ran back into the woods on the other side of the path and they could not catch him, but the one who was stabbed died.

Here the standard appears more significant than human life – its importance lies in its symbolism. It links Hákon to King Magnús. A similar
identification seems to lie behind the decision of Eysteinn Haraldsson's
men to destroy a ship – *drekann mikla er inn fyrri Eysteinn hafði gøra
látit (Msk.* II, 239) 'the great dragon ship that Eysteinn the Elder had had
built' – rather than have it fall into enemy hands. The value of this ship
for Eysteinn the Younger lies probably not least in the fact that it connects
him with the popular and wise Eysteinn Magnússon. Previously, King Eysteinn had destroyed the connection with his noble namesake by having
his boat sheds burned (*Msk.* II, 237), which turned out to be fateful, leading indirectly to his fall. It is significant that Eysteinn Magnússon had the
sheds built because Eysteinn Haraldsson is unlike his elder namesake yet
fervently desires to be like him, but in fact succeeds only in destroying his
work.

When Magnús the Good gave Haraldr half of Norway in one sprig,
Haraldr came up with a reciprocal gesture:

> Ok síðan lét Haraldr konungr upp lúka féhirzlunum ok mælti
> síðan til Magnúss konungs: 'Þér veittuð oss fyrra dags ríki
> mikit er þér hofðuð áðr unnit með sœmð af óvinum yðrum
> ok várum ok tókuð oss til samlags við yðr, ok var þat vel
> gørt, enda hofðuð ér mikit til. Nú er hér í annan stað at sjá.
> Vér hofum verit útanlendis ok þó í nokkurum mannhættum
> áðr en vér hafim þessu gulli saman komit. Ok skulu vér nú
> skipta þessu í tvá staði öllu, ok skulu þér nú, frændi, eignask
> hálft gullit við oss, þar er þér vilduð at vér ættim hálft landit
> með yðr.' Lætr nú Haraldr konungr bera upp gullit ok bera
> til reiðlur ok skipta milli sín. Ok þykkir þetta mikil furða,
> hverjum er sér, er í Norðrlond skal svá mikit gull vera komit
> í einn stað (*Msk.* I, 127).

King Haraldr then ordered that the money chests be opened
and then said to King Magnús: 'The other day you gave us
a great kingdom that you had previously won with honour
from your enemies and mine, and you took us into your fellowship. That was well done, even though you were well
off. Now is an occasion to look at matters otherwise. We

have been abroad and in some danger before we managed
to gather together this gold. Let us now divide it all into two
portions, and you, kinsman, shall now have half since it was
your wish that we own half of the land with you'. King Haraldr then had the gold heaped up and the scales brought out
to divide the gold between them. And everyone who looks
on thinks that it is a marvel that so much gold has been collected in one place in the northern lands.

Haraldr's dramatic gesture is striking. The spectacle in itself is sufficient:
we are told about the amazement of the onlookers and take part in it
ourselves. But the event is also the beginning of tension between the kings;
immediately thereafter there is dissatisfaction about the ring that Magnús
wishes to give in return. It turns out that Haraldr is still thinking about
these gifts a year later when Magnús has become terminally ill:

> Þá spurði Haraldr konungr: 'Hversu mikit er eptir gulls þess
> er vér fluttum í land ok gáfum í yðvart vald ok þér þáguð
> hálft við oss?' Magnús konungr mælti: 'Lít hér á borðin,
> frændi', segir hann, 'er skipuð eru góðum drengjum ok dýr-
> ligum. Þeim sǫmum hefi ek gefit gullit ok haft í móti gullinu
> ást þeira ok hollostu' (*Msk.* I, 169).

> Then King Haraldr asked: 'How much remains of the gold
> which I brought to the country, half of which I gave into
> your keeping, and which you accepted?' King Magnús
> spoke: 'Look here at the tables, kinsman', he says, 'at which
> are seated good men and noble. To those same men have I
> given the gold and have received in return their devotion
> and loyalty'.

Magnús considers that he has looked after Haraldr's gift well, but Haraldr
leaves without saying a word and appears to be offended by the fact that
Magnús has given his gift to others. On his deathbed Magnús the Good
gives various things to his friends:

> Síðan mælti konungr við skósvein sinn: 'Hefi ek nǫkkut
> minnzk þín?' 'Ekki nú at sinni', segir hann. Konungr rétti þá

til hans kníf ok belti, ok var þat hvárttveggja gersimi, sem
ætla má, er þvílíkr maðr hafði átt ok borit. Ok er sveinn-
inn tók við gripunum þá leit hann til konungs, ok var hann
þá beint í andlátinu. En honum, sveininum, brá svá við ok
fekksk svá mikils at hann fell í óvit. Ok er hann vitkaðisk
þá váru í brottu gripirnir í þys þeim inum mikla er þá var,
ok aldri sá hann þá síðan (*Msk.* I, 171).

Then the king spoke to his page: 'Have I remembered you in
any way?' 'Not yet', he says. The king handed him his knife
and belt, both of them great treasures, as can be imagined
since they were owned and worn by such a man. And when
the page took the gifts, he looked at the king, who died at
that moment. And the page was so moved that he fell unconscious, and when he came to, the gifts had disappeared in
the commotion of the moment and he never saw them again.

The king shows the page his affection, but the boy, once the king is dead,
does not benefit from the objects any longer than did the king himself.[26]
Previously Magnús the Good desired to seal his bond of faith with
Sveinn Úlfsson with a gift:

Ok einn dag við drykkju gaf konungr honum skikkju sína, er
skorin var af inum dýrasta guðvef, ok þar með eina skál fulla
af mjǫð ok bað hann drekka mótsminni. 'Ok hér með', segir
konungr, 'vil ek gefa þér jarls nafn ok þvílíkt af landsgæzlu
í Danmǫrk sem þá viljum vér hafa á kveðit, er vér komum
þar'. (*Msk.* I, 51)

One day while they were drinking the king gave him his
cloak, which was cut from the most precious material, and
along with it a bowl full of mead, bidding him to drink a
toast, 'and with it', says the king, 'I wish to bestow the title
of Earl upon you and the benefits of the land in Denmark
that I will specify when I come there'.

---

26 The fate of the treasures could suggest that the boy also did not long benefit from his
loyalty.

Sveinn *tekr við skikkjunni ok kastar eigi yfir sik, gefr þegar einhverjum sínum manni* (*Msk.* I, 51) 'accepts the cloak, but did not put it on; instead he gives it immediately to one of his men' He ostentatiously degrades the gift (thereby prompting Einarr Paunch-Shaker's biting remark '*ofjarl, ofjarl, fóstri*' 'too fine for an earl, too fine for an earl, my foster-son' and rejects the bond between a king and a nobleman that the gift is meant to symbolise. Gifts are important but sensitive forms of exchange. The interest in their worth can be seen in the chapters from the later years of King Haraldr the Severe's reign (*Msk.* I, 217–239). It is an honour for Auðun of the Westfjords that the King of Denmark accepts his gift (of the polar bear); but Þorvarðr krákunef 'Crow-nose' is humiliated by Haraldr's refusal of his sail (*Msk.* I, 237–239).

Gifts reify social intercourse.[27] The author's emphasis on such reification is a sign of the general interest in material objects.[28] They can however also have their own validity as precious objects, as attested in the story of Sigurðr the Crusader:

Þá mælti konungr ok tók bókina þá ina dýru er hann hafði haft í land ok ǫll var gullstǫfum ritin, ok eigi hafði meiri gersimi komit í land í einni bók. Dróttningin sat hjá honum. Þá mælti konungr: 'Mart kann skipask á manns ævinni. Ek átta tvá hluti þá er mér þóttu baztir er ek kom í land. Þat var bók sjá hérna ok dróttningin, er nú þykki mér hvárr ǫðrum verri, ok þat á ek svá í eigunni er mér þykkir verst allra hluta. Dróttning finnr eigi hvernug hon er, því at svá sýndisk sem geitarhorn stœði ór hǫfði henni, ok því betri sem mér þótti dróttning,' sagði konungr, 'því ǫllu verri þykki mér hon nú.' Þá kastaði konungr bókinni fram á eldinn er gǫrr var, en laust dróttningu kinnhest. (*Msk.* II, 139).

27 In this discussion I have benefited from the ideas of Marcel Mauss (*The Gift: Forms and Functions of Exchange in Archaic Societies*) and Gurevich (*Categories of Medieval Culture*, pp. 215–39).
28 Objects can also be booty (e.g., *Msk.* I, 193, *Msk.* II, 82), chapters in the adoration of saints (*Msk.* I, 96, 253, 328), calumny (*Msk.* I, 162–163, 178) or precious objects (*Msk.* I, 105, 131, 209, 238, 286, *Msk.* II, 148).

Then the king spoke and took the precious book that he had
brought to Norway and everything was written in gold letters and never had a more costly treasure in the form of a
book ever come into the country. The queen sat next to him.
Then the king said: 'Many things can change in the life of an
individual. I owned two things that seemed to me the most
costly when I arrived in the country, one was this book before you and the queen, and now each seems worse than the
other, and I own that which seems to me the worst of all
things. The queen does not seem to know who she is, since
it seems as if goat's horns are sticking out of her head, and
the better the queen once seemed to me', said the king, 'the
worse she seems to me now'. The king threw the book into
the fire that had been made and smacked the queen in the
face.

The king's madness is revealed in his hatred of his precious possessions.
The treatment of his book and his queen confirms that he has taken leave
of his senses. The book is not just a symbol of his earlier esteem. It is
important for the king as an object until it abruptly loses its importance
– at the same time as the king ceases to love his wife. His attachment to
the book has become almost fetishistic. For Sigurðr it is equivalent to the
queen without really being her. We may say the same about the retainers'
preference for artefacts generally. This could easily turn into fetishism,
with material objects becoming more important than the values that they
represent.[29] The decoration on the stage is thus its anchor within which
resides merit, a magnificence that the life of the court revolves around. He
who rejects it loses his position in life. Sigurðr's disgust with this object
throws his life out of kilter, as the golden book had been the anchor of his
life up to this point.

The *Morkinskinna* stage is never so well decorated as in its description
of Sigurðr's crusade. In Constantinople Emperor Alexios puts on games to
honour the Norse king.[30] The games are a substitute for gold for Sigurðr,

29 See Elias, *The Court Society*, pp. 85–86.
30 See part IV, chapter 2. On the description, see Paul Riant, *Expéditions et pèleri-
    nages des Scandinaves en Terre Sainte au temps des croisades*, pp. 199–203 ; Sigfús

who has indeed chosen them instead of red gold.[31] They are in addition accompanied by songs, the sounds of musical instruments and many kinds of carnival entertainment. Sigurðr's life is as colourful as the book that in his derangement he casts into the fire. When it burns, it is not just the treasure that is damaged – the hurt extends to the king himself.

In the saga's fondness for material objects, symbolic thinking appears when the external and the internal are in close association with each other. At the same time the things identified as desirable create the glamour of courtly society that was far removed from an Icelandic audience.

A world full of wonders

A considerable part of *Morkinskinna* takes place in distant countries. The narratives devoted to the youth of Haraldr the Severe and Sigurðr the Crusader are more detailed in this than in any other saga. The world of the saga is also more comprehensive. Not only does it embrace the whole of Europe, but Haraldr is said to have done battle with *konunginn sjálfan í Affríka* (*Msk*. I, 94) 'with the king himself in Africa'.[32] The wide-ranging saga world bears witness to a romantic interest in the exotic, as when Haraldr the Severe is captured in Constantinople and he is made to contend with a serpent in a dungeon (*Msk*. I, 109–111).[33] In a world full of wonders there are wonders and treasures everywhere but also dangers and monsters, as in folk tales.[34] The boundary between the normal and paranormal is unclear.

Blöndal, *Væringjasaga: Saga norræna, rússneskra og enskra hersveita í þjónustu Miklagarðskeisara á miðöldum*, pp. 31–35 and 212–217.

31 In contrast the Danish King Eiríkr took the gold, and in *Knýtlinga saga* much space is devoted to explaining Eiríkr's poor 'cash flow' situation that caused him to make such a choice. Finally, it is observed: *Ok greinask menn at því, hvárt hǫfðinglegar þótti kosit vera* (*Danakonunga sǫgur*, p. 237) 'And there was disagreement as to which of the two chose more nobly'.

32 See Andersson and Gade, *Morkinskinna*, p. 83.

33 Later he purges a worm from a woman rumoured to be his mistress (*Msk*. I, 234). The incident may be connected to abortion, and dragons are associated with childbirth (Ásdís Egilsdóttir, 'Drekar, slöngur og heilög Margrét').

34 See Lönnroth *Njáls Saga: A Critical Introduction*, pp. 55–61, who considers that it is the miraculous, as much as the alleged 'realism,' of medieval Icelandic sagas that accounts for their charm. As he puts it: 'it is readable partly because it is unreadable,

In the twelfth and thirteenth centuries the saga writers' interest in ancient times grew steadily. Against the background of known history, saga writers created a prehistory, and when facts were wanting, they resorted to the structures of fantasy stories. In *Morkinskinna* an interest in old customs of every kind is discernible, as in the detailed description of the court customs of Óláfr the Quiet.[35] In the saga we find the relatively recent past described – that is to say, events dating back over the previous two centuries, though not within the previous sixty years. On the other hand, we find folk-tale motifs that bear witness to a delight in richly exotic narrative. Here we also see the emergence of the notion that the past is always a kind of fairy tale. Sveinn Úlfsson once flees from a battle against Haraldr the Severe into the world of fairy tale, encountering an old woman in a cottage who – not recognising the king – criticises him roundly in his hearing. The narrator then announces that at this point we have left behind historical reality for *gamans frásǫgn ok eigi sǫguligt eins kostar* (*Msk.* I, 252): 'a story told for pleasure and not particularly historical'. We are moving into the world of the folktale and the comic tale that has various parallels in the apocryphal fables of later times.[36]

It is generally believed that the more fairy-tale elements that occur in a saga, the more fictional it is. However, the presence of wondertale motifs need not mean that the work is unhistorical; it may instead indicate that the writer's understanding of history was a less narrow and more flexible one, embracing elves, trolls, flying dragons and every kind of marvellous

i.e. difficult to fully understand' ('Saga and Jartegn: The appeal of mystery in saga texts,' p. 122)

35 In W. P. Ker's words (*Epic and Romance: Essays on Medieval Literature*, p. 184), Old Icelandic sagas are generally 'immersed in matter.'

36 This comic story has several medieval parallels, notably the tale of King Alfred and the cakes, which in fact resembles its *Heimskringla* variant even more closely (Joaquin Martinez Pizarro, 'Kings in Adversity: A Note on Alfred and the Cakes'; Harris, 'The King in Disguise. An International Popular Tale in Two Old Icelandic Adaptions'). We have an apocryphal saga about a king who is not recognised by one of his lowly subjects. As several scholars have pointed out (for example, Harris, see above, and John Lindow, '*Hreiðars Þáttr heimska* and AT 326: An Old Icelandic Novella and an International Folktale') much *þættir* narrative is of a wondertale and folkloric nature. The extent of such material in *Morkinskinna* (and not just in the *þættir*) is worth further examination.

creature. It was the story that mattered most. In the episode of Karl the Luckless the hero is tied up in a darkened room,

> Ok eptir þat leitar Karl út frá þeim í brot, en hendr hans váru bundnar á bak aptr, en fjǫtr á fótum. Hann ekr sér þá þar at sem lá øx eins þeirra varðmannanna ok færir þar ofan á bakit ok nýr hǫndunum við eggina unz hann fekk skorit strenginn, ok váru þá lausar hendr hans (*Msk.* I, 14).

And afterwards Karl sought to escape from them but his hands were tied behind his back and his feet in fetters. He crawled to where an axe of one of the guards lay and turned over on his back and rubbed his hands onto the edge of the axe until he managed to cut the bonds and freed his hands.

We have here a classical wondertale motif, and in a similar vein the chapter closes with a boat race (*Msk.* I, 15–17). Numerous such incidents occur in *Morkinskinna*.[37] We also encounter the killing of dragons and berserks who are impervious to weapons. In this narrative world when something really important happens, it happens three times.[38] Haraldr the Severe gives Hákon Ívarsson three choices, and Hákon chooses the one that most resembles a fairytale test (*Msk.* I, 259–261). Hreiðarr the Simple is reminiscent of a *kolbítr*, who *varla sjálfbjargi fyr vits sǫkum* (*Msk.* I, 152) 'scarcely had the wit to take care of himself', but turns out to have a quick and undisciplined tongue. Stereotypical characters throw light on historical personages, and historical events are given the form of fairy tales.[39] An episode concerning Bishop Magnús Einarsson and Haraldr Gilchrist reveals the yawning gap between the two worlds. When the bishop

---

37 One incident begins with an Icelander witnessing a search for money: *þá sá hann ... at tveir menn gengu þangat leyniliga með graftól ok grófu þar í jǫrð niðr, ok þat ætlar hann at þeir muni fjár leita* (*Msk.* I, 208) 'then he saw ... that two men were walking along there stealthily with digging tools and then dug down into the ground, and he thought they must be looking for treasure'. Another concerns a game of hide and seek wherein *leystir sporhundar í skóginn, ok þegar villtisk þeim vegr* (*Msk.* II, 51) 'the bloodhounds were let loose in the forest and immediately lost the trail'.

38 For example, see *Msk.* I, 135, 140–141, 201–202, *Msk.* I, 147.

39 John Lindow, 'Þáttr,' pp. 661–662, and Marianne E. Kalinke, 'Sigurðar Saga Jórsalafara,' pp. 158–159, have drawn attention to this point.

comes to court, the king is in difficulty and thinks that he is short of gifts to present. He takes a drinking vessel and gives it to the bishop, and the queen gives him the cushion she is sitting on, and in Iceland,

> var þá rætt um hvat af borðkerinu skyldi gera, þess er kon-
> ungi gegndi bezt. Byskup leitaði ráðs við menn. Mæltu sum-
> ir at selt myndi ok gefit fátœkum mǫnnum verðit. Þá mælti
> byskup: 'Annat ráð vil ek taka. Gøra skal af kalek hér at
> staðnum, ok vil ek svá fyrir mæla at hann njóti ...' Ok sá
> kalekr er mestr at staðnum í Skálaholti (*Msk.* II, 167).

> there was some discussion as to what should be done with
> the drinking vessel that would best reflect on the king. The
> bishop conferred with his advisors. Some said that it should
> be sold and the money given to the poor. Then the bishop
> said: 'I have a different plan. I will make it a chalice for
> the church and I recommend that it should be used in this
> way ...' And the chalice is the largest in the church at Skál-
> holt.

Gifts that a king dispenses to people when nothing better is at hand become the greatest of treasures in an impoverished Iceland. There is an
enormous gap between Iceland and richer countries, and descriptions of
wealth and riches of foreign countries create tension between the world of
the saga and that of of the saga audience.

The exotic and the foreign go hand in hand in *Morkinskinna*. Though
the saga begins in Russia, with Denmark and England featuring prominently from the start and with the Wends as enemies nearby, it is only when
the travels of Haraldr the Severe begin that names such as Saxony, France,
Lombardy, Rome, and Puglia begin to appear.[40] Haraldr the Severe spends
a long time in Constantinople as, later, do Sigurðr the Crusader and Erlingr skakki 'the Crooked'. Constantinople was at the time one of the rare
urban centres in Europe, and there was nothing in Western Europe to com-

---

40 Here the author makes full use of the poetic sources where many of these places are
mentioned; for the poems he uses, see *Skaldic Poetry of the Scandinavian Middle
Ages II: Poetry from the Kings' Sagas* 2, ed. Kari Ellen Gade.

pare with it.[41] The astonishment of the Norsemen as they contemplate the splendour of the court there finds expression when the Emperor Alexios puts on the games for his guest Sigurðr the Crusader:

Þat segja þeir menn er verit hafa í Miklagarði at paðreimr sé á þá leið gǫrr at veggr hár er settr um einn vǫll, at jafna til víðs túns kringlótts, ok gráður umhverfis með steinveggnum, ok sitja menn þar á, en leikr er á vellinum. Eru þar skrifuð margs konar forn tíðendi, Æsir ok Vǫlsungar ok Gjúkungar, gǫrt af kopar ok málmi með svá miklum hagleik at þat þykkir kvikt vera. Ok með þessi umbúð þykkir mǫnnum sem þeir sé í leiknum, ok er leikrinn settr með miklum brǫgðum ok vélum; sýnisk sem menn ríði í lopti, ok við er ok skoteldr hafðr, ok sumt af forneskju. Þar við eru hǫfð alls konar sǫngfœri, *psalterium* ok organ, hǫrpur, gígjur ok fiðlur ok alls konar strengleikr (*Msk.* II, 97–98).

People who have been in Constantinople say that the arena is so constructed that a high wall is built around a plain that is comparable to a large circular hayfield; steps that people sit on are built into the stone wall while the games are played on the field. On the walls many kinds of old legends are portrayed, the Æsir, the Volsungs and the Gjukungs, wrought in copper and iron with such great skill that they seem alive. And with this arrangement the spectators feel they are part of the games. And with the games set up with so many illusions and devices, it seems as if the athletes are riding in the air, while flames shoot out, sometimes by magic. There are all kinds of musical instruments on display, psalteries,

41 On Norsemen and Constantinople, see Sigfús Blöndal, *Væringjasaga: Saga norrænna, rússneskra og enskra hersveita í þjónustu Miklagarðskeisara á miðöldum.* Gustav Storm ('Harald Haardraade og Væringerne i de græske Keiseres Tjeneste') and Sigfús Blöndal (see above, pp. 108–168) discuss the historical kernel of the sagas of Haraldr the Severe in Constantinople. See also Bagge, 'Harald Hardråde i Bysants: To fortellinger, to kulturer'; Claus Krag, 'Harald Hardrådes ungdomsår og kongesagaene: Forholdet mellom sagaprosa, skaldekvad og muntlig tradisjon'; Jan Ragnar Hagland, 'Olavslegender frå Bysants.' Both Bagge (p. 175) and Hagland (p. 195) ignore narratives in *Morkinskinna* about Haraldr's youth, though for different reasons.

organs, harps, violins and fiddles and all kinds of stringed instruments.

Although the Norsemen act confidently when abroad, it is viewing the arena and its wonders through their incredulous eyes that confirms, despite their outward nonchalance, that they appear to feel like unsophisticated rustics underneath.

The *Morkinskinna* audience will have heard references to many countries: Sicily, Jerusalem, the Bosporus, the Gibraltar Strait, and Hungary. Sigurðr the Crusader arrives at the island of Ibiza (*Msk.* II, 84–85). He spends time in Lisbon and in the south of Spain where the Moors are at home. He meets the Holy Roman Emperor in Swabia (*Msk.* II, 99). We may imagine the thrill Icelandic readers must have felt when seeing their fellow-countrymen mentioned in a saga about a Norwegian king who is treated as an equal by the Holy Roman Emperor himself. All kings receive Sigurðr graciously and exchange gifts with him. His travelogue shows that a Norwegian king is the equal of any other kings even though Norway is a small country.[42]

Norsemen had long before secured a firm foothold in England. When the saga begins Knútr the Great's family rules both Norway and England. England is described in great detail when Haraldr the Severe makes his way there on his last military campaign. Conditions on the river banks of the River Ouse are described in detail (*Msk.* I, 306–307) before battle is joined between the attacking forces and the armies of the Earls Waltheof and Morkere. Events are so thoroughly described that the text seems designed for listeners who have little acquaintance with the terrain, although England and Normandy are clearly not alien countries, at least no more foreign than the Orkneys, Ireland, Germany and Constantinople.[43]

---

42 Kalinke, 'Sigurðar Saga Jórsalafara,' p. 157. She notes that Icelandic romances pay detailed attention to the linguistic accomplishments, education and cosmopolitanism of the hero.

43 On the connection between Scandinavians and the English in the Middle Ages, see, among others, Henry Goddard Leach, *Angevin Britain and Scandinavia*; M. K. Lawson, *Cnut: The Danes in England in the early eleventh century*, pp. 4–8, 163–174. In the tale about Styrkárr the Marshall and the local man in a cart, the native Englishman realises that he is facing a Scandinavian; English people seem to be used to them (*Msk.* I, 321). At the time the saga was written, England and France were

The world is not just vast in a physical sense, it also embraces the past and eternity, and much that is now considered either not to exist or to be beyond the normal world.[44] Though *Morkinskinna* is a relatively secular saga, as attested by a comparison with *Heimskringla*,[45] it has more than one level: both God and Óláfr the Saint are a part of society, and they appear in dreams and give various signs. It is necessary to take God and his saints into consideration, and many kinds of communication take place between the spiritual and the secular. Þórir of Steig does not take part in Haraldr's military campaign in England *fyr því at hann hafði dreymt illa um konung* (*Msk.* I, 303) 'because he had an unsettling dream about the king'. Without a doubt, Þórir has simply sensed the likely outcome, and the fateful portents certainly continue. Women appear and chant, and Haraldr dreams fateful verses.[46]

Saints are accessible on their feast days, and various events in the saga are connected to them.[47] It makes a difference what happens after death; emphasis is laid on where the departed kings are buried.[48] A man's ancestors and descendants can be seen in genealogies. Skúli Tóstason the king's foster-father is said to be the ancestor of King Ingi and Earl Skúli (*Msk.* I, 327). There is not always a sharp distinction drawn between Christian and heathen traditions: *Þetta var Matheusmessuaptan, en hon stóð þá á óðinsdegi* (*Msk.* I, 308) 'It was on the evening before Saint Matthew's

culturally very close, and links between Scandinavia and France were also strong; see, among others, Peter Foote, 'Aachen, Lund, Hólar'; 'Latin Rhetoric and Icelandic Poetry: Some Contacts.'

44 See Ármann Jakobsson, 'History of the Trolls?,' pp. 53–55. Davíð Erlingsson ('Fótaleysi göngumanns: Atlaga til ráðningar á frumþáttum táknmáls í sögu af Hrólfi Sturlaugssyni, ásamt formála,' 340–356) criticises the tendency of modern scholars to read back into authors and characters in Old Icelandic sagas their own empiricism, and to lack understanding of everything that the modern mind regards as unrelated to realism. See also Davíð Erlingssson, 'Saga gerir mann.'

45 See Sverrir Tómasson, 'Snorri Sturluson als Hagiograph,' pp. 275–286.

46 Sigurðr the Crusader's dream before the arrival of Haraldr Gilchrist in Norway is another example of a sinister dream containing paranormal matter. Anne Holtsmark ('Harald Gille, en sending,' pp. 84–89) notes that Haraldr can be seen as a kind of *sending,* 'a curse' or 'a spell', connects him with sorcery, and observes that the same wording is also used in *Sverris saga.*

47 See, for example, *Msk.* I, 171, 308, *Msk.* II, 66, 177, 202 and 234.

48 See, for example, *Msk.* I, 174, 327, *Msk.* II, 16, 113, 138, 152 and 210.

Day, which fell on Óðinn's day [Wednesday]'. Here Óðinn and Matthew are mentioned in the same breath. The world of *Morkinskinna* is Christian, but much has survived that, while not Christian, is nevertheless part of the Christian world. Although the retainers of Haraldr the Severe are Christian and the saga author also thinks it is not out of the question that Haraldr and his daughter María *eins manns fjǫr [...] bæði* (*Msk.* I, 324) 'both had the same life', since they died on the same day.

Óláfr the Quiet, as we have noted, respected customs but was still an advocate of empirical knowledge, as is clear in the tale about a man who was said to understand the language of crows. As Óláfr remarks, '*Slíkt mun hégómi mikill ok trúi ek ekki á*' (*Msk.* II, 12) "'That is a lot of nonsense, and I do not believe it for a minute"', he seems to be regarded in much the same way as are clairvoyants nowadays – a courtly diversion rather than a seer to be taken seriously. When the king is next in the vicinity of the farmer, he decides to test him empirically. He has one of the farmer's horses stolen and decapitated. The farmer works this out, even though he has no other sources than the crows that fly cawing overhead. This tale unites empirical method and everyday magic. The conclusion is that the man does in fact understand the language of crows.

With respect to the medieval Icelandic literary corpus, *Morkinskinna* is a relatively contemporary saga in that the events that it narrates deal with the recent past, dating back just two centuries at most. Nevertheless, the past and tradition do matter. A great degree of interest is shown in the strange and the exotic, whether it manifests itself in ancient customs or foreign countries; it is as important as the saga's love of material objects. This saga is characterised by its learning and its desire for entertainment.[49] The author recognises two perspectives – the world of analytic history, and the world of miracles and adventures, in which the story itself and its wonders are as important as its names and facts. The saga is knowledgeable about the past, the singular, former events, and those individuals who are involved in the saga at particular times and places. But all the stories are

---

49 As Andersson and Gade (*Morkinskinna*, p. 57) put it: 'This person ... was more of a storyteller than a critical historian.' It is uncertain whether the author of *Morkinskinna* would have made such a distinction.

also universal in their meaning, like fairy tales, and the author of *Morkinskinna* gives full expression to that element.

2. Courteous Brutality

Three hangings

At one point in *Morkinskinna* a dispute arises between the Icelander Ásu-Þórðr and the arrogant Norwegian chieftain Ingimarr Sveinsson. On Ingimarr's ship Þórðr discovers a boy who had run off with his tenting, upon which Þórðr *tekr sveininn hǫndum ok rekr heim fyri sér í garðinn ok lætr þar varðveita* 'has the boy seized and taken to his house and kept there'. This act angers Ingimarr, who demands that Þórðr hand over the boy, and in turn Þórðr counters that he has no intention *at láta ganga ódæmdan þjóf um bæinn* (*Msk.* II, 110) '"of letting an unsentenced thief run around loose"'. A dispute then arises between Ingimarr and Þórðr's friends in the court of King Eysteinn. Finally, an appeal is made to the king:

> Konungr biðr taka þjófinn ok leiða á mót, ok var svá gǫrt, ok var bundit tjaldit á bak honum, sem siðr er til. Síðan var hann dœmðr ok festr upp út á Eyrum. Þá mælti konungr: 'Hvat ætlar þú, Ingimarr, hvat þjófrinn mun hafa í ǫðrum heimi?' 'Gott,' svarar Ingimarr. 'Nei,' segir konungr, 'beint helvíti.' (*Msk.* II, 112–113)

> The king ordered the thief to be apprehended and led forth, and this was done. The tenting was tied to his back, as was the custom. Then he was condemned and hanged at Eyrar. Then the king spoke: 'Ingimarr, what do you think the thief will experience in the other world?' 'Good things', said Ingimarr. 'No', said the king, 'pure hell'.

No pity is shown to the boy who is hanged, even though his crime might seem to us a considerably minor one. We are not told why he took the tenting, although the suspicion remains that Ingimarr had put him up to

169

it, but the punishment, hanging, is public and severe.[1] Hanging was regarded then as a humiliating form of death, which men of rank were usually spared; the boy's sentence is carried out, and the object that he stole fastened to his back.[2] And, of course, the punishment, in the world of the saga at least, is not over: the king sends him directly to hell after his death.[3] It is difficult to understand what lies behind the king's words. Is the king reminding Ingimarr of his own responsibility for the fact that his servant is on his way to hell? The king appears to be unnecessarily harsh, and yet this is the same King Eysteinn who had previously cured the melancholic Ívarr with such exceptional tact.

The thief himself is not granted any last words, and it is difficult to form an opinion of him or to believe that he deserves the punishment. The only thing we know about him is that he is a *sveinn*, which can mean 'a young man', scarcely beyond puberty or adolescence, or a servant or slave. In any case he is clearly without any power. The description of the hanging is virtually without context, simply the hanging of a young man about whom it is difficult to say much since no evaluation is made aside from the words of the king. The narrative is so restrained as to border on cruelty.[4]

Previously, the saga has told of Steigar-Þórir's revolt against Magnús Barelegs which fails because his supporters run away. At the time Þórir

1 Executions nowadays in the western world are generally not so physically brutal (no more hanging, drawing and quartering, for example), nor are they public, but all of these elements were widespread as late as the eighteenth century. In France public executions were common into the twentieth century. Michel Foucault (*Discipline and Punish: The Birth of Prison*, pp. 3–16) called attention to the spectacle of punishment and the connection between revenge and punishment.
2 Kari Ellen Gade, 'Hanging in Northern Law and Literature,' pp. 161–168.
3 Both in England and France the custom of denying the condemned person confession and extreme unction was known (Johan Huizinga, *The Waning of the Middle Ages: A Study of the Forms of Life, Thought, and Art in France and the Netherlands in the Fourteenth and Fifteenth Centuries*, p. 23) and perhaps the same attitude is at work here.
4 William Brandt (*The Shape of Medieval History: Studies in Modes of Perception*, pp. 133–135) notes that what seems cruel to us is often simply a lack of compassion; courtiers could not have felt sympathy for the thief since they could not have imagined any common bond with him. This scarcely applies to the description (see below) of the execution following the unsuccessful revolt instigated by Steigar-Þórir.

must have been about sixty-three years old and hardly able to walk: *var Þórir borinn í borum um fjallit, því at hann var hrumr mjǫk fyr elli sǫkum* (*Msk.* II, 24) 'Þórir was carried over the mountain on a stretcher because age had greatly weakened him'. Þórir's old age and decrepit state are emphasized, but he is given the chance to express himself. When he mocks his men for running away from the island after all their boasting, his sarcasm humanises him. Nor is he short of an answer to the taunts of his opponents:

> Þá er skipin renndu saman, áðr en Þórir yrði handtekinn, kallaði Sigurðr ullstrengr á Þóri: 'Ertu heill, Steigar-Þórir?' Hann svaraði: 'Heill at hǫndum en hrumaðr at fótum' … Þá mælti Sigurðr: 'Feitr ertu, Þórir'. 'Matr minn veldr því ok mungát,' segir Þórir … Ok er Þórir sér gálgann ok banann opinn fyri sér, en þeir váru tveir einir eptir, þá mælti Þórir ok glotti við … Mǫrg hermðarorð mæltu menn við Þóri … Þat segja menn at Víðkunnr Jóansson mælti þá er Þórir var leiddr til gálgans ok hann reikaði af gǫtunni, er hann var fóthrumr: 'Meirr á stjórn, Þórir,' sagði hann, 'meirr á bakborða.' (*Msk.* II, 25–26).

When the ships approached each other before Þórir was captured, Sigurðr Woolly-Band called out to him, 'Are you in good health, Steigar-Þórir?' He answered, 'Hale of hand, but halt of foot' … 'You have grown fat', said Sigurðr. 'Food and drink are the cause' … and when Þórir saw the gallows and death so close, and only the two of them left, he spoke smiling … Many harsh words were uttered to Þórir … People say that Víðkunnr Jóansson spoke when Þórir was led to the gallows and he stumbled, since he was unsteady on his feet: 'More to starboard, Þórir', he said, 'more to port'.

Þórir reacts heroically to the taunting. Although it appears that people are not averse to taking revenge, the audience experiences a crippled man seized, mocked, and dragged to the gallows.[5] The execution proves violent when Þórir takes leave of his life in a brutal fashion on a gallows that cannot bear his weight.

Egill Áskelsson, Þórir's son-in-law, is left behind – the only man who did not turn tail and, when led ashore, is said to be *inn kurteisasti maðr ok allra manna vaskastr* (*Msk.* II, 25) 'the most courteous and the bravest of men'. After Egill witnesses his father-in-law's hanging, he was

> leiddr undir gálgann, en þrælar konungs skyldu hengja hann. Ok þá mælti Egill við þrælana: 'Eigi munu þér af því þetta við oss gera, at festa oss upp, at eigi væri hverr yðar makligri til.' (*Msk.* II, 27).

> led to the gallows where the king's slaves were to hang him, and then Egill said to them: 'Just because you are able to hang me does not mean that each of you would not be more deserving of such a fate'.

Egill regards it as a humiliation that slaves should hang him – since hanging is not the punishment for a nobleman. Egill is as honourable in appearance as in character and bears up bravely during the spectacle:

> Þá mælti Egill: 'Þat ætla ek at nú hyggi menn hér gott til at sjá fótalætin vár í dag.' Hann var í hálfskiptum kyrtli. Þá svǫruðu menn honum: 'Ætlar þú eigi at þú munir því ráða hversu þér skal bregða við banann?' 'Þat mun nú sýnask,' svarar Egill, 'hvárt ek má nekkvi um ráða.' Ok síðan var virgill dreginn á háls honum. Ok er hann hóf upp þá sté hann fœtinum ǫðrum á ristina ok brásk ekki við, ok þar lét hann líf sitt. Ok allir hǫrmuðu slíkan dreng er hann skyldi svá fara. (*Msk.* II, 27–28).

> Then Egill said: 'I imagine that people are happily anticipating my footwork today.' He was clad in a two-coloured

---

5   It might be mentioned that he later, posthumously (*Msk.* II, 102), becomes King Eysteinn Magnússon the Good's father-in-law when the king marries his daughter Ingibjǫrg.

cloak. The reply came: 'You don't think that you will be able to control how you face death?' 'It will be seen', said Egill, 'how well I can manage things'. Then a noose was put around his neck, and when he was borne aloft, he pressed one foot on the other and did not move. And there he took leave of his life and everybody mourned the passing of such a man.

Then we are told that the king would probably have spared Egill's life had he been asked, but clemency could not be granted without such a request. The description is stark. Egill's reference to 'footwork' suggests the full extent of the macabre spectacle. Another kind of effect is created along with sympathy for the crippled Þórir.[6] The audience admires the gallantry of a man whose greatest concern is his own reaction during the performance, but at the same time they look death and horror in the eye. The three hangings are performances, and members of the saga audience are cast in the role of spectators at the brutal and well-orchestrated death of another person.

These three hangings receive considerable coverage in the saga. In addition, the execution of Sigurðr the Noisy is described in detail. It is said to have been so brutal and torturous that *alþýða manna gekk frá ok vildu eigi á sjá* (*Msk.* II, 208) 'people left, not wishing to watch'. The boundaries have been breached; Sigurðr becomes a martyr, exalted rather than brought low by his almost superhuman behaviour. The severity of the executions and torture creates a fraught reaction among those who know the victims. Ívarr skrauthanki 'Decorative Handle' is a witness to the execution of Ívarr dynta 'the Conceited':

> Ívarr dynta var leiddr á land upp ok hǫggvinn ... Þat sagði
> Ívarr at þat hafði svá liðit yfir hann at honum þótti mest er

6   In *Heimskringla* (Vol. 3, pp. 216–217) this description is briefer; Egill's appearance is not described, Þórir has less dialogue and nothing is said about *fótalæti* 'footwork'. In *Morkinskinna* when Einarr Paunch-Shaker's son Einriði is killed, the latter's excellence is also emphasised: *er allra manna var vaskastr ok gǫrviligastr* (*Msk.* I, 216) 'the bravest and the most accomplished of all men'. Clearly, the loss of a man of such abilities seems regrettable.

nafni hans var leiddr á land upp undir øxi ok hvarf til þeira
ok bað þá heila hittask. (*Msk.* II, 206).

Ívarr the Conceited was led ashore and executed ... Ívarr
[Decorative Handle] said that what had moved him the most
was when his namesake was led ashore and under the axe
and embraced them and expressed a wish to see them safe
and well.

The brutality goes hand in hand with sentimentality, which makes the
other unpleasant accounts ambiguous.

Norbert Elias considers the medieval European attitude towards death
paradoxical. Death and violence were not to be thought about; it was important to ignore them and be cheerful. To those who exercised power,
using it against others seemed like a natural law.[7] Cruelty and deriving
pleasure from torture and executions could seem desirable qualities rather
than a likely cause of social exclusion among those professionally involved
in killing people. The knightly ideal – bravery, courtesy, honour, gallantry
towards women and so on – was ennobling, but the job of the knight was
essentially to do battle.[8] Hostilities were thus to be enjoyed, and men parti-
cipated gladly in their war games when there was no opportunity to engage
in real fighting.[9] The expression of emotions was heightened: weeping
and fainting, frenzy, physical assault and violence went hand in hand with
an almost manic hilarity or even exaggerated gentleness.[10] In medieval
Iceland violent deeds that border on sadism occur, and this is depicted

7   Norbert Elias, *The Civilizing Process*, pp. 158, 161–162 and 170–171; Huizinga, *The Waning of the Middle Ages*, pp. 9–11 and 22–25.
8   See Maurice H. Keen, *Chivalry*, pp. 1–17, 143–178 and 219–238; Joachim Bumke, *Studien zum Ritterbegriff im 12. und 13. Jahrhundert*, pp. 35–60 and 88–150.
9   Elias, *The Civilizing Process*, pp. 158–160 and 167. As Keen points out (*Nobles, Knights and Men-at-Arms in the Middle Ages*, pp. 1–20) chivalric culture was by its very nature a culture of war: 'Chivalry was quintessentially bellicose, setting the fighting man on a pinnacle of honour' (p. 18).
10 Elias, *The Civilizing Process*, pp. 157–159, 161, 164 and 175–176. See Huizinga (*The Waning of the Middle Ages*, pp. 23–25). Elias has been criticised for oversimplific-ation (by, among others, Sverre Bagge, *Mennesket i middelalderens Norge: Tanker, tro og holdninger 1000–1300*, pp. 225–232; Richard W. Kaeuper, 'Chivalry and the "Civilizing Process"'). C. Stephen Jaeger's theories (*The Origins of Courtliness: Civilizing Trends and the Formation of Courtly Ideals 939–1210* and *The Envy of An-*

especially in *Sturlunga saga* and the Sagas of Icelanders. Humiliation of an adversary seems as important as his death, as can be seen repeatedly in *Sturlunga saga*.[11] There the culture of violence in the society can be observed finding an outlet.[12] We register the paradoxical feelings inherent in saga violence: on the one hand, pity for the person executed, while on the other hand the pleasure in violence.[13]

In *Morkinskinna* brutality and sentimentality are two sides of the same coin. Twice a man is struck in the eye or the throat so that the shaft comes out at the nape of the neck, and this is regarded as a remarkable shot since all other body parts are fully protected. Brutality turns into joy after a fortunate victory. In the saga there are many descriptions of battles in which opponents are cruelly slain as if they were cattle.[14] Violence is simply a

gels: Cathedral Schools and Social Ideals in Medieval Europe, 950–1200) on chivalric ideals offer a necessary revision of Elias's views.

11 Gade, '1236: Órækja meiddr ok heill görr'; Gade, 'The Naked and the Dead in Old Norse Society'; Gunnar Karlsson, 'Siðamat Íslendingasögu'; Guðrún Ása Grímsdóttir, 'Um sárafar í Íslendinga sögu Sturlu Þórðarsonar'; Guðrún Nordal, '"Eitt sinn skal hverr deyja": Dráp og dauðalýsingar í Íslendinga sögu'; Ármann Jakobsson, 'Sannyrði sverða: Vígaferli í Íslendinga sögu og hugmyndafræði sögunnar.' Generally, the emphasis on violence seems to intensify according to the proximity of the event described to the present.

12 William Ian Miller, *Humiliation and Other Essays on Honor, Social Discomfort, and Violence*, pp. 53–92. On violence in the medieval and early modern periods, see Natalie Zemon Davis, *Society and Culture in Early Modern France: Eight Essays*, pp. 152–187; Jørn Sandnes, *Kniven, ølet og æren: Kriminalitet og samfunn i Norge på 1500- og 1600-tallet*; Guy Halsall, 'Violence and society in the early medieval west: an introductory survey.'

13 Jeffrey Jerome Cohen (*Of Giants: Sex, Monsters, and the Middle Ages*, pp. 152–166) argues that the concept of pleasure entails cruelty, sadism and masochism. The enjoyment experienced at an execution is presumably sadomasochistic; people enjoy the torture and humiliation of others but experience horror in recognising that the same thing could happen to them.

14 The art of war is rarely spoken of in the saga, except when cities are won with tricks. In this respect the saga resembles other Norse kings' sagas. See Bagge, *Society and Politics in Snorri Sturluson's Heimskringla*, pp. 90–97; Bagge, *From Gang Leader to the Lord's Anointed: Kingship in Sverris saga and Hákonar saga Hákonarsonar*, pp. 38–51. On medieval battle strategies, see, for example, Philippe Contamine, *War in the Middle Ages*. Shaun F. D. Hughes ('The Battle of Stamford Bridge and the Battle of Bouvines') has noted the strong influence of contemporary battle practices on the battle depictions in *Morkinskinna* and other thirteenth-century royal biographies.

part of life. Victims are often the ones who were previously the aggressors, as in *Sturlunga saga*.[15] This observation applies to both Steigar-Þórir and Sigurðr the Noisy. Magnús the Blind is said to be violent, but one of the cruellest deeds in the saga is when Haraldr Gilchrist's slaves put out Magnús's eyes, cut off his feet and then castrate him. Good fortune in battle is fleeting: he who lives by the sword dies by the sword.

One day as they sat drinking

When members of the saga audience on an Icelandic farm turn from their memories of violence, like those treated above, to scenes of good manners, luxury and colourful play on the *Morkinskinna* stage, they will doubtless seek to emulate the actors and actions depicted in the saga. Events take place *í hǫllunni* (*Msk.* I, 58) 'in the hall [or palace]' or in *drykkjustofunni* (*Msk.* II, 135) 'in the drinking parlour'. They begin when kings and his advisers are *einn dag við drykk* 'one day sitting drinking' or *yfir matborðum* 'sitting at table' or *einn dag við snæðing* (*Msk.* I, 51, 56, 143) 'dining one day'.[16] Christmas or another major holiday or feast is often mentioned. Sometimes descriptions of the customs of celebration follow: *hann drakk aldregi svá í skytningum at eigi drykki húskarlar hans allir með honum* (*Msk.* II, 231) 'he never drank in taverns without having all of his retainers drink with him'. The confusion of the endless feasts is part of a world of kings and noblemen that revolves around pleasure rather than hard work. Celebrations also serve to bring adventures to a happy conclusion, as when the son of a commoner is betrothed to or marries the daughter of a king. But though all this talk of feasts can make a saga seem remote it can also brings matters close to home; it is more than likely that *Morkinskinna* was enjoyed as entertainment during a feast.

The Sneglu-Halli tale begins when a ship sails into a fjord and long ships quickly close in on it. On the foremost ship is a man in a red tunic

15 See Ármann Jakobsson, 'Sannyrði sverða,' pp. 57–76.
16 Gerd Althoff ('Friendship and Political Order,' pp. 94–95) has written about the importance of banquets for the friendships and political alliances of kings and magnates. See also Bagge, *Mennesket i middelalderens Norge*, pp. 55–63; Rudolf Meissner, *Die Strengleikar: Ein Beitrag zur Geschichte der altnordischen Prosalitteratur*, pp. 127–129.

who turns out to be King Haraldr. After that the narrative is staged *með hirðinni* (*Msk*. I, 271) 'at court', where tricks are performed, verses are spoken, humorous tales are told, men place bets with each other, and spend a good deal of time drinking or eating. It is a crowded scene, full of life and energy. The tale is a composite of stories about the games of adult men. The king and Halli begin their acquaintance by exchanging coarse insults:

> Maðrinn mælti: 'Sarð hann yðr eigi þá Agði?' Halli svarar: 'Eigi enna.' Maðrinn mælti: 'Var þó nǫkkut til ráðs um?' 'Já, herra,' svarar Halli, 'beið hann at betri manna, vænti þín þangat í kveld.' (*Msk*. I, 270–271).

> The man said: 'Didn't Agði screw you?' Halli answered: 'Not yet'. The man spoke. 'Was there some reason for that?' 'Yes, sir', said Halli, 'he was waiting for a better man; he is expecting you there this evening'.

Certainly, the gloves come off in this kind of coarse banter, and the king's insulting of Halli is reminiscent of childish bullying in school, but Halli replies in kind and matches him insult for insult. This indicates that words are not being used seriously, certainly not for their literal meaning, but as the tools in a game in which the goal is to demonstrate verbal ingenuity in outwitting one's adversary; the nature of this game explains why Halli lives to compose verse on another day. The next chapter in the *þáttr* is another kind of word game. The king gives Þjóðólfr the task of composing a poem about the quarrel between a tanner and a blacksmith and to portray them first as Þórr and Geirrøðr and then as Sigurðr and Fáfnir. Þjóðólfr passes the test and *of kveldit var tíðrætt of vísurnar* (*Msk*. I, 271–272, at 272) 'in the evening the verses were discussed'. In *Morkinskinna* the court always discusses what is happening in their world.

In an aforementioned scene at court (see part II, chapter 3) a man, Túta, is *til sýnis ... lágr sem dvergr ok digr ... ok hlæja menn at honum* (*Msk*. I, 273) 'on display ... he was dwarflike and fat ... and the others laughed at him'. A dwarf is an example of the grotesquery that was striking in games during the Middle Ages.[17] Today it is seen as cruel to laugh at dwarfs or others with physical abnormalities. To us the laughter of the courtiers appears harsh and tasteless.[18] The king promises to reward the poet who can compose a poem about Túta. Halli succeeds and earns the king's favour but falls into disfavour when he later leaves the king's company in order to eat gruel. (His hunger for gruel implies that the king is starving him at the dinner table.) Later that evening the king has more gruel served to Halli than the latter can eat, and, in order to redeem himself, Halli is required to compose a poem very quickly. This he succeeds in doing and his transgression is forgiven (*Msk.* I, 273–276). Although the king threatens Halli with death, the occasion is frivolous and the tone of the narrative is such that everything appears comic rather than serious, as if all games contained a serious element. The later dispute between Þjóðólfr and Halli is not a game, but it is settled in a comic way. Their competition for poetic fame ends in their both being required to compose for the king the worst poem that each has composed in his life. Halli narrates the grotesque tale of the death of Þjóðólfr's father and how he ate his father's killer. The seriousness is sufficiently restrained so that the king makes peace between them, but things could have got out of hand; this seems to be the nature of games in such an age. Then another game begins, in which Halli bets with another courtier that he will receive compensation from Einarr the Fly. Then several stories concerning Halli's tricks follow (*Msk.* I, 276–284).[19] The frivolous tone of the episode agrees well with the whole of *Morkinskinna* and not least with the part in which King Haraldr is the leading character. This is readily apparent in Haraldr's conflict with King Sveinn. Though in deadly earnest, their clash bears considerable resemblance to a tournament or competitive game in which the Kings must incite their

17 The grotesque and its importance in medieval culture has been much discussed, especially on the basis provided by Mikhail Bakhtin's *Rabelais and His World*. See Helga Kress, 'Bróklindi Falgeirs: Fóstbræðrasaga og hláturmenning miðalda.'
18 See Elias, *The Civilizing Process*, pp. 156–68; Huizinga, *The Waning of the Middle Ages*, pp. 9–29.
19 On the nature of the humour in this episode, see, among others, Hermann Pálsson, 'Hirðskáld í spéspegli'; Skúli B. Gunnarsson, 'Hið íslenska hirðfífl: Um fíflsku Sneglu-Halla og Hreiðars heimska'; Björn Gíslason, 'Klám og gróteska í Sneglu-Halla þætti.'

men to perform in a manner not unlike that of modern athletics coaches (*Msk.* I, 199–203).

That warfare and killing are regarded as a game is not merely a medieval phenomenon, since duelling has been such a large part of the courtly, or at least aristocratic, world almost up until the present; boys will indeed be boys. Medieval courtly life was characterised by sports, games and pranks. Throughout thirteenth-century courtly culture, joy is an important condition for royal knights.[20] At the beginning of the tale about Ívarr Ingimundarson the king asks Ívarr *hví hann væri svá ókátr* (*Msk.* II, 103) 'why he was so downcast'. It is unseemly for a knight (and even more for a poet) to be sad even when there is apparent cause. Judging by the king's inquiries regarding his woes and the solutions that he offers, it appears a given that he should be joyful in himself and a source of joy for others.

Transient joy

The crowded stage of *Morkinskinna* is a veritable hurly-burly of activity. However, the noise is sometimes so intense that it generates considerable problems. At one point in the saga, during an assembly in Denmark it is said,

> er menn mæltu þar málum sínum þá varð þar háreysti mikit … Ok annan dag er þeir koma á þingit þá er þar eigi minni gnýr en fyrr ok hlamm ok óp ok hvers kyns skvál ok kliðr. (*Msk.* I, 282).

> as matters were being discussed, voices became very loud … And the next day when they came to the assembly, there was no less noise than before, what with the shouting and yelling and all kinds of din and noise.

Though the various 'stages' in *Morkinskinna* portray great merriment and joy, the tale of the assembly in Denmark reminds us, however, that merriment can soon become noise, and joy can turn to rage and violence. The

---

20 Elias, *The Civilizing Process*, pp. 158–162; Jaeger, *The Envy of Angels*, pp. 102–103; Jaeger, *The Origins of Courtliness*, pp. 161–173.

commotion there is almost terrifying and is a reminder that at public meetings unmitigated joy is a transitory commodity.

When eating and drinking are involved things can go either way. Courtly society's unconditional demand for merriment involves an element of toughness and, even, of emotional shallowness. No one can always be happy, but in the court men are required to keep up at least the appearance of good humour. The joy of court, like that of an honour society itself, must thus always entail a degree of stress.[21] For all the eating and drinking, the fun and games, the assignations and romances, in the harsh chivalric world joy can be transitory. Teasing can lead to mockery and, in no time at all, a round of cheerful banter can turn into a harsh dispute.[22] Magnús the Good and Haraldr the Severe have a falling out at a feast. At first *eru konungar kátir* (*Msk.* I, 126) 'the kings are merry'. Then Magnús gives Haraldr a ring that Haraldr claims was stolen from his father. In the same way, things turn out badly when Haraldr invites Einarr Paunch-Shaker to a feast (*Msk.* I, 214–216), and Einarr dozes while the king relates tales from his youth in Constantinople. Those exploits are a key element in the king's image of himself, and so is his skill as a storyteller. The insult is thus doubled.[23]

In several romances and other narratives with a court setting a similar stock scene occurs: an important king is at a feast together with his champions and the rest of his court. In his good humour he claims that everything is perfect and that such a valiant troop is nowhere else to be found. He then receives an answer that is the equivalent to the loss of paradise: the person answering destroys the king's ideal world by pointing out something that spoils the picture.[24] *Morkinskinna* in fact begins with such a scene when King Jarizleifr, the ruler over Garðaríki 'Russia

---

21 As Cohen points out in his remarks on *Gawain and the Green Knight* (*Of Giants: Sex, Monsters, and the Middle Ages,* pp. 152–166) there is a fierce side to merriment and laughter in medieval courtly society.

22 'A moment ago they were joking, now they mock each other, one word leads to another, and suddenly from the midst of laughter they find themselves in the fiercest feud' (Elias, *The Civilizing Process*, p. 164). See also Huizinga, *The Waning of the Middle Ages*, pp. 9–29.

23 See also part IV, chapter 2 and 3.

24 See other such events in *Hrólfs saga kraka* (Desmond Slay ed., pp. 86–87) and *Þiðreks saga* (Unger ed., pp. 182–183), and a variation on the theme in *Karlamagnús saga*

(or Kievan Rus)', in the best of humour, asks his queen whether she knows of a hall equal in splendour to his own. The queen does not respond in the way that he would have wished: joy is thus destroyed (*Msk.* I, 3–4).

The court can thus be a tough world. The joy of the feast is fleeting, and behind the civilization of the hall and the throne, the games and costly objects, the food and drink, lurks the man who is also a bestial murderer. At any time a feast can be spoiled, and a game can turn into a dispute and a brawl. Despite the frills, violence is never far beneath the surface. When Einarr Paunch-Shaker dozes during King Haraldr's tale, the king has his kinsman Grjótgarðr wake Einarr. Grjótgarðr does so and farts in the process (*Msk.* I, 215). Einarr regards this as so shameful that he has Grjótgarðr killed.[25]

For the uninitiated the court is difficult of entry. Icelanders could be subject to bullying. Such a greenhorn in the court is Hreiðar the Simple:

> 'Bú þik þá sœmiliga at klæðum eða vápnum … skipask margir menn vel við góðan búning, enda er vandara at búa sik í konungs herbergi en annars staðar, ok verðr síðr at hlœgi gǫrr af hirðmǫnnum' … Svá er þó mót á manninum, er þeir Þórðr eru með hirðinni, at Hreiðarr verðr í fyrstu fyr miklum ágang af hirðmǫnnum. Ok breyttu þeir marga vega orðum við hann ok fundu at hann var ómállatr. Kom við sem mátti, ok hendu þeir mikit gaman at því at eiga við hann (*Msk.* I, 157–158).

> 'Provide yourself in an appropriate fashion with clothes and weapons … many men are impressed by fine clothes, and of course it is harder to dress well in the king's quarters than elsewhere, and you will be made less of a laughing stock by

(Bjarni Vilhjálmsson, ed., pp. 739–741). See Ármann Jakobsson, 'Le Roi Chevalier: The Royal Ideology and Genre of Hrólfs saga kraka,' pp. 146–47.

25 Gade ('Einarr Þambarskelfir's Last Shot') has discussed the connotations of this term in light of Einarr's nickname, since *þǫmb* could have meant both 'curve/bow/bend' and 'stomach/belly', and implied that Einarr's shots were silent unless they came from the intestines. See William Sayers, 'The Honor of Guðlaugr Snorrason and Einarr Þambarskelfir: A Reply,' pp. 540–544; Gade, 'Einarr Þambarskelfir, Again'; Anatoly Liberman, 'Gone with the Wind: More Thoughts on Medieval Farting'; Lotte Motz, 'More Thoughts on Einar Þambarskelfir.'

the courtiers' ... but he was such a curious specimen that when Þórðr and he were at court, Hreiðarr at first suffered a good deal of teasing from the courtiers. They found him chatty in their many exchanges with him. Things turned out as might be expected and they had fun at his expense.

Clothes make the man. At court, excluding the king, no one is allowed to stand out. Even though Hreiðarr cleaned up his appearance somewhat, he is dealt with harshly early in his stay because of his odd behaviour:

> verðr Hreiðarr skauttogaðr mjǫk ok fœrðr í reikuð. Hann er málugr ok hlær mjǫk, ok þykkir mǫnnum ekki at minna gaman at eiga við hann. Ok verðr honum nú fǫrin ógreið (*Msk.* I, 154).

> and Hreiðarr was handled very roughly and pushed around a lot. He talked and laughed at lot, which did not make him less fun to push around, and his road turned rocky.

The Norwegian court would have seemed formidable to many Icelanders at the time *Morkinskinna* was written.

Greenhorns at court did not need to be as strange as Hreiðarr in order to have difficulty establishing themselves. In the Stúfr episode the king had to consult with his leading retainers to determine whether Stúfr should be granted a place at court (*Msk.* I, 292–293). Elsewhere in the saga there were courtiers who were eager to prevent parvenus from acquiring access to the king and respect among the courtiers.[26] Þjóðólfr Arnórsson the poet is said to be *nǫkkvat ǫfundsjúkr við þá menn er kvámu til hirðarinnar* (*Msk.* I, 271) 'somewhat envious of those who came to court'. When Sneglu-Halli gains a modicum of prestige Þjóðólfr is *fátt um* (*Msk.* I, 273) 'not best pleased', but when Halli makes a blunder *þykkir Þjóðólfi þetta hlœgligt er Halli hefir til tekit* (*Msk.* I, 275) 'Þjóðólfr considers Halli's

---

26 Among others, Áki, steward to the Danish King Sveinn in 'Auðunar þáttr' (*Msk.* I, 218–219) and Árni Shore-skewed in 'Þórarins þáttr stuttfelds' (*Msk.* II, 135–136). This motif is not confined to Icelanders – we find it in the arrival of Haraldr Gilchrist in Norway (*Msk.* II, 142). Þjóðólfr Arnórsson is an Icelander, although he acts like a native Norwegian in 'Sneglu-Halla þáttr.'

misstep amusing'. In the back of his mind there is the glimmer of insecurity about his own status and a fear that turns out to have its roots in his humble origins. Þjóðólfr is sensitive, and Halli exposes this weakness. In the tale of Þorgils the fisherman (*Msk.* I, 284–288) the king provokes a dispute between the proven retainer and a newcomer. The fisherman composes some lines for the king, and the king demands a verse from Þjóðólfr in return, but the latter is obliged to suffer the king's derision for having rhymed *grǫm* and *skǫmm* (the former consists of a long syllable and the latter is short). Clearly, Þjóðólfr does not stand up well to such teasing:

> Konungr mælti: 'Þjóðólfr, yrk nú í móti.' En Þjóðólfr lézk
> eigi myndu yrkja. 'Bæði er,' segir konungr, 'Þjóðólfr, at þú
> yrkir vel, enda ertu vandlátr um.' (*Msk.* I, 287).

> The king said: 'Þjóðólfr, compose something now in response'. But Þjóðólfr said he would not compose any verse. 'It is the case', said the king, 'Þjóðólfr, that you compose well, but that you are fastidious about it'.

This is doubtless the reason why the king chooses him as the butt of the joke.[27]

At the beginning of the saga, as we have seen, King Magnús as a child is fostered by King Jarizleifr in Russia. The king and the queen treat him *eigi með minni ást ok elsku* (*Msk.* I, 5) 'with no less love and affection' than their own sons, but some courtiers turn against him despite the royal couple's solicitations. At court each has to worry about his own place in the scheme of things. Honour could often be a zero-sum game: a rise in status for one person might be at the expense of someone else.[28] Thus a

27 Bjarne Fidjestøl, 'Tåtten om Harald Hardråde og fiskaren Þorgils.'
28 Helgi Þorláksson, 'Virtir menn og vel metnir,' pp. 17–19. This is also apparent in the contest between Haraldr Gilchrist and Magnús Sigurðarson (*Msk.* II 148–150) and in the animosity between Sigurðr the Crusader's men and those who stayed behind in Norway when the former return from Constantinople (*Msk.* II, 131). This aspect of court society is reminiscent of medieval Icelandic society as depicted in the *Íslendingasögur*; see Preben Meulengracht Sørensen (*Fortælling og ære: Studier i islændingesagaerne*, pp. 249–65) on Kjartan Ólafsson's social status. Constant competition and conflict characterise both societies, although the status of the king changed a good deal. It must be borne in mind that here we are talking about the representation

man unhappy at hearing another praised must fear that such praise involves the disparagement of someone else, that is, of himself. This fear lies at the heart of all envy, whether medieval or modern.

At court, rivalry for influence and power is endemic. This small society is characterised by dissension, envy and slander. On one occasion conflict between King Magnús and Einarr Paunch-Shaker was only just avoided. There was much talk that displeased the king:

> Magnúsi konungi líkar þungt, ok mæla menn þat fyr honum at eigi sé allsœmiligt, svá mikla sem hann gerði þá feðga yfir ǫllum Þrándheimi, at nú skyli þeir halda þá menn er lagabrot gøra ok hann hefir reiði á. Konungr svarar þeim fám orðum. (*Msk.* I, 141).

> King Magnús was unhappy. People speak of this to him that it is unseemly, given that he had made father and son rulers over all Þrándheimr, that they should now be having dealings with those men who break the law and with whom he was angry. The king answers them in few words.

The people at court are opposed to the friendship between the king and Einarr, but the king retains his composure. When Sigurðr the Crusader believes the slander about Sigurðr Hranason and accuses him of theft, the latter points out to the king that everybody has envious detractors. He is referring to *er yðr er sagt* (*Msk.* II, 120) '[that which] you were told' and puts his finger on an important characteristic of court society, its incessant gossip. The court is like a village and this situation generates talk, which is a potent force in such a society. Everyone at court is constantly under discussion and under scrutiny.[29]

In the saga court talk is not just background chatter but can be an important element in the drama, as was the case with the storytelling Icelander who speaks of Haraldr the Severe's foreign adventures:

of society in *Morkinskinna*, and not social conditions in eleventh- and twelfth-century Norwegian society. That said, a great deal of competition and discord did prevail during that period.

29 On the social functions of gossip, see Patricia Meyer Spacks, *Gossip*. Helga Kress ('Staðlausir stafir: Um slúður sem uppsprettu frásagnar í Íslendingasögum') discusses gossip in the *Íslendingasögur* and has adduced several interesting examples.

> Taka menn at drekka ok rœða margir um at þó sé djǫrfung í
> þessu er hann, Íslendingr, segir þessa sǫgu, eða hversu kon-
> ungi muni virðask. Sumum þykkir hann vel segja, en sumir
> vinnask minna at. (*Msk.* I, 236).

> The men took to drinking and many discussed whether it
> was audacious for this man, an Icelander, to tell this story,
> and how the king would respond. Some thought he spoke
> well but others thought less of it.

Court talk here creates suspense, especially since the king remains silent and adopts a poker face. It is also clear how much is at stake for the
Icelander. As a foreigner in the court, he is regarded as an upstart. The
episode reveals the position of any Icelander in the Norwegian court –
this is a key theme in the saga as a whole.

In this case, two points of view are presented. Some think that the
Icelander is a good story-teller, and others do not. Court talk is used in
identifying opposing viewpoints and allowing them to compete with one
another.[30] This creates a multifaceted view of the events recounted in the
saga, also apparent in Hreiðarr's circumspection of the king discussed
above. All events can be viewed in different ways; the author of *Morkinskinna* uses court talk to underline their complexity, and although – in his
tale – the sovereign's word is paramount, the opinion of the court nevertheless retains a certain importance.

Soon after Magnús the Good and Haraldr the Severe have taken over
joint rule of Norway discord between the two kings becomes apparent,
and court talk plays a role in fomenting it:

> Kǫlluðu nú menn Magnúss konungs at hann hefði rétt at
> mæla, en þeir er óvitrari váru kǫlluðu Harald í þessu nakkvat
> svívirðan. En Haraldsmenn sjálfir mæltu þat at eigi væri
> skilt á aðra leið en Magnús konungr skyldi lægit hafa ef þeir
> kvæmi báðir senn til, en Haraldr væri eigi skyldr at leggja
> í brot ef hann kœmi fyrr. Ok tǫlðu þeir at Haraldr hefði af

<hr>

30 *Menn lǫgðu hér til misjafnt, mæltu sumir með sveini en sumir með hirðmanni*
(*Msk.* I, 6) 'People were divided on the matter; some favoured the boy but others
the retainer.'

þessu vel ok vitrliga. En þeir er verr vildu um rœða tǫlðu at Magnús konungr vildi rjúfa sættina ok hann vildi gera ósœmð ok rangt frænda sínum, Haraldi konungi. (*Msk.* I, 130).

King Magnús's men considered that he was justified, but those less subtle considered Haraldr to have been somewhat dishonoured in this affair. But Haraldr's men said that the only way to view that matter was that King Magnús had a right to the anchorage if they had arrived at the same time, but that Haraldr was not obliged to choose another anchorage if he arrived first. They considered that he had behaved properly in the matter. However, those less well disposed in their comments considered that King Magnús wanted to break the settlement and to dishonour and wrong his kinsman King Haraldr.

Though the kings reach an agreement that at first seems clear and simple, all agreements are subject to interpretation, and court gossip is used by the author to promote this notion. The *óvitrari* 'less subtle' followers of Magnús appear to be boasting. Those followers of Haraldr 'less well disposed in their comments' take offence on his behalf. Men in both camps heighten the difference between the kings, and, in turn, their talk influences both men.

'Return to your natural state'

When King Haraldr the Severe suppresses an uprising among the Upplanders, he receives an invitation to visit one Úlfr the Wealthy. There everything proves *stórmannlig, borðbúnaðr ok ǫlgǫgn, ok hallarbúningr var með miklu yfirbragði ok bæði ok fémikill* (*Msk.* I, 227) 'splendid, the table settings, the drink and the hall decorations were both lavish and costly'. During the feast the king stands up and says that he wishes to express his thanks by telling a story. The reaction of the guests is – unsurprisingly – unanimous:

Allir svǫruðu ok kváðu þat veizlunni mikla prýði ok sóma ef slíkr maðr skemmti. (*Msk.* I, 227)

All responded and said that the feast would be greatly honoured and privileged if such a man entertained them.

This proves to be the first of many mistakes that Úlfr makes.

Haraldr's story deals with a young king and his *karl* 'retainer', whom
the slave Álmsteinn drives into exile because he has collected taxes and
misappropriated them. The slave has himself crowned king but is unpopular, especially as he seizes noble women and keeps them for as long as
he pleases and fathers children with them (*Msk.* I, 227–228). He believes
that he has killed the king and his retainer by burning down a house with
them inside, but they escape and capture Álmsteinn in a surprise attack:

> Álmsteinn bað sér útgǫngu, en Hálfdan kvað þat makligt at
> hann tœki nú slíkan dóm á sik sem hann hafði honum hugat:
> 'En fyr þá sǫk,' segir hann, 'at vér erum ekki jafnmenni þá
> gøri ek þér þann kost at þú skalt hverfa til náttúru þinnar,
> vera ávallt þræll meðan þú lifir ok ǫll ætt þín, sú er frá þér
> kømr.' Ok þat kýs Álmsteinn. Ok þá fekk Hálfdan honum
> með þrælsnafninu kyrtil hvítan ok lítt vandaðan. (*Msk.* I,
> 228–229).

> Álmsteinn asks for safe passage, but Hálfdan said it was
> fitting that he now suffer the same fate as he had devised
> for him, but 'because we are not equals I will give you the
> choice that you return to your natural state, to be a slave for
> as long as you live, together with all your family who come
> after you'. And Álmsteinn chose this, and Hálfdan gave him
> a plain white tunic along with his designation as slave.

The slave returns to his 'nature' and receives the white tunic of a slave.

As in all good stories the moral comes at the end,

> 'Álmsteinn þræll átti mart barna, ok ætla ek þá vera ætt þína,
> Úlfr,' segir konungr, 'at Álmsteinn væri fǫðurfaðir þinn, en
> ek em sonarsonr Hálfdanar konungs.' (*Msk.* I, 229).

> 'Álmsteinn the slave had many children and I believe them
> to be your family, Úlfr', said the king, 'and that Álmsteinn

was your paternal grandfather, but I am the grandson of King Hálfdan'.

Storm clouds quickly form on Úlfr's horizon, for Hálfdan had condemned Álmsteinn's entire family to slavery:

'Tak nú hér, Úlfr,' segir Haraldr konungr, 'kyrtil einn hvítan, þann er Hálfdan fǫðurfaðir minn gaf Álmsteini fǫðurfǫður þínum, ok þar með ættar nafn. Ver ávallt þræll heðan í frá, því at svá var fyrr til skipat, þá er Hálfdan hafði þingit, sem fyrr gat ek, at afi þinn tók kyrtilinn at þar kómu mœðr barna hans til þingsins, ok tóku þá ǫll bǫrn hans þess konar klæði, ok skyldi svá allt þat er frá þeim kvæmi.' (*Msk.* I, 229).

'Now, Úlfr', says King Haraldr, 'you shall adopt a white tunic like the one my grandfather Hálfdan gave your grandfather along with the designation of slave. You will be a slave henceforth as was proclaimed previously by Hálfdan at the assembly, as I just related, when your grandfather received the tunic and when the mothers of his children came to the assembly and all his children adopted this style of dress and so must all those who follow in your line'.

In the eyes of the king Úlfr the Wealthy is little better than a thief, and, in the end,

konungr tekr upp ǫll ǫlgǫgn hans ok aðrar gersimar. Ok sér eignar konungr ǫll ǫnnur bú hans en þat it eina er hann gaf honum. (*Msk.* I, 230).

the king gathers up all Álmsteinn's drinking vessels and other treasures and seizes for himself all his other farms excepting the one he gave him.

On the other hand, Úlfr is permitted to keep his freedom and a single farm and his reaction had been to take only that which was his due: *hann treystisk nær eigi ǫðru en taka til kyrtilsins* (*Msk.* I, 230) 'he trusted himself only to accept the tunic'.

Here is a parable within a parable. The saga of Haraldr has a general message, and so does this episode; but what is that message? There may in fact be two of them. Sverrir Tómasson sees in the saga a flattering irony: Haraldr perpetrates an injustice on Úlfr and the saga is designed to show him as an unjust king.[31] Of course, Haraldr deprives someone of his possessions because of his origins as a slave. But thirteenth-century perspectives on such matters differ considerably from those of the present day. Álmsteinn was granted his life although his family is condemned to slavery from then on. The phrase *hverfa til náttúru sinnar* 'to return to his nature' also refers to Úlfr. Slaves cannot own anything, and thus King Haraldr is completely within his rights, and indeed merciful, when he grants Úlfr his freedom and one farm. The parable does not portray Haraldr as unjust but rather charts the rise of a nasty parvenu in society whose upward mobility, almost by definition, has been occasioned by ill-gotten gains. Úlfr thinks he has risen above his family by virtue of his wealth and has positioned himself between social classes on his own initiative, and in the face of a specific legal agreement.

But even if slaves were required to keep to their true station in life and never seek to be the equals of chieftains, the picture of society in the saga is far from straightforward. Though the viewpoint of the ruling elite is prominent at all times, another kind of attitude is also discernible.[32] At one point Họgni, a wealthy farmer, rejects the title of a landed man on the following grounds:

> 'Með þọkkum vil ek taka yðra vingan, herra, ok allt þat
> er ek má skal ek yðr gott gøra, en lends manns nafn, þat
> vil ek eigi hafa, því at ek veit hvat rœtt mun þá er lendir
> menn koma saman: Þar sitr Họgni ok er minnstr allra lendra
> manna, hann er búanda ættar. Þat er mér ekki til virðingar

31 Sverrir ('Vinveitt skemmtan og óvinveitt,' p. 67) alleges that 'Úlfs þáttr' (*Msk.* I, 226–230) and 'Brands þáttr' (Msk. I, 230–232) explore the same themes, and, of course, a cloak occurs in both tales. He detects in both of them the influence of the doctrines of John of Salisbury. Magnus Olsen ('En skjemtehistorie av Harald Hardråde') also discusses 'Úlfs þáttr.'

32 The mindset of the elite is always dominant in society and the common people then adopt it. See Antonio Gramsci, *Selections from the Prison Notebooks*, pp. 52–60; T. J. Jackson Lears, 'The Concept of Cultural Hegemony: Problems and Possibilities.'

heldr til háðungar ok at athlœgi. Nú vil ek heldr vera mestr bœndanna, ok sé þat mælt hvar sem menn koma saman at Hǫgni er þeira fremstr; ok verðr mér sú umrœða miklu vinveittri ok mér skapfelldri.' (*Msk.* I, 214).

'I will accept your friendship with thanks, lord, and I will do the best I can for you, but the title of landed man is something I do not wish to have, for I know what will be said when the chieftains meet: There sits Hǫgni, the least of all landed men; he is by nature a farmer. That would not honour me but rather be a source of mockery and ridicule. I would rather be the greatest among farmers and have it acknowledged wherever men gather that Hǫgni is the first among them. Such a reputation would be preferable to me and more positive'.

This seems nobly spoken. Nobility lies not in a title alone, but this saga suggests that every individual has a station in life and should not aspire to another. In *Morkinskinna* there are tales about the aforementioned Óttarr the Trout, *búandason ok kertisveinn, ok skyldi þá þjóna, svartr á hárslit, lítill ok vaskligr ok kurteiss, døkklitaðr ok þó vel um sik.* (*Msk.* II, 139) 'a landowner's son and chamberlain in [King Sigurðr's] service, dark-haired, small in stature but manly and courtly, of dark complexion and a man of some worth'. King Sigurðr at first reacts negatively when the newcomer retrieves a book that the king has cast into the fire (see part III, chapter 1) and then sees fit to offer him sound advice: '*Hvat muntu kenna mér ráð, inn versti kotkarlsson ok innar minnstu ættar?*' (*Msk.* II, 140) '"Who are you to give me advice, the lowest of peasants from the least distinguished of families?"' The conclusion, however, is that the king is finally able to judge Óttarr on his merits:

'Hér sátu inir œztu vinir mínir, lendir menn ok stallarar, skutilsveinar ok allir inir beztu menn í landinu, ok varð ǫngum manni jafn vel til mín sem þessum er yðr mun þykkja lítils verðr hjá yðr. Hann unni mér nú mest, ok var þar Óttarr birtingr ...' (*Msk.* II, 140).

'Sitting here are my closest friends, landed men, marshals, officials at court, and all the best men in the land, and none was as well-intentioned towards me as this man, who will seem to you of little worth. It was Óttarr the Trout who honours me now most of all …'

And the king eventually promotes Óttarr to the rank of landed man:

'Hann er áðr kertisveinn; nú skal hann vera lendr maðr minn, ok mun þat þó fylgja er meira er, at hann mun merki-ligastr maðr vera af stundu lendra manna minna. Gakk nú í sæti hjá lendum mǫnnum ok þjóna eigi lengr.' (*Msk.* II, 140).[33]

'He was previously a chamberlain, but now he shall be my landed man, and moreover it will turn out that he will be the most important of my landed men. Go and take your place among the chieftains and no longer be my servant'.

Nobility is not always a matter of family origins, but in the world of *Morkinskinna* a definite hierarchy prevails, and the way to advancement lies in winning the favour of the king.

Haraldr the Severe mocks Þórir the King's Brother by claiming that his father was called *Hvinn-Gestr* (*Msk.* I, 138), Gestr 'the thief'. It is one thing to be the king's brother and quite another to be the son of someone called Hvinn-Gestr. In the saga there are terms such as *búandaliðið* (*Msk.* I, 265) 'militia' used in a pejorative sense and on one occasion Sigurðr the Crusader divides his men into chieftains and *þá er lítils eru verðir* (*Msk.* II, 115) 'those who are of little significance'. Although there are some admirable sons of farmers, that does not mean that farmers are generally equal to chieftains. It is far from the case that all men are equal. The hierarchical power structure is a given, but the world is transitory.[34] The wealthy bully Geirsteinn says to some of the 'little men' before he is killed:

33 See also the example of Áslákr hani 'the Rooster' (*Msk.* II, 145).
34 Elias, *The Civilizing Process*, p. 171.

'Upp hefjask nú í móti oss litlir menn ok af smám ættum ok
ætla við oss at jafnask.' (*Msk.* II, 226).

'Insignificant men from modest families are rising up and
see themselves as our equals'.[35]

In *Morkinskinna* few have less influence and enjoy less prestige than
farmers. Styrkárr stallari 'the Marshall' gets into trouble while fleeing
after King Haraldr's demise in England, when a 'man in a wagon', a
'farmer', expresses the desire to kill him but proves not to be armed, so
Styrkárr simply lops off his head instead (*Msk.* I, 321–322). This is the situation of the common people; they exist and they are different, but there is
no need to be much concerned with them.[36] In this incident the little man
is simply treated as a figure of fun.

Nevertheless, the voice of the common people finds expression on one
occasion. King Sveinn of the Danes and some of his men are forced to seek
refuge in a small farm, when he encounters *ein gǫmul húsfreyja* (*Msk.* I,
252) 'an old housewife'. They keep their true identity secret, so that the
old woman speaks her mind freely and complains bitterly:

'hví hefir gegnt óp þetta eða hlamm er verit hefir í nótt er
vér hǫfum eigi fengit ró fyrir né svefn?' (*Msk.* I, 252).

'what was last night's terrible racket all about – there was
no peace for the wicked and no-one slept a wink?'

In the middle of the clash between the kings we are placed in a cottage
with an old woman who values her own sleep more than any historical
event. This mundane voice forces its way unexpectedly into the saga and
is unafraid to subject the king to some straight talk:

Þá mælti kerling mikit fólskumál: 'Vesǫl erum vér konungs
ok æ vei verði oss. Vér eigum konung hvárttveggja haltan
ok ragan.' (*Msk.* I, 252).

35 This is reminiscent of the words spoken by Jón Loptsson to the effect that things have
   reached a desperate state: '*ef þat skal eigi rétta, er skillitlir menn drepa niðr höfðingja*'
   (*Sturlunga saga* 1, p. 230) '"if justice will not be achieved when insignificant men kill
   chieftains"'.
36 See Elias, *The Civilizing Process*, p. 172.

> Then the old woman spoke with great foolishness: 'We are
> ill served with respect to our king, and all misfortune befalls
> us, for we have a king who is both lame and limp'.

The king is obliged to put up with this. In the middle of the king's story
we are suddenly presented with a new setting, a cottage, and there an old
woman, and not the king, who has the floor and holds forth. There is little
surprise that the saga writer should offer a partial apology for telling such
a story (*Msk.* I, 252).

Morkinskinna takes place in a courtly society. But there is more to the
world than that, and in *Morkinskinna* the nature of that 'more' is revealed.
Although the old woman in the cottage is largely a figure of fun (as are
ordinary folk in stories of noble persons), she enjoys her fifteen minutes
of fame. At that moment, hers is the only voice in the saga, completely cut
off from other people, but she serves as witness to the fact that the world
of the saga is only part of the story. Despite the apology that this tale is
not historically accurate, the old woman reminds us that the tale told in
Morkinskinna is not the whole story.

3. A History of Private Life

Medieval emotions

Although emotions have always existed, emotional reactions vary according to social and cultural contexts.[1] While in the description of kings and great men moderation is repeatedly emphasised,[2] *Morkinskinna* shows both moderate and excessive, both discreet and unreserved reactions. When Haraldr the Severe puts Brandr the Bountiful to a certain test, Brandr does not speak. From this reticence, the king concludes that Brandr is *maðr skapstórr ok mun vera mikils háttar maðr er honum þótti eigi þurfa orð um at hafa* (*Msk.* I, 231) 'a proud man and must be truly distinguished if he does not feel the need to say anything'. In *Morkinskinna*, controlling one's feelings is hardly the same as having no feelings.

The saga is also full of examples of uninhibited expression of feelings. Emotional extravagance was fashionable in medieval courtly society, but was a thorn in the side of the church, whose clerics and other churchmen preached the virtues of moderation.[3] Strong emotional expressions accompanied the death of King Magnús the Good. His men could hardly speak because of their grief (*Msk.* I, 169, 172) and *[y]fir hans grepti stóðu margir góðir menn ok vaskir grátandi* (*Msk.* I, 176) 'many good and valiant men stood crying over his grave'. This bears witness to the affection in

---

1 See William Ian Miller, *Humiliation and Other Essays on Honor, Social Discomfort, and Violence*; Miller, 'Emotions and the Sagas,' pp. 89–109; Peter N. and Carol Stearns, 'Emotionology: Clarifying the History of Emotions and Emotional Standards.'

2 Ármann Jakobsson, *Í leit að konungi*, pp. 222–228.

3 Norbert Elias, *The Civilizing Process*; C. Stephen Jaeger, *The Origins of Courtliness: Civilizing Trends and the Formation of Courtly Ideals 939–1210*; Jaeger, *The Envy of Angels: Cathedral Schools and Social Ideals in Medieval Europe, 950–1200*. Violent public expressions of grief were customary in the fifteenth century; see Johan Huizinga, *The Waning of the Middle Ages*, pp. 11–14.

which the king was held.[4] Such cultivation of feelings seems at odds with the sometimes brutal nature of the saga society, but these sharp contrasts harmonize with its ever mutable nature.

Various kings in the saga are men of strong spirit. Magnús the Good becomes blood-red in the face when he considers the death of his father at Stiklastaðir. This reaction is sufficient to induce Kálfr Árnason to mount his horse and flee the country (*Msk.* I, 30). When Sigurðr Hranason falls into the hands of Sigurðr the Crusader in the middle of a fight with King Eysteinn and his men, Eysteinn became *svá rauðan at honum mátti einum fingri dreyra vekja* (*Msk.* II, 129) 'so red in the face that he could have bled from any finger'. Yet he does not lose his temper.

In the saga outward appearances and somatic responses are sometimes indicative of otherwise hidden emotions. Frequently, such feelings are suppressed until they suddenly erupt. When, at the instigation of King Jarizleifr and Queen Ingigerðr of Russia, Norwegian chieftains visit in order to take Prince (later King) Magnús back to Norway, the king and queen are at first evasive. Einarr Paunch-Shaker thinks it is *eigi hǫfðingligt at skipta svá skjótt skapi sínu fyrir engin tilefni* (*Msk.* I, 20) 'not befitting a chieftain to change one's mood so quickly for no reason', by which he is obviously not pleased that the king and queen are reversing their previous position on Magnús's return to Norway. One may well sense the anger beneath the surface of Einarr's calm demeanour. When Haraldr the Severe disliked one of the verses in Arnórr the Earls' Poet's poem, he insisted '*Lofa konung þenna sem þú vill, ... en lasta eigi aðra konunga*' (*Msk.* I, 144) '"Praise this king if you like ... but do not condemn other kings"'. The rhythm of the sentence is sharp and aggressive, and its effect is similar to a sword being drawn from its scabbard. Magnús's comments before he goes red in the face at the thought of Stiklastaðir are charged with emotion: '*Taka myndi øx þín þá til fǫður míns*' (*Msk.* I, 30) '"Your axe would have reached my father, then"'. As the king blushes, the threat in his words increases, which in turn signal his frame of mind.

4   The same was said of Eysteinn Magnússon (*Msk.* II, 138), and when Hákon Þórisfóstri 'Þórir's foster-son' dies *allir grátandi, því at náliga unnu honum allir menn hugástum* (*Msk.* II, 18) 'all cried because nearly everyone loved him dearly'.

There was always the need for caution when approaching the royal hall. The kings in *Morkinskinna* are invariably on their guard and take note of body language of every kind. They are the highest authority in the land, and at court many people are not all that they seem and do not know how to temper their words in the presence of the king. No one is to be trusted, and kings must be on their guard and constantly test their retainers' loyalty. Often this wariness can seem to be exaggerated touchiness, even paranoia. The killing of Einarr Paunch-Shaker may be attributed to his falling asleep in his old age (and in his cups) during King Haraldr's recitation of his adventures in Constantinople, but the king feels that Einarr *óvirði frásǫgnina* (*Msk.* I, 215) 'dishonoured the story' (see also part IV, chapters 3 and 4).

The characters in the saga are not only representatives of groups in society, but they also have emotional lives that are important in their own right. The Hreiðarr episode is about the maturation of Hreiðarr, if King Magnús's remarks are any guide:

> 'Þetta kvæði sýnisk mér undarligt ok þó gott at nestlokum. En kvæðit mun vera með þeim hætti sem ævi þín; hon hefir fyrst verit með kynligu móti ok einrœnligu, en hon mun þó vera því betr er meirr líðr á.' (*Msk.* I, 164).

> 'This poem seems to me rather strange but also good towards the end. In this respect the poem resembles your own life. At the outset it has been strange and singular but it will get better as time passes'.

Perhaps the tale can be understood as a kind of parable about the origins of intelligence. Hreiðarr matures but it is not clear exactly how or why. At the end it is said that the *kynjalæti er hann sló á sik* (*Msk.* I, 164) 'the idiosyncrasies that stood out' in his early life disappeared later. The true Hreiðarr emerges gradually but his personality does not really change. It may be that Hreiðarr ought to be regarded as a *kolbítr*. It is not so much that *kolbítar* mature but rather that, in modern parlance, they 'need to get a life' and accomplish something. The problem with Hreiðarr is that he has never been angry (*Msk*. I, 156–157),[5] a state of affairs that changes during the course of the story (*Msk*. I, 157–164). That is to say, Hreiðarr's problem is a lack of emotion, and perhaps a lack of experience. He does not know how to be angry – which makes him dangerous, a danger to himself and a simpleton. Once acquainted with this emotion he will become less eccentric.

Oddness and singularity are *leitmotifs* in the saga. Idiosyncratic forms of expression, such as those deployed by the old woman in the cottage, who calls the clash of weapons *óp þetta eða hlamm* 'that din and racket', occur repeatedly.[6] So, too, when King Magnús the Good makes Sveinn Úlfsson an earl, Einarr Paunch-Shaker says '*ofjarl, ofjarl*' (*Msk*. I, 51) '"too fine for an earl, too fine for an earl"'. The repetition of this term lends it additional weight in serving to describe accurately the relations between Magnús and Sveinn. In the tale of Þórarinn Shortcloak we find references to men called Hákon Lard-Arse and Árni Shore-Skewed (*Msk*. II, 135).[7] Sneglu-Halli reduces a whole assembly in Denmark to silence by saying,

> 'Ek skal kæra af óðindælu mína sjálfs. Mér er horfin ok hein ok heinarsufl, nál ok skreppa ok allt skjóðuskrúð, þat er betra er at hafa en missa.' (*Msk*. I, 282).

> 'I must complain of an accident of my own making. I have lost a whetstone and some whetstone oil, a needle and a bag and everything that goes with it, and they are better to have than to lose'.

---

5 A common saga motif; it features in an international folktale (AT 326), of which there is an Icelandic version about a boy who knew no fear; see Einar Ólafur Sveinsson, *Verzeichnis isländischer Märchenvarianten*, p. 23.

6 Throughout the saga command of language is presented as being very important. We note that Haraldr Gilchrist is mocked because he is not fluent in Norwegian (*Msk*. II, 148), and those kings who receive the most attention are linguistically gifted, as with Haraldr the Severe and Eysteinn Magnússon.

7 Diana Whaley ('Nicknames and Narratives in the Sagas') cites examples of nicknames causing conflict in *Morkinskinna*. This Árni is also named in *Þorgils saga ok Hafliða*. His nickname has yet to be explained: Finnur Jónsson, 'Tilnavne i den islandske Old-litteratur,' p. 323.

His listeners find Halli's remark strange and fall into a curious silence, since people often tend to listen to and reflect on what they do not understand.[8]

The author of *Morkinskinna* is interested in the inner life of individuals and has a remarkable understanding of human emotions. This is well attested in the Ívarr episode discussed above (see part II, chapter 3).[9] Their relationship is so close that King Eysteinn immediately senses Ívarr's unhappiness. Ívarr, however, does not wish to confide in the king: '*Þat sem er, herra, má ek ekki frá segja.*' (*Msk.* II, 103) '"I cannot speak about this matter, Sire"'. Perhaps Ívarr is simply reluctant to speak spontaneously of his pain, as is often the case with people in a state of depression. King Eysteinn is able to help by guessing the roots of Ívarr's unhappiness and then offering psychological support. The plan is adopted, Ívarr soon forgets the woman and stays with the king.[10] The story is an example of the emotional relationships that matter most in *Morkinskinna*, those between kings and their retainers.[11] They are *ástsamlig* 'affectionate', but the term describes the love between a man and a king rather than a man and a woman.[12]

8   In medieval Icelandic sagas it is very often the case that verbal ambiguity is used in connection with bluffing, see e. g. *Hungrvaka* (ed. Ásdís Egilsdóttir, pp. 10, 14–15) and *Laxdæla saga* (ed. Einar Ól. Sveinsson, pp. 178 and 181) plus the famous case in *Króka-Refs saga* (ed. Jóhannes Halldórsson, pp. 153–55).

9   A similar thing happens with Eysteinn's brother (*Msk.* II, 106). Marianne E. Kalinke ('Sigurðar Saga Jórsalafara,' pp. 159–161) suggests that the author of *Morkinskinna* knew several medieval medical cures for lovesickness.

10   As Anne Heinrichs points out ('Wenn ein König liebeskrank wird: Der Fall Óláfr Haraldsson,' p. 44) this strategy was not unknown in the Middle Ages, and lovesickness was very fashionable (pp. 27–30). See Mary F. Wack, *Lovesickness in the Middle Ages: The Viaticum and Its Commentaries*, especially pp. 146–176; Charlotte Kaiser, *Krankheit und Krankheitsbewältigung in den Isländersagas: Medizinhistorischer Aspekt und erzähltechnische Funktion*, pp. 243–269; Theodore M. Andersson, 'Skald Sagas in their Literary Context 3: The Love Triangle Theme,' pp. 272–284.

11   R. Howard Bloch (*Etymologies and Genealogies: A Literary Anthropology of the French Middle Ages*, p. 226) states that in the courtly mindset social issues were often transformed into psychological ones, and this may be the case here.

12   The vocabulary used to describe relationships between kings and their favourite retainers resembles closely that used to depict affairs of the heart; see C. Stephen Jaeger, *The Envy of Angels: Cathedral Schools and Social Ideals in Medieval Europe, 950–1200*, p. 104; Jenny Jochens, 'Representations of Skalds in the Sagas 2: Gender Relations,' pp. 309–332.

When people discuss whether psychology can be used in the interpretation of medieval narrative, we should note that here modern psychological methods are being used to explain events in a saga that is older than most Sagas of Icelanders. A psychological dimension is also apparent in the description of Sigurðr the Crusader, who suffers from a serious *ógleði* 'unhappiness' that causes others grief (*Msk.* II, 106). This condition is described obliquely:

> sá menn at konungr var með miklu vanmegni ok þungu bragði ... Konungr leit yfir lýðinn ok arðgaði augunum ok sá umhverfis sik um pallana. (*Msk.* II, 139).[13]

> His retainers saw that the king was in a greatly weakened and melancholic condition ... The king looked over his retinue and rolled his eyes and looked around him at the benches.

Some kings in the saga are famous for their good relations with retainers. In addition to Eysteinn Magnússon, Magnús the Good may be mentioned, as well as Ólafr the Quiet, Haraldr Gilchrist and Ingi Haraldsson. Moreover, Haraldr the Severe is a friend to his friends, and his men follow him to the end. The warmth that characterises Haraldr's dealings with his men is obvious; like Eysteinn he is quick to sense the unhappiness of the story-wise Icelander (*Msk.* I, 235–236). Despite their conflict, the exchanges between Halldórr Snorrason and Haraldr conclude with Haraldr requesting that Halldórr, by this time living in Iceland, send him some foxskins. Halldórr responds by saying: '*Eldisk árgalinn nú*' (*Msk.* I, 187) "'the old cock is getting on in years'". When such tough individuals begin to use nicknames about each other, we may conclude that they are by no means indifferent to each other's fate. We learn later that Haraldr is pleased that Halldórr recalls their long friendship (*Msk.* I, 236–237).

13 There are other instances of mental illness in the saga. Haraldr the Severe explains the condition of a boy who has lost his memory: he has been *draumstoli, en þat hlýðir ǫngum manni, ok er ekki ǫðli til þess at menn dreymi ekki ok at þat megi hlýða* (*Msk.* I, 147) 'deprived of his dreams, and that is not good for anyone, and it is unnatural not to dream, and that will cause harm'. Kaiser (*Krankheit und Krankheitsbewältigung in den Isländersagas*, p. 223–43) discusses images of mental illness in the *Íslendingasögur* but not those in *Morkinskinna*.

When the earl Tostig Godwinson appeals unsuccessfully to the Danish King Sveinn for help, Tostig says: '*Frændr várir gørask oss fjándr. Þeira fjándmenn skulu ok þá vera mínir frændr*' (*Msk.* I, 301) '"Our kinsmen become our enemies, and so their enemies will be my kinsmen"'. Shortly thereafter Tostig becomes the 'kinsman' of Haraldr the Severe, Sveinn's enemy. The role of kinsmen is to support each other, and Tostig neatly takes on new kinsmen when he has exhausted his store of old ones. In this case friendship serves as a social institution connected to one's political activities. Yet devotion can accompany this friendship to the grave.[14] In early and high medieval Germanic societies, friendship was an important ingredient in politics and was formalised through oaths.[15] The wording of such oaths throughout the Middle Ages, however, was often emotionally charged.[16] The relationship between Magnús the Good and Sveinn Úlfsson is political but described in terms of personal friendship. When Sveinn refuses to accept a gift from Magnús, we are told that Sveinn *roðnar við mjǫk* (*Msk.* I, 51) 'blushes profusely'. He shows his emotional reaction at the same time as he pledges his loyalty to Magnús. Their friendship is bound up with politics, but the language of love is used. We should note that notions of affection, love and friendship in male relationships throughout thirteenth-century courtly love literature were nourished by clerical ideology.[17]

Magnús the Good's upbringing in Russia is described thus: *En Magnús er með hirð konungs, ok fæddr upp með mikilli ást* (*Msk.* I, 6) 'Magnús was raised with great love at the king's court'. Magnús is also the foster son of Einarr Paunch-Shaker, and his behaviour as king reveals their close

---

14   On friendship as a social institution, see Jón Viðar Sigurðsson, 'Friendship in the Icelandic Commonwealth,' pp. 205–215; 'Forholdet mellom frender, hushold og venner på Island i fritatstiden,' pp. 325–229; *Frá goðorðum til ríkja: Þróun goðavalds á 12. og 13. öld*, pp. 81–126; *Goder og maktforhold på Island i fristatstiden*; *Chieftains and Power in the Icelandic Commonwealth*. Jón Viðar derives many of his ideas from the writings of Gerd Althoff.

15   Gerd Althoff, 'Friendship and Political Order,' pp. 92–93; Jón Viðar Sigurðsson, *Frá goðorðum til ríkja: Þróun goðavalds á 12. og 13. öld*, pp. 112–16. For a long time marriage was primarily a business transaction.

16   See Peter Burke, 'Humanism and Friendship in Sixteenth-Century Europe,' p. 266.

17   Jaeger, *The Envy of Angels*, pp. 310–322, Jaeger, *Ennobling love: in search of a lost sensibility*.

relationship: *Konungr ríss upp ok eptir honum ok leggr hǫnd á háls Einari* (*Msk.* I, 142) 'the king rose, went after him and put his arm on Einarr's neck'. Although their relationship is based on mutual vested interests, it is still an emotional one, and Magnús promises that their friendship will not be broken. Vested interests and feelings come together; the division between the diplomatic and the personal is far from clear.

Bedtime stories

Morkinskinna opens with a quarrel between the Russian king and queen, which concludes with their fostering Óláfr the Saint's illegitimate son, Magnús the Good. The destiny of Norway is thus decided by a marital spat. Later Hákon Ívarsson recaptures King Magnús's standard from one of Haraldr the Severe's soldiers and carries it off in a swashbuckling manner. King Haraldr comments,

> 'kann ek eigi skaplyndi Ragnhildar frændkonu ef honum yrði auðvelt at komask yfir rekkjustokkinn hennar ef hann hefði látit merkin, en nú munu þau sættask' (*Msk.* I, 267).

> 'I would be much mistaken about my kinswoman Ragnhildr's temper if it had proved easy for him, having lost the standard, to regain access to her bed, but now they will be reconciled'.

Morkinskinna is in part a saga about family life and significant events sometimes take place in private spaces such as bedrooms. Kings and noblemen are involved, and their private lives are, at the same time, public events. Kingship alone is, however, not the only cause of the dual nature of courtly lives. In the Middle Ages neither life nor death was a private matter.[18]

---

18 See Georges Duby, 'Communal Living,' pp. 35–85; Norbert Elias, *The Civilizing Process*, pp. 134–138; Huizinga, *The Waning of the Middle Ages*, pp. 9–14. On the ideas and vocabulary of public and private, see Jürgen Habermas, *The Structural Transformation of the Public Sphere: An Inquiry into a Category of Bourgeois Society*, pp. 1–26.

Where society and family are interlinked, sex can impact significantly on that society. The chivalric world is a culture of men, and a knight is defined in terms of military service and warfare.[19] However, the nature of knighthood involves honouring women. Traditional masculine and military virtues are softened and refined, and warriors are idealised.[20] Although men in *Morkinskinna* are expected to show moderation, violent explosions of emotions are sometimes viewed indulgently. The image of the knight has contradictory elements, and the medieval masculine ideal involves a fusion of attitudes associated with both the warrior and the cleric. Various men of the church, adopting the strategy that offence is the best form of defence, sternly criticised the 'feminine' customs of some courts, notably long or unnaturally curly hair or pointed shoes. This criticism has been connected to twelfth- and thirteenth-century uncertainty about sexuality.[21] In reaction to problematic aspects of femininity, traditional masculine values were elevated, notably killing and warfare.[22] Beards were the single most common symbol of masculinity, but they clashed with clerical custom and, sometimes, courtly fashion. In medieval Iceland men were reproached for beardlessness, crying and sensitivity, and for alleged passivity, which was regarded as effeminate.[23]

In *Morkinskinna*, however, men are seldom criticised for lack of masculinity. Greater interest is shown in the relations amongst men than between men and women. Men seem able to dress lavishly without fear,

19 Simon Gaunt, *Gender and Genre in Medieval French Literature*, pp. 22–121.
20 Jaeger, *The Origins of Courtliness*; Jaeger, *The Envy of Angels*. This notion of masculine identity is still resonant, with chivalric behaviour regarded as a male virtue; it finds expression in the cowboys of the Wild West as they were once represented in American movies.
21 See, among others, Jo Ann McNamara, 'The Herrenfrage: The Restructuring of the Gender System, 1050–1150,' p. 9; Jaeger, *The Origins of Courtliness*, pp. 176–94; Gabor Klaniczay, pp. 58–65.
22 This process is described by Jaeger (*The Origins of Courtliness*, p. 195): 'The ultra-conservative mentality always equates restraint with cowardice, and sees heroism and manhood threatened by the advance of civilization ... In any case this mentality has a store of *topoi* which are effective in stirring up primitive aggression and making hatred and violence appear as noble instincts, and revenge a heroic act.'
23 Ármann Jakobsson, 'Ekki kosta munur'; Ursula Dronke, *The role of sexual themes in Njáls Saga: The Dorothea Coke Memorial Lecture in Northern Studies, University College London, 27 May 1980.*

show their feelings towards and love for each other without incurring disgrace. Characteristics that our modern age often associates with feminine behaviour do not at all appear to be feminine in *Morkinskinna*.

Kings' affairs with women constitute one of the energising forces in Norwegian history as depicted in the kings' sagas.[24] Haraldr the Severe began his expedition in search of fame and fortune abroad after failing to win the hand of Ellisif, the daughter of the king of Russia, because he lacked money and a kingdom (*Msk.* I, 86). Haraldr Gilchrist is renowned for his womanising (*Msk.* II, 166), and it is this which causes his downfall when Sigurðr the Noisy tricks him into revealing where he will be spending the night (*Msk.* II, 177–178). The king is eventually killed while lying half-asleep with Þóra Gothormsdóttir, thinking that Þóra is treating him roughly.[25] Þóra is seen only in bed and her only role in the saga is that of the king's sexual companion. Another 'ladies' man', King Sigurðr munnr 'the Mouth' Haraldsson, is also killed in the presence of a woman, Sigríðr the Grass Widow (*Msk.* II, 233). Earlier he had also fathered a child with the serving woman of a rich man:

> er konungr reið um bœinn þá heyrði hann í hús nakkvat
> kveðandi svá fagra at honum fannsk mikit um. Hann reið
> til hússins ok sá at þar stóð kona ein við kvern ok kvað við
> ágæta vel. Konungr sté af hestinum ok bað menn sína bíða
> úti, en hann gekk inn einn til konunnar. (*Msk.* II, 215).

---

24 In *Heimskringla* Haraldr hárfagri 'Fairhair' unifies Norway because of a woman (ed. Bjarni Aðalbjarnarson, Vol. 1, *ÍF* 26, pp. 96–97). This romantic motif is at odds with notions of the alleged realism of the saga. The conflict between Harold Godwinson and the Norman King William I is also explained in terms of an affair involving women (*Msk.* I, 328).

25 The passage is: *en konungr hafði drukkinn niðr lagzk ok svaf fast ok vaknaði við þat er menn vágu at honum ok mælti þat í óvitinu: 'Sárt býr þú nú við mik, Þóra.' En hon hljóp upp ok mælti: 'Þeir búa sárt við þik er verr vilja þér en ek.' Þar lét Haraldr konungr líf sitt* (Msk. II, 178) 'and the king had gone to bed drunk and slept deeply and woke up when men were beating him and said groggily: "You are treating me rather roughly, Þóra". She jumped up and said: "Those who are treating you roughly wish you much worse than I do". There King Haraldr lost his life'. Similarly, considerable bad blood arises between Sigurðr the Crusader and Sigurðr Hranason (and later between King Sigurðr and King Eysteinn) due to an affair (*Msk.* II, 116)

when the king rode by the farm, he heard in a certain house singing of such beauty that it much affected him. He rode up to the house and saw a woman with a handmill standing there and singing wondrously well. The king dismounted his horse and ordered his men to wait outside, while he went in to the woman.

The woman appears at first to enthral the king with her singing as in a fairy tale, but he takes the initiative and allows nothing to restrain him from satisfying his desires.[26] In the episode dealing with Margrét Þrándardóttir a different point of view emerges: that a man is discouraged from sleeping with a woman against her will. Margrét has no desire for a brief encounter with King Magnús (*Msk.* I, 149–151), and the king eventually changes his mind after a warning received from Ólafr the Saint.[27]

In *Morkinskinna*, it is also common for men to engage in coarse banter with each other, and only on rare occasion with women (*Msk.* I, 89).[28] In the Sneglu-Halli episode the dealings between Halli and King Haraldr involve coarseness, not least in the assertion that certain men have allowed themselves to be buggered.[29] There are examples of male sexual aggres-

---

26 Bagge ('Kvinner i politikken i middelalderen,' pp. 23–24) points out that this woman did not even have the status of a concubine, which was not considered demeaning. On concubinage in medieval Norway, see Else Ebel, *Der Konkubinat nach altwestnordische Quellen: Philologische Studien zur sogenannten 'Friedelehe'* and Auður G. Magnúsdóttur, *Frillor och fruar: Politik och samlevnad på Island 1120–1400*. In these works, however, there is little discussion of the life of the concubine in the Norwegian kings' sagas.

27 On this motif in the saga, see Andersson, 'Skald Sagas in their Literary Context 3,' and the notes in his and Kari Ellen Gade's translation (*Morkinskinna*, pp. 431–432, 454 and 456). Jochens ('The Politics of Reproduction: Medieval Norwegian Kingship,' p. 338) thinks that this story demonstrates a clash between the concerns of men and women in sexual matters. The point of the story is that women have the right to decline the king's advances. Later Sigurðr the Crusader satisfies his desire with Sigríðr Hranadóttir and disgraces her brother, but nothing is said about Sigríðr's attitude (*Msk.* II, 116–117, 124). A king is then presumably obliged to acknowledge the responsibility for the harm that later plagues him.

28 '[T]he necessary myth of constant, uncontrollable potency has to be ritually strengthened in male gatherings through boasts and dirty jokes and occasional group aggression against women' (McNamara, 'The Herrenfrage,' [see note 26] p. 10).

29 In *Morkinskinna* this is especially true at the beginning of the tale (*Msk.* I, 270) whereas in *Flateyjarbók* a special chapter is added for this purpose (*Flateyjarbók* III,

sion, King Magnús is thus castrated at the same time as he is blinded (*Msk.* II, 162),[30] but attacks on women are rare.[31] In Haraldr the Severe's military expeditions in Denmark the Norwegians capture *bæði konur ok fé* 'both the women and money', but there is no mention of the women being abused. Haraldr mocks the Danes for these defeats but when beating a hasty retreat he frees the women (*Msk.* I, 198, 201–202).

In foreign romances we find traces of both anti-feminism and the veneration of women.[32] In *Morkinskinna*, while some women are the playthings of men, others fill a more dignified role. Generally, the saga is a saga of men. The Ívarr episode appears at first to be about Ívarr and the woman he loves, but in fact it is about the friendship between Ívarr and the king. Ívarr had said that he *sér um hana mest vera allra kvenna* (*Msk.* II, 103) 'valued her above all women', but this love develops into sickness that the king is required to treat.[33] Engaging with women neither

426–428; *Flateyjarbók* IV, 213–215). The chapter deals with, among other things, the friendship between a king and a retainer whom the queen dislikes (see Joseph Harris, 'Gender and Genre: Short and Long Forms in the Saga Literature,' pp. 59–60).

30 King Óláfr the Saint is satisfied with blinding King Hrærekr (*Heimskringla II*, p. 105) in order to make him *óvirkan* 'powerless' as a rival for power, so that castration seems primarily designed as sexual humiliation; see Henric Bagerius, 'Vita vikingar och svarta sköldmör: Föreställningar om sexualitet i Snorre Sturlassons kungesagor,' pp. 24–25. The association of castration and eyes is accounted for in Annette Lassen, 'Øjets sprog: En undersøgelse af blikkets og blindhedens symbolværdi i den norrøne litteratur,' 123–125.

31 Noted by Andersson and Gade (*Morkinskinna*, pp. 436 and 441). Finnr Árnason's angry words aimed at his sister are not of this nature, and the narrator tells us that he is scarcely in control of his emotions (*Msk.* I, 251). Earl Vilhjálmr kills his wife for having preferred Harold Godwinson to himself (*Msk.* I, 329).

32 Gaunt, *Gender and Genre in Medieval French Literature* (see note 24); E. Jane Burns, *Bodytalk: When Women Speak in Old French Literature*. See also Sverrir Tómasson, 'Hugleiðingar um horfna bókmenntagrein,' pp. 211–212. Love in courtly literature is depicted in a wide variety of ways (Kaj Aalbæk-Nielsen, *Kærlighed i middelalderen*, pp. 113–172).

33 See Harris, 'Gender and Genre,' pp. 60–61. Generally, the episodes in *Morkinskinna* deal with the relations between men. Harris thinks this feature defines *þættir* as a literary genre. Though very few of his examples are drawn from *Morkinskinna*, his view is certainly applicable to its *þættir*.

can nor ought to be a substitute for the masculine responsibilities of bearing arms, fighting and supporting the king.[34]

In *Morkinskinna*, while little attention is paid to the general social status of women,[35] aristocratic women are granted pride of place as the saga deals with aristocrats rather than peasants.[36] Female rulers appear, such as Queen Zóe in Constantinople,[37] who approaches a place where the Norsemen are behaving arrogantly and requests a lock of Haraldr's (alias Norðbrikt's) hair. In return he requests '*hár ór magaskeggi þínu*' "'one of your pubic hairs'". This is an outrageous piece of vulgarity and foolhardiness, but Zóe *gaf ekki gaum at ok gekk leið sína* (*Msk.* I, 89) 'paid no attention and went on her way'. Such self-control is to be expected from a monarch, but it may be that she has something else in mind.[38] It is said that *hún sjálf drottningin vildi hafa hann* (*Msk.* I, 106, compare *Msk.* I, 109) 'the queen herself wanted him'. A conflict develops between the two, including Haraldr's kidnap and return of her niece (*Msk.* I, 113–114). In this

34 The exemplary knight Lancelot refuses to marry precisely because he does not want to cease engaging in quests, battle, and adventures: 'Girls, then, seem to spoil the boys' games and possibly bring bad luck, and there is no question of whether love or war comes first' (Graham D. Caie, 'A City Built to Music: An Introduction to the Story of Arthur,' p. 18).

35 Jenny Jochens has dealt in great detail with the status of women in medieval Norwegian society, making particular use of the sagas as sources. She directs our attention to the actual status of women (*Women in Old Norse Society*) and the images of women that form people's sense of femininity (*Old Norse Images of Women*). See also Agnes S. Arnórsdóttir, *Konur og vígamenn*, pp. 173–197; Shulamith Shahar, *The Fourth Estate: A History of Women in the Middle Ages*, pp. 126–173.

36 Relatively little has been written about women in the Norwegian kings' sagas (though see Jochens, 'The Female Inciter in the Kings' Sagas'; Jochens 'Politics of Reproduction'). On women in Danish historical writing, see Nanna Damsholt, *Kvinnebilledet i dansk højmiddelalder*, pp. 84–167; Birgit Strand, *Kvinnor och män i Gesta Danorum*.

37 According to some local sources she was a mighty witch, a sexually deranged man-eater and a half-troll. In Norwegian sources she is more like the king's mother Gunnhildr or Sigríðr stórráða, both of whom were human but with the same disposition. See Lönnroth, 'The Man-Eating Mama of Miklagard: Empress Zoe in Old Norse Saga Tradition,' pp. 37–41.

38 As interpreted by Lönnroth, 'The Man-Eating Mama of Miklagard,' p. 40. It may be that the queen takes Haraldr's coarse humour as an indication of his desire for her, and her persecution of him does not begin until he begins to flirt with her niece María. Then Zóe treats Haraldr as her equal, since queens were not allowed to pursue non-aristocratic men.

battle, the queen is reminiscent of the king's mother Gunnhildr in *Brennu-Njáls saga*.[39] The difference is that whereas Hrútr in that saga is a retainer who lies with the queen in order to increase his prestige, perhaps Haraldr regards himself as a king who cannot submit to the desires of the queen.[40] He nevertheless behaves courteously towards her niece, and there is no further mention of his behaving dishonourably towards women. It is only Zóe who needs to be humiliated because of her tyrannical behaviour.[41] In *Morkinskinna* the women are powerful and thus, whether good or evil, they threaten men.[42]

Haraldr the Severe marries Ragnhildr, the daughter of Magnús the Good, to Hákon Ívarsson and promises him the title of Earl as part of the bargain.[43] This appears to have been necessary to secure Ragnhildr's love (*Msk.* I, 256) and once Hákon returns from visiting the king, Ragnhildr receives him with laughter and calls him *jarl*.[44] He is forced to confess his lack of an earldom, but she decides to stay with him, which turns out

39 Ármann Jakobsson, 'Ekki kosta munur,' pp. 22–24; Jochens, *Women in Old Norse Society*, pp. 73–74

40 The situation is different in the relationship between Þórðr and Ása (*Msk.* II, 109); some find the woman and her family to be dishonoured by her liaison with the Icelander.

41 In this respect the story of Haraldr and Zóe represents a kind of 'queen's saga.' Bagerius ('Vita vikingar och svarta sköldmör,' pp. 20–22) and Kalinke ('The Misogamous Maiden Kings of Icelandic Romance,' and *Bridal-Quest Romance in Medieval Iceland*) discuss sagas of this kind.

42 Another outstanding figure appears in Ingiríðr, the mother of Ingi Haraldsson. She is Haraldr Gilchrist's queen (*Msk.* II, 153, 166), but really begins to make her presence felt as the mother of a king. She reacts quickly to he husband's death, calling the king's retainers and the landed men to deliberations (*Msk.* II, 178–179). It is she whom the men of Vík follow, and although power devolves to her son, it is once again she who leads the party associated with King Ingi when she demands that he take revenge after the death of Sigurðr skrúðhyrna 'Dandyhat' (*Msk.* II, 232).

43 Much has been written about medieval marriage. The position of women varied widely, and the ideology of marriage was no less heterogeneous. See, among others, Jochens, 'Consent in Marriage: Old Norse Law, Life, and Literature'; Agnes S. Arnórsdóttir, *Konur og vígamenn*, pp. 124–172; Duby, *Love and Marriage in the Middle Ages*; Duby, *Le chevalier, la femme et le prêtre: Le mariage dans la France féodale*; Christopher N.L. Brooke, *The Medieval Idea of Marriage*.

44 Here she is reminiscent of Hildigunnr (another woman who will only marry a *goði*) when she receives Flosi in *Brennu-Njáls saga* (ed. Einar Ól. Sveinsson, ÍF 12, pp. 289–92) and calls him *jarl*.

well for her. Hákon still does not dare to return home later in the narrative without the King Magnús standard that she had given him (*Msk.* I, 262, 267). Ragnhildr is a woman who can incite fear, although she is primarily a spectator who watches her husband's great deeds and for whom great deeds are (at least ostensibly) done.

The saga boasts of other distinguished women, some mysteriously so and mentioned only in passing. Einarr Paunch-Shaker travels to an assembly meeting with sixty men in order to support King Haraldr's levying of taxes and

> hafði verit áðr með ekkju nakkvarri ríkri er Ingibjǫrg hét, ok fekk hon honum liðit. (*Msk.* I, 137).

> had previously been the guest of a certain wealthy widow named Ingibjǫrg, who provided him with the support.

Nothing more is said about this woman, but it is clear that she is an important friend for Einarr. Such extra-familial friendly relations between men and women are rare in the saga.[45] A different Ingibjǫrg has a relationship with Haraldr and is said to be

> í vináttu við konung, ok jafnan var konungr þar á veizlum ok var með þeim Ingibjǫrgu tíðrœtt. Kunni hon of marga hluti vel at hjala ok hyggiliga.' (*Msk.* I, 232).

> a friend of the king's, and the king was often present at feasts there, and they conversed a good deal. She knew how to speak sensibly about many things.[46]

---

45 Platonic friendships between men and women became fashionable during the twelfth century (McGuire, *Friendship and Community*, p. 229, works cited therein). The Icelandic saga particularly concerned with such matters is *Laxdœla saga*, in which the emphasis is placed on the friendship between Guðrún Ósvífrsdóttir and, for example, Gestr Oddleifsson and Snorri goði. Guðrún is clearly the intellectual equal of these men.

46 Things do not turn out well for her, and finally she enters a nunnery at the king's request; he seems to regard her as spoiled through being possessed by a *vendværan gest* (*Msk.* I, 234) 'an implacable spirit'.

These mysterious women in *Morkinskinna* could indicate an uncertainty towards or even a fear of the female sex.

Although the relationships amongst men seems to be of central importance in *Morkinskinna*,[47] there is an example of a woman, another Ragnhildr, who is well respected and praised in verse at the behest of King Eysteinn (*Msk*. II, 223), much as in French romance (*romans courtois*).[48] Similarly, Magnús Barelegs appears the most courteous of kings when, behaving like a troubadour, he composes verses for the noble Maktildr, and enjoys her good will (*Msk*. II, 60–62).[49] Such courtesy associated with the praise of women is also a prominent feature in the *skáldasögur*.[50] These, however, are among the few such examples in *Morkinskinna*, and despite the respect that these women enjoy they are essentially passive figures. The ordinary woman's role in medieval Icelandic sagas is that of

47 Gaunt (*Gender and Genre in Medieval French Literature*) and Burns (*Bodytalk*, p. 13) note that this applies generally to medieval romance literature. Duby (*Medieval Marriage: Two Models from Twelfth-Century France*, pp. 11–15; *Love and Marriage in the Middle Ages*, pp. 32–35 and 56–63) sees the relationships between two men as the main theme in love triangle chivalric romances.

48 Even though the role of women is greater in these romances than in other chivalric literature, they deal primarily with the formation of masculine identity, as, for example, in the *chansons de geste*. See Gaunt, *Gender and Genre in Medieval French Literature*, pp. 71–121.

49 See Bjarni Einarsson, *To skjaldesagaer*, pp. 22–23, where he points to several examples of kings in the saga composing love poetry for women; on the one hand the verses of Haraldr the Severe for 'Gerðr í Görðum,' and on the other the love poem that Magnús the Good composes that appears without explanation or context (*Msk*. I, 148). See Poole ('Some Royal Love-verses') for a discussion of these and additional love verses composed by kings. Rosemary Power ('Magnus Bareleg's Expeditions to the West,' pp. 121–122) considers that here Matilda, the daughter of Melkólmr king of the Scots, is the woman in question, and there is no known emperor's daughter of this name from this time.

50 For discussion of *skáldasögur*, their verses, the origin of the *Íslendingasögur* and the influence of romance, see Bjarni Einarsson, *Skáldasögur: Um uppruna og eðli ástarskáldasagnanna fornu*; Andersson, 'Skalds and Troubadours'; Bjarni Einarsson, 'The Lovesick Skald: A Reply to Theodore M. Andersson'; Bjarni Einarsson, *To skjaldesagaer: En analyse af Kormáks saga og Hallfreðar saga*; Alison Finlay, 'Skalds, Troubadours and Sagas'; Alison Finlay, 'Skald Sagas in their Literary Context 2: Possible European Contexts.'

the onlooker, the voice of the people, and the person who incites others, either actively or just by their very presence (*Msk.* II, 232).[51]

Morkinskinna is a story of private life, but the story is also a public one as 'there is no private life which has not been determined by a wider public life'[52] and vice versa. The same could be said for all kings' sagas, yet *Morkinskinna* strikes out in a new direction, becoming more detailed and moving in the direction of private life and the family, the two principal concerns of the Sagas of Icelanders, the earliest of which can be dated to just a little after *Morkinskinna*.[53] In *Morkinskinna* we appear to have the same kind of interest in love, family and private life that also helped to create the courtly literature of the period.[54] Daily and inner life is worth telling about in *Morkinskinna*.[55] In this respect it is much in keeping with the *zeitgeist*.

51   Bjarne Fidjestøl ('Ut no glytter dei fagre droser: Om kvinnesynet i norrøn litteratur') sees the main role of women in skaldic poetry as that of onlookers. He traces this notion to the somewhat impolite words of Finnr Árnason: '*Eigi er nú undarligt at þú hafir vel bitizk, er merrin er með þér*' (*Msk.* I, 251) 'It is not surprising that you bite well when the mare is with you'. This also reflects the role of women in jousts whose presence and beauty arouse and sustain the contestants' competitive spirit. Frank ('Why Skalds Address Women,' pp. 67–83) notes that this makes women important in the art of skaldic poetry. On the role of women in Old Icelandic sagas – for example, in inciting vengeance – see, among others, Rolf Heller, *Die literarische Darstellung der Frau in den Isländersagas*, pp. 98–122; Jochens, 'The Politics of Reproduction'; *Old Norse Images of Women*, pp. 162–203; and Meulengracht Sørensen, *Fortælling og ære*, pp. 226–248.

52   George Eliot, *Felix Holt, the Radical*, p. 70.

53   The *Íslendingasögur* are often called 'family sagas' in English, an issue that Andersson addresses in 'Why do Americans say "Family Sagas"?,' pp. 297–307. The history of Iceland that they help to create takes the form of a collection of stories about the private lives of chieftains. W. P. Ker (*Epic and Romance: Essays on Medieval Literature*, p. 251) argued that such tales bore the stamp of a particular form of society in Iceland: 'The public history of Iceland lies all in the lives of private characters.'

54   Robert Hanning, *The Individual in Twelfth-Century Romance; Gaunt, Gender and Genre in Medieval French Literature*.

55   Interest in family history, everyday history and the history of individual private lives has increased over the last few years (see, among others, Peter Burke, *History and Social Theory*, pp. 38–43; Stefanie Würth, 'New Historicism und altnordische Literaturwissenschaft,' pp. 193–208; Duby, *Love and Marriage in the Middle Ages*, pp. 129–216).

Part IV.

PORTRAITS OF MEN

1. The Guise

Who is that man?

Þat sama haust er Magnús konungr lá skipum sínum við Skáney sá þeir einn dag at skip sigldi austan fyrir land. (*Msk.* I, 80).

That same autumn when King Magnús anchored his ship along Skáney, they one day saw a ship sailing from the east along the coast.

The ship was decorated in gold and had magnificent dragons' heads and sails made of fine double-strength fabric. Naturally, King Magnús is eager to learn who is on this vessel. The man who speaks for the newcomers does not identify himself, but *talaði mál Haralds Sigurðarsonar, sem hann væri sendimaðr hans* (*Msk.* I, 81) 'spoke on behalf of Haraldr Sigurðarson as if he were his emissary'. The emissary speaks of Haraldr's wisdom, strength and great deeds abroad and states that it would *horfa til mikils váða eða vanda ef hans viðrtaka verðr eigi með sæmð eða æru* (*Msk.* I, 81) 'turn out to be dangerous and difficult if his reception is not honourable and respectful'. The unidentified man is *mikill vexti ok með tíguligu yfirbragði, þat er hann mátti á sjá, en ávallt var nǫkkur hulða á dregin* (*Msk.* I, 81) 'large and of noble appearance as far as could be seen, but there was always something indistinct about him'. The man is in disguise, a virtual shape-shifter abetted by mysterious subterfuge. He then returns to the ship, and proves to be Haraldr Sigurðarson himself. The narrative consists of a double scene: the narrative of *Morkinskinna*, and the scene that Haraldr stages where he takes on an alien guise.[1]

At the conclusion of this play-within-a-play a lengthy flashback presents the biography of King Haraldr. The account begins when he escapes with his life from the battle at Stiklastaðir by disguising himself: the

---

1   For an earlier version of this chapter, see Ármann Jakobsson, 'Dulargervið.'

farmer's son who tells the story says '*[s]á hafði steypt hettinum, ok mátti ek fyrir því ekki sjá í andlit honum*' (*Msk.* I, 83) '"he had on a hood, and for this reason I could not see his face"'. Disguise is a commonplace in the story of Haraldr. When Haraldr arrives at Constantinople and joins the king's service, it is once again under an assumed name:

> nefndisk hann sjálfr Norðbrikt, ok var þat eigi í vitorði al-
> þýðu at hann væri konungborinn, heldr bað hann alla sína
> því leyna, því at þat er að viðrsýn gǫrt ef útlendir menn eru
> konunga synir. (*Msk.* I, 88).

> He called himself Norðbrikt and it was not commonly
> known that he was of royal blood, because he requested all
> his men to keep it secret, explaining that foreigners who are
> the sons of kings tend to be mistrusted.

Haraldr always disguises himself for a purpose: to escape, to avoid trouble or to be victorious in battle. This is a mark of cunning and slyness, but many causes call for the same response, the disguise.

The common man needs no disguise, since, according to the viewpoint of the upper class, he is by his very nature anonymous. But because Haraldr stands above the ordinary man, a disguise is sometimes necessary and is a measure of his special status. At Stiklastaðir, because he is the brother of the fallen king, he disguises himself. It is common for a legitimate heir to a throne or for a king to escape persecution in this way: Christ fled from Herod, and Óláfr Tryggvason from the king's mother Gunnhildr.[2] In Constantinople, because he is the son of a king, Haraldr must adopt a disguise in order not to create an imbalance in the society: the presence of two kings in the same place at the same time, the saga suggests, leads to friction, divided loyalties and open conflict. Upon arrival in Norway he adopts yet another guise, and while his motivation is less clear, it appears that he must always be on guard. Haraldr is not always everything he seems to be.

2 Ármann Jakobsson, 'The Hunted Children of Kings: A Theme in the Old Icelandic Sagas.'

But he is not the only one to adopt disguises in *Morkinskinna*, where they are everywhere. Often it is noblemen who try to conceal their status. Before the battle at Lyrskov Heath it is said,

> Ok nú taka þeir þat ráðs, konungr ok Einarr, at þeir fara leyniliga eitt kveld ok dyljask í herinum, ok kenndu menn þá eigi, því at þeir hǫfðu breytt búningi. (*Msk.* I, 59).

> And the king [Magnús the Good] and Einarr decide to go out secretly one evening and mingle in disguise among the soldiers, and the men did not recognise them because they had changed their clothing.

Here the king and Einarr, like all spies, must keep their real identity secret, and the device works well, allowing them to covertly assess the morale of their men.

The scene is a familiar one. There are folk tales about kings who disguise themselves in order to test their men and administer justice. The most famous version appears in *The Arabian Nights*, but there are others involving Charlemagne and Óláfr the Saint. In this saga the disguise serves the truth: the king disguises himself in order to see and understand something clearly.[3] Behind this device is the premise that the nobility of the king causes men to hide their true face and intentions in his presence. In order to perceive the truth the king needs to adopt the guise of the ordinary man, to become, like him, anonymous. The story tells a paradoxical truth: reality is full of falsehood, and sometimes only deception brings out the truth.

'The handsome one in the silk shirt'

In *Sturlunga saga* there is an *exemplum*, *Geirmundar þáttr heljarskinns*, about the limitations of physical appearance. A queen trades her two sons for the beautiful son of a slave woman, but at a young age the supposed king's son demonstrates his faint-heartedness, while the alleged slave's

---

3 Joseph Harris ('The King in Disguise: An International Popular Tale in Two Old Icelandic Adaptions,' 57–81) provides a full list of examples concerning this saga.

children increase in vigour the older they grow, until the queen watches them, at play, pull the slave's son from the high-seat.[4] This is clearly royal behaviour. One conclusion to be drawn from the episode is that beauty is not everything, although the external can provide an indication of the internal. The body is not an unequivocal social phenomenon.[5]

The kings in *Morkinskinna* are of distinguished appearance and are often said to be easily recognisable.[6] Their appearance is frequently described in detail in *Morkinskinna*, whereas the appearance of women is never described.[7] Magnús the Good is called *sá inn fríði ... í silkiskyrtunni* (*Msk.* I, 63) 'the handsome one ... in the silk shirt' by his adversaries; Sveinn Úlfsson gains support by being *virðuligr sýnum* (*Msk.* I, 51) 'worthy in appearance'; and Haraldr the Severe is *með tíguligu yfirbragði* (*Msk.* I, 81) 'of noble appearance'.

The superior appearance of kings can be clearly observed in the settlement at Konungahella. There the kings of Norway, Denmark and Sweden meet, and, in the narrator's estimation, each proves to be more splendid than the other:

> þá rœddu liðsmenn þat sem þótti, at varla myndu fásk aðrir þrír hǫfðingjar jafn tíguligir. Ok var Ingi konungr mest aldri farinn ok var einna mestr af ǫllum þeim ok þrekligastr, ok þótti hann af ǫllum þeim ǫldurmannligastr. Eiríkr Danakonungr hafði fegrsta ásjánu ok ítrmannligsta, en Magnús Nóregskonungr var af þessum ǫllum miklu kurteisastr ok vaskligastr ok hermannligastr, ok váru þó allir þeir miklir ok sterkir. (*Msk.* II, 59–60).

> their liegemen said, as seemed to be the case, that three other such noble chieftains could scarcely be found. King

4 *Sturlunga saga* 1, pp. 5–7. The tale also occurs in *Hálfs saga ok Hálfsrekka*.
5 For discussion of the body and its different symbolic values in the Middle Ages, see Lars Lönnroth, 'Kroppen som själens spegel – Ett motiv i de isländska sagorna,' pp. 63–64; Joachim Bumke, 'Höfischer Körper – Höfische Kultur,' pp. 67–102.
6 See Ármann Jakobsson, 'Konungasagan Laxdæla,' pp. 97 and 106; Margaret Arent Madelung, 'Snorri Sturluson and Laxdoela: The hero's accoutrements,' pp. 45–92.
7 The same applies, at least, to *Laxdæla saga*; see Ármann Jakobsson, 'Laxdæla dreaming: a saga heroine invents her own life.'

Ingi was the oldest, tallest and most powerfully built, and
he seemed the most impressive of them all. King Eiríkr of
the Danes was the best looking and the stoutest. But King
Magnús of Norway was the greatest of them all in courtliness and manliness and military bearing, and yet they were
all large and powerfully built.

Here excellence in physical attributes is defined: size, facial beauty, masculinity, and courtliness. In *Morkinskinna* kings are handsome, and they
are also tall.[8] Óláfr the Quiet is described thus:

Óláfr konungr, sonr Haralds konungs, var mikill maðr á
vǫxt, ok þat er allra manna sǫgn at engi hafi sét fegra mann
eða tíguligra sýndum. Hann hafði gult hár ok bjartan lík-
ama, eygðr manna fegrst, limaðr vel (*Msk.* II, 3).

King Óláfr, the son of King Haraldr, was a large man and
everyone said that no one had seen a more handsome man
or one of more noble appearance. He had blond hair and a
light complexion, beautiful eyes, and was well built.

Magnús, Óláfr's son, is *manna fríðastr sjónum, þegar frá var tekinn Óláfr
faðir hans, ok manna hæstr var hann* (*Msk.* II, 9–10) 'the handsomest of
men, with the exception of his father, and a very tall man'. A cross in
St Mary's Church in Kaupangr shows that Magnús was shorter than Óláfr,
who is shorter than Haraldr the Severe, the tallest of them all, as expressed
in the remarks of Harold Godwinson about his demands for land: '*Hann
skal hafa sjau feta rúm, eða því lengra sem hann er hæri en flestir menn
aðrir*' (*Msk.* I, 315) '"He shall have seven feet of space or more since he
is taller than most other men"'.

Descriptions of men's appearance in *Morkinskinna* are not always as
extensive as is sometimes the case in Sagas of Icelanders, but they are generally more thorough than in the chivalric romances, where small details
are often omitted, although it is stated that characters are handsome and
of pleasing proportions.[9] Indeed, general descriptive words often suffice:

8   Ármann Jakobsson, *Í leit að konungi*, pp. 96–111.
9   Eyvind Fjeld Halvorsen, 'Riddersagaer,' pp. 177–178.

Þá steypir Magnús konungr af sér brynjunni er hann var í ok hefir ekki klæða nema eina silkiskyrtu. (*Msk.* I, 61).

Then Magnús cast off the coat of mail that he had been wearing and had nothing under it but a silk shirt.

Magnús is not described in detail, and the saga audience is allowed to visualise him standing before them in his shirt. The saga's admiration for the splendid kings sometimes grows in indirect proportion to the amount of clothing they are wearing.[10] Sigurðr the Noisy attracts great admiration for his shirt:

Sigurðr ... var í skyrtu einni ok hafði ekki á hǫfði ... ok heldr vaskligr maðrinn, því at allra manna var hann snǫfurligastr. (*Msk.* II, 191).

Sigurðr was dressed in a shirt and had nothing on his head ... and a rather dynamic man, since of all men he was the most energetic.

The author seems to have a special liking for Sigurðr and does not refrain from using extravagant language to signal this.[11] He is described as fully as most heroes in the Sagas of Icelanders:

Sigurðr var mikill maðr ok vænn, jarpr á hár ok nakkvat ennisnauðr, bláeygr ok réttleitr, liðr á nefinu, afrhendr ok fimr ok hverjum manni gǫrvari at sér um alla hluti. (*Msk.* II, 192).

10 Consider this description of Haraldr Gilchrist when he races on foot against Magnús the Blind's horse: *Haraldr var í línbrókum nafarskeptum ok lét knéit leika laust í brókinni. Hann var í stuttri skyrtu ok hafði mǫttul á herðum ok kefli í hendi* (*Msk* II, 149) 'Haraldr was dressed in linen trousers that were baggy around the knees. He wore a short shirt and had a cloak over his shoulders and a stick in his hand'. Later in the saga there is a more general description of Haraldr.

11 Sigurðr frequently undresses in the saga. This use of adjectives may have been borrowed from *Hryggjarstykki*; see Bjarni Guðnason, *Fyrsta sagan*. Elsewhere the author remarks that Sigurðr is *at allri atgǫrvi ... umfram langt alla sína jafnaldra ok náliga hvern mann annan í Nóregi* (*Msk.* II, 168) 'in all acomplishments ... far ahead of his contemporaries and nearly every other man in Norway'.

The Guise

Sigurðr was a large and handsome man, with brown hair and a somewhat low forehead, blue eyes and regular features, and a curved nose, dextrous and athletic and more accomplished than any other man in every respect.

The king's body receives attention, but more frequently attention is drawn to the kings' clothes. This focus is in keeping with the great amount of time devoted in the saga to material things and the emphasis on every kind of costume.

Kings are recognisable primarily because they are dressed differently from others, as becomes apparent in this description of Magnús Barelegs:

> Magnús konungr var auðkenndr. Hann hafði hjálm gylldan á hǫfði ok skjǫld fyri sér, ok var skrifat á leó með gulli, sverð í hendi er kallat var Leggbiti; váru at tannhjǫlt ok vafiðr gulli meðalkaflinn ok var allra sverða bitrast. Hann hafði dregit silkihjúp rauðan um útan skyrtuna, ok var þat allra manna mál at eigi hefði sét vígligra mann með jafn mǫrgum vápnum eða tíguligra höfðingja. (*Msk.* II, 68).

> King Magnús was easily recognisable. He had a golden helmet on his head and a shield in front of him on which a golden lion was emblazoned, a sword in his hand called 'Legbiter'; it had an ivory hilt and the grip was bound in gold, and was the sharpest of swords. He was wearing a red silk jacket over his shirt, and everybody said that never had they seen a more courageous man with so many weapons or a nobler chieftain.

A king dresses like a king, but in the saga the clothing of courtiers is also shown to be worthy of attention. Brandr the Bountiful is dressed in *skarlatskyrtli ok hafði skarlatsskikkju yfir sér, ok var bandit uppi á hǫfðinu* (*Msk.* I, 231) 'in a fine red tunic with a fine red cloak bound up on his head', Eysteinn orri 'the Heathcock' is dressed *í skarlatskyrtli rauðum* (*Msk.* I, 238) 'in a fine red tunic' and Egill Áskelsson goes to the gallows *í hálfskiptum kyrtli* (*Msk.* II, 27) 'in a two-coloured tunic'. Kings and courtiers in *Morkinskinna* repeatedly dress up for the parts they must play.

Elaborately clad men appear to be works of art, as the *zeitgeist* of courtly culture required. Thus in *Morkinskinna* clothes really do make the man.

Reality playhouse

Usually kings are easily recognisable but sometimes, as we have seen, they appear incognito. A monarch's appearance can matter a great deal – who knows them and who does not.[12] Magnús the Good allows himself to be deceived by the appearance of Sveinn Úlfsson (*Msk.* I, 51) assuming that the outer and the inner man are of a piece, but *Morkinskinna* confirms that this is not always the case. Thus the many costumes worn by characters in *Morkinskinna* condition this recognition that appearances sometimes deceive.

In *Morkinskinna* great emphasis is placed upon other kinds of tests as well. Kings are constantly testing their subjects. Even when disguises do not feature directly in the saga, every aspect of a courtier is defined, at least in part, by his costume. For this reason the king has to test the man hiding under the surface to discover his true identity.[13] But the tables can be turned so that the courtiers test the king instead, just as the fisherman with whom Haraldr the Severe exchanges remarks proves to be a soldier in disguise (*Msk.* I, 288). Such tests seem to be an almost daily event in the courtly society of the saga.

Of all the kings in *Morkinskinna* Haraldr the Severe is the one most often encountered in a guise other than his own. But in his disputes with Hákon Ívarsson, Hákon also frequently appears in costume. On one occasion he plays a game similar to that of Robin Hood, by dressing in rags and then casting off his disguise after arriving in the woods, where his men discover that they *hafa … þá fundit Hákon jarl* (*Msk.* I, 268) 'were indeed face to face with Earl Hákon'. The common disguise motif, ever present in fairy tales, is discernible in all this description. Shortly before King Haraldr falls at Stamford Bridge, Harold Godwinson fools him with a disguise

---

12 Ármann Jakobsson, *Í leit að konungi*, pp. 130 and 274–75.
13 This can be observed in the tales of Haraldr the Severe (for example, *Msk.* I, 230–232) and Óláfr the Quiet (*Msk.* II, 12–16). Boberg (*Motif-Index of Early Icelandic Literature*, pp. 147–162) cites various examples of tests in Old Norse literature.

(*Msk.* I, 315). It is symbolic of the setting sun of Haraldr the Severe's fortunes that he should now be on the wrong side of such a ruse. Earlier he had captured a city with a trick that required him to play the part of both a corpse and a pallbearer (*Msk.* I, 102–106). But there is sometimes no need for special clothing when the basic deportment of men is sufficient, since there is little to choose between a well-designed play and the play of life itself. Thus King Eysteinn has his men pretend to be prepared for hostilities in the lawsuits with Sigurðr (*Msk.* II, 122). The most important factor is not actually to be well armed but to appear to be.

Disguises are woven into the entire narrative texture of *Morkinskinna*, and it appears that everyone wears a variety of costumes in courtly society. Time and again unknown men appear whose identity is subsequently revealed. These events are a reminder of the narrative manner of the saga. We repeatedly observe people from the outside: from their faces, words and deeds. The saga audience of *Morkinskinna* is often placed in the position of the chieftains in *Brennu-Njáls saga*, who see an unknown man who arouses their curiosity, and this, in turn, occasions the repeated description of Skarphéðinn Njálsson.[14] One of the leitmotifs of the Sagas of Icelanders is an amazing appearance: again and again unknown men in some form of disguise are encountered, even if it provides nothing more than the mask of anonymity.[15]

In the mid-twentieth century the sociologist Erving Goffman sought to examine society in a new way by making use of Shakespeare's famous insight that 'all the world's a stage'. He took the metaphor seriously and reflected on society and people's behaviour with the help of three related concepts – *role*, *performance* and *guise*.[16] Thus he notes how social structure is socially and culturally constructed and how its rules could be explained by the metaphor of the play. In modern gender studies Judith

---

14 *Brennu-Njáls saga*, pp. 297–306.
15 See the essays by Susan Crane ('Knights in Disguise: Identity and Incognito in Fourteenth-Century Chivalry,' pp. 63–79) and Janet L. Solberg ('"Who Was That Masked Man?" Disguise and Deception in Medieval and Renaissance Comic Literature,' pp. 117–138).
16 *The Presentation of Self in Everyday Life* (New York, 1959). Johan Huizinga had previously developed his theory that play was the key to a culture (*Homo ludens: A Study of the Play Element in Culture*), and cited examples from the *Poetic Edda*.

Butler employed a similar method using the important concepts of *masquerade* and *performance* to explain how sexuality is culturally constructed.[17] Butler emphasises that the process is in its nature dramatic, as the word '"performance" suggests a dramatic and contingent construction of meaning'.[18] These ideas echo the way people in the Middle Ages thought. Stephen Jaeger considers that masks and costumes were characteristic of medieval courtly societies. There the actions of people were governed by custom; language and gestures were dictated by formal rules. With all behaviour socially and culturally constructed, the courtier himself becomes a work of art. His experience is a narrative, and court life a kind of performance art of reality with its own style, aesthetics and actors.[19]

In medieval Europe, people used literary and historical concepts to shape their worlds, not least at court. Kings adopted the Round Table whereby their men named themselves after King Arthur's knights and acted out the parts revealed in the Arthurian tales.[20] The story served as a model, not just for the court but also for clerics and the ordinary citizenry. Kings, dukes and even the pope pretended to be Caesar, Alexander, Hannibal, Arthur and Charlemagne. Knights imitated Tristan, Roland and Lancelot. Poets and historians emulated Virgil, Tacitus and Livy. These exemplary models were everywhere, in texts read, sung, preached from the pulpit, played at festivals or depicted in paintings.[21] And in the process the boundary between life and art grew increasingly unclear, to the point where life imitated art, the *raison d'être* of the *exemplum*, rather than the reverse.

17 *Gender Trouble: Feminism and the Subversion of Identity*. Butler derives her idea of the masked play from the work of the psychoanalyst Joan Riviere.
18 Butler, *Gender Trouble*, p. 139
19 C. Stephen Jaeger, *The Origins of Courtliness: Civilizing Trends and the Formation of Courtly Ideals 939–1210*, p. 258; Norbert Elias, *The Civilizing Process*, pp. 48–56; William Brandt, *The Shape of Medieval History: Studies in Modes of Perception*, pp. 114–125.
20 Roger Sherman Loomis, 'Arthurian Influence on Sport and Spectacle,' in *Arthurian Literature in the Middle Ages: A Collaborative History*, pp. 553–559. On King Arthur in the north, see Hermann Reichert, 'King Arthur's Round Table: Sociological Implications of its Literary Reception in Scandinavia,' pp. 394–414; Foster W. Blaisdell, Jr., 'The Figure of the King: Arthur vs. Hrólf'; Marianne E. Kalinke, *King Arthur North-by-Northwest: The matière de Bretagne in Old Norse-Icelandic Romances* .
21 Klaniczay, *The Uses of Supernatural Power*, p. 95, who draws on Huizinga (*The Waning of the Middle Ages*).

In recent decades scholars have discussed the concept of the individual, especially the complex relationship between the emerging sense of individual identity during and after the twelfth century, and the importance of the exemplary and the commonplace in medieval societies.[22] There is no clear distinction between the individual and society; individuals live in a society, and its structure shapes their lives.[23] In medieval Europe exemplary figures, be they saints or knights, cast a long shadow. The life of each individual was not regarded as unique; it was often said that all saints' lives were one and the same, for the reason that they had so much in common, with the events of one life seeming to resemble those in another. Repetitions and references confirmed that the individual and the secular were less important than the general and the divine.[24] Increased interest in individuals and individuality in the twelfth and thirteenth centuries involved an element of paradox, since at the innermost core of each individual lay that which was common to all – the image of God. All individual self-scrutiny involved a search for the general rather than the particular.[25] Another paradox involved the effect of an ever-expanding twelfth-century secular and ecclesiastical structure of administration – authority, once local and real, grew increasingly distant and symbolic.[26] It may also seem paradoxical that growing interest in the individual was

---

22 Walter Ullmann, *The Individual and Society in the Middle Ages*; Peter Dronke, *Poetic Individuality in the Middle Ages: New Departures in Poetry 1100–1150;* Colin Morris, *The Discovery of the Individual 1050–1200*; John Benton, 'Consciousness of Self and Perceptions of Individuality'; Robert Hanning, *The Individual in Twelfth-Century Romance*; Caroline Walker Bynum, 'Did the XIIth Century discover the individual?'; Caroline Walker Bynum, *Jesus as Mother: Studies in the Spirituality of the High Middle Ages*, pp. 82–109; William Brandt, *The Shape of Medieval History: Studies in Modes of Perception*; Thomas J. Heffernan, *Sacred Biography: Saints and their Biographers in the Middle Ages*; Aaron J. Gurevich, *Das Individuum im europäischen Mittelalter*; Gurevich, *Categories of Medieval Culture*, pp. 19–88. See also Ármann Jakobsson, 'The Individual and the Ideal: The Representation of Royalty in Morkinskinna.'
23 Elias, *The Civilizing Process*, p. 168.
24 Heffernan, *Sacred Biography*; Bynum, *Jesus as Mother*, pp. 80–109; Georges Duby, 'The Diffusion of Cultural Patterns in Feudal Society'; Brandt, *The Shape of Medieval History*, pp. 106–146; Ásdís Egilsdóttir 'Um biskupasögur,' pp. 49–52.
25 Bynum, *Jesus as Mother*, pp. 80–109.
26 C. Stephen Jaeger, *The Envy of Angels*, pp. 4–15.

accompanied by increased preoccupation with fraternity and human society.[27]

The characters presented in *Morkinskinna* are thus to be viewed both as individuals and as models and exemplars whose words and deeds can have more general applicability. The overall courtly society in the saga is depicted by focusing on certain representative figures. Although some five hundred named individuals appear in the work, there are just two main dramatic roles, king and retainer. The dramatic form of the saga is connected to ideas about the nature of society and the individual; in the drama of the saga we are presented with playlets set on the stage of human existence. In one scene King Magnús and his mother first speak to each other in secret and then play out for others the substance of their conversation (*Msk.* I, 166–167). Immediately afterwards a man appears *með góðum riddarabúnaði* 'in fine chivalric livery' to the king and his forces, and sets his horse to *fagrliga burdeigja* 'prance around elegantly', before he performs *marga leika með mikilli list* (*Msk.* I, 167) 'many manoeuvres with great artistry'. This man (who turns out to be King Sveinn) behaves as if he were on a stage, which, of course, in one sense he is.

We can reflect on whether King Magnús was just having fun when he started snooping around among his troops or whether this was a serious mission, not least because he took Einarr Paunch-Shaker along with him, the great champion who had established himself so unmistakably in the saga that the idea he should now adopt a disguise seems comical. In comedy, disguise represents one element in the reversal of a reality that must eventually be restored. Its success depends, of course, on dramatic irony, the audience seeing through the deception while few if any of the characters in the play do so. In this respect the comic episodes in *Morkinskinna* resemble other comedies through the ages; in Shakespearean comedy, for example, disguises and mistaken identity play a major role.[28] In the most thoroughgoing comic episode in *Morkinskinna*, the tale of Sneglu-Halli,

27 Bynum, *Jesus as Mother*, pp. 59–109; Heffernan, *Sacred Biography*.
28 Solberg, '"Who Was That Masked Man?" Disguise and Deception in Medieval and Renaissance Comic Literature.' By the end of *Víglundar saga* one important character turns out to be different from the person he had pretended to be. The motifs of double-identity and disguise are closely linked, though the matter is too complex to be discussed here.

Haraldr the Severe appears more or less in disguise, as so often before. At the beginning of the tale he and Halli exchange insults without the king identifying himself, so that later we need to be told that [þ]*ar var Haraldr konungr er orðum skipti við Halla* (*Msk.* I, 271) 'it was King Haraldr who exchanged words with Halli'. In another comic scene Sigurðr Woolly-Band is sent in disguise to trade insults with Sveinki Steinarsson, who turns out to be in an even better disguise (*Msk.* II, 29–34). The key comic moment can involve the actor seeing through a disguise but pretending not to have done so, as when Sveinn the Russian and his men pretend to be monks in order to get close to Þrándr of Upplǫnd (*Msk.* I, 135–136).

We may say that no play can exist without disguise. This applies to most early forms of narrative, whether they deal with tricksters like Robin Hood or courageous knights who disguise themselves for other reasons.[29] Although it could appear paradoxical the disguise motif is most often associated with kings and champions, those who are more elevated or are in some way better than mankind in general. The avowed purpose of the costume is to conceal, but in fact it signals a special status: men dress up in costumes because they stand out from other people.[30]

In a saga such as *Morkinskinna* the disguise motif recalls the general and symbolic value of the narrative.[31] Although we are dealing here with

29 Boberg (*Motif-Index of Early Icelandic Literature*, pp. 168–87) lists instances of every kind of hoax and costume in saga narrative. The trickster motif occurs in *Færeyinga saga, Njáls saga* (where Gunnarr plays Kaupa-Héðinn) and *Króka-Refs saga*. Grettir often appears in disguise, and the saga deploys a special sub-motif, borrowed from *Tristrams saga*, where the hero dresses in rags (as in the tales of Robin Hood). *Gylfaginning* in *Snorra Edda* is a special tale with costumes in which the one who is deceived (Gylfi) is himself in disguise. This accounting is virtually endless. Disguise was very common in nineteenth-century adventure stories (as in Scott's *Ivanhoe* and Dumas's *The Count of Monte Cristo*) which are, in a sense, thus a continuation of a medieval tradition.

30 As Susan Crane ('Knights in Disguise: Identity and Incognito in Fourteenth-Century Chivalry,' p. 63) notes: 'chivalric incognito, as a motif of romance and as a historical practice, amounts to a peculiar kind of self-representation, a self-dramatization that invites rather than resists public scrutiny.'

31 Bengt Holbek, *Interpretation of Fairy Tales: Danish Folklore in a European Perspective*, pp. 187–403; Holbek, *Tolkning af trylleeventyr*, pp. 88–91; Davíð Erlingsson, 'Fótaleysi göngumanns: Atlaga til ráðningar á frumþáttum táknmáls í sögu af Hrólfi Sturlaugssyni, ásamt formála.'

an historical narrative, full of names and events that are unique and historical, the universal is also consistently and simultaneously in sight. And the
general truth behind all the disguises in *Morkinskinna* is perhaps not so
different from the theories of Goffman and Butler. The frequent disguises
help to call attention to the disguises that all must adopt – the roles that
people play in that society.

2. The One

The individual and the ideal

While the circle that Hreiðarr the Simple traces around Magnús the Good (see part II, chapter 3 and part III, chapter 2) is emblematic of the structure of *Morkinskinna*, it also shows how form and content coalesce. Hreiðarr's understanding of the king requires this circumspection; the changing form of the saga depends upon viewing kings from all sides, not least from the point of view of the retainers while they are gathered around him. Its contents influence the structure of the episodes that in turn give substance to its meaning, including the definition of royal power. *Morkinskinna*'s circumspection of the chief characters in the *þættir* functions to deepen their characterisation; the interest in characterisation informs the structure of the saga. The description of the kings, finally, becomes the history of Norway.[1]

Ideas about the special bond between kings and the divinity are an important cultural resource that served royalty well in acquiring and maintaining power. The kings' sagas are formed out of and live from such general myths as the divine nature of royal power, much like saints' lives are concerned with holiness and the role of saints in society. The kings in *Morkinskinna* are both individuals and moral exemplars. Every king consists of a complex symbolic valency that is created and modified by his culture. Each king is an individual, but his unique nature is inseparable from his general role. This role is adaptable; in the thirteenth century royal power meant something different from what it does today, and in Iceland the kings' sagas played a key role in shaping this meaning.[2] Although all

1   Andersson, 'The Politics of Snorri Sturluson,' p. 16. Kalinke, ('Sigurðar Saga Jórsala-fara: The Fictionalization of Fact in Morkinskinna,' p. 156) considers character de-lineation, rather than conflict, the driving force of the saga. Andersson and Gade (*Morkinskinna*, p. 2) express a similar view.
2   Ármann Jakobsson, *Í leit að konungi: Konungsmynd íslenskra konungasagna.* Though *Morkinskinna* also looms large in that study, the present work will deal only

kings require definite qualities to fulfill their roles, they are endowed with them in unequal proportions. But all kings, whatever their endowments, always have a role to play.

Medieval man's image of himself was formed in various ways. People identified themselves with exemplars and role models, family, possessions or things. A king could never be simply a man, and the creation of a king's identity – a central concern of the kings' sagas – is complex, embracing both the human and the godly, the secular and the spiritual.[3] In the image of each monarch the kings' sagas simultaneously portray an individual man and a complex social phenomenon.

All texts about societies deal with power. In the kings' sagas the power of the king is the essential ingredient. The discussion of kings in *Morkinskinna* focuses on the nature of this power. This discussion would achieve no definition if it simply described kings in isolation; it is only when the king is shown among his courtiers, in society, that royal power assumes meaning. *Morkinskinna* is an important source for discovering ideas about royal power precisely because kings do not hover over the proceedings but rather have both feet placed firmly upon the ground, among their retainers. The kings in the saga are complex individuals who discharge their roles and are also symbols of a higher reality. How individual kings are measured against the general notion of the nature of a king and what shapes the personal identity of individual kings will be the subject of the present discussion. In *Morkinskinna* the king is a part of court society.

'Where have you ever seen as fine a hall?'

Individual kings in *Morkinskinna* are not just measured against ideal exemplars but are also compared to each other. Such comparisons are the principal means by which an author can advance his ideas about royal power. In the initial incident in *Morkinskinna* the Russian King Jarizleifr has a great hall built, which Queen Ingigerðr enters *með fagrligri kvenna*

---

with those parts of the saga's discussion of royal power that are most important for the interpretation of the saga as a whole.

3 Ármann Jakobsson, 'The Individual and the Ideal: The Representation of Royalty in Morkinskinna'; *Í leit að konungi*, pp. 117–132.

sveit (*Msk.* I, 4) 'with a fine retinue of ladies-in-waiting'. The king rises to welcome her and then asks:

> 'Hvar sáttu jafn dýrliga hǫll eða jafn vel búna, fyrst at sveit-inni slíkra manna sem hérru saman komnir ok í annan stað búningr hallarinnar með miklum kostnaði?' (*Msk.* I, 4).

> 'Where have you ever seen as fine a hall or one as well endowed with a troop of such men as are assembled here, and also a hall as lavishly appointed?'

The queen duly speaks well of it, but then declares that the hall '*er Óláfr konungr Haraldsson sitr í, þó at hon standi á súlum einum*' (*Msk.* I, 4) '"which King Óláfr occupies, although it stands on piles"' is finer. After Jarizleifr strikes her a blow in the face, she twists the knife in the wound: '*Miklu mun ykkar þó meiri munr ... en ek mega orðum svá til skipa sem vert er*' (*Msk.* I, 4) '"much greater though is the difference in worth between the two of you ... than I can express in words"'. The saga, then, begins with a feast that goes wrong. The king's question has many parallels in chivalric kings' sagas, and the reactions are always the same: something happens that casts an ominous shadow over the splendour and joy. When true harmony seems finally to have been achieved, trouble is just around the corner.[4]

The opening of the saga shows that, whatever else happens, kings will always be compared. The king falls into a rage and slaps the queen's face; understandably she reacts negatively and expresses a desire to leave the king. He, in turn, is forced to relent, and invites her to accept whatever she desires as compensation. Since the dispute concerns Óláfr the Saint, she decides that Jarizleifr should foster Óláfr's illegitimate son, adding, '*því at sannligt er þat með ykkr, er mælt er, at sá er ógǫfgari er ǫðrum fóstrar barn*' (*Msk.* I, 5) '"for it is true what they say of you men that he is the lesser man who fosters the other's son"'. Again a familiar motif occurs: the lesser man fostering the son of the greater man.[5] When something

---

4   This is a familiar romance motif (Ármann Jakobsson, 'Le Roi Chevalier. The Royal Ideology and Genre of Hrólfs saga kraka'). See also part III, chapter 2.

5   As Einar Ólafur Sveinsson has noted (*Laxdæla saga*, note 75) this motif occurs widely. See Ármann Jakobsson, *Í leit að konungi*, p. 133.

important happens, the narrative is generously furnished with well-known saga topoi.[6]

King Jarizleifr's reaction shows his moderation and intelligence. He acknowledges the superiority of Óláfr:

> 'una megum vér því þó at Óláfr konungr sé oss meiri [maðr],
> ok eigi virði ek til óvirðingar þótt vér fóstrim honum barn.'
> (*Msk.* I, 5).

> 'and I do indeed accept that King Óláfr is the greater man,
> and I do not consider it dishonourable to foster his child'.

He later even violates the trade agreement with Norway because of the circumstances occasioning King Óláfr's death (*Msk.* I, 6–7). Although the saga begins with comparison and competition between Jarizleifr and Óláfr, a brotherly spirit eventually develops between them, and the former eventually extends the hand of friendship to Haraldr, Óláfr's brother (*Msk.* I, 85–86, 114–118). Jarizleifr deals with Norwegian kings as if they were closely related to him. All kings appear to be brothers under the ermine, the avatars of the same heavenly king and the representatives of an earthly royal community. For this reason, it is right and proper to compare them repeatedly, helping us to understand the nature of royal power itself and to link the individual with the general. But the saga also examines whether it is right for more than one king to rule at the same time.

'I did not see you there'

The flyting episode between Sigurðr and Eysteinn Magnússon, who ruled Norway jointly for twenty years,[7] is a final note in the drama of their re-

---

6   Some biblical associations may be noted here. The queen uses biblical language, as with *sannligt* 'true/truly'. King Magnús becomes king in much the same way as Christ himself, in exile while others occupy the country that is his by right. A king is not merely himself, he resembles other kings.

7   On the flyting, see Lönnroth, *Den dubbla scenen*, pp. 53–80; Kalinke, 'Sigurðar Saga Jórsalafara,' 162–165; Hallvard Lie, *Studier i Heimskringlas stil: Dialogene og talene*, pp. 66–68. On its general aesthetic character, see Clover, 'The Germanic Context of the Unferþ Episode'; Clover, 'Hárbarðsljóð as Generic Farce'; Lönnroth, 'The double scene of Arrow-Odd's drinking contest,' pp. 97–109.

gency. Of course the comparison between the two has begun long before the narrative reaches this point.[8] Their dispute does not involve family nobility or the legitimacy of claims to the crown but rather the virtues, roles and obligations of a king. Sigurðr boasts of being the stronger and the better swimmer; Eysteinn claims he is more dextrous and better at chess. Sigurðr says he is good with weapons and capable of participating in many a *turniment* but people turn more readily to Eysteinn to receive his judgement in their legal matters. Sigurðr claims that he is more reliable in keeping his word; but Eysteinn says that Sigurðr promises nothing. Eysteinn thus appears the more flexible, Sigurðr more rigid.

The contest between the kings reaches its height when the specific achievements of the kings in office are compared. Sigurðr plays his trump card – his crusade:

> 'Fór ek til Jórdánar, ok kom ek við Púl, ok sá ek þik eigi þar. Vann ek átta orrostur, ok vartu í øngarri. Fór ek til grafar Dróttins, ok sá ek þik eigi þar. Fór ek í ána, þá leið er Dróttinn fór, ok svam ek yfir, ok sá ek þik eigi þar. Ok knýtta ek þér knút, ok bíðr þín þar. Þá vann ek borgina Sídon með Jórsalakonungi, ok hǫfðum vér eigi þinn styrk eða ráð til.' (*Msk.* II, 133).

> 'I went to the river Jordan and was in Apulia, and I did not see you there. I won eight battles and you were in none of them. I went to the grave of the Lord, and I did not see you there. I went into the river, by the route that the Lord took, and swam over it and I did not see you there, and I tied a knot that still awaits you there. Then I won the city of Sidon with the King of Jerusalem, and we did not have your support or advice'.

Eysteinn shows himself capable of fighting fire with fire:

---

8 Compare Kalinke, 'Sigurðar Saga Jórsalafara,' p. 154. Andersson ('Snorri Sturluson and the saga school at Munkaþverá,' p. 16) sees the *mannjafnaðr* as highlighting the contrasting images of the merciful and harsh kings that he sees as a key element in *Morkinskinna*.

'Norðr í Vágum setta ek fiskimannavist, at fátœkir menn
mætti nœrask til lífs ok hjálpar. Þar lét ek ok kirkju reisa ok
settak þar prestvist ok lagðak fé til kirkjugerðar, en náliga
var áðr heiðið. Munu þeir menn muna at Eysteinn konungr
hefir verit í Nóregi. Á Þrándarnesi lét ek ok kirkju gøra ok
lagðak fé til, ok munu þeir menn muna at Eysteinn konungr
hefir verit í Nóregi. Um Dofrafjall var fǫr ór Þrándheimi.
Urðu menn þar opt úti ok fóru hǫrðum fǫrum. Lét ek þar
sæluhús gøra ok leggja fé til, ok munu þeir menn muna at
Eysteinn konungr hefir verit í Nóregi. Fyr Agðanesi váru
ørhœfi ok hafnleysi, ok fórusk þar jafnan mǫrg skip. Þar er
nú hǫfn gǫr ok gott skipalægi ok kirkja gǫr. Síðan lét ek
vita gera á háfjǫllum. Munu þeir menn muna er þess njóta
at Eysteinn konungr hefir verit í Nóregi. Nú munu njóta
þessa fiskimenn ok kaupmenn er gœðin flytja landi þessu,
ok missir þá eigi alls konungdómrinn. Hǫllina lét ek ok gøra
í Bjǫrgyn ok Postolakirkju ok rið í milli. Munu konungar
muna, þeir er síðarr eru, þetta verk. Mikaelskirkju lét ek ok
gera, ok settak þar munklífi. Skipaða ek lǫgunum, bróðir,
at hverr mætti hafa réttendi við annan, ok ef þau eru haldin mun betr fara landsstjórnin. Þeim Jamtum hǫfum vér ok
snúit undir þetta ríki, meirr með blíðyrðum ok viti heldr en
með ágang. Nú er þetta smátt at telja, en eigi veit ek víst at
landsbúinu gegni þetta verr eða sé óhallkvæmra en þótt þú
brytjaðir blámenn fyrir inn raga karl ok hrapaðir þeim svá í
helvíti.' (*Msk*. II, 133–134).

'North in Vágar I established a shelter for fishermen so that
poor men might be nourished and thus keep body and soul
together. I had a church built there and endowed a living
for a priest and gave money for building the church – the
area was once nearly pagan. Those people will remember
that King Eysteinn was in Norway. I had a church built
in Þrándarnes and I gave money for its maintenance, and
those people will remember that King Eysteinn was in Norway. A trail leads from Þrándheim over the Dofri Mountains

[Dovrefjell]. Men were often out in the elements and had a tough passage. I had shelters built and also gave money, and those people will remember that King Eysteinn was in Norway. Off Agðanes there was bare coastline and no harbours and many ships were lost there. Harbours have now been built there and good anchorages and churches. Then I had beacons built on the mountains. Those who enjoy these benefits will remember that King Eysteinn was in Norway. Now fisherman and merchants who bring their blessings to this country will enjoy these benefits, and the kingdom will lose none of them. I had a hall built in Bergen and the Church of the Apostles and a bridge between them. Kings who come later will remember this work. I also had Saint Michael's Church built and established a monastery. I made laws, brother, so that everyone might have justice from others, and if they are adhered to, the better will be the governance of the land. We have also made Jamtaland part of the country, more with warm words and wisdom than with aggression. Now all this may not amount to much, but I am not sure that the inhabitants of the land are worse off or have profited less than when you butchered Africans for the devil and sent them to Hell'.

The style of this passage is marked by repetition and enumeration that establishes pace and a regular rhythm. Sigurðr repeatedly completes his sentences with a phrase, '*sá ek þik eigi þar*' "'I did not see you there'", that captures his brusqueness and energy. On the other hand, Eysteinn inserts into his enumeration the words '*munu þeir menn muna at Eysteinn konungr hefir verit í Nóregi*' "'those people will remember that King Eysteinn was in Norway'", a longer and more harmonious phrase that makes mention not just of Eysteinn but also of those whom he serves.

Sigurðr first recounts his exploits in battle, all of which have been accomplished for the glory of God. In contrast, Eysteinn counters with church-building and the establishment of monasteries, the formulation of a body of laws, construction of harbours and wayside shelters, and he singles out merchants and fishermen amongst those who have benefited from his activities. As the oft-repeated phrase implies, Eysteinn is working for the benefit of others and doing so in Norway. He is a king for merchants, seamen, and peaceful citizens who require good roads, harbours, stable and equitable laws, and monasteries that are institutions devoted to both spirituality and culture. Sigurðr's crusades and courtliness are certainly remarkable, but they are of less practical use to his subjects in their daily lives than Eysteinn's achievements.

The flyting serves as a 'kings' mirror', revealing the virtues and functions of the two kings. Although Eysteinn emerges the victor, Sigurðr's merits are obvious. Earlier in saga it had been shown that these very dissimilar kings govern well when they put their minds to it.[9] But this is clearly not lasting. Just before the episode of the flyting comes the 'Þinga saga' episode (*Msk.* II, 117–131), an *exemplum* about the conflict between the two monarchs, in which Sigurðr's stubbornness and strength are opposed by Eysteinn's legal chicanery. They manage to settle matters eventually, but *eptir þetta varð þó aldregi m[art] milli þeira brœðra né blíða eða ástsemð* (*Msk.* II, 131) 'after this there was never much ... between the brothers, neither joy nor affection'.

Nevertheless, Eysteinn and Sigurðr remain the most successful joint rulers in *Morkinskinna*, where in all there are six periods in which two or more kings rule at the same time; Magnús the Good and Haraldr rule together for a year; the sons of Haraldr, Magnús and Óláfr, for three years; their sons for one year; Magnús Barelegs's sons rule, at first all three together and then just two, Eysteinn and Sigurðr, over a period of twenty years; Magnús the Blind and Haraldr Gilchrist vie for power for five years; and the sons of King Haraldr rule together for twenty years. In some cases the land is divided, but it is always joint rule to some degree.[10] Magnús the Good gives Haraldr the Severe half of his kingdom, but it turns out that when they are together Magnús is to be *fyrimaðr okkarr í heilsun ok þjónkun ok sæti* (*Msk.* I, 126) 'first between the two of us in greetings, service and seating' and is to enjoy priority when docking at the king's pier.

9   Kalinke, 'Sigurðar Saga Jórsalafara,' p. 164.
10 On the division of Norway, see Ármann Jakobsson, *Í leit að konungi*, pp. 139–141 (and the works cited therein).

This arrangement lasts for a year, and in *Morkinskinna* no year in the history of Norway is reported in such great detail, in this case constituting just over a tenth of the saga (*Msk.* I, 124–173). The arrangement turns out to be seriously ill-conceived. The two kings may be foremost and equal, but their equality is not such as to correspond to the heavenly order of the Catholic Church where emphasis is laid on the unity of the highest power.[11] All the narrative episodes involving the realm of these kings point to the disadvantages of a land being ruled by two kings. The distinction that is drawn between them is the cause of their disagreements. Magnús will not be satisfied unless he is the more prominent king, yet at the same time Haraldr finds it intolerable to be second in anything. In their mutual dealings it is always apparent that

> at vant var til at gæta ok gera svá at báðum líkaði vel … Ok þvílíkar greinir gerðusk brátt á umrœðum manna, ok hafa verit fleiri þeir hlutir er nǫkkur grein hefir á orðit með þeim frændum. Og heldu nú landinu um vetrinn (*Msk.* I, 130).

> it was difficult to arrange matters so that both of them were pleased … and such differences soon did the rounds among their men, and many other things led to differences between the kinsmen, and in this state they ruled the country over the winter.

From the outset Haraldr attempts to outdo Magnús with outlays of gold and displays of magnificence. Then Haraldr is insulted over a ring that Magnús wishes to give him and appears to envy Magnús his saintly father (*Msk.* I, 128). Haraldr then tries to anchor at the royal mooring, in direct contradiction of the formal agreement; when Magnús proves adamant and Haraldr is forced to back down, the latter tries to patronise Magnús (*Msk.* I, 130). Subsequent episodes show their subjects inevitably taking sides in the discord, to Haraldr's disadvantage. Two of his retainers who have served many kings regard Magnús as behaving in a way that befits a king (*Msk.* I, 131–133). Then there is the incident in which Haraldr persecutes friends of Magnús (*Msk.* I, 134–139) and cannot bear the idea of

11 Ármann Jakobsson, *Í leit að konungi*, pp. 133–143.

Magnús being the more loved by their subjects.[12] In the story of Haraldr's levying of taxes an old man claims that if two men are kings and the first is accepted at the Eyraþing, then '*ætlum vér þat at sá mun mest vald á oss eiga, þegnum sínum*' (*Msk.* I, 138) '"we think that he is the one who must have more power over us, his subjects"'. Naturally, this greatly upsets King Haraldr.

The episode about Arnórr the Earls' Poet deals with this comparison and the differences it reveals. Arnórr intends to recite poems in praise of both kings in their presence, and since one poem must obviously precede the other and in light of the agreement reached between the two kings that Magnús should have priority in all things, the first poem ought to be the one in praise of Magnús. But when Arnórr appears in front of the kings Haraldr speaks up and clearly attempts to provoke Arnórr into re-citing Haraldr's poem first. Arnórr succeeds in not insulting Haraldr and is allowed to proceed with a poem in praise of Magnús, but the matter remains unresolved, for the following lines occur in the poem: '*manngi veit ek fremra annan ... hverr gramr es þér stóru verri*' (*Msk.* I, 143–144) '"I know of no more prominent man ... every king, in comparison to you, is much inferior"'. Haraldr understands perfectly the significance of these lines and cries out: '*Lofa konung þenna sem þú vill ... en lasta eigi aðra konunga*' (*Msk.* I, 144) '"Praise any king you choose ... but do not demean other kings"'. The poem about Magnús turns out to be much better, at least in the estimation of King Haraldr; on the other hand, Arnórr succeeds in ranking Magnús higher without earning Haraldr's enmity, an accomplish-ment that not all Haraldr's retainers manage to achieve.

Not only does the competition between the two kings continue for as long as their joint rule lasts, but, almost as importantly, it does not end even when Magnús predeceases Haraldr. Shortly before the death of Magnús, Sveinn Úlfsson states that they are '*ójafnir konungar*' (*Msk.* I, 167) '"unequal kings"'. After Magnús's death, when Haraldr wishes to

---

12 The following sentence is typical: *spurði Haraldr konungr þetta. Þótti Þrándr brátt hafa á litit ok sýnt sik í því at hann vildi meira sóma gera Magnúsi konungi en sér. Ok líkar honum illa ok leggr til Þrándar mikinn óþokka* (Msk. I, 134) 'King Har-aldr learned of this. He reckoned that Þrándr had not thought matters through when he showed himself willing to honour King Magnús more than him. And he was dis-pleased with this and developed a great dislike for Þrándr'.

take a large troop with him to Denmark, where he intends to be crowned before Sveinn, Einarr Paunch-Shaker says he prefers '*at fylgja Magnúsi konungi dauðum en hverjum ǫðrum konungi lifanda*' (*Msk.* I, 173) '"to serve King Magnús in death rather than any other king living"'. Magnús himself warns his mother against relying on the protection of Haraldr (*Msk.* I, 166) and thinks it likely '*at sumum verði myrkari ok kaldari ráð Haralds konungs, frænda míns, en mín*' (*Msk.* I, 171) '"that for some the counsels of my kinsman King Haraldr will be darker and colder than mine"'. Thus, Haraldr was repeatedly forced to endure the unfavourable comparison for as long as he lived.

When Hreiðarr the Simple learns of Haraldr's arrival in Bergen, he says that he is not widely travelled, '*en mér er mikil forvitni á at sjá tvá konunga senn í einum stað*' (*Msk.* I, 159) '"but I am very curious to see two kings at once in the same place"'. At first glance this seems a foolish observation, but it highlights a key element in the ideology of *Morkinskinna*, to the effect that a country is the worse off for having two kings. When Haraldr demands the Norwegian throne, Einarr Paunch-Shaker says: '*ekki fýsumsk vér at tvískiptask milli hǫfðingja. Hǫfum vér jafnan einum senn þjónat*' (*Msk.* I, 121) '"we are not eager to be split up between chieftains. We have always served one at a time"'. When Haraldr originally asks the farmers to call him king, *þorði engi maðr þar at gøra fyri ríki Magnúsar konungs at láta heita annan mann konung at honum lifanda* (*Msk.* I, 125) 'no man dared to allow anyone else to be called king while King Magnús was still alive because of how powerful he was'. Having two kings guarantees trouble. Still, at this time there is *friðr ok mikil gæzka í landinu fyr árferðar sakir ok annarra hluta* (*Msk.* I, 130) 'peace and great prosperity in the land on account of plentiful harvests and other matters'. With Haraldr the Severe's death there are once again two kings in the land, but not for long, since Magnús Haraldsson dies sooner than expected (*Msk.* I, 325). The sons of Magnús and Óláfr the Quiet thus both seize power at Óláfr's death, and trouble seems inevitable when Hákon Þórir's foster-son dies suddenly (*Msk.* II, 18). The consequences are even more dire when Magnús the Blind, Haraldr Gilchrist and Sigurðr the Noisy compete for power over the land. Of the years when Haraldr's sons rule there is mention only of the discord and dissent that eventually led to their deaths.

The landed men are getting above themselves

Conflict over power is a feature of *Morkinskinna* even when two kings are not contending with one another, as others can threaten a king. Thus it may be said that a country's leadership consists of two people when there is a powerful earl in the country, as was the case in the days of Erlingr the Crooked and Magnús, Hákon galinn 'the Furious' and Ingi Bárðarson, Skúli Bárðarson and Hákon. Such a division of power leads to as much conflict as when there are two kings, but in such cases it appears that audience sympathy tends toward the king.

An example of such a conflict also appears in the dispute between Haraldr the Severe and Einarr Paunch-Shaker. Prior to the killing of Einarr, two short narratives (*Msk.* I, 208–214) dramatise the basic principle. The long-standing feud between Einarr and the king heats up considerably when King Haraldr says: *'Ríkr ertu, Einarr, ef þú ert konungr yfir landinu heldr en ek, þó ek sé svá kallaðr'* (*Msk.* I, 211) 'Powerful you are, Einarr, if you rather than I are king over the land even though I am so called'. Earlier it was said,

> Haraldr konungr varð ósáttr við Einar þambarskelfi fyrir þá
> sǫk at Einarr vildi jafnask við konung í ríkdóm sínum allt
> í Þrœndalǫgum, ok aldri kom hann svá til kaupstaðarins þá
> er Haraldr konungr var fyrir at eigi hefði hann mikit lið, ok
> varla mátti konungr koma fram málum sínum fyrir ofríki
> Einars. Ok þat kapp gørði Einarr í kaupstaðnum at hann tók
> af móti sannan þjóf, ok náði konungr eigi at dœma hann, ok
> var Haraldr konungr sjálfr á mótinu. (*Msk.* I, 207).

> King Haraldr was at odds with Einarr Paunch-Shaker be-
> cause Einarr desired to be equal in power to the king in
> Þrœndalǫg. Einarr never came to town when King Haraldr
> was present without having a large following, and the king
> could scarcely carry out his business because of the sheer
> force of Einarr's presence. And Einarr went so far in the
> town as to remove from the assembly a proven thief and the
> king was not able to adjudicate the case against him, even
> though King Haraldr was present at the assembly meeting.

Beforehand the farmers had knuckled under to Haraldr and later agreed to pay taxes to him rather than to Magnús the Good. Then Einarr attends a meeting and humiliates Haraldr. Haraldr becomes furious and accuses Einarr of overweening pride: '*góðr væri sá dagr er þinn ofsi steypisk, ok svá sem nú ertu hǫfði hæri en aðrir skyldir þú brátt hǫfði lægri*' (*Msk.* I, 138) 'Good will be the day when your pride brings you down, and just as you are now standing a head taller than everyone else, you will soon be a head shorter'. Later Einarr refuses to join the military expedition to Denmark that Haraldr undertakes in order to secure his rule there (*Msk.* I, 173); indeed, from the beginning Einarr had opposed Haraldr's receiving the crown (*Msk.* I, 120–121).

While King Magnús is alive, Einarr appears to be completely within his rights, but when he and Haraldr fall out subsequently, Einarr loses credibility. At the beginning of the saga he is said to be *frægr maðr ok kunnigr at mǫrgum góðum hlutum* 'a famous man and known for many good deeds' and *fyrirmaðr allra lendra manna í Nóregi* (*Msk.* I, 20) 'the head of all the chieftains in Norway'. His pride makes him reluctant to swear an oath of fidelity to Magnús, but in the end he humbles himself and swears the oath that Queen Ingigerðr requests. Afterwards, he supports the king loyally. In the Þorsteinn Síðu-Hallsson episode it becomes clear that Magnús and Einarr will allow nothing to damage their friendship (*Msk.* I, 140–143). On the other hand, from the beginning he is no friend to Haraldr the Severe. From the evidence of *Morkinskinna*, however, we must conclude that Haraldr leaves him in peace for a long time. On one occasion Einarr does not wish to support King Sveinn of Denmark against Haraldr, stating '*[o]k hvern enda sem á með okkr Haraldi konungi þá mun ek ekki svíkja hann né land undan honum*' (*Msk.* I, 212) '"and whatever conclusion is reached in my dealings with King Haraldr, I will not betray him nor the land he rules"'. Haraldr regards such a manner of speaking '*beint ván at honum at drengiliga myndi hann mæla ok af ǫngri hollostu við mik*' (*Msk.* I, 212–213) '"to be expected from him: that he would speak boldly and show little devotion towards me"'. Still, in comparison with others who were tested by the bribe ruse, Einarr's response demonstrates that he is a man of honour, which not only earns him sympathy with the saga audience but, we may surmise, provides him with borrowed time.

The final blow, however, occurs when Haraldr invites Einarr to a reconciliation meeting. During the meeting, Einarr, by this time well advanced in years, falls asleep while Haraldr is reciting one of his yarns, thereby insulting the king (*Msk.* I, 214–215).[13] After this incident the king no longer seeks reconciliation, and when Einarr next meets with the king, Einarr and his son are killed (*Msk.* I, 215–216). The author then heaves a sigh of relief over this conclusion:

> Nú leið svá at Einari lǫng heipt ok fjándskapr er Haraldr konungr hafði lengi bundizk ok stilltan sik at, sem til vísar fyrr í þessu máli, ok var þó mǫrg ǫnnur áminning milli þeira áðr en á þessa lund lykisk. (*Msk.* I, 216).

> This was the result for Einarr of the long hatred and enmity that King Haraldr had harboured and suppressed, as was indicated previously in this matter, but there had been many other warnings between them before things ended in this fashion.

In the author's view Haraldr has shown moderation. Although Einarr is always described as a noble and worthy man, the suggestion is that chieftains do not have the right to place themselves on an equal footing with a king. Just as Magnús had had the law completely on his side in his conflict with Haraldr, the law is now on Haraldr's side. At another instance in the saga, when Sveinki Steinarsson showed Magnús Barelegs some resistance, the king launched a tirade against chieftains who do not pay sufficient attention to the honour of a king (*Msk.* II, 34). The just Kolbeinn klakka 'Cluck' warns Sveinka against wishing '*at óreyndum sǫkum eflastk móti konungi þínum réttkosnum ok ættbornum til lands þessa, ok hefir þat ǫngum vel gefizk*' (*Msk.* II, 35) '"for no good reason to contend against your lawfully chosen king and one destined by birth to rule this land – that has never done anyone any good"'. This is as clear a statement as can be found of *Morkinskinna*'s view of this political doctrine.

<hr/>

13   Kari Ellen Gade, 'Einarr Þambarskelfir's Last Shot,' 153–162.

In this respect there is a clear difference of emphasis between *Morkin-skinna* and *Heimskringla*.[14] It is tempting to view this variance in the light of early thirteenth-century Icelandic history. As discussed earlier, both sagas were probably put together at some point during the two decades following 1220, and at that time a king and an earl, Hákon and Skúli respectively, ruled Norway. The *Morkinskinna* view is that only one of these figures, the king, should rule; the author of *Heimskringla* appears to be more tolerant towards joint rule, even if someone other than a king is involved. Snorri Sturluson was a follower of Earl Skúli and fell out with the king for this reason. In *Morkinskinna* sympathy for the king's point of view seems to be more pronounced. But though the attitude towards contemporary politics helps to form the ideology of *Morkinskinna*, the view developed in the saga has a more universal validity. The heavenly king is symbolised by all earthly kings, whose power derives from him and who are his representatives. He alone rules and is the one who guarantees justice on the earth below.[15] In *Laxdæla saga* there is an incident in which an argument breaks out as to who should take over the helm of a ship that had lost its bearings out at sea. The suggestion is made that the decision should rest with those *er fleiri váru* 'who are in the majority'. When this view is put to Óláfr pái 'the Peacock', who is also on board, he responds: *'því verr þykki mér sem oss muni duga heimskra manna ráð, er þau koma fleiri saman'* '"it seems much worse to me that we have to suffer the counsel of stupid men when they are in the majority"'.[16] The *Morkin-skinna* view of democracy seems to echo this sentiment. It is a king's duty to guarantee justice and it is the best and simplest solution for just one person to shoulder this burden.

Royal portraits

In the tale of each of the kings in *Morkinskinna* there is one unifying element, self-control, which defines the nature of a king's power. The story

14 Ármann Jakobsson, 'Rundt om kongen: En genvurdering af Morkinskinna,' pp. 75–78; Ármann Jakobsson, 'Kongesagaen som forsvandt: Nyere kongesagastudier med særligt henblik på Morkinskinna.'
15 Ármann Jakobsson, *Í leit að konungi*, pp. 117–125.
16 *Laxdæla saga*, p. 53.

of Magnús Óláfsson concerns his transformation from young king who *gørisk brátt ríkr ok vinsæll ok var ... fullgǫrr með afli ok vizku ok stjórn* (*Msk.* I, 29) 'quickly became powerful and popular and was ... mature in strength and wisdom and authority' into a 'Magnús the Severe' (*Msk.* I, 30–31, 34), and back again, becoming Magnús the Good. When a king, who is in most respects an exemplary figure, ceases to practice moderation, his strength ceases to be a virtue and becomes excessive. Magnús' excellence and nobility is evident during his youth. After killing a courtier in Russia his foster-father, King Jarizleifr remarks *'Konungligt verk, fóstri'* (*Msk.* I, 6) '"a royal deed, my son"'.[17] But his transformation from a tyrannical to an exemplary king only comes when he learns to control himself. Having regained his virtue, and having ruled as an exemplary figure, nearer the end of the Magnús' life Hreiðarr justifiably tells the king, *'þannug myndi hverr sik kjósa sem þú ert, þó at sjálfr mætti ráða'* (*Msk.* I, 156) '"everyone who could decide for himself would choose to be like you"'. The depth of description of Magnús the Good in the saga derives from the fact that his temperament is revealed from the beginning. For a while it affects his leadership to the point that he becomes a veritable tyrant, but with greater moderation he becomes a model king.

The saga of Haraldr the Severe, the most complex character in *Morkinskinna*,[18] also deals with self-control. Haraldr is a paragon among men, endowed with intelligence, shrewdness and practicality, but also bears resemblance to the classical sly fox.[19] Two additional traits that are frequently associated with Haraldr are his delight in stories and poems, and

17 Kings, when it comes to other kings, see further beyond the horizon than others (Ármann Jakobsson, *Í leit að konungi*, pp. 130–132.
18 Bjarni Aðalbjarnarson, ed., *Heimskringla* III, *ÍF* 28, p. xviii. Bjarni, Finnur Jónsson (*Morkinskinna*, pp. xxiv–xxv) and Indrebø ('Harald Hardraade i Morkinskinna,' pp. 173–180) considered the portrait of Haraldr in *Morkinskinna* rather a mixture of elements that resulted from a failure to harmonise conflicting character traits in the various versions of the saga. Others have attempted to interpret Haraldr as he appears in the saga as it is now preserved (Andersson, 'The Politics of Snorri Sturluson', and Ármann Jakobsson, 'The Individual and the Ideal').
19 Haraldr's physical appearance also offers mixed signals. He is *vígligr maðr ok fǫllitaðr, stórmannligr ok skolbrúnn ok nǫkkut grimmligr* (*Msk.* I, 84) 'a warlike man, pale, masculine, with heavy eyebrows and somewhat fierce-looking', radiating ferocity and terror, even though he is the protagonist of the chapters that follow.

his friendship with Icelanders, which greatly increases his closeness to the author of *Morkinskinna*. Haraldr is wiser and stronger than most other kings.[20] But the third chief virtue of a king is restraint, and there's the rub. Often Haraldr's aggressiveness and lack of restraint are evident.[21] Nearly half of the *Morkinskinna* text (243 of the 569 pages in the Íslenzk fornrit edition) is devoted to the story of Haraldr the Severe. In characterising him no punches are pulled, and the author seems to relish describing both Haraldr's virtues and vices. Touchiness and impatience, a thirst for revenge and immoderation, envy and parsimony are described with the same gusto as are wisdom, courage, friendship towards Icelanders, humour and wit, a delight in poetry, a passion for testing men and a rough exterior that often conceals benevolence towards poets, court jesters and Icelanders. In the end, it is also an exemplary narrative about the virtues of restraint, attested by its conclusion as Haraldr undertakes his final military expedition to England. Just before the final battle at Stamford Bridge, Haraldr summons Earl Tostig and asks his advice. Yet, when the time comes, he does not act on the shrewd Earl's advice, who observes: '*Þér skuluð ráða þessu, herra, sem ǫllu ǫðru*' (*Msk.* I, 312) '"you should decide this, sire, as with everything else"', and when all is said and done Haraldr has nobody to blame but himself. His strategic skills had repeatedly been apparent up to this point, not least an antipathy towards foolhardiness in battle (among other places, *Msk.* I, 100–106, 110–111, 113–114, 201–203, 254, 264–268). The story concludes soon afterwards:

> Nú fær Haraldr konungr lag framan í óstinn, svá at þegar kom blóðboginn út í munninn. Þetta var hans banasár, ok því næst fell hann til jarðar. (*Msk.* I, 319).

> Then King Haraldr received a spear in his throat and blood came gushing out of his mouth. This was his death-wound, and he then fell to the ground.

His death is quick, as is that of Earl Tostig and finally Eysteinn the Heathcock. The narrative becomes tragic when a simple statement about the

---

20 Ármann Jakobsson, *Í leit að konungi*, pp. 202–222.
21 Ibid., pp. 225–226.

passing of time reminds the audience of the transitoriness of life: *Þar fell náliga allt stórmenni Norðmanna, ok var þá inn øfri hlutr dags* (*Msk.* I, 321) 'There nearly all the prominent Norsemen fell, and it was then towards the end of the day'. Although the author is reticent on the subject, it seems very likely that he regrets the death of Haraldr the Severe – as, doubtless, did many in the saga audience.

Óláfr the Quiet ruled Norway longer than any other king from the days of Haraldr Fairhair to those of Hákon Hákonarson, twenty-seven years in all. Nevertheless his impact on Norwegian kings' sagas is remarkably slight, though the narrative in *Morkinskinna* about him (*Msk.* II, 3–16) is more detailed than elsewhere. In Óláfr's story he is repeatedly compared to his father Haraldr the Severe, with the former often recalling his father's power, sometimes at the expense of his own. However, Óláfr also says that he is pleased to see '*á lýð mínum gleði ok frelsi ... En á dǫgum fǫður míns var lýðr þessi undir aga miklum ok ótta*' (*Msk.* II, 10) '"in my people joy and freedom ... whereas in my father's days these people lived under strong discipline and anxiety"'. Here the difference between the reigns of Haraldr and Óláfr is emphasised, with the former described as a despot. But this does not necessarily mean that the author prefers Óláfr to Haraldr.[22] Óláfr is the personification of magnaminity, and is cheerful, generous and merciful. Moreover, he is popular, and his regime results in additional freedom and joy for his subjects. On the other hand, Haraldr excels when it comes to wisdom, leadership and discipline. There are, however, several similarities between Óláfr and his tough-minded father, but where his father's story was one of inflexibility, the story of Óláfr the Quiet demonstrates, on the other hand, that a king can be resolute but at the same time magnanimous and moderate in temperament.

Magnús Barelegs, like his grandfather, is an uncompromising ruler but he lacks several of Haraldr's virtues. The decisive difference between the two is that Haraldr's retainers follow him to the death, while Magnús Barelegs's forsake him. He is less clearly delineated character than his father or grandfather. His private life is for the most part shrouded in mist, we never see him in times of peace, and there are few references to any dealings with poets and Icelanders. Of his reign we may perhaps conclude that

22 Andersson ('The Politics of Snorri Sturluson,' pp. 66–68) argues this point.

too much severity and constant warfare offered little joy to his subjects. It is Magnús's fate to die alone and abandoned on a foreign shore, full of rancour towards and bewilderment at the cowardice of his men. Popularity depends upon generosity of spirit in dealing with one's subjects; without that popularity the strongest and most courtly king can suddenly find himself alone and abandoned.

The two sons of Magnús, Eysteinn and Sigurðr the Crusader, rule together but are contrasting figures. Eysteinn is an example of a king who can govern calmly. He is a blessing to his subjects and his passing is greatly mourned. In the meantime Sigurðr is one of the most complex kings in *Morkinskinna*.[23] He wins fame for Norway in his youth heading south on a crusade and is everywhere received with open arms. He travels from land to land and the receptions become even grander and more elaborate and the merriment more pronounced. His greatest victory comes during a feast with the emperor of Constantinople, but just when the the king's honour is at its highest, a serpent rears its head in the form of a prophet who spoils the happiness:

> Þat mælti spekingr einn í Miklagarði at svá myndi fara virðing Sigurðar konungs sem it óarga dýr er vaxit, geyst í bógunum ok aptr minna; lét at svá myndi fara hans konungdómr at þá myndi mest um þykkja vert en síðarr minna. (*Msk.* II, 99).

> A wise man in Constantinople prophesied that the fame of Sigurðr would resemble the frame of a wild beast, broad in the shoulders and tapering towards the rear; so would his kingship fare, that though at that time he was of great renown he would decline later.

The life of a king reminds the wise man of a wild animal. Though comparison derives from the shape of a lion, it reminds us at the same time of the animal that dwells in every civilised man.[24] King Sigurðr is now

---

23 See my further work on him: 'The Madness of King Sigurðr: Narrating Insanity in an Old Norse Kings' Saga;' 'Image is Everything: The Morkinskinna Account of King Sigurðr of Norway's Journey to the Holy Land.'

24 On lion metaphors in Old Icelandic sagas, see Heinrich Beck, 'Hit óarga dýr und die mittelalterliche Tiersignificatio.'

a star in the firmament, but there dwells within him that which will lead to his downfall. Echoing the feast in Constantinople, later in life Sigurðr continues to feast, but everything has changed:

> Sigurðr konungr sat með mǫrgum mǫnnum gǫfgum í stirð-
> um hug. Var þat frjákveld eitt at dróttsetinn spurði hvat til
> matar skyldi búa. Konungr svaraði: 'Hvat nema slátr?' Svá
> var mikil ógn at honum at engi þorði í mót at mæla. Váru nú
> allir ókátir, ok bjoggusk menn til borðanna. Kómu inn send-
> ingar ok heitt slátr á, ok váru allir menn hljóðir ok hǫrmuðu
> konungs mein. (*Msk.* II, 144).

> King Sigurðr was sitting with many noble men in a sad state
> of mind. One Friday evening the steward asked what food
> should be prepared. The king answered: 'What else besides
> blood sausage?' So great was their fear of him that no one
> dared to contradict him. Everyone was unhappy and people
> prepared to eat. Steaming platters of blood sausage were
> borne in, and everybody was quiet and lamented the king's
> indisposition.

There is no joy here; the prophecy has proved true. The crusader king is now demanding to eat meat on Friday, thereby violating Christian law.

For Marianne Kalinke the saga confirms that Eysteinn and Sigurðr rule best together and then enjoy the greatest goodwill. Norway is best served when Sigurðr increases his fame abroad while Eysteinn attends to the needs of the country and its people at home.[25] The solidarity between the brothers is certainly unique; where two kings rule in *Morkinskinna* dissension normally reigns. But there is little said in the saga about the good years. More space is devoted to the final period, during which Eysteinn's qualities come to the fore. It is, though, the prominence given to

---

25 Kalinke, 'Sigurðar Saga Jórsalafara,' 164: 'Either ruler, had he been charged with sole responsibility for the realm, would have been deficient … Only as a team, albeit one with contrary tendencies, can the Norwegian monarchy … be considered to have had considerable impact both at home and abroad.' See Andersson, 'The Politics of Snorri Sturluson,' pp. 69–71.

Sigurðr's mental illness in those last years that compromises the reputation that he earned in his youth. Precisely because of how much is made of his youthful exploits abroad, his story ends up a sad one.

Many stories dealing with the king's mental illness take place at feasts as he sits contentedly on his throne with his courtiers and his story veers towards sadness when he loses his grip on his mental capacities. Sigurðr's misfortune then becomes Norway's misfortune, as these brothers are followed by many disastrous kings: Magnús the Blind is cruel (*Msk.* II, 148–150, 175); Haraldr Gilchrist is incompetent (*Msk.* II, 175); Sigurðr the Noisy commits numerous atrocities in his quest for power (*Msk.* II, 177). The saga concludes with the sons of Haraldr Gilchrist. None of them is an outstanding king, but Ingi is the best of them when he resolves to do great deeds.

Theodore M. Andersson has pointed out how neatly the author of *Morkinskinna* divides the kings into two groups: Magnús the Good, Óláfr the Quiet and Eysteinn Magnússon are peaceful, beloved and devoted to domestic welfare; Haraldr the Severe, Magnús Barelegs and Sigurðr the Crusader, on the other hand, are bellicose and concern themselves more actively with conquest than with tending their own gardens. Andersson believes that the saga clearly shows a preference for the kings portrayed in the former group. Haraldr, Magnús and Sigurðr are formidable individuals but less impressive kings.[26]

The author of *Morkinskinna* measures individual kings against the ideal role of the king and pays attention to their reputations, popularity and magnanimity. Magnús the Good, Óláfr the Quiet and Eysteinn are certainly presented in a favourable light. On the other hand, the description of Haraldr the Severe is hardly as thoroughly negative as Andersson would have us believe. Despite everything, Haraldr is a commanding figure in many respects, and the author pays a great deal of attention to him. Haraldr is far and away the most interesting picture of a king in the saga. The characterisation of Sigurðr the Crusader is also positive in many ways, even though the last years of his reign cannot be ignored. The kings in

---

26 Andersson: 'The Politics of Snorri Sturluson'; 'Snorri Sturluson and the saga school at Munkaþverá,' p. 16; 'The Unity of Morkinskinna'; 'The King of Iceland.'

Morkinskinna are exemplary figures but also complex individuals – these two elements are never in conflict in *Morkinskinna*.

Each individual king represents a composite of royal virtues. Some kings lack one or two of these virtues and are thus either partially deficient in their roles, or, in extreme cases, completely unqualified for royal office. Haraldr the Severe and Sigurðr the Crusader have faults, and Magnús Barelegs and Eysteinn Haraldsson are eventually abandoned by their men. Magnús the Blind, Haraldr Gilchrist and Sigurðr Haraldsson are almost totally unfit for their roles. In *Morkinskinna* the ideal is always present as a reference point when an individual king is represented. Individual kings certainly find it hard to meet all the demands of ideal kingship. No individual king has all the virtues, and all shortcomings and faults are revealed, even those of Magnús the Good and Eysteinn Magnússon. Yet, though nothing is suppressed, the concept of royal power is not challenged, and we are made aware how carefully this theme must be treated. The *Morkinskinna* author explores the idea of royal power in a positive but discriminating way.[27]

---

27 For a more thorough examination of the reigns of each of these kings and the manner in which the author of *Morkinskinna* explores the notion of royal power through their respective stories, see Ármann Jakobsson, *Staður í nýjum heimi*, pp. 191–222.

3. Kings and Subjects

'Your freedom is my joy'

In *Morkinskinna* the most important knights are the kings. Magnús Bare-legs is said to be *manna kurteisastr* (*Msk.* II, 10) 'a very courteous man', more so than the kings of both Sweden and Denmark (*Msk.* II, 60). Although accounts of the meetings of the three Scandinavian kings oc-cur in other sagas, the word *kurteisi* 'courtesy' is used only in *Morkin-skinna*. What does the word mean? Here it might have special reference to Magnús's appearance, bravery and skill in arms, and indeed shortly afterwards it is said that the emperor's daughter thought *slíkr konung ... sœmiligr sem Magnús konungr var* (*Msk.* II, 62) 'such a king ... was as becoming as King Magnús'. Courtesy can embrace every kind of physical grace. Magnús the Good, in his youth, was *kœnn við marga leika ok íþrótt-ir* (*Msk.* I, 5) 'accomplished in many sports and skills', and in one verse Haraldr the Severe prides himself on his skill in eight *íþróttir* (*Msk.* I, 116) 'arts'.[1] Noble-mindedness and generosity convince Emperor Alexios of the courtesy of Sigurðr the Crusader (*Msk.* II, 96–99). Courtesy also in-volves waging war honourably. Terms such as honour, excellence, glory and noble-mindedness are often used in this context.

All these elements of courtesy can be called external courtesy.[2] An-other category is the internalised form that affects interpersonal dealings,

---

1   The term *íþrótt* refers to all kinds of abilities that now would be called arts, among them sports in our modern sense. There is considerable overlap even today: in most countries dance is an art form, while in others it is regarded as an athletic contest and is called a 'sport.' Magnús the Good's courtiers were known for their *kurteislegan róður* (*Msk.* I, 149) 'courteous rowing', Sigurðr the Noisy is *allra manna fóthvatastr* (*Msk.* II, 176) 'very fleet of foot' and *manna best syndr* (*Msk.* II, 207) 'a very good swimmer', Haraldr Gilchrist can run faster than a horse (*Msk.* II, 149–150) and Ey-steinn Magnússon and Sigurðr the Noisy are good at chess (*Msk.* II, 132 and 174). See Lönnroth, 'Charlemagne, Hrolf Kraki, Olaf Tryggvason,' pp. 29–52.

2   See Jaeger, *The Envy of Angels*, pp. 106–116. See, among others, Bjarni Einarsson ('On the status of Free Men in Society and Saga,' p. 49) on the word *courtesy*.

and such dealings are, of course, essential for kings. Although kings stand alone at the top of the social pyramid, they must know their people and be able to deal with them.[3] Magnanimity is one important virtue for a king, and the term entails both generosity and mercy. The use of one word to signify two things could suggest that generosity with money and mercy have been thought of as two sides of the same virtue. In the tale of Auðun Haraldr's generosity in sparing Auðun's life is comparable to Sveinn's generosity in giving him money. This story reminds us also that gifts can lie at the heart of relationships.

Generosity with material wealth helps to define a man. On one occasion Magnús gives one of his aged subjects a ring to which the man replies: '*Konungliga er gefit, herra*' (*Msk.* I, 133) '"This is royally given, sire"'. Generosity is a key element in royal behaviour. Conspicuous generosity can certainly buy popularity, as attested when Gregoríus Dagsson uses his money in order to support King Ingi (*Msk.* II, 229) and to maintain

> betr húskarla sína en hverr annarra lendra manna, því at
> hann drakk aldregi svo í skytningum at eigi drykki húskarlar
> hans allir með honum. (*Msk.* II, 231).

> his own followers better than those of any other landed man,
> since he never drank in taverns without having all of them
> with him.[4]

Among kings famed for their generosity Haraldr Gilchrist occupies an important position. We are told that Bishop Magnús Einarsson from Skálholt visited him and received priceless gifts (*Msk.* II, 167), and Haraldr's generosity is so much a part of his nature that he gives the bishop the cushion

3 Max Weber (*Wirtschaft und Gesellschaft: Grundriss der Sozialökonomik*) distinguished between governance by charisma and by power and authority alone. Elias (*The Court Society*, pp. 117–145) notes that even seventeenth-century despots needed to tread carefully in human affairs, and such restrictions applied all the more to kings within a feudal system.

4 Here Gregoríus's behaviour recalls the strategy of politically powerless men who reinforce their high social standing by holding feasts (see, for example, Helgi Þorláksson, 'Draumar Dalamanns,' pp. 43–49). *Ǫrlæti* 'generosity' is at the same time a virtue in Viking chieftains and romance kings, as attested in certain kennings in skaldic poetry (see Ármann Jakobsson, *Í leit að konungi*, pp. 236–239).

upon which he and his Queen are sitting (see part III, chapter 1). Unfortunately, his other qualities are not on a par with this, but it is generosity that, for all his other faults, accounts in part for Haraldr's popularity in life and death. On the other hand, Eysteinn Haraldsson is left in the lurch by his men, who tell him to use his 'chests of gold' to defend the land. Eysteinn was ill-served by having chests *full* of gold, and he would have been better advised to share his wealth with his retainers, as did Magnús the Good and Haraldr Gilchrist. Eysteinn's gold is, when it comes to the crunch, of no use to him.

Mercy is a royal virtue, and a king is obliged to give quarter to an adversary in accordance with definite rules.[5] Those who surrender and place themselves at the king's mercy always receive it. Sveinn Úlfsson refuses to kill some Norwegians who asked for his 'mercy', even though he is urged to do so (*Msk.* I, 204). But despite this rule there is no doubt that when men surrender to the king, he has the power of life and death over them. Magnús the Good's anger is palpable when his mother decides, on her own initiative, to spare Þorkell geysa (*Msk.* I, 165–166). A king owns the lives of his prisoners; no one else can pardon them. Despite Haraldr the Severe's often demonstrated severity, he offers a truce to those who surrender in the wake of his conquest of various towns in Sicily; he returns the last of these towns to its ruler, whom he considered a noble adversary (*Msk.* I, 105–106). It seems a token of Haraldr's good fortune that, rather than burning and plundering,

> hvar sem hann fór um Jórsalaland váru náliga allar borgir ok staðir upp gefnir í hans vald; svá fylgði honum mikil hamingja. (*Msk.* I, 106–107).

> wherever he went in the Holy Land nearly all the towns and villages surrendered to him; thus good fortune accompanied him.

When Finnr Árnason is Haraldr's prisoner, he is forced to accept mercy against his wishes, though Haraldr cannot resist boasting about it. Concerning this event the author comments: *þar líknaði sá er valdið átti,*

---

5 Ármann Jakobsson, ibid., pp. 232–236; Ármann Jakobsson, 'Hákon Hákonarson – friðarkonungur eða fúlmenni?'

ok vegr var þat en eigi lítilrœði (Msk. I, 253) 'the one who wielded power demonstrated mercy, and there was honour in that and no small-mindedness'. This, in a nutshell, is the *Morkinskinna* view.

An adversary who has surrendered is rarely executed. Nevertheless, Sigurðr Haraldsson is killed after asking his brother for a truce (*Msk.* II, 234). When Magnús Barelegs routs Steigar-Þórir, a large troop is *á konungs vald (Msk.* II, 25) 'in the king's power'. The word *vald* 'power' is a precise synonym for one sense of *grið* 'mercy', since those who request a truce enter the king's sphere of influence – that is, they are at his mercy. Kings should show mercy, but Magnús is *reiðr (Msk.* II, 28) 'angry', and seems blind to that obligation. Although the prisoners executed are traitors, the executions are still an unhappy stain on his reign (compare part III, chapter 2 and part IV, chapter 2).

Courtesy is developed in dealings with others. The magnanimous king is the centre of a society and is surrounded by his subjects. He must be cheerful and mild in manner in order to obtain the loyalty of those subjects. Magnús the Good is generous and merciful according to both the letter and spirit of those qualities. When he comes to a farm, we are told that *allir menn leggja ástúð til hans (Msk.* I, 149) 'all people love him', and the reactions to his death are intense and personal, as is sometimes the case with the death of prominent personalities even today. Poor people were *eigi lengi orðum upp koma fyrir harmi (Msk.* I, 174) 'in their grief unable to utter a word for a long time' and few eyes remained dry. Óláfr the Quiet is likewise generous with his wealth, but also compassionate, cheerful and affectionate towards his subjects:

> Ok í þessu má marka hver hans gœzka hefir verit ok ástsemð við lýðinn. Þá má marka nǫkkut af þeim orðum er hann mælti einn dag í Miklagildi; var hann þá kátr ok í góðu skapi, ok gørðusk þeir menn til er þetta mæltu: 'Herra, mikill fǫgnuðr er oss á því er þú ert svá kátr.' Hann svarar: 'Nú skal ek kátr vera er ek sé bæði á lýð mínum gleði ok frelsi, ok sitk í samkundu þeiri er helguð er inum helga Óláfi konungi frænda mínum. En á dǫgum fǫður míns var lýðr þessi undir aga miklum ok ótta, ok fálu þá flestir menn gull sitt

ok gersimar, en nú sé ek á hverjum yðrum skína þat er á, ok er yðart frelsi mín gleði.' (*Msk.* II, 10–11).

and this may be seen in his goodness and affection towards his people, and also in certain of those words that he spoke one day at the Great Guild. He was expansive and in good spirits, causing people to say: 'Sire, it gladdens us much that you are so happy'. He said: 'I should be happy when I see my people both happy and free and when I sit in an assembly devoted to my kinsman Saint Óláfr. But in my father's days these same people lived in fear and terror, and many hid their gold and treasures, but now I see shining on each of you the things that you own, and your freedom is my joy'.

Óláfr is a courteous king, as can be seen in the good cheer, affection and warm words he directs towards his subjects. In the description of Óláfr this courtesy also involves his characteristic self-control, and he is said to be *glaðr við ǫl ok fagrmæltr við vini sína ok hófsmaðr um alla hluti* (*Msk.* II, 3) 'happy at the ale-drinking and supportive in speech towards his friends and a man of moderation in all respects'.

Haraldr the Severe is also happy in good times, as the saga frequently reveals, and when the fateful day dawns his men are determined to follow him to the death (*Msk.* I, 319). Hákon Þórir's foster-son is *allra manna vinsælastr við bændr* (*Msk.* II, 17) 'the most popular with the farmers', and there is widespread grief at his death. Sigurðr the Noisy composes some lines about the happiness of his subjects: *Gótt vas í gamma / þars vér glaðir drukkum / ... vasa þar gamans vant / at gamans drykkju / þegn gladdi þegn ...* (*Msk.* II, 193) 'It was pleasant in the turf hut where in our happiness we drank ... there was no lack of cheer at the cheerful drinking, retainer delighted retainer ...'. The sons of Magnús Barelegs are described in the beginning as *listuligir, róir ok friðsamir við sína undir-menn* (*Msk.* II, 71) 'magnificent, calm and peaceful with their subjects' and having made friends *í mǫrgu lagi við landsmenn ok alla alþýðu* (*Msk.* II, 71) 'in many ways with their countrymen and ordinary folk'. At first, then, both the brothers are exemplary figures, but slowly their differences become clear. Eysteinn Magnússon turns out to be *inn mildasti af fé, ok allra konunga ... ástsælastr við sína menn* (*Msk.* II, 102) 'the most generous of all kings ... and very affectionate towards his people'. This is confirmed when he helps Ívarr Ingimundarson. Thus, a model king is prepared to support his subjects and make them happy, and Eysteinn is appropriately mourned (*Msk.* II, 138). Sigurðr the Crusader also shows great and frequent generosity (*Msk.* II, 130–131). When he returns from his crusade all of his people turn out to welcome him and verses are composed about *hversu fegnir menn urðu honum er hann kom heim í land* (*Msk.* II, 100) 'how glad people were when he arrived home'. But it is not long before he becomes *fálátr ok ómálugr, lítt talaðr á þingum* (*Msk.* II, 105) 'reserved and taciturn, and spoke little at assemblies' and starts to have fits (*Msk.* II, 106). Still later he is gloomy at a feast, and Eysteinn feels the need to remind him that it is *'várr sómi at gleðja menn vára'* '"our honour to entertain our men"'. Sigurðr answers him: *'Ver þú svá kátr sem þér sýnisk. Lát mik ráða minni gleði'* (*Msk.* II, 131) '"You can be as happy as you choose; allow me to decide on my own happiness"'. By being unhappy, Sigurðr is letting his men down. Kings should be happy, and when they are unhappy the whole court suffers (see *Msk.* II, 139–140).

The emphasis on the good cheer and happiness, the affection and popularity of a king, stems from the author's interest in society and the dealings among its members. Courtesy is a virtue of a new age, and is more important than the arts of war, courage and joy in battle. Though such qualities also have a part to play in *Morkinskinna*, it is magnanimity and cheerfulness that feature more prominently.[6]

Weighty obligations

Queen Ingiríðr, the widow of Haraldr Gilchrist, is on her way from church one day when she virtually trips over the body of Sigurðr Dandyhat, one of Haraldr's old courtiers. She hastens to her son, King Ingi, and says *'hann lengi mundu lítinn konung ef hann vildi ekki at hafask þótt hirðmenn hans væri drepnir annarr at ǫðrum sem svín'* (*Msk.* II, 232) '"he would not

---

6   J. David Burnley (*Courtliness and Literature in Medieval England*, pp. 64–75) considers the two types of magnanimity the highest virtues in the ideology of the courtiers, along with self-control; see also Jaeger, *The Origins of Courtliness*, pp. 28–48; *The Envy of Angels*, pp. 102–106 and Sverrir Jakobsson, 'Uppruni nútímans á 13. öld.'

amount to much of a king if he failed to react when his courtiers were killed one after another like swine"'. Gregoríus Dagsson adds that Ingi's brothers would become even more assertive

> '[n]ú er þeir sjá at þú hefsk ekki at þá munu þeir taka þik af konungdóminum er vinir þínir eru drepnir áðr.' (*Msk.* II, 233).

> 'when they now see that you do not react, and they will deprive you of your kingdom after they have killed off your friends'.

Were Ingi not to react to this emergency, he might well be toppled from his throne.

Royal power demands determination and kings have certain responsibilities to discharge. The deeds of Óláfr the Quiet reveal his sense of the monarch's role: *sá hann hvat konungdóminum hæfði, ok eru mǫrg verk hans at telja, þau sem bæði eru góð ok konunglig* (*Msk.* II, 10) 'he saw what was good for the kingdom, and many works of his may be counted as both good and worthy of a king'. Mention is made of his support of the church, the adoration of Saint Óláfr and the keeping of the peace. Kings ought to help towns to thrive and to preserve the peace for the benefit of merchants.[7] So seriously does Magnús Barelegs take the task of keeping peace that when the Þrændir rise up in revolt, he says he cannot be called a king *'nema ek gefa stǫkk þessum ófriði'* (*Msk.* II, 22) '"unless I suppress this insurrection"'. The *Morkinskinna* view on war and peace seems to be that it is better to win land through stealth and guile rather than iron and blood (see *Msk.* II, 101, 133). Merchants and farmers always want peace rather than conflict where they conduct their affairs and the king is obliged to bring this about.[8] Kings in *Morkinskinna* are repeatedly shown as judges and lawgivers. For some royal officials, this seems to have been a difficult lot. A young reeve in England complains about his judicial role:

---

7 Ármann Jakobsson, *Í leit að konungi*, pp. 179–180; Sverrir Jakobsson 'Griðamál á ófriðaröld.'

8 See Sverrir Jakobsson ('Griðamál á ófriðaröld' and 'Friðarviðleitni kirkjunnar á 13. öld') on peace negotiations in the Middle Ages and the concept of the 'king's peace.' Ármann Jakobsson (*Í leit að konungi*, pp. 179–180) discusses the obligations of the king to the non-combatant classes, such as clerics and merchants.

'ek em þó maðr ungr ok lítt vanr at sitja yfir málum manna,
ok er mér enn mart ókunnigt þat er þessu fylgir.' (*Msk.* II,
55).

'I am a young man and little accustomed to sit in judgement
of legal matters, and there is still much in all this that I am
ignorant of'.[9]

The kings in *Morkinskinna* are social institutions. The saga does not distinguish between the individual and the communal; kings are both. However,
the social dimension is unstable, for kings are not absolute rulers who seize
power and hold it without effort. In the society of the saga, power, law and
justice, money and fame, are all contested. These matters are constantly in
a state of flux, no less than in the society of the Sagas of Icelanders. Despite its decorative surface, *Morkinskinna* society is harsh, and no one can
be certain of his or her position, not even a king. Kings find themselves
in a continual struggle to maintain their position in society, either against
other kings or powerful chieftains. Kings need to carry out their obligations and maintain their power base. Although Ingi is a king, his mother
and Gregoríus Dagsson are able to compel him to kill his brother Sigurðr.

The saga in its extant form ends with King Eysteinn Haraldsson suffering defeat at the hands of his brother Ingi. He hides in the bushes, but
is found by Símon skálpr 'the Scabbard': *Símon mælti ok heilsaði honum:
'Heill, lávarðr,' segir hann. Konungr svarar: 'Ek ætla nú at þú þykkisk
ekki síðr minn lávarðr'* (*Msk.* II, 239) 'Símon spoke and greeted him:
"Greetings, my lord". The king answered: "I imagine you regard yourself
as my lord"'. An unbridgeable gap separates king and cottager, but with
society in constant flux it is impossible for everyone to know what tomorrow will bring for them. In *Morkinskinna* only two kings, Óláfr the Quiet
and Sigurðr the Crusader, live past their thirty-fifth year and die in their
beds; and one of those, Sigurðr the Crusader, only after suffering from a
protracted mental illness. It is hard to be king in such a society, as the cut-
ting words of King Eysteinn in response to Símon the Scabbard remind us.

---

9   On the king's role as judge, see Ármann Jakobsson, *Í leit að konungi*, pp. 180–185.
    One of the most remarkable discussions about kings, conduct of lawsuits and law
    occurs in 'Þinga saga.'

Although Símon addresses him with due decorum, the words and title that he uses are largely formulaic. In their dealings from that point onwards, only Símon can make the important decisions. Eysteinn can despise but not defeat him; he has nothing to offer but words.

A noble man worth his weight in gold

While Magnús the Good lies on his deathbed, Haraldr the Severe asks him what he had done with the gold he had presented to him as gift:

> 'Lít hér á borðin, frændi,' segir hann, 'er skipuð eru góðum drengjum ok dýrligum. Þeim sǫmum hefi ek gefit gullit ok haft í móti gullinu ást þeira ok hollostu, ok er víst betri fylgð ok framganga eins góðs drengs en mikit fé.' (*Msk.* I, 169).

> 'Look around the tables here, kinsman', he said, 'which are occupied by noble and excellent men. To these same men I have given gold and in return for the gold I have received their love and loyalty, and it is certainly better to have the loyalty and devotion of a good man than a lot of gold'.

Such a sentiment is to be expected of a generous king. In *Morkinskinna* there is a keen interest in everything that unites retainer and king. When Sigurðr the Crusader embarks on a crusade he has *með sér fjǫlmennt ok gott mannval, ok þó þá eina er sjálfir vildu fara ok veita honum fylgð ok fǫruneyti* (*Msk.* II, 71–72) 'with him a numerous and select company of men but only those who wanted to go and give him support and fellowship'. In warfare, a king and his men form something resembling a competitive team. In the saga, robbing and plundering, ransoming captives and inciting each other prior to battle are important functions of combat units, while the king delivers rousing speeches and lays down battle plans, as can also be seen in *Sverris saga*.[10] Kings are the wise fathers who can be relied upon – not least Haraldr the Severe (*Msk.* I, 99). The chief virtues of

---

10 See Ármann Jakobsson, *Í leit að konungi*, pp. 257–64 and 212–22, and Bagge, *From Gang Leader to the Lord's Anointed: Kingship in Sverris saga and Hákonar saga Hákonarsonar*, pp. 20–49.

a brave retainer are obedience and loyalty. The disobedient are punished, but devotion, the positive side of obedience, is also clearly shown. Sometimes we encounter devoted subjects who have served many kings. One of them is Þorkell dyðrill 'the Fop', who claims,

> 'Ek hefi nú verit með nǫkkurum konungum ok þjónat þeim af minni kunnostu. Fyrst með Ólafi konungi Tryggvasyni er ek unna mest allra manna. Síðan var ek með feðr þínum, ok myndi hann eigi þess til mín geta at ek mynda svíkja son hans.' (*Msk.* I, 132).

> 'I have now been with various kings and served them as well as I knew how. First with King Óláfr Tryggvason, whom I loved best of all. Then I was with your father, and he would not expect me to be capable of deceiving his son'.

Þorkell's trust in Magnús the Good is an impressive endorsement, coming as it does from an old man who served *með feðr þínum í hernaði, ok unna ek honum sem sjálfum mér* (*Msk.* I, 133) 'in battle with your father, whom I love as I do myself'.[11]

During battle the devotion of retainers is tested to the limit. When Haraldr the Severe's men are offered clemency after his death, they refuse it and *vilja sigrask á óvinum sínum eða liggja þar allir um konung sinn* (*Msk.* I, 319) 'wish to defeat their enemies or all remain there with their king'. Things turn out differently when Magnús Barelegs urges his men on, noting '*Kann ok vera at nú megi þat sýnask hvat þér vilið veita yðrum konungi*' (*Msk.* II, 67) '"It may also be that it may now be revealed how you wish to serve your king"'. But when the men of Upplǫnd ought to be shooting at the Irish as they crossed the fen, they

> kǫstuðu þó heldr skjǫldum á bak sér ok runnu sem þeir máttu af taka til skipanna.
>
> Þá kallaði Magnús konungr á Þorgrím húfu ok mælti: 'Óvitr var ek þann dag er ek gerða útlagan Sigurð hund, ok var

---

11 Þorgils the fisherman and Sigurðr Dandyhat are two other courtiers who likewise served more than one king (*Msk.* I, 288 and II, 232).

hitt þó miklu fíflsligra er ek gørða þik lendan mann, ok
ódrengiliga skilsk þú nú við mik, ok minnask mætta ek
þessa, ok eigi myndi Sigurðr svá fara ef hann væri hér.'
(*Msk.* II, 68).

put their shields on their backs and ran as fast as they could
to their ships.

Then King Magnús called out to Þorgrímr the Cap, saying:
'I was unwise on that day when I outlawed Sigurðr the Dog
although it was much more foolish to have made you a chieftain. You take your leave from us in a dishonourable way,
and this ought to be remembered, and Sigurðr would not
behave in this fashion if he were here'.

Víðkunnr Jónsson proves to be a better man and enhances his fame in
the service of his king (*Msk.* II, 69–70). The same applies to Sigurðr
Hranason, who later sends men to Eysteinn Magnússon for supporting
troops and states that

'ok ef konungr hefir nǫkkurar tregður í at fara, segið honum
at ek ætla at síðarsta lagi skilðumk ek við fǫður hans vestr
á Írlandi.' (*Msk.* II, 112).

'if the king is somewhat reluctant to come, tell him that I
think it was only at the last moment that I left his father
west in Ireland'.

Eysteinn needed little persuasion. Sigurðr and Víðkunnr turn out to be
worth their weight in gold in their devotion. Later Sigurðr Hranason is
reluctant to befriend Sigurðr the Crusader, claiming

'hvé mikit fé sem við liggr, ok þótt líf mitt liggi við, þá mun
ek ǿngan mann virða meira um aldr en Eystein konung meðan ek lifi.' (*Msk.* II, 130).

'no matter how much money is involved and though my life
depends upon it, I will never honour any man more than
King Eysteinn for as long as I live'.

Despite the coolness between the brothers, King Sigurðr can only accept this expression of loyalty.

The importance of the devotion a subject owes his king is symbolised in the image of a courtier bearing the king in his arms. Just as Aeneas carried his father on his back at the fall of Troy, Hreiðarr Grjótgarðsson takes Magnús the Blind in his arms in an attempt to escape with him. It is said of Hreiðarr: *Ok þat mæltu allir at hann þótti vel ok prúðliga hafa fylgt sínum lánardróttni, ok gott er hverjum er slíkan orðróm getr (Msk.* II, 203) 'And everyone said that he had followed his lord well and valiantly, and it is good for anyone who receives such praise'. Such behaviour was widely regarded as exemplary, and the voice of the saga confirms this. Hreiðarr demonstrates by his deeds what the word service really means.

The relations between subjects and kings in times of conflict are explored at length in several kings' sagas, whereas *Morkinskinna* affords greater prominence to peacetime relations.[12] When individual subjects are described, attention is also focused at the same time on the general run of retainers. Medieval culture promoted exemplary behaviour and figures, and the saints and knights of chivalric romances were models that could help to promote the service mentality that was a necessary precondition for any hierarchical society, whether we mean an actual feudal system or not.[13] In Iceland exemplary figures and behaviour could be found in works such as *Morkinskinna.* Everyone must find someone to serve; kings serve subjects, but the court and all the people in the country serve kings. Service, of course, works both ways. Though subjects obey their king, kings too must carry out their side of the bargain.[14] A king that does not protect his men is a king in name only, as Queen Ingiríðr points out to her son Ingi when his men are being killed *sem svín* 'like swine'. An envoy of Magnús Barelegs's describes the pact between kings and subjects in this way:

'en nú vill konungr sýna sik í allri blíðu til allra sinna manna, þeira er til hans vilja þjóna, býzk til forystu ok at

12 *Sverris saga* also dramatises the dealing of kings and subjects, often in times of conflict, whereas in *Morkinskinna* the focus is more on peacetime relations.

13 Lars Bisgaard, *Tjenesteideal og fromhedsideal: Studier i adelens tænkemåde i dansk senmiddelalder,* pp. 23–40.

14 On reciprocity in human intercourse, see, among others, Peter Burke, *History and Social Theory,* pp. 69–71.

vera brjóst fyr ǫllum Nóregsmǫnnum, stórum ok smám. Þar
í móti vill hann hafa af sínum landsmǫnnum góða þjónostu
ok sœmilga fylgð' (*Msk.* II, 31).

'but now the king wishes to show himself in the most bene-
volent way to all his men, to those who wish to serve him –
he offers to lead and be a bulwark for all Norwegians, great
and small. In return he wishes to receive from his countrymen good service and all due obedience'.

The message is, in this instance, not well received. But the principle applies in general: the king defends his subjects, and they serve him. Each
has their obligations that are important in the saga's representation of society.

This pact does not mean that subjects must always remain silent and
serve blindly. An unnamed man reproaches Magnús the Good for allowing
a heathen with magical powers to kill his men *sem búfé* (*Msk.* I, 62) 'like
cattle'. They duly rout the heathens, and long afterwards the man rewards
the king for having accepted his advice *lítillátliga* (*Msk.* I, 133) 'humbly'.
Kings cannot rule without good advice. While King Óláfr the Quiet reigns,
there is even a special office for the most eminent of men, the *konungs
ráðgjafi* 'king's advisor' (*Msk.* II, 8). Such a man is Sigurðr Sigurðarson
who is said to be one of the wisest men in Norway (*Msk.* II, 125), and
when he advises Magnús Barelegs to retreat from Ireland, the king fails
to take his advice and subsequently falls in battle (*Msk.* II, 65–66).

The saga also contains many examples of subjects who admonish a
king. Sigvatr the Poet is the first. King Magnús has become unpopular
and *þótti nú vinum hans þǫrf á at nǫkkurr segði konunginum hvar komit
var* (*Msk.* I, 31) 'and his friends thought the time had come for someone
to tell the king how far matters had deteriorated'. Chosen by lot for the
task, Sigvatr composes *Bersǫglisvísur*. The king considers *þessum ráðum
ok áminningum sem Sigvatr skáld hefir til skipat í kvæðinu* (*Msk.* I, 42)
'the counsels and admonitions that Sigvatr had woven into this poem',
and accepts this counsel, not least because Sigvatr composes a poem in
his honour and manages to praise him although with concealed condem-
nation. Brandr the Bountiful succeeds in admonishing Haraldr through
symbolic gestures, delivering a pointed message that does not offend him

(*Msk.* I, 230–232). Again, Stúfr the Blind manages to criticise Haraldr without insulting him, by inexplicably bursting into laughter (*Msk.* I, 291). Haraldr grasps the implication of his remarks, and both maintain their dignity.

During the period when Sigurðr the Crusader is suffering from his mental illness, there are four incidents in which a subject reprimands the king or takes some action to preserve him from some misfortune. The king needs these interventions and is always grateful, even if he cannot always control his temper. Óttarr the Trout is one of these impetuous subjects, and the king praises him for choosing '*svá orðunum at mér yrði at virðing*' (*Msk.* II, 140) "'his words in such a way as to respect me'". If someone seeks to act in the best interests of the king but without his approval it is essential to proceed with caution. Kolbeinn Cluck does Magnús Barelegs a favour by reconciling him with Sveinki Steinarsson (*Msk.* II, 35–37). The negotiations are conducted without the king's knowledge, but the point seems to be that such actions can be taken on behalf of the king if they are in his best interest. For example, Earl Ormr Skoptason offers a truce to Sveinn Úlfsson without consulting King Magnús in advance and thereby risks incurring the king's anger. Instead, however, he is rewarded by a king ready and able to recognise a valuable initiative (*Msk.* I, 133). The relations between kings and their subjects are marked by moderation, and these relations are the foundation of the society that is depicted in *Morkinskinna*.

'Too fine for an earl'

Although kings are the chief characters in *Morkinskinna* the deeds of their greater and lesser subjects are also recounted in considerable detail. The tales of each and every one of them are examples of service to a king.

Early in the saga Einarr Paunch-Shaker is chosen to be Magnús the Good's foster-father and guardian, and the Russian king and queen trust no one more than Einarr (*Msk.* I, 19). Once the kingdom is safely in the hands of Magnús, the king takes offence at Kálfr Árnason, and Einarr has a hand in fuelling the king's displeasure (*Msk.* I, 29). Einarr is ruthless, and obviously considers it his job to protect the king from those who are getting above themselves in Norway. When Sveinn Úlfsson is angling for the friendship of the king, Magnús receives him well, gives him gifts and the title of Earl, but when Einarr sees Sveinn's disdainful refusal of Magnús's gifts,

> mælti hann: 'Ofjarl, ofjarl, fóstri,' segir hann. Konungr segir styggiliga: 'Fátt ætli þér at eg kunna at líta ok øngva mann-raun muni kunna at því at yðr þykkir sumt ofjarlar en sumt ekki at manni.' (*Msk.* I, 51).

> he said: 'too fine for an earl, too fine for an earl, my foster-son', he says. The king responds angrily: 'You think that I see little and have no experience of men, since you think some too fine to be Earls but some not fine enough to be a man'.

The relationship between the king and Einarr resembles that between parents and children – the latter wish to choose their own friends and think that parents have no faith in their judgement. The power relations involved are, however, very different, and Einarr recognises this and knows his place. He proves to be correct on this occasion. Einarr finds himself opposing the king's actions when Haraldr the Severe lands in and wishes to conquer Norway:

> Síðan eru til heimtir ríkismenn ok upp borit af Magnúsi kon-ungi hvers Haraldr beiddisk. Þá svaraði Einarr þambarskelf-ir fyrst ríkismanna: 'Fjarri vartu þá, Haraldr, er vér unnum land af Knýtlingum.[15] Ok ekki fýsumsk vér at tvískiptask milli hǫfðingja. Hǫfum vér jafnan einum senn þjónat, ok svá mun enn vera meðan Magnús konungr heldr ríkinu ok lífi sínu.' Eptir þessi rœðu hneigjask allir ríkismenn í sínum svǫrum (*Msk.* I, 120–121).

> Then the country's elite were summoned, and Magnús raised the matter that Haraldr had requested. Then Einarr Paunch-Shaker answered first for the governors: 'You were

---

15 The Knýtlingar are the family of the Danish kings, the descendants of King Knútr the Powerful (sometimes known as the Knútlingar). The reference here is to the fact that Knútr's son was king of Norway before Magnús.

far away, Haraldr, when we won the land from the Knútr family, and we are not eager to be divided between two rulers. We have always served one at a time, and such will be the case while King Magnús lives and rules the kingdom'. After this speech all the governors tended the same way in their answers.

Einarr spoils the case for Haraldr, and Magnús comes to believe later that he was ill-advised (*Msk.* I, 122–123). However, the story of this joint rule of the kings implies that there is much in what Einarr says.

In the disputes between Haraldr and Magnús, Einarr takes it upon himself to look after Magnús's interests and, at a meeting with Haraldr (*Msk.* I, 137–138), wrecks the latter's attempts to impose taxes at the assembly. Relations remain cool between Einarr and Haraldr when Magnús dies, and the situation is not improved when Einarr prefers to accompany Magnús' body north to be buried rather than to go with Haraldr on a military expedition against Denmark (*Msk.* I, 173). Matters do not come to a head until much later, however. Despite all their differences, Haraldr desires to maintain peaceful relations with Einarr. Similarly, Einarr emphatically rejects the chance to betray Haraldr. Both men, of course, are domineering and ruthless, but wise enough to keep the peace. In the end, Einarr's emotional excess brings about his own demise, so that we can say that his own term *ofjarl* applies to him as well. Although Haraldr has previously been furious with Einarr (*Msk.* I, 138), he tolerates him until Einarr strikes. When Haraldr puts Einarr's loyalty to the test, he asks his envoy: '*Hversu fóru orð með yðr Einari kappanum á Gimsum?*' (*Msk.* I, 212) '"What was the result of your exchange with that old scrapper Einarr at Gimsar?"'. There is, of course, a comic element in the word *kappi*, literally 'warrior', here 'scrapper'; despite everything, Haraldr enjoys a wry joke at Einarr's expense. For his own part, Einarr is able to make a joke at his own expense, referring to himself on one occasion as *gamall oxi* (*Msk.* I, 28) 'an old ox', and accompanying King Magnús in a comically implausible disguise to spy on his men (*Msk.* I, 59).

The relationship between King Magnús and Einarr is a loving one, and the king always calls him *fóstri* 'foster-father'. When he becomes ill, Einarr is by his side and, on his deathbed, Magnús requests Haraldr to be '*vinir vina minna*' (*Msk.* I, 168) "'a friend to my friends'". Haraldr promises to do so, but Einarr has his doubts and understands very well how great a personal loss Magnús's death is for him. His grief runs deep: the friendship between Magnús and Einarr is put to the test when Þorsteinn Hallsson, while in the king's disfavour, offers Einarr some stud horses. Einarr refuses them, but his son Einriði does not. This gift obligates father and son to Þorsteinn, an obligation that in turn endangers the friendship between Einarr and the king. Einarr is thus disinclined to visit the king over Christmas, but Einriði prepares to go in spite of this. Einarr then decides to go after all and is upset with Einriði:

> 'Allkynlig er þín ætlun, sœkja heim Magnús konung ok Þor-
> steinn með þér. Far heim heldr á Gimsar, en ek mun hitta
> konung, ok mun ek alls við þurfa at sættir verði teknar. En
> ek kann hvárntveggja ykkarn konung at ekki mynduð it svá
> stilla ykkrum orðum at þat myndi hlýða' (*Msk.* I, 141–142).

> 'Your intention to visit King Magnús and take Þorsteinn
> along is strange indeed! Return home to Gimsar instead, and
> I will visit the king. I will have a great deal of trouble be-
> ing reconciled with the king, but I know both you and the
> king well enough to know that you are incapable of choos-
> ing your words fittingly'.

Einarr regards the king as no less of a son than Einriði, and he cannot abide conflict between them – he is in the position of a father reconciling two sons.[16] Finally, Einarr visits the king, who receives him well but does not wish to discuss the matter of Þorsteinn before Einarr flies off the handle. Einarr's angry outburst and his dramatic behaviour are sufficient:

---

16 Conflicts between fathers and sons are less frequent in the *Íslendingasögur* and can
entail a clash between old and new customs; see Paul Schach, 'Some Observations on
the Generation Gap Theme in the Icelandic Sagas.' The dispute between Einarr and
Einriði may be interpreted as an *exemplum* about the rashness of youth and the wisdom
of age. On the social position of young men, see Georges Duby, 'Les "jeunes" dans
la société aristocratique dans la France du Nord-Ouest au XIIᵉ siècle'; compare Brian
Stock, *The Implications of Literacy. Written Language and Models of Interpretation
in the Eleventh and Twelfth Centuries*, pp. 476–489.

Konungr ríss upp ok eptir honum ok leggr hǫnd á háls Einari ok mælir: 'Kom heill ok sæll, fóstri,' segir hann; 'þat skal aldregi verða at okkra vináttu skili' (*Msk.* I, 142).

The king went after him and laid his arm on Einarr's neck, saying: 'Be assured of our affection, foster-father', he says, 'nothing will ever damage our friendship'.

Friendship wins out over pride.

Although the saga seems to favour Haraldr in his feud with Einarr, at the end the narrative perspective focuses on Einarr. The old man sees the writing on the wall, but still attempts to save Einriði:

Ok Einarr gekk at hǫllinni ok inn síðan. Þá mælti hann: 'Myrkt er í málstofu konungs.' Einarr bað Einriða son sinn, standa í forstofunni ok lézk ætla at konungr myndi eigi á hann ráða ef hann væri eptir. Ok er Einarr kemr í stofuna þá bera þeir menn vápn á hann er þar eru fyrir. Einarr veðr þá at þar er konungr er ok hǫggr til hans, ok sakar hann ekki, því at hann er fyr í tveim brynjum. Þá mælti Einarr: 'Hvat bíta nú hundar konungs.' Ok er Einriði heyrði þat þá stenzk hann eigi ok hleypr inn, ok er sá maðr Árni nefndr er honum varð at bana. Ok var þar nú drepinn Einarr ok Einriði sonr hans er allra manna var vaskastr ok gǫrviligastr. (*Msk.* I, 216).

Einarr approached the hall and went in. Then he spoke: 'It is dark in the king's chamber'. Einarr told his son Einriði to wait in the antechamber and said he thought the king would not attack him if he stayed behind. When Einarr entered the king's room, he was attacked by armed men who had been waiting there. Einarr rushed forward to where the king was located, striking at him but failed to wound him because he was wearing two coats of mail. Then Einarr spoke: 'The king's dogs bite hard'. When Einriði heard that, he could not hold back any longer and ran in, and the man who killed him was named Árni. And then Einarr and Einriði his son, a most valiant and accomplished man, were killed.

The point of view focuses on Einarr, and Einriði's death was all the more poignant for that. King Haraldr had long since gained control over his temper, and because of that this deplorable act appears even more unnecessary and mournful than if it had occurred simply in a moment of ungovernable rage.

Concurrent with the early stages of Einarr's story is that of Kálfr Árnason, a nobleman in the service of Sveinn Álfífuson, who

> [h]afði ... heitit verit jarlsdómi af Knúti konungi ef hann felldi Óláf konung frá landi, ok svá var virðing hans mikil at hann skyldi leggja skip sitt næst konungsskipinu jafnan hvar sem þeir lágu í hǫfnum. (*Msk*. I, 16).

> had been promised an earldom by King Knútr if he drove King Óláfr from the country, and his honour was so great that he was granted the privilege of always anchoring his ship next to that of the king wherever they were anchored in a harbour.

In the Karl the Luckless episode, however, things take an unexpected turn when Kálfr captures Karl and takes refuge from King Sveinn.[17] Sveinn becomes suspicious of Kálfr's integrity, and wishes to be the first to betray him. Realising this, Kálfr sets sail for Russia and joins up with Magnús, who accepts his service and prefers, perhaps, to have Kálfr as his dubious ally than his certain enemy (*Msk*. I, 18). Einarr and Kálfr together become the king's counsellors; Kálfr dispenses wisdom, and Einarr provides the muscle (*Msk*. I, 23). Nevertheless, Kálfr eventually falls into disfavour, but once again shows his quick-wittedness and flees to the Orkneys (*Msk*. I, 30). What saves his life seems to be his swiftness under fire. Indeed, this has been demonstrated in a short and amusing tale (*Msk*. I, 28) that shows how he is ready for anything. Later he learns that Magnús would like him to rejoin his retinue if he will support the forces of Earl Rǫgnvaldr

---

17 It is not clear what became of the title of jarl that Kálfr was promised. Perhaps it is implied that Kálfr has at this point in the saga grown tired of petitioning for his reward. This is not the only promised jarldom that fails to materialise; Hákon Ívarsson leaves King Haraldr's service and joins up with King Sveinn of Denmark following Haraldr's failure to honour his promise to Hákon (see *Msk*. I, 257–258).

of Orkney, but it turns out that he changes sides yet again, this time in the middle of a battle, and does not return to the court of the Norwegian kings, but *hann leggsk í hernað eptir þenna bardaga ok gørisk víkingr mikill* (*Msk.* I, 44) 'he harried widely after that battle and became a great Viking'.[18]

In contrast to Einarr Paunch-Shaker, who remains faithful to Magnús even after the king is dead and buried, Kálfr Árnason is quick to switch allegiances. Both men are useful to the king, but he who fights on one side today and on another tomorrow can hardly be an exemplary figure. Yet even Einarr's steadfastness can arouse suspicion. His devotion to Magnús the Good is greater than his loyalty to the monarchy in general even though, finally, he has no wish to deceive Haraldr.

Sveinn Úlfsson's role in the saga is ambiguous, as he is at some point both king and retainer. He approaches Magnús the Good, speaks in *fagrmæli* 'flattering terms' and promises King Magnús *ǫllum sínum trúnaði ok vinfengi, ef hann vildi sæma hann í nǫkkuru léni til forráða* (*Msk.* I, 51) 'his complete loyalty and friendship if he will grant him some modest position'. He then betrays Magnús and later attempts to reel in Haraldr the Severe in order to betray him in the same manner (*Msk.* I, 119). With the growing coolness between Magnús and Haraldr, Magnús's feelings towards Sveinn become more generous. Shortly before Magnús' death, Sveinn says:

> 'Ek em níðingr fyr Magnúsi konungi, ok slíkt sama er Har-
> aldr konungr fyr mér, ok ójafnir konungar eru þeir, Magnús
> konungr ok Haraldr konungr.' (*Msk.* I, 167).

> 'I betrayed King Magnús, and King Haraldr did the same
> to me, and they are unequal kings, King Magnús and King
> Haraldr'.

By this time King Magnús regards him as a *gersimi* 'treasure' and his treachery is all but forgotten. On his deathbed he recommends that Sveinn be allowed to keep Denmark and to rule well and adds '*ef ek hefi nǫkkut*

---

18 On the figure of Kálfr, see Wolfgang Fleischhauer, *Kalf Arnason: Die Berührungen zwischen Heldenlied und Königssaga*.

í átt, ok ek ann honum nú ok bezt at njóta, því at mér þykkir hann rétt-
ligast til kominn' (*Msk.* I, 169) '"if I ever had any claim I now wish him
to have it and prosper in it and I think he has the just right to it"'. Sveinn
receives the news during his preparations for departure, intending to leave
the kingdom (*Msk.* I, 171–172) Instead, a long war begins against Haraldr,
who tirelessly slanders Sveinn as a traitor, and recalls *'hversu hann helt*
eiðana við Magnús konung' (*Msk.* I, 193) '"how he kept his oaths to King
Magnús"'. And, though Haraldr has the upper hand for a time, in the end
his men go over to Sveinn, who is said to be more popular (*Msk.* I, 216,
242). Thereafter Sveinn's situation improves steadily and his clashes with
Haraldr conclude in a stalemate.

Haraldr the Severe also has loyal retainers who follow him from beginning to end. One is Úlfr stallari 'the Marshall' whom we first encounter
in the king's service when Haraldr conquers various Sicilian towns by diverse ruses (*Msk.* I, 103) and is subsequently thrown into a dungeon along
with the king and Halldórr Snorrason (*Msk.* I, 109–111). Úlfr is thereafter
repeatedly seen in the service of the king (*Msk.* I, 206, 243–245), but dies
shortly after Haraldr embarks on his final military campaign to England
(*Msk.* I, 303). Halldórr, on the other hand, becomes estranged from the
king (*Msk.* I, 181–187) because of a series of rather undignified squabbles
revealing character flaws in both men.[19] Halldórr receives neither a position of honour equivalent to that of Úlfr nor does he marry into the king's
family; he is perhaps a better liegeman in war than in peace. Nevertheless,
Halldórr seems to occupy a place in the king's affection despite their contentious leave-taking as he is happy to learn that Halldórr later tells tales
of their foreign exploits while home in Iceland (*Msk.* I, 236). Sometimes
friendships simply deteriorate and friends cease to see eye to eye, so that
it matters little what had previously gone before.[20]

In the story of Magnús Barelegs, loyalty to the king is the key theme.
Steigar-Þórir has been introduced into the saga much earlier. When Haraldr the Severe arrives in Norway, he clearly wishes to reach an agreement

---

19 Bárðr upplenski 'the Uplander' asks Haraldr to remember *'skap Halldórs ok stirðlæti'*
   (*Msk.* I, 184) 'Halldórr's temper and stubbornness', but in the episode a similar character flaw in the king is clearly revealed.
20 Another of Haraldr's devoted followers is Eysteinn the Heathcock Þorbergsson, who
   leads the Norwegians in battle after the king's death (*Msk.* I, 321).

with Magnús the Good, but adopts the strategy of having himself crowned prior to their meeting, doubtless in order to strengthen his position. But no one dares to assign him the title before he arrives in Guðbrandsdalr. Then *einn maðr af búǫndum ... en þat var Þórir á Steig er síðan var mikill hǫfðingi, en þá var Þórir fimmtán vetra gamall er hann gaf Haraldi konungs nafn* (*Msk.* I, 125) 'a man among the landowners ... [enters the tale], Steigar-Þórir, who later becomes a great chieftain, but was then merely fifteen years old when he bestowed the title of king on Haraldr'. Already in his youth Þórir is eager to do what others dare not do: to go against the will of a king. At this time he supports King Haraldr, who later decides to test him and many other chieftains by offering them money ostensibly from King Sveinn. Þórir, like some others, accepts the money, but learns of the trick and *hvert víti þeir hǫfðu hreppt er við fénu hǫfðu tekit* (*Msk.* I, 213) 'what punishment those who had taken money had suffered'. He goes directly to meet Haraldr and says he had decided to '*taka við fénu, ok þótti mér betr komit at þér hefðuð en Danir*' (*Msk.* I, 213) '"accept the money, as it seemed better for you to have it rather than the Danes"'. Then he pretends that he must hurry away to settle a dispute, but does not show up at the feast for Haraldr:

> Þá mælti konungr: 'Hafi þik troll svá slægan, en þar er sá maðr er sízt má vita hvat í skapi býr, ok er þetta nú nǫkkut vant at skilja með hverju hann ferr, en ekki munu vit hann nú hafa at sinni. En svá segir mér hugr um at ósýnt sé hversu hans mál leiðir til lykða, fyrir sakir pretta hans ok ótrúleika.' (*Msk.* I, 213–214).

> The king spoke: 'May the trolls take you, you old fox, and here is a man who can least be seen through and it is pretty tough to work out what he is up to. We can do nothing to him for the time being, but I suspect that it will be difficult to see how things will end with him because of his deceit and lack of loyalty'.

Steigar-Þórir is harshly judged here; he has two fatal character traits, deceit and infidelity. He succeeds in avoiding Haraldr's wrath, but when it comes time to accompany Haraldr on his fateful campaign in England, Þórir is nowhere to be seen *því at hann hafði dreymt illa um konung* (*Msk.* I, 303) 'because he had an ominous dream about the king'.

Steigar-Þórir had been exposed as deceitful before Magnús Barelegs came to power. He acts for his own benefit, and for a long time has got away with it. When Óláfr the Quiet dies, the Þrændir choose Þórir's foster-son, Hákon Magnússon, as king. Power over the land seems within Þórir's grasp when his foster-son dies unexpectedly. Then Þórir goes a step too far and is the chief instigator behind the decision of the Þrændir to take as their king a Sveinn of dubious background (*Msk.* II, 18). This troop begins a campaign of plundering and violence. An uprising is mounted, which is put down bloodily, and Þórir is executed despite his advanced age and frail health. The description is detailed and brutal and clearly creates sympathy for Þórir, who is witty and sarcastic (see part III, chapter 2). His men joke that

> 'Ok eigi mun gǫrt hafa verit jafn frítt skip síðan Ormr inn langi var gǫrr. Þetta er ok vǫskum drengjum skipat ok eru glíkligir til góðrar varnar.' (*Msk.* II, 24)

> 'no fairer ship will have been built since the Long Serpent. It is also manned with brave men, and they will surely make a brave defence'.

But they then flee like scared rabbits, leaving Þórir and Egill Áskelsson to their own devices. Then Þórir says:

> 'Vera má at várt skip sé eigi verr skipat en Ormr inn langi var, en þess get ek at fleiri felli þar, en hér renni fleiri.' (*Msk.* II, 24).

> 'It may be that our ship is not less well built than the Long Serpent, but I wager that more men died there, and more run away here'.[21]

---

21 Þórir may be said to be partly vindicated later since King Eysteinn marries his daughter (*Msk.* II, 102). Andersson has pointed out that Steigar-Þórir's family might be one of the sources for the saga here, and this could explain the obvious empathy with his plight (Andersson and Gade, *Morkinskinna*, pp. 429, 437 and 448).

Although King Magnús appears to be a complete scoundrel, Þórir is nevertheless deceitful. The king's might undoubtedly makes right.

Magnús Barelegs has a model liegeman, Víðkunnr Jónsson, who serves him to the end (*Msk.* II, 69–70). It is Magnús's cruel fate to be, like Steigar-Þórir, abandoned by his men. Víðkunnr is often mentioned among the followers of the sons of Magnús. He is so faithful that although he has sympathy with King Eysteinn in 'Þinga saga', he decides to back King Sigurðr since he is his vassal (*Msk.* II, 119–120). He fosters Sigurðr's son Magnús and supports him in his clash with the sons of Haraldr (*Msk.* II, 193). By this time Víðkunnr is an old man, but his loyalty is as strong as ever. Sigurðr Hranason is also said to have followed Magnús to Ireland when others ran away (*Msk.* II, 112). When he falls out with Sigurðr the Crusader, severe strife breaks out between the two kings. Then Sigurðr Hranason chooses to place his fate in King Sigurðr's hands and trust to his mercy, as befits a loyal subject. Following a violent period, order is established under the rule of Magnús's sons as subjects obey their kings.

Toward the end of the story of Sigurðr the Crusader another model subject makes his appearance, Óttarr the Trout. He is first a chamberlain, but then gains access to the king with his heroic behaviour and courtly bearing (see part III, chapter 2), and is thereafter in the first rank of Norwegian courtiers. He is in the loop when the Þrændir made Sigurðr Haraldsson king when he was four years old (*Msk.* II, 179). Afterwards he is at the forefront of Sigurðr's troop and persuades others that it is right and proper that the brothers join together against Sigurðr the Noisy (*Msk.* II, 200). He then married Ingiríðr, the widow of King Haraldr Gilchrist, and became a *mikill styrkðarmaðr ríkis Inga konungs meðan hann var í barnæsku* (*Msk.* II, 212) 'a great supporter of the rule of King Ingi while he was a child'. Sigurðr, Ingi's brother, understandably regards Óttarr as biased against him and finally Óttarr is killed (*Msk.* II, 212).

These tales about subjects all address the same theme, how to be a good subject to a king. Kings require noble and courageous subjects, but such leaders should not become *ofjarl* 'too fine for an earl', and loyalty must be treated with care.

4. The Icelandic Identity

Icelandic and Scandinavian images of the self

'Nú skal jafnmæli með okkr,' segir konungr; 'skaltu nú standa upp ok leggja af þér skikkju, ok vil ek sjá þik.' Hreið-arr fleygir af sér feldinum ok hefir saurgar krummur – maðr-inn hentr mjǫk og ljótr – en þvegnar heldr latliga. Konungr hyggr at honum vandliga (*Msk.* I, 156).

'Now it is my turn', said the king. 'Stand up and take off your cloak so that I can see you'. Hreiðarr threw off his cloak, revealing gnarled and dirty hands; the man had quite ugly hands that were badly cared for. The king studied him closely.

When Hreiðarr the Simple has circled Magnús the Good, the king has an opportunity to return his gaze and so does the saga audience. All eyes are on the Icelander's large and filthy hands. His scruffy bearing cannot help but make us think of the *kolbítr*, the fairy-tale hero who in the end wins half of the kingdom along with the princess. In Hreiðarr's case the treasure that is granted to him is not a princess but rather a king's friend-ship. At their parting Magnús wishes to give him an island off the coast of Norway, which, while small, has good grazing and excellent farmland. Hreiðarr responds: '*Þar skal ek samtengja með Nóreg ok Ísland*' (*Msk.* I, 164) '"There I shall unite Norway and Iceland"'. The king does not think much of this notion and decides to give Hreiðarr money instead, since the Icelander's continued stay in Norway would have involved considerable danger from King Haraldr.[1] Hreiðarr had acted as though he were a dip-

---

1 Andersson and Gade (*Morkinskinna*, p. 433, note 21) considers that this 'peculiar idea … suggests some larger theme'; here 'a real parodistic edge' may be discerned and reference is made to Óláfr the Saint's attempts to obtain Grímsey in Eyjafjörður as a gift from Icelanders.

lomatic representative of Iceland. But all fun contains a serious element. In *Morkinskinna* Iceland and Norway are united.

In Norway it appears as though the Icelander is the clown or the alien who in a real sense represents the viewpoint of the saga, not least in the narrative episodes. The viewpoint is also the author's, who is probably an Icelander himself and who, when he first came to Norway, found himself, as it were, more or less in Hreiðarr's shoes. Stories are instrumental in creating identities,[2] and they have their roots in life and in the understanding of an author's sense of his own identity. In the stories of Icelanders who come to Norway and enter into the service of a king, the author may well be indirectly indulging himself in a form of autobiography. *Morkinskinna* does not just treat kings but also Icelanders in Norway.[3]

When the loss of life among the troops of Magnús the Blind is recounted, the narrator remarks: *Þá fellu tveir íslenzkir menn, Sigurðr prestur, sonr Bergþórs Mássonar, annarr Klemet sonr Ara Einarssonar (Msk.* II, 205) 'And two Icelanders fell there – Sigurðr the Priest, the son of Bergþórr Másson, and Klemet, the son of Ari Einarsson'. Not only is special reference made to Icelanders in these important events but also to their families in order that the contemporary saga listeners recognise them.[4] They achieve a certain amount of attention because they are abroad. Similarly, it is said that Auðun is from the Northwest of Iceland and that Sneglu-Halli is from the north although their genealogies are not mentioned. It clearly matters what part of Iceland somebody comes from.

Morkinskinna is a testimony to the personal image of Icelanders in the Middle Ages. But the words *nationality* and *national consciousness* are problematic: Icelanders were not only citizens of Iceland but also Christians, people from a particular valley, or Sturlungs. It matters little until one goes abroad whether a person is Danish, Norwegian or Icelandic, but, equally, the further an individual ventures from home, the less important it becomes with each new day. In Constantinople Icelanders were an unnamed subset of the group of Scandinavians:

2   Davíð Erlingsson, 'Saga gerir mann: Hugleiðing um gildi og stöðu hugvísinda.'
3   See also Ármann Jakobsson, 'Konungurinn og ég: Sjálfsmynd Íslendings frá 13. öld.'
4   The saga narrator commonly speaks with familiarity about Icelanders and their affairs. In the account of Sigurðr the Noisy's stay with Þorgils Oddason it is clearly assumed that the contemporary saga listener knows who Þorgils is (*Msk.* II, 173–175).

En mikill fjǫlði var þar áðr fyrir Norðmanna, er þeir kalla
Væringja. Þar var sá maðr íslenzkr er Már hét ok var Hún-
røðarson, faðir Hafliða Mássonar (*Msk.* I, 88).

A great multitude of Scandinavians was already there, and
they were called Varangians. A man named Már was also
there, the son of Húnrøðr, the father of Hafliði Másson.

Again, Eldjárn from Húsavík is called a Norwegian in England (*Msk.* II,
54–55). It is primarily in Norway that it is important to be an Icelander,
but this does not suggest an inherent opposition to the Norwegian king
and his authority. Icelandic nationality is not implicit in the political independence of Iceland but rather in the image Icelanders have of themselves
in Norway.[5]

The sense of self that is shared by Scandinavians in remote lands was
formed in a similar fashion. Foreign countries catalyse an individual's personal image. This is perhaps most apparent in the disputes between the
Varangians under the leadership of Haraldr the Severe (calling himself
Norðbrikt) and Gyrgir, a kinsman of the queen:

Þá kom til hǫfðinginn Gyrgir ok bað Væringja flytja í brot
tjǫld sín. Norðbrikt segir: 'Ekki er þat réttligt, ok ekki hefir
þat verit Væringja háttr at flytjask í dalverpi undan Grikkj-
um.' (*Msk.* I, 91).

Then the chieftain Gyrgir arrived and ordered the Varangians to move their tents. Norðbrikt said: 'That is not lawful,
and it has never been the custom of the Varangians to move
into a ditch for the Greeks.

Haraldr regards it as natural that Scandinavians are superior to Greeks, yet
they are visitors in the land of one of the world's then greatest superpowers.

---

5 My remarks here are based on Sverrir Jakobsson, 'Hvers konar þjóð voru Íslendingar
á miðöldum?'; 'Defining a Nation: Popular and Public Identity in the Middle Ages.'
A remarkable contribution to the emergence of such group consciousness in historical writings can be found in James Fentress and Chris Wickham, *Social Memory*,
pp. 162–72, who find examples in medieval Icelandic society.

Icelandic nationality has no special importance in Constantinople, but being Scandinavian does. Among the Greeks, moreover, Scandinavians have much in common with other westerners; Norðbrikt is not only the leader of the Scandinavians in battle for the emperor but also of *latínumenn* (*Msk.* I, 93) 'westerners'.[6]

The narrative accounts of the foreign travels of Sigurðr the Crusader (see part III, chapter 1 and part IV, chapter 2) throw no less light on the kings of Norway and the Norwegians themselves. In such travelogues men measure themselves against the world. Although the splendour in Constantinople is greater than in the far north, the two kings are presented as equals. Sigurðr and his Norwegians are elevated through this trip. Their achievements are often mentioned with pride, and the trip is a showcase for Norwegian modesty and military prowess (*Msk.* I, 75–96).[7] In the wars with Danes and Gautar 'Geats', Norwegians seem to be a unit. Generally, adversaries are lumped together under a national designation and referred to as the followers of a specific king. Often Norwegians are a part of Danish or Swedish troops, even in an army led by a Norwegian pretender, as when Magnús the Blind and Sigurðr the Noisy attempt to topple the sons of Haraldr. There are nevertheless times where particular characteristics are attributed to nations. Haraldr the Severe accuses the Danes of being more willing to raise pigs than to fight (*Msk.* I, 197), and the Gautar appear to be ill-suited to the rigours of military life (*Msk.* I, 24, 173, 177–178, 188, 193, 199–202, 240, 259, 265–266, II, 11–12, 58–59, 182–183). Although Magnús the Good is king of Denmark, rightfully so in his view (*Msk.* I, 169), he values his own native ground (*Msk.* I, 125), and the Danes perceive a difference between Magnús and their own kings, although he has a strong army (*Msk.* I, 52–53, 165).

6   Examples of solidarity among 'westerners' are rare in medieval Icelandic writings (Sverrir Jakobsson, 'Hvers konar þjóð voru Íslendingar á miðöldum?,' p. 122), but the term could refer to the friction in Constantinople between Greeks and Roman Catholic westerners at the beginning of the thirteenth century.

7   See *Msk.* I, 269. It is unclear whether Scandinavians as a group are being referred to or whether a distinction between them and southern Europeans is being made (see Sverrir Jakobsson, 'Hvers konar þjóð voru Íslendingar á miðöldum?,' 129–30). We need not assume that the English cart driver is drawing a distinction between Styrkárr the Marshall and Danes just because he calls him a Norwegian (*Msk.* I, 322).

Conflict among Norwegians is no rarity in the saga. The Þrœndir, guilty of inflated posturings on more than one occasion, even refer to themselves as *hǫfuð Nóregs* 'the head of Norway', and it is easy to exploit their sense of grandeur: '*Þrœndir váru þá ok ríkir menn, en nú skulu þeir vera þrælar konungs greifa hér í Nóregi*' (*Msk.* I, 31) '"The Þrœndir were powerful men then, but now they are supposed to be slaves of a king's steward here in Norway"'. At the beginning of the saga they follow Einarr Paunch-Shaker and still do so when Haraldr the Severe tries to incite his men to war in Denmark (*Msk.* I, 173). The country is often divided between kings but only after the death of Óláfr the Quiet does the first real break up of the country seem imminent. Then the Þrœndir follow Hákon Þórir's foster-son and not Magnús Barelegs and, at Steigar-Þórir's instigation, take another man (Sveinn Haraldsson) as their king against Magnús (*Msk.* II, 18). When the sons of Magnús divide the land, Eysteinn is the king of the Þrœndir, and in 'Þinga saga' it emerges that each part of the country has its own system of law. Later Sigurðr Haraldsson is the king of the Þrœndir and then the hostility between the men of Vík and Bergen towards the Þrœndir is palpable (*Msk.* II, 199–200). Other Norwegians are less arrogant, but still Haraldr the Severe comes down hard on the Upplanders when they demand legal rights beyond those granted to others in Norway (*Msk.* I, 223–226). Later in the saga these demands do the Upplanders no credit when reference is made to their cowardly flight during Magnús Barelegs's final battle in *Úlaztír* 'Ulster' (*Msk.* II, 68).

It is commonplace that personal identity is a composite. In Norway men are Þrœndir, and in King Magnús's army Norwegians, while in Constantinople they become Scandinavians.[8] But the most important group of people in *Morkinskinna* are the Icelanders. More than in other kings' sagas this work defines the role of Icelanders in Norway as more important to a sense of Icelandic nationality than their life in Iceland. The difference is most marked in the *Íslendingaþættir*, the so-called 'tales of the Icelanders'. They become significant as a class of tales within a saga about Icelandic courtiers and their place in the world.

---

8   Sverrir Jakobsson, 'Hvers konar þjóð voru Íslendingar á miðöldum?'; 'Defining a Nation,' 91–101.

'No worse a family in Iceland'

As noted above, Haraldr the Severe is the king in *Morkinskinna* who receives the most attention. In a saga without a single main character he comes closest to playing this role. There are many chapters in his story, within most of which Icelanders occupy a key position because King Haraldr is well disposed towards Iceland:

> Hann hefir verit allra Nóregskonunga vinsælastr við Íslendinga. Þá er á Íslandi var mikit hallæri þá sendi Haraldr konungr fjǫgur skip ok hlaðin ǫll með mjǫl ok kvað á at ekki skippund skyldi dýrra en þrim mǫrkum vaðmála. Hann leyfði útanferð ǫllum fátœkum mǫnnum, þegar er þeim fengisk vistir um haf, ok fór fjǫlði útan fátœkra manna. Ok þaðan í frá nœrðisk landit til árferðar ok batnaði er áðr var at þrotum komit af hallæri því er á gekk. Haraldr konungr sendi út til Íslands klukku til kirkju þeirar er inn heilagi Óláfr konungr sendi viðinn til ok aðra klukkuna, ok sú kirkja var sett á Þingvelli, þar sem alþingi er sett. Þvílíkar menjar hafa menn hans á Íslandi ok þar með margar stórgjafir er hann veitti þeim er hann sóttu heim. Úlf Óspaksson, íslenzkan mann, hann gørði Haraldr konungr stallara sinn ok veitti honum þar með inn mesta metnað ok valði honum kvánfang virðuligt, Jórunni Þorbergsdóttur Árnasonar. (*Msk.* I, 205–206).

Of all the Norwegian kings he was the most popular among Icelanders. When there was a great famine in Iceland, King Haraldr sent four ships loaded with flour and specified that every 275 pounds should not cost more than three marks of homespun. He allowed all the poor men to go abroad when they secured passage on a ship and many poor men did indeed go abroad, and from then on the country became more prosperous and things improved after having reached a low point because of the famine that had persisted so long. Haraldr sent to Iceland a bell to the church for which Saint Óláfr had sent wood to build and another bell, and that church was built at Þingvellir where the *alþing* is convened. His men in Iceland had such mementos of him, and in addition he gave many magnificent gifts to those who visited him. King Haraldr appointed an Icelander, Úlfr Óspaksson, as his marshall and in so doing paid him a great honour and made a good marriage for him with Jórunn, the daughter of Þorbergr Árnason.

Úlfr is a follower of the king from his youth in Constantinople and dies just before him when the military expedition to England is in the planning stage. Haraldr says at his graveside: *'Hér liggr nú sá maðr er dyggvastr var ok dróttinhollastr'* (*Msk.* I, 303) "'here lies the most loyal of men and the most faithful to his lord'". Úlfr is a model retainer and the king is his benefactor, choosing for him the sister of the queen as a bride. It is stated that Haraldr's remarks about Úlfr are a *gott vitni Msk.* I, 303 'a great tribute', and they apply to Icelanders in general. Úlfr is a credit to Iceland, and Haraldr's words are doubtless quoted chiefly in order to document this fact.

Nevertheless, it is far from the case that the dealings between kings and Icelanders in the saga are invariably positive. On the contrary, things often become tense and strained to breaking point. In the first of the *þættir* in the saga (*Msk.*, XXII) Þorsteinn Síðu-Hallsson refuses to pay Magnús the Good a land tax and also exempts his men from the same tax. For this transgression Magnús outlaws Þorsteinn, even though he is ultimately reconciled with him, not because of his own insights or because Einriði Einarsson thinks him *gott mannkaup* 'a fine figure of a man' (*Msk.* I, 141), but rather to maintain his friendship with Einarr Paunch-Shaker. Later Þorsteinn approaches King Magnús on his deathbed, who no longer has material wealth to bestow, and requests permission to name his son after the king. Although the king is not really pleased by this request, stating *'þó nǫkkur svá djǫrfung ótígnum mǫnnum at kalla bǫrn sín eptir mér'* "'somewhat presumptuous for a commoner to name his children after me'", he does not withhold his permission from Þorsteinn (*Msk.* I, 170).

The next of these tales concerns Arnórr the Earls' Poet, who behaves audaciously not only with kings but also with Norwegian courtiers. Arnórr calls himself the kings' poet and does not even bother to clean the tar from his hands before appearing in front of the kings (*Msk.* I, 143). The description of this confident Icelander seems to be a comic creation. However, Arnórr proves himself able to tread carefully and retain the respect of both kings. He becomes their friend, and in *Morkinskinna* a king's friendship is always a good measure of a man's worth.[9]

At first glance it is hardly possible to find two Icelanders more dissimilar than the experienced Arnórr and the provincial Hreiðarr the Simple. Though the structure of the Hreiðarr episode suggests a symbolic character, its narrative substance portrays an Icelander at the Norwegian court wherein Hreiðarr becomes a personification of the Icelandic nation. Icelanders seem to subscribe to this notion as when it becomes known, chiefly through Hreiðarr's wholesale broadcasting of the news after being sworn to secrecy by his brother, that he is scheduled to accompany Þórð to Norway *firna allir Þórð um ef hann flytr útan afglapa* (*Msk.* I, 153) 'they all criticise Þórð for taking the fool abroad'. Hreiðarr does not seem much of an ambassador for his country, but the king is eager to meet him. Hreiðarr does not understand what lies behind the invitation: *er Hreiðarr heyrði sagt at konungr vildi hitta hann þá gengr hann uppstert mjǫk ok nær á hvat sem fyrir var, ok var hann því óvanr at konungr hefði beizk fundar hans* (*Msk.* I, 155) 'when Hreiðarr heard it said that the king wanted to meet him, he walked around swollen with pride and bumped into everything in his path, so unprepared was he that the king had asked to meet him'. He behaves much like a child, but it is hard to see that the nation suffers much loss of prestige as a result. On the contrary, it turns out that King Magnús understands the situation of the unknown simpleton at court and predicts that things will turn out well for him.

Although, on the other hand, he is an old retainer of King Haraldr the Severe's and his situation is unlike Hreiðarr's, yet it is possible to discern prejudice against Icelanders in the Halldórr Snorrason episode. A Norwegian ship captain, Sveinn of Lyrgja, is insulted when the king informs him that he is being replaced as captain by Halldórr: *'Eigi kom mér þat í hug at þú myndir íslenzkan mann til þess velja, en taka mik frá skipstjórn'* '"it never occurred to me that you would choose an Icelander for this position and remove me from the captaincy'". It seems obvious that Sveinn considers Icelanders to be a race apart, but the king counters:

> 'Hans ætt er eigi verri á Íslandi en þín hér í Nóregi, ok eigi hefir enn alllangt síðan liðit er þeir váru norrœnir er nú byggja Ísland'. (*Msk.* I, 184).

> 'His is no worse a family in Iceland than yours here in Norway, and besides that it was not all that long ago when Norwegians settled Iceland'.

Doubtless it now seems more natural to refer to the unique position of Icelanders, but Haraldr takes the opposite position in the matter, saying he considers Icelanders to be equal to Norwegians and will treat them well for this reason.

Antipathy towards Icelanders often appears in the saga. Auðun of the Westfjords is laughed at in Denmark (*Msk.* I, 221) after returning from a pilgrimage to Rome and suffering great hardship. When an Icelander amuses the court with stories from Haraldr the Severe's youth, *ræða margir um at þó sé djǫrfung í þessu er hann, Íslendingr, segir þessa sǫgu* (*Msk.* I, 236) 'many comment that it was audacious for him, an Icelander, to tell this tale', the man's nationality emphasised. Later the overbearing Ingimarr attempts to humiliate Ásu-Þórðr and *lézt eigi mega heita lendr maðr ef hann hefði eigi við stafkarlinum einum íslenzkum* (*Msk.* II, 110) 'said he did not deserve to be called a landed man if he could not handle a beggar of an Icelander'. It seems to him that the king is making a lot of *hluta mǫrlandans* (*Msk.* II, 113) 'the matter of this suet-eater'. In the face of such antipathy kings tend to protect Icelanders and guard their rights, as when Haraldr admonishes Sveinn of Lyrgja.

Nevertheless, Haraldr refuses the sail offered by Þorvarðr Crownose, saying that he had accepted '*segl at yðr, Íslendingum*' "'a sail from you Icelanders'" that turned out to be of poor quality (*Msk.* I, 237), obviously tarring all Icelanders with the same brush. Matters are eventually put right, and generally the king takes up the cause of Icelanders. This is an essential theme in *Morkinskinna*: Icelanders are complex individuals and should be measured according to their merits, and not as a group. Two nameless Icelanders have roles in an episode that takes place in the time of Haraldr the Severe. One is the storytelling Icelander (*Msk.* I, 235–237), and the other is someone from the north, who behaves foolishly and is finally sent from the country by Einarr Paunch-Shaker and told not to return to Norway '*meðan Haraldr konungr er yfir landi*' (*Msk.* I, 210) '"while King Haraldr rules the land"'. The story of this fool shows that Icelanders come in different shapes and sizes.[10] Generally, however, they prove to be men of distinction, and their tales turn out well. This is especially true of Hreiðarr the Simple, Auðun of the Westfjords and Brandr the Bountiful.[11]

The tales involving Sneglu-Halli (*Msk.* I, 270–284) and Stúfr the Blind (*Msk.* I, 290–293) demonstrate how Icelanders win the king's favour through eloquence and poetic skill, arts highly appreciated by Haraldr the Severe. Sneglu-Halli was *svá farit at hann var skáld ok foryfldisk heldr fás í orðum sínum* (*Msk.* I, 270) 'of such a temperament that he was a poet and not particularly reticent in what he said to anyone'. When Halli arrives *á fund konungs ok kveðr hann* 'approaches the king and greets him', the king warns him that the court is a difficult place for '*útlendum mǫnnum*' (*Msk.* I, 271) '"foreigners"'. Halli turns out to be erratic in his behaviour, and the king rather touchy: '*Hvat skyldir þú fara útan af Íslandi til ríkra manna ok gørask svá at undrum*' (*Msk.* I, 274) '"why did you leave Iceland to visit powerful men and make such a fool of yourself"'. The origins of the Icelander are once again used as a whip against him. Halli is more or less an oddity at court, coarse and uncivilised, scarcely housebroken. He earns the king's favour, though, after having been pitted against the skald Þjóðólfr, creating an opposition between the two Icelanders who appear at first glance to be poles apart in their natures. Þjóðólfr is a venerated

10 Oddr Ófeigsson occasions the displeasure of the king for forbidden dealings with the Lapps. With him is a courtier named Þorsteinn, a kinsman of Þórir hundr 'the Dog' (*Msk.* I, 293–299), and the king well remembers the deception practiced by Þórir: '*kann vera at ⟨þú⟩ segisk í ætt þína um svikin*' (*Msk.* I, 298) 'it may well be that treachery is a family trait'. Alfred Jakobsen ('Har det eksistert en skriftlig saga om Tore Hund og hans ætt?,') thinks that a saga about Þórir hundr existed at one time. Oddr is the chief figure in *Bandamanna saga*, and there this deception is not regarded as important. Indeed, this saga is scornful of kings (Ármann Jakobsson, 'Royal pretenders and faithful retainers: The Icelandic vision of kingship in transition,' p. 50; Andersson, 'The King of Iceland,' pp. 923–924).
11 Shorter tales about Gizurr Ísleifsson (*Msk.* I, 289) and Magnús Einarsson (*Msk.* II, 166) also show how highly Norwegian kings value Icelanders from renowned families.

skaldic poet and courtier, whereas Halli is foul-mouthed, scurrilous, and lacking in all refinement. But examined more closely, both are simply impoverished Icelanders whose humble origins provide a striking contrast with the splendour of the court. The king, of course, appears to sense all this from the beginning. Ultimately Halli fits in at court because the king desires it.

Stúfr's Icelandic background also plays a role in his tale. The king is quick to see that he is an Icelander and thus makes fun of his father's nickname, which was Þórðr kǫttr 'the Cat' – he was the foster-son of Snorri *goði*.[12] Stúfr laughs at himself and succeeds without insulting King Haraldr to remind him that his own father had a disreputable nickname (*sýr* or 'the sow'). Then Stúfr proceeds to amuse the king so thoroughly that he is offered a place at court, though only after the agreement of his courtiers is obtained (*Msk.* I, 292). On this occasion permission is easily obtained, but sometimes Icelanders are not so well received by other retainers. Then they have to make their own way, often with eloquence and poetic arts as their only weapons. This was the gist of the tale of Þórarinn Shortcloak, which happened in the days of Sigurðr the Crusader (*Msk.* II, 135–137). Like Arnórr the Earls' Poet, Halli, Stúfr and Þórarinn are all skilled in poetry. This gift is a major asset for Icelanders at the court and continues to be important even after Haraldr disappears from the stage. Einarr Skúlason enjoys the good will of kings because of his ability as a poet. He is nevertheless different and more than an entertainer; he first makes his presence felt when Sigurðr the Crusader sends him on an errand; he then gives a report of his experiences, of course, in verse form (*Msk.* II, 124). But his career is most identified with Eysteinn Haraldsson; there he is the marshal and advisor in the disputes with King Ingi, and offers his advice in verse form (*Msk.* II, 222). Although Einarr speaks through his poetry, he is taken seriously. The poet (who was also a priest and thus not suited to fighting) discharges his obligations at court as an envoy and all-round diplomat; he enjoys trust precisely because his language is his only weapon.[13]

---

12 Compare Anne Holtsmark, 'Kattar Sonr.'
13 Bjarne Fidjestøl, 'The king's skald from Kvinesdal and his poetry,' pp. 73–79.

PORTRAITS OF MEN

With Einarr Skúlason the circle that begins with Úlfr the Marshall has been closed. Úlfr and Einarr are not just as good as the Norwegian courtiers, but rather better. Úlfr and Einarr are the confidants of their kings. Their nationality seems to give them bonus points; as Icelanders they are not dependent on anyone in Norway, apart from the king, and thus he can rely on them more than on others. At the same time the trust of a king attests to the merits of Icelanders. They establish themselves at court because of their own abilities.

In *Landnámabók* it is stated that the value of writing of this historical nature is such that,

> vér þykjumsk heldr svara kunna útlendum mǫnnum, þá er þeir bregða oss því, at vér séim komnir af þrælum eða ill-mennum, ef vér vitum víst várar kynferðir sannar[14]

> we think we will be able to answer foreigners when they accuse us of coming from slaves or evildoers if we are ac-quainted with our true ancestors.

In medieval Icelandic sagas several examples can be found of Icelanders recognising that the outside world takes little note of their arrival on the scene. In various Icelandic sagas reference is made to the earliest settlers regarding Iceland as remote and unremarkable.[15] The pejorative epithet *mǫrlandar* 'suet-eaters' occurs frequently.[16] In *Morkinskinna*, as in sev-

14 *Íslendingabók*, ed. Jakob Benediktsson, ÍF 1, p. 336, note 1. This observation is from the *Þórðarbók,* and probably also the *Melabók* redactions. Guðrún Ása Grímsdóttir ('Fornar menntir í Hítardal: Eilítið um íslenska tignarmenn og ættartölurit á 17. öld,' p. 50) has pointed out that it reflects as much the temperament of Icelandic chieftains of the seventeenth century as that of previous centuries.

15 See, for example *Laxdæla saga*, ÍF 5, p. 5; *Vatnsdæla saga*, ÍF 8, p. 29. Both of these sagas describe families that are defined using foreign concepts of royalty and nobility (Ármann Jakobsson, 'Konungasagan Laxdæla'; 'Royal pretenders and faithful retain-ers: The Icelandic vision of kingship in transition'). Clunies Ross ('From Iceland to Norway: Essential Rites of Passage for an Early Icelandic Skald') has discussed the position of Icelanders as a marginal nationality and describes their status in various narratives about Icelanders in Norway thus: 'individual Icelanders ... are, on a case-by-case basis, represented as better, cleverer, and more gifted than any individual Norwegian, except for perhaps the Norwegian king' (57).

16 Bogi Th. Melsteð, 'Töldu Íslendingar sig á dögum þjóðveldisins vera Norðmenn?,' p. 30.

eral other Old Icelandic narratives, we find a response to these insults.[17] The Icelanders in the saga are a mixed bunch and some turn out badly. Sometimes other fellow countrymen have to pay for these shortcomings. Among the finest qualities associated with Icelandic courtiers are aristocratic boldness, the ability to compose poetry, and the capacity to entertain the court.[18] It appears that one part of the more general myth about Icelanders is reflected in Magnús the Good's remark that they are *hugkvæmir* (*Msk.* I, 156) 'ingenious'. This feature can also be seen in tales of Icelanders in the Sagas of Icelanders who boldly visit a king and are said to be *einráðir* 'eccentric'.[19] But despite this eccentricity the road to success in life is closely linked to the king and his court.[20]

The author of *Morkinskinna* has a fondness for eccentric men. Despite eccentricity – and sometimes because of it – Icelanders are entertaining and useful retainers in the service of a king. Although occasionally a certain tension arising from their Icelandic origins is discernable, the general rule is that as retainers they are as good as others – and sometimes better.

A *Bildungsroman* on two levels

In *Morkinskinna* Icelanders are often persons of humble means. But there are, of course, others, one being Karl the Luckless. Jarizleifr sees in him a mismatch between his origins and his capacities: '*þú ert vitr maðr þótt þú sér smárar ættar*' (*Msk.* I, 10) '"you are an intelligent person although your

---

17 This includes skalds' sagas: see Diana Whaley, 'Representations of Skalds in the Sagas 1: Social and Professional Relations,' pp. 305–308.

18 The idea can be found repeatedly in sagas and elsewhere, for example in the prefaces of Theodoricus Monachus and Saxo Grammaticus, that Icelanders are experts in history and antiquities. Preben Meulengracht Sørensen ('Social institutions and belief systems of medieval Iceland (c. 870–1400) and their relations to literary production,' p. 13) puts this wittily: 'Icelanders were professionals, a kind of literary Swiss Guard, which was called upon when it became necessary to relate history in poetry or in writing.'

19 See, among other works, *Laxdæla saga*, ÍF 5, p. 213. Tanja Brünger ('"Hugkvæmir og höfðingjadjarfir": Urteile und Vorurteile über Isländer in zwei Kurzerzählungen des 13. Jahrhunderts') and Vésteinn Ólason ('Den frie mannens selvforståelse i islandske sagaer og dikt') have discussed Icelandic *þættir* as portraits of Icelanders.

20 Clunies Ross, 'The Skald Sagas as a Genre: Definitions and Typical Features,' pp. 47–48.

family does not amount to much'". Óttarr the Trout is another retainer who turns out better than his family origins might have augured (see part III, chapter 2). Both Karl and Óttarr manage to climb up the ladder of success by virtue of their services to a king, and that is one sure way for a member of a lesser family to reach the top. This is true not least for Icelanders. In Norwegian society they are aliens, and that is always a difficult cross to bear.[21]

One of a Norwegian king's duties was to secure equally the rights of all his courtiers – great and small, foreigners and Icelanders. This theme occurs often in *Morkinskinna*; for example, in the Auðun episode, in the tale of the storytelling Icelander, and in the Sneglu-Halli and Þórarinn Short-cloak episodes. Generally, kings are well disposed towards Icelanders and support them against the attacks of jealous courtiers. Haraldr the Severe is, as we have seen, the Icelanders' best friend, and the saga repeatedly stresses this point. The tales in *Morkinskinna* involving Icelanders deal-ings with a king define the relationship between these two key characters in the saga. The conclusion is that Icelanders very often prove useful to kings and, of course, vice versa. There are, of course, exceptions. Haraldr does not respond well to Hreiðarr the Simple, and the king's friendship with Halldórr Snorrason eventually suffers an irreparable breach. Haraldr can sometimes be his own worst enemy, but usually makes amends. Thus the episodes of Arnórr the Earl's Poet, Brandr the Bountiful and Þorvarðr Crownose all conclude on an upbeat note.

There is no denying that sometimes kings and Icelanders do not always get along, that Icelanders are not always universally loved, but nowhere are the disagreements between royalty and Icelanders dramatised as a clash of Nordic nationalities. Theodore Andersson identifies a negative attitude in *Morkinskinna* towards kings, especially towards those of a militaristic disposition.[22] Though there are certainly examples of this, there are no in-stances of the king falling out with Icelanders because of their nationality.

---

21 Sverrir Jakobsson ('Útlendingar á Íslandi á miðöldum') has discussed the correspond-ing position of Norwegians in Iceland. See Hallvard Magerøy, 'Skaldestrofer som retardasjonsmiddel i islendingesogene,' pp. 586–599.

22 See, among other works, 'Snorri Sturluson and the saga school at Munkaþverá,' pp. 16–17; 'The Politics of Snorri Sturluson,' pp. 56–58; 'The Unity of Morkinskinna,' p 5.

The animosity against Icelanders is most obvious in the Halldórr episode but it is precisely there that King Haraldr takes offence when an Icelander is singled out for discrimination. There he states clearly the view, repeated in *Landnámabók*, that Halldórr's family in Iceland is no worse than Sveinn of Lyrgja's family in Norway. The author of *Morkinskinna* seems to regard it as right and proper that the Icelandic aristocracy is no less highly regarded than the Norwegian nobility.

The narrative focus in *Morkinskinna* is certainly Icelandic, but it is also very close to that of the kings in the saga. Little attention is paid to Icelanders from the moment they leave Iceland until they suddenly appear at the Norwegian court, and then they are viewed from a Norwegian perspective. The commonest type of Icelander to appear in the episodes is the one so well represented by Sigvatr the Poet, Arnórr the Earls' Poet, Brandr the Bountiful, Ívarr Ingimundarson and Einarr Skúlason. This composite Icelander is a cosmopolitan traveller. He is a well-bred man of the world who knows how to behave in the presence of kings and is a diplomat down to his finger tips. Einarr plainly plays such a role in the saga, and Sigvatr, Arnórr and Brandr all manage to perform this highly sensitive balancing act with equal expertise. All of these men are skalds, but their art lies not only in their command of words, but also in their demeanour, refinement and good habits. They themselves are works of art in a culture where the whole man is the product of courtly instruction. They are perfectly rounded courtiers, polished and artistic and are duly honoured at court.[23]

Ole Bruhn has suggested that the new world of which the author of *Morkinskinna* was conscious was characterised by a freedom to choose one's own lifestyle and personal image (see part V, chapter 2). Many chose to look to the ancient art of skaldic verse and become skalds who flourished in the new courtly world, while at the same time maintaining a presence in the disappearing world of traditional poetic art.[24] Poetry and storytelling represent major elements in the courtliness of the poets Sigvatr, Arnórr, Ívarr and Einarr. Such individuals do not just compose

23 Such courtiers are well and widely described in Jaeger's work (for example, *The Origins of Courtliness*, p. 258).
24 Ole Bruhn, 'Earl Rognvald and the Rise of Saga Literature,' p. 242.

poems – they are poets.[25] And, further, their image of themselves unites the old and the new; they are not exclusively poets but are also courtiers. We may imagine that the author of *Morkinskinna* may have been an individual of a similar type. He was an Icelander, surely well travelled, and very probably a courtier, and as far as his art is concerned, *Morkinskinna* itself is sufficient testimony to his gifts. But another tale lies behind this one. Refined and courtly men of the world like Sigvatr, Arnórr or Einarr Skúlason do not pop out of Zeus's head fully formed. Behind every Earls' poet is another tale, the story of a Hreiðarr the Simple. Although the author of *Morkinskinna* and other Icelandic royal courtiers in thirteenth-century Norway could see themselves in figures such as Sigvatr and Arnórr, most of them had no doubt also (and perhaps more often) endured experiences resembling those of Hreiðarr the Simple, Auðun of the Westfjords or Sneglu-Halli when they first went abroad. Behind every perfectly turned out courtier is the child who understood nothing and stuck out like a sore thumb at court. More than a few listeners to *Morkinskinna* had probably been in the position of this child who knows nothing of the world. Even the author himself knows there is a Hreiðarr the Simple inside every courtly royal poet from Iceland.

The story of the Icelanders in *Morkinskinna* is a *Bildungsroman* on two levels in which may be seen both Hreiðarr the Simple and Arnórr the Earls' Poet. They are, in a real sense, two sides of the same coin, yet they are separated by the vast chasm of a sophisticated courtly culture that distinguishes successful poet from bumpkin *kolbítr*. Arnórr the Earls' Poet is, of course, an unusual courtier – in a sense a jester who shows up in the presence of the kings covered in tar and greets them affably, as if nothing were amiss. But his grasp of courtly customs elevates his extraordinary behaviour to a virtue, whereas for a lesser poet and courtier such conduct would constitute a fatal false step. Arnórr is so certain in his otherness that he dresses himself in a brilliant costume of the eccentric poet, an image by no means out of fashion in our world. Arnórr understands the structure of the court and makes use of a new role of the Icelander as court jester. It is in this that his courtliness lies, newly defined. He awakens

---

25 This is another poetic myth but is modelled on tales such as *Egils saga* and *Kormáks saga* (Alison Finlay, 'Pouring Óðinn's Mead: An Antiquarian Theme?' pp 85–99).

admiration for being different, whereas Hreiðarr's otherness gains him, at least initially, nothing but derision. They can hardly be more unlike, but they are nevertheless the same man, before and after their time at court.

This can also be seen in the story of Þjóðólfr Arnórsson, who seems the politest of royal court poets and despises uncultivated Icelanders like Sneglu-Halli.[26] But behind the polite figure lay his own origins in Iceland, brought up in abject poverty as a child and living on charity. When Halli says that Þjóðólfr ate his father's killer, a murmur can be sensed among the courtiers, since such a notion is at odds with refined and stylised courtly life. Then it is revealed that Þjóðólfr lived on the edge of starvation in his childhood. His father was unable to support his family, and a collection was taken up at the local assembly meeting where one chieftain was so generous that he donated a calf for the family. The father, on the other hand, is so clumsy that he contrives to get himself hanged by the calf, who is attached to a rope that the man had tied around his own neck. Afterwards the children led the calf home and ate it (*Msk.* I, 277–278). For Þjóðólfr this is all very humiliating: abject poverty, the charitable handouts, and the ridiculous fate of his father. At the same time this tale is proof that he has led a double life. He is a skald to kings and considers himself above Sneglu-Halli. But he is in fact two men. Behind the mask of the poet is a penniless child who lived by scrounging on the outer reaches of society. It is not surprising that Þjóðólfr grows angry and wishes to strike Halli. In the saga it comes to light that behind the pose of a cultivated court poet stands an impoverished and uncultivated islander.

The self-image of the Icelander that develops in *Morkinskinna* is two-fold. We find the otherness of the islander and the insignificance of the foreigner, but we also observe that Icelanders can be useful and worthy retainers of a king, not least in their poetic and storytelling skills. An inferiority-complex and self-assurance repeatedly clash with each other; first Arnórr gets the upper hand, and then Hreiðarr takes over. The poor dirt farmer is always in search of recognition from the wealthy rancher

26 Margaret Clunies Ross has explored the 'colonial experience' of the Icelandic court poet in her article, 'From Iceland to Norway: Essential Rites of Passage for an Early Icelandic Skald'.

and wishes to secure it by being considered equally as accomplished. And yet, at the same time, he also wishes to preserve his individuality.

Part V.

WE TELL OURSELVES STORIES

1. Metanarratives

Two biographies

Within the story of Haraldr the Severe there is a short episode called *Fra scemton Islendings* 'Concerning the Entertainment of an Icelander',[1] which takes place *eitthvert sumar* 'one summer' during his reign (*Msk.* I, 235–237). In addition to the king an unnamed Icelander who is said to be *ungr ok fráligr* 'young and quick' plays a primary role.[2] He approaches the king who is obviously well disposed towards him and eager to avail himself of the young man's services. As for the Icelander, his first thought is of stories when the king asks what he is good at:

> Konungr spurði ef hann kynni nǫkkverja frœði, en hann lézk kunna sǫgur. Þá segir konungr at hann mun ⟨taka⟩ við hon-um, en hann skal þess skyldr at skemmta ávallt, er vildi, hvergi sem hann bæði. Og svá gørir hann, ok er hann vin-sæll við hirðina. Ok gefa þeir honum klæði, ok konungr gefr honum vápn í hǫnd sér. Ok líðr nú svá fram til jóla. (*Msk.* I, 235).

> The king asked if he possessed any special talents, and he said he knew a lot of stories. Then the king said he would (take) him on, but that he would be required to entertain at the king's bidding and command, and so he did. He was popular with the court and they gave him clothes, and the king gave him weapons, and time passed until Christmas.

---

1 *Morkinskinna*, ed. Finnur Jónsson, p. 199.
2 The unclear chronology and anonymity of the Icelander is reminiscent of fairy tales, which take place at unspecified times ('once upon a time') and deal with unnamed characters (the son of a cottar and the daughter of a king). In the *Flateyjarbók* version of this tale the Icelander, on the other hand, is identified as Þorsteinn, a very common name for a hero in such tales.

Clearly we are dealing with a poor man (he has no money for clothes or weapons) and a foreigner. His only capital is the art of storytelling, but that is a major resource.

The conflict in the episode begins when the Icelander becomes unhappy and is reluctant to reveal to the king the source of his gloom. The king gets to the bottom of the mystery: the Icelander has run out of stories. It turns out he has one left to tell, an account of Haraldr's youthful exploits abroad. The Christmas entertainment at court for the year in question turns out to be the Icelander's recitation of this tale. There is considerable suspense as to how the king will like the story. The Icelander receives the king's assistance in making sure that the saga lasts to the end of the Christmas holidays. Several of the courtiers regard the Icelander as presumptuous in venturing to tell this tale, but it turns out that the king enjoys it immensely and is even more pleased to hear who the authority behind the stories is, his old friend and adversary Halldórr Snorrason (*Msk.* I, 236).

This story covers the same ground as another story that has already been told in the saga (*Msk.* I, 82–120). We are in the presence of a special kind of dramatic irony. The narrator of *Morkinskinna* offers the saga audience a story about an Icelandic storyteller who offers his listeners a story that the same narrator has already told to the same audience. Among those listening are the king himself, who has lived the events of the tale, and his courtiers who have heard the tale more than once.[3] The narrative is

3   This tale has generated discussion of how long it would take to tell a tale that would correspond to Haraldr's travels abroad (see, among others, Clover, *The Medieval Saga*, p. 195; Stephen A. Mitchell, *Heroic Sagas and Ballads*, p. 98). It is also an excellent example of oral saga telling (see also Heinrich Matthias Heinrichs, 'Die Geschichte vom sagakündigen Isländer (Íslendings þáttr sögufróða): Ein Beitrag zur Sagaforschung'). There is, however, no mention of how many of the overseas events find expression in the tale or of how detailed the account is. Lönnroth ('The Man-Eating Mama of Miklagard,' pp. 47–48) points out that the tale shows how historical knowledge was spread; tales of Haraldr's youth were told to the court and more people were involved than just the king. Although this tale is not more reliable than the tale of the journey abroad itself, it still creates the sense that all of this really happened. Jürg Glauser ('Erzähler – Ritter – Zuhörer: Das Beispiel der Riddarasögur: Erzählkommunikation und Hörergemeinschaft im mittelalterlichen Island') has speculated about the position of the saga listener in courtly romances, where it is quite common for the tales to be delivered orally.

self-reflexive; a well-informed Icelander (the author), who has frequented the courts of kings and told of the overseas travels of Haraldr the Severe, tells a tale of a well-informed Icelander who is telling the same tale at the court of a king. And when the tale is told to Icelandic listeners – and it is at least partly designed for them – they listen to a tale about one of their compatriots entertaining the Norwegian court with a tale that he heard at Þingvellir. This autobiographical episode is like a reproduction of the text within the text, an instance of *mise en abyme*, a meta-narrative.[4]

In *Sverris saga* the hardships of Sverrir's youth are compared to *þá er konunga bǫrn urðu fyrir stjúpmœðra skǫpum* (*Sverris saga*, p. 12) 'when kings' children fall under the spells of stepmothers'. Kings' sagas commonly regard people's lives as stories. In the story of the 'saga-learned Icelander' the life of Haraldr the Severe is narrative material and not for the first time, since Haraldr had already told Magnús the story, and later entertained Einarr Paunch-Shaker with his youthful adventures (*Msk.* I, 214). The story of the Icelander who narrates his own biography to the king is not the first such tale told in *Morkinskinna*; earlier, Sigvatr the Poet had composed biographical verses for King Magnús. The story about the saga of a king is repeated; it tells of the position of Icelanders at court and in the world, and of the central importance of poetry in the construction of the Icelanders' self-identity.

This all happened

On Lyrskov Heath Magnús the Good engages in a battle with some pagans. A bell is heard ringing in the sky above them and *í þessum þys kemr þar búkarl einn ok brýzk fram í milli manna ok kvazk eiga skylt erendi við konunginn* 'in the confusion a farmer came forward among the men and said that he had an important matter to discuss with the king'. He tells the king a dream about Saint Óláfr on a white horse and adds: *'ok at þú grunir eigi mína sǫgn þá hefi ek sannar jarteinir til at sanna sǫgu mína'* (*Msk.* I, 61) '"and so that you do not doubt my story, I have true tokens to prove my tale"'. On this occasion tokens are necessary; it matters whether the story

---

4 See also Ármann Jakobsson, 'Textreferenzen in der Morkinskinna: Geschichten über Dichtung und Geschichten'.

is true. The author has, of course, stated a little earlier that a man had been with the king there *Oddr hét ok var Gellisson. Hann hefir sagt suma hluti frá þessum tíðendum* (*Msk.* I, 60) 'named Oddr Gellison. He has related some aspects of these events'. Although a source is mentioned, the events narrated are all the more incredible:

> ok svá varð mikit mannfallit, sem ólíklegt mun þykkja er frá
> er sagt, at svá stórir valkestir lágu í ánni ok svá þykk at stíga
> mátti búk af búk ok fara svá þurrt yfir ána. (*Msk.* I, 62).

> and so many were the casualties that, unlikely as it may
> seem, it is said that the pile of bodies in the river was so
> large and dense that it was possible to cross the river by
> stepping from corpse to corpse and remain dry.

The storyteller is not always sure of his claims, as when he speaks of Magnús: *rak hann svá mjǫk lengi einn samt flóttann at engi maðr fylgði honum, en sumir segja at hann ræki við þrettánda mann* (*Msk.* I, 63) 'he pursued the fleeing troops so long that no one accompanied him, but some say that he did it with twelve men'. It is the *sumir segja* that betrays the uncertainty and provides the disclaimer in the face of anticipated scepticism.

The author of *Morkinskinna* is a writer of history. He does not possess complete freedom as to how he narrates the events of the story, but rather is dependent upon available sources and also presumably on oral tradition. In earlier *Morkinskinna* episodes the listener is reminded of this. Far from emphasising his independence the author signals his dependence on others. The saga writer is one link in a long chain. He can shape his materials and modify them for his own purposes and to promote his overall meaning. But, rather than calling attention to this, the narrative emphasises that we are dealing with a saga whose author does not have complete control over his materials and that his knowledge derives from others.

In *Morkinskinna* reference is sometimes made to sources, as Eiríkr Oddsson and his authorities for the saga of Sigurðr the Noisy are discussed at length (*Msk.* II, 185).[5] Reference is also made to the saga of King Knútr

---

5 Allusions to sources are frequent in the narrative, which may well derive from *Hryggjarstykki* (Bjarni Guðnason, pp. 12–32; on the sources of *Hryggjarstykki*, pp. 72–94).

(*Msk.* II, 12) but more often the allusions are to authoritative persons or poems,[6] sometimes to both:

> Með þessum hætti segir Þorgils, vitr maðr, ok kvað sér segja Goðríði, dóttur Gothorms Steigar-Þórissonar, ok hann lézk sjá mǫsurbollann ok mǫttulinn er Haraldr konungr gaf Þóri ok var þá skorinn í altaraklæði. Þessi mál sannar Bǫlverkr skáld (*Msk.* I, 128).

> Þorgils, a wise man, spoke thus; and he said he had been told by Goðríðr, the daughter of Gothormr Steigar-Þórisson, and he said he had seen the maple bowl that King Haraldr had given Þórir and also the cloak that had been made into an altar cloth. This matter has been confirmed by the poet Bǫlverkr.

Sometimes poems are accompanied by observations on the validity of sources: *[O]k til þess at þetta sé eigi logit þá segir Arnórr svá jarlaskáld* (*Msk.* II, 8) 'and in order to ensure that there is no untruth being spoken, Arnórr the Earls' poet states'. When we are told that Haraldr blinded the King of the Greeks, two verses and this comment follow:

> eigi þarf orð at gera hjá því at sjálfan Grikkjakonung blind-aði hann. Jafn vel mætti nefna til þess greifa einnhvern eða hertoga, ef þat þœtti sannara, en í ǫllum kvæðum Haralds konungs segir þetta eina lund. (*Msk.* I, 113).

> there is no need to doubt that he blinded the King of the Greeks. Some count or duke might just as well be cited if that would make things seem more true, but in all King Haraldr's poems this is stated unanimously.

It is clear to the author that the accuracy of any narrative account may be doubted, and he regards this as a justification for discussing his sources

6 See, for example, *Msk.* I, 71, 255, 321, *Msk.* II 38–39, 168, 186, 171, 201, 204 and 209–210.

and their reliability.[7] Sometimes reference is made to how poets work: *Þat sannar Stúfr er heyrt hafði Harald konung frá segja þessum tíðendum* (*Msk.* I, 107) 'Stúfr confirms this, and he had heard King Haraldr tell of these events'. The narrative of Haraldr's journey to Jerusalem is thus partly based upon Stúfr's poem that, in turn, relies upon Haraldr's narrative. Since the narrative of Haraldr's youthful exploits corresponds to what Haraldr tells Magnús when they finally meet for the first time, we are here dealing with a special kind of source: Haraldr cites a poet who has borrowed the narrative from him!

The gold that Haraldr brought to Norway is said to be the wealth of the King of the Greeks: *sem allir menn segja at þar sé rautt gull nær húsum fullum* (*Msk.* I, 127) 'which everyone says is enough red gold to fill more than one house'. Here reference is made to persons in the know, but there is an *aðalhending* 'full internal rhyme' in the sentence (*gull – fullum*), suggesting that a poetic source lay behind this.

Such remarks about truth can be found in other kings' sagas and in *Sturlunga saga*, but mostly in legendary sagas. They are, on the other hand, rare in Sagas of Icelanders. Thus it appears that the more unbelievable the sagas are, the more their authors felt the need to insist upon their value as true sources.[8] In *Morkinskinna*, truth is most often spoken of in the fairy-tale-like narratives of Haraldr the Severe's youth and in the saga of Sigurðr the Noisy. Sometimes the reliability of a narrative is reinforced by first presenting a certain point of view and then stating that some sources do not agree:

Þat er flestra manna sǫgn at Magnús konungr hafi skotit,
en þó stóð annarr maðr hjá konungi háleyskr, ok skutu þeir

7   See Jón Helgason, ed., *Morkinskinna: MS. No. 1009 fol. in the Old Royal collection of The Royal Library, Copenhagen*, p. 13. The *Morkinskinna* author's examinations of and reflections upon his sources are quite extensive when compared to other medieval works (see Peter Burke, *The Renaissance Sense of the Past*, pp. 19–20).
8   On the attitudes of medieval Scandinavian saga authors to truth and history, see Sverrir Tómasson, *Formálar íslenskra sagnaritara á miðöldum: Rannsókn bókmenntahefðar*, pp. 189–260. Preben Meulengracht Sørensen (*Fortælling og ære: Studier i islændingesagaerne*, pp. 33–78; 'Modernitet og traditionalisme: Et bidrag til islændingesagaernes litteraturhistorie, med en diskussion af Fóstbræðra sagas alder,' pp. 156–57) has pointed out that discussions of truth occur very often in narratives of a fairy-tale character (for example, the legendary sagas).

báðir senn, ok hefir annarr hvár þeirra ǫrina átta. En þó vís-
ar Þorkell hamarskáld svá til at Magnús konungr ætti ǫrna,
sem hér segir … Ǫnnur ǫrin kom á nefbjǫrgina hjálmsins
ok festi þar, ok nú fyr þá sǫk hafa menn nǫkkut deilzk at
hvárri konungr skaut at þeir stóðu nær ok hvárt skotit fylgði
ǫðru, er þeir skutu jafn snemma báðir. (*Msk.* II, 45–46).

Most people say that King Magnús shot the arrow, but another man, a Hálogalander, was standing beside the king,
and they both shot at the same time and (so) it was one of
them who shot the arrow that struck the target, but Þorkell
Skald from Hamarr indicates that Magnús shot the arrow
as is stated here … Another arrow struck the nosepiece of
the helmet and stuck there, and for this reason it has been a
source of debate as to which man shot the arrow in question,
since the two men were standing so close together, and as
to which arrow followed the other when they both shot with
equal speed.

Here the discussion focuses on a battle taking place in the British Isles.
The same problem over disputed actions occurs when Sigurðr the Noisy
picks up Magnús the Blind from the monastery at Hólmr:

Fór Sigurðr slembir til Hólms ok tók þar með valdi ór klaustr-
inu Magnús frænda sinn af nauðgum munkum. En sú er
fleiri manna sǫgn at Magnús fœri at vilja sínum (*Msk.* II,
180).

Sigurðr the Noisy went to Hólmr to take Magnús his kinsman by force from the monastery against the will of monks,
but many people said that Magnús went of his own free will.

It is by such comments that the saga writer blunts the impact of any poten-
tial scepticism by disclaiming perfect knowledge of the past: *hér greinir
eigi um hvárt þeir fundusk síðan (Msk.* II, 137) 'it is not stated whether
they ever met again'.[9]

9 The same intention may lie behind statements noting that the distance between the
events and their narration is considerable. On one occasion reference is made to the

Such allusions are, however, valued as much for their aesthetic merit as for their truth value. When Haraldr the Severe invades England, *segja svá allir þeir er nǫkkur frásǫgn er kunnig hér um at eigi hafi betra mannval búizk af Nóregi til einnar ferðar en þetta (Msk.* I, 302) 'all those who have any knowledge of the story say that never has a more magnificent troop of warriors been sent from Norway on such a campaign'. In this statement the knowledge of the people who report on Haraldr's army is no more important than the appearance of this imposing group of men. The many allusions to sources in the saga thus have an important structural and thematic role. They demonstrate that while the intention is to present the saga as a historical work, based upon sources that are measured in a critical manner,[10] the author is able to create a vivid image of formidable forces at work in the service of the king. These references serve to confirm eye-witness evidence that in those days giants trod the earth.

Another feature that implies the historicity of the narrative is the plethora of personal and place names in the saga. When we are told of the death of Einriði Einarsson, we learn that *er sá maður Árni nefndr er honum varð at bana (Msk.* I, 216) 'the man who killed him was named Árni'. The man has not been referred to before and his name is never cited in a verse. It is mentioned only for the sake of being mentioned; all historical knowledge is important, and there is no reason to hold back on it. In Haraldr the Severe's invasion of England mention is made of the king's standard, *er þeir kǫlluðu Landeyðu. Friðrekr hét sá maðr er merkit bar (Msk.* I, 312) 'which was called "land-ravager". Friðrekr was the name of the man who carried the standard'. This same Friðrekr then immediately disappears from the saga. Why is he mentioned? The answer is an aesthetic one: saga listeners are encouraged to believe that they are listening to a true story, in which people of all shapes and sizes are mentioned simply because they were there at the scene. There is no need to name fictional characters that have no important influence on the story, but when actual

---

men who had news of the Varangians in the east: *þat segja menn, þeir er verit hafa í Miklagarði, at Væringja minni svá frásagnar (Msk.* I, 109) 'people who have been in Constantinople say that the Varangians remember accounts'.

10 William Manhire, 'The Narrative Functions of Source-References in the Sagas of the Icelanders.'

people are involved, they may be named – because they existed and were present.

Sometimes characters that have nothing to do with the saga are mentioned because of their family connections with other characters that do.[11] Now and then reference is also made to family members who do not play a role in the saga.[12] In various battles many men are tallied up among the supporters of the kings, a habit that becomes more frequent as the saga moves on and approaches the time of the saga writer. Near its end *Morkinskinna* becomes reminiscent of *Sturlunga saga*. Characters are repeatedly mentioned who mean nothing to readers today, but who, we can assume, were known at least to some of the saga audience at the time.[13] Thus reference is made to Þorgrímr the Cap and Sigurðr the Dog and there is clearly a story behind these references (*Msk*. II, 68), but nothing more is stated about these characters.[14] These names have no importance for the development of the saga, but nevertheless create a feeling for the truth of the narrative and underscore the portrait of the society of the saga – the kings of Norway did not exist in a vacuum but in an environment in which many people had their own stories. Some names are connected to places, and some also have lively nicknames, but others stand alone as a memorial to a man who is now only a name.

The saga sometimes makes mention of foreign kings as proof that here we are in the presence of a historical narrative. When Eysteinn Haraldsson's military campaign is narrated, there is this addition: *þá var Stefnir konungr á Englandi* (*Msk*. II, 219) 'at that time Stephen was king of

---

11   This probably applies to Ketill krókr 'the Hook', who is the ancestor of *mart stórmenni* (*Msk*. I, 326) 'many distinguished personages'.

12   See, for example: *Var þar mest fyrimaðr Jóan Mǫrnefsson, faðir Einriða er fell undir Serk, lendr maðr ok gǫfugr* (*Msk*. II, 125) 'the most important man was Jóan Mörnefsson, Einriði's father, who fell at Sekkr, a landed man and an excellent man'.

13   In sagas contemporary with *Morkinskinna*, for example *Sverris saga* and *Hákonar saga*, characters are often named who are not accounted for in the sagas and whom the reader cannot identify without editorial help. The expectation seems to be that all saga listeners recognise such characters. We may, however, be dealing with the author's attempt to create a bogus authenticity. This applies also to *Morkinskinna*, especially in the latter part. On historiography in medieval Icelandic literature, see Ármann Jakobsson, 'History of the Trolls? *Bárðar saga* as an historical narrative.'

14   *Morkinskinna* in fact does not bear comparison with other authorities on these chieftains; see Andersson and Gade, *Morkinskinna*, pp. 450–451, note 2.

England'. Somebody in the group of the listeners would have recognised King Stephen, the last Norman king, Stephen of Blois, who was king of England from 1135 to 1154.[15] Another way of reminding the listeners that the narrative is historical is to refer to the present. The saga maintains two present times. On the one hand the historic present is often used to enable the listener to become a participant in the saga happenings. Suspense is created when arrows are raining down on King Sigurðr Haraldsson: *er nú liðit mjǫk gengit af hǫndum honum* (*Msk.* II, 234) 'and now his troops are much decimated'. We know that this *nú* refers to the present of the narrative, but the present tense is also used to connect the historic past with the present. Haraldr the Severe sees Saint Ólafr on a street in Constantinople and the saga man steps out of the saga for a while and become a guide: *þar er nú gǫr kapella Ólafs konungs* (*Msk.* I, 109) 'there King Ólafr's Chapel has now been built'. When mention is made of the crypt of King Magnús an addition is made: *en nú er þat innan kórs fyrir rúmi erkibyskups* (*Msk.* I, 176) 'but now it is inside the choir and outside the archbishop's chamber'. Relics connect the past to the present. Einarr Paunch-Shaker was killed in a room at the River Nið *þar sem nú er höllin* (*Msk.* I, 216) 'where the hall now stands'. After the death of Sigurðr the Crusader it is stated: *Liggr hann nú í steinveggnum útarr frá kórnum* (*Msk.* II, 152) 'he now lies in the stone wall that is outside the choir'. Sigurðr disappears from the saga but the saga listener knows that he is lying inside the stone wall.

When mention is made of Skúli the Kings' foster-father his family is traced to Ingi and Skúli Bárðarson. It may be assumed that Skúli was still alive when the saga is told, but that Ingi had recently died (in 1217). Also mentioned is the archbishop Eysteinn (d. 1188), who had Haraldr the Severe's remains moved more than a generation after his fall (*Msk.* I, 327). The characters in the saga are connected to the time of the saga author.[16] The historical perspective of the work can be seen when sometimes that which had not yet happened is accounted for. For example, in the saga of

15 Indeed, Andersson and Gade (*Morkinskinna*, pp. 74–77) call attention to the *Morkinskinna* author's indifference to chronology. For him history is clearly not simply a matter of chronology.

16 Awareness of the continuum between generations reflects the mindset of the medieval aristocracy (Lars Bisgaard, *Tjenesteideal og fromhedsideal: Studier i adelens tænkemåde i dansk senmiddelalder*, pp. 100–102).

the mistress of Sigurðr the Crusader a priest named Sigurðr appears and mention is made of what lies ahead of him: *ok síðan var byskup* (*Msk.* II, 150) 'and later [he] was a bishop'. In the time of the saga he is just Sigurðr the priest, but the saga listener learns in addition something about his future career.

On one occasion the author turns not only to the present but all the way to Iceland and connects the long dead Haraldr Gilchrist with objects that are probably well known to the saga audience:

> Ok sá kalekur er mestr at staðnum í Skálaholti. En af pellunum er yfir váru dregin hœgindin, ok konungr ok dróttning gáfu honum, eru nú gervar fyrisǫngskápur þar at staðnum. (*Msk.* II, 167).[17]

> And that chalice is the largest in the church at Skálholt, and from the rich fabric that covered the cushion that the king and the queen gave him were made robes for the chanting before the services in the church.

As the author disappears for a while the guide takes over and reminds the listener that everything that has been narrated is true; anybody who wants to prove it can do so by simply going to Skálholt and inspecting the chalice.

The author of *Morkinskinna* lets the saga audience know in a variety of ways that he is engaged in the act of history writing – a true story based upon sources, but it remains, for all of that, that his narrative is still a work of art. *Morkinskinna* deals with the past, of course, but the author's interest in tradition derives from contemporary thoughts and ideas and his own instincts.

Beautifully composed

Accounts of power struggles, deception, feasts and business dealings all contribute to the rich tapestry of life in *Morkinskinna*. Tales and poems are among the historical events in this narrative and can themselves be

17 *Hungrvaka* also speaks of these gifts (p. 29).

elements in any struggle for power. This is apparent at the beginning of the saga when King Magnús reviews the transgressions of his subjects against his father. As part of this process he wishes to hear the story of the death of Saint Óláfr. Kálfr Árnason, on the other hand, has no wish for this event to be revisited in narrative form. The retelling includes one of the major events of the saga. This retold story of the king's death marks the beginning of the end of the friendship between King Magnús and Kálfr (*Msk.* I, 29–30). It also marks the beginning of King Magnús's tyranny, which only comes to an end through another literary initiative, Sigvatr's *Bersǫglisvísur* (*Msk.* I, 31–42). The story of Magnús's tyranny is framed by a tale and a poem.

In the story of Úlfr the Wealthy, Haraldr the Severe tells a tale (including some verse) that proves to be *óvinveitt skemmtun* (*Msk.* I, 230) 'a mixed bag of pleasures' for Úlfr the Wealthy, since the story is the king's way of relieving Úlfr of his possessions. The story is a speech act; its effect is that Haraldr vanquishes Úlfr.[18] Throughout the saga speech acts are a substitute for battle. The flyting between Eysteinn and Sigurðr is one such struggle, and Haraldr the Severe and Sveinn Úlfsson often wage a war of words before engaging in battle (*Msk.* I, 199–200). King Magnús the Good teaches his half-brother Þórir to compete in verse against Haraldr the Severe. Þórir is said to be *fámálugr ok ekki orðhittinn* 'rather taciturn and not quick with words'. Haraldr finds it dishonourable to be seated opposite him and composes a verse against him: '*Þegi þú, Þórir! / Þegn estu ógegn; / heyrðak at héti / Hvinn-Gestr faðir þinn*' '"Shut up, Þórir / you are a contentious subject / I heard that your father / was called thief-guest"'. Þórir becomes furious *en þóttisk engu kunna at svara* 'but was unable to respond', but Magnús teaches him this verse: '*Gǫrði eigi sá / garð um hestreðr, / sem Sigurðr sýr. / Sá vas þinn faðir*' '"he never enfolded / the penis of a horse / as your father / Sigurðr the sow, did"'. Haraldr,

---

18 A similar example can be found in *Hákonar saga* (*Hákonar saga Hákonarsonar etter Sth. 8 fol., AM 325 VIII, 40 og AM 304,4 40*, p. 155) when Earl Skúli stands up and recites a verse about an eagle who was sitting on a stone, repeating the statement three times within the verse. Here Skúli uses poetry to deflect guilt from his own person, and it is this use of language that is equivalent to an exchange of weapons; Skúli's grasp of sarcasm makes a big difference. See also *Skaldic Poetry of the Scandinavian Middle Ages II: Poetry from the Kings' Sagas 2*, ed. Kari Ellen Gade, p. 849.

sensitive about his father, flies into a rage and draws his sword (*Msk.* I, 138–139).[19]

Within the overall saga are shorter episodes, and within these even shorter tales are told.[20] Just before Einarr Paunch-Shaker is slain, a feast hosted by Haraldr the Severe is recounted. This tale deals with a story that Haraldr tells Einarr, perhaps the same one that the storytelling Icelander later recites at Christmas. Einarr falls asleep during the tale and is, of course, *gamall mjǫk* 'very old'. Because of his advanced age, Einarr cannot stay awake, but Haraldr takes offence, and is sensitive on two accounts: he is proud of his youthful exploits and of his reputation as a master storyteller and poet (see part IV, chapter 2).[21]

In the Sveinki Steinarsson episode men come into their own not only through their language but also in the speeches they make. Sigurðr Woolly-Band makes one such:

> 'Guðs kveðju ok sína sendir Magnús konungr Guðs vinum ok sínum ok einkum ǫllum lendum mǫnnum ok ríkum búǫndum ok allri alþýðu út í frá' (*Msk.* II, 30).

> 'King Magnús sends God's greetings and his own to God's friends, to his own friends, and especially to all the landed men and powerful farmers and all the people besides'.

Here and elsewhere the saga displays its borrowings from and tendency towards an elevated style, not least in letters and speeches that are often alluded to.[22] Here it will suffice to quote a description of the military campaign of Haraldr the Severe to England:

19 Later this dispute turns out to be postponed rather than forgotten (*Msk.* I, 169–172).
20 Andersson and Gade (2000, *Morkinskinna*, p. 82) have called attention to the author's interest: 'he shows a curiosity about literary transmissions that appears nowhere else in Icelandic literature.'
21 The coolness between Haraldr and Einarr has earlier appeared in verse; when the king is displeased with Einarr he goes off by himself and murmurs a verse that is potentially threatening for Einarr, and mention is also made in the verse about the size of the forces that often accompany Einarr (*Msk.* I, 207–208). These verses mark the beginning of the rupture of the friendship between the two.
22 See, for example, *Msk.* II, 199. The same applies when battles are described or knights accompany a king; see, for example, *Msk.* I, 96, 98, 111 and *Msk.* II, 71–72. As Finnur Jónsson has pointed out in his edition of *Morkinskinna* (p. viii) there are many loan

ok lǫgðu þeir eptir brynjur sínar, en gengu upp með skjǫldum ok hjálmum ok kesjum ok váru gyrðir sverðum, ok
margir hǫfðu skot ok boga. Þeir váru kátir mjǫk ok hugðu
nú til enskis ófriðar. Ok er þeir sœkja í nánd borginni sjá
þeir jóreyki mikla ok þar undir því næst fagra skjǫldu ok
hvítar brynjur (*Msk.* I, 311).

And they left their byrnies behind and marched with shields
and helmets and pikes and were girded with swords and
many had bows and arrows. They were in good spirits and
did not think of any hostilities, and when they came into
the vicinity of the city they saw a great cloud of dust and
beneath it beautiful shields and white byrnies.

Vocabulary and other devices from an elevated register help to create the
saga's image of society. However, the author's interest in language is also
an aesthetic one. His saga is not just a narrative of events long past but
also work of great verbal artistry.

The continual recital of stories in the saga is a mark of its highly developed consciousness of form. Mention is made of narrative limits and
restrictions: *verðr hér frásǫgn at hvílask fyrst, því at eigi má allt senn
segja* 'we will allow the story to remain where it is for a while, since not
everything can be told at once'. It goes without saying that a pause is made
when suspense is high and use of the historic present allows the listener
to take part in what is happening:

> Magnús konungr er nú áhyggjufullr, því at liðsmunr er mik-
> ill ... en konungr vill þó fyrir ǫngvan mun flýja, en allillr

words in the saga related to court life and knightly culture, among them *príss, jaga,
gráðr, próvendor, jungfrú, raufarar, burdeigia, turniment* and *cisterna.* Kari Ellen
Gade has compiled a list of loan words and hapax legomena in *Morkinskinna, Sverris
saga* and *Óláfs saga helga* and generously made it available to me. These lists show
that in *Morkinskinna* there are considerably more such loan words than in the other
works, and very many are related to court life. Prominent among them are *herra* and
kurteislegr. In *Morkinskinna* the word *kurteisastr* is used in the description of Magnús
Barelegs at a meeting in Konungahella (*Msk.* II, 60), but not in the corresponding
place in the text of *Heimskringla* (vol 3, ÍF 28, p. 229) or *Fagrskinna* (*Fagrskinna –
Nóregs konunga tal*, ÍF 29, p. 311).

kvittr er í þeim Dǫnunum, ok þykkir þeim sér stýrt til váða. (*Msk.* I, 55).

King Magnús is now concerned because of the great difference in the size of the fighting forces, but the king desires under no account to flee, but there is a very bad feeling among the Danes, and it seemed to them that they were being led to disaster.

Thus, the narrator makes it clear that a tale is being told, but at the same time uses all the devices of narrative art to keep the reader fully engaged.

When the events of the saga are narrated, a discussion of that narration – a meta-narration – often occurs, as, for example, in the account of the last of Magnús Barelegs's battles. Most of the king's men desert him and few are left to tell the tale; only those who have remained with the king to the end can say what happened:

þat sagði Víðkuðr sjálfr at þá er menn runnu ok hann rann frá konunginum at fáir myndi þá kunna frá þeim tíðendum at segja er þar váru eptir á vettvanginum. (*Msk.* II, 69–70).

then Víðkunnr himself said later that when he and other men ran away from the king few were left on the battle field who would then be able to tell these tidings.

All battle feats are connected to the narrative. King Sigurðr the Crusader points out to his men that in the one battle in the south something could happen '*þat er frásagnar þykki vert*' (*Msk.* II, 75) '"that seems worthy of telling about"'.[23] And the greatest battle feats become skaldic verse that also appears in the saga. The narrative of an event merges with the meta-narrative (in poems) of the same event.

When Haraldr the Severe escapes from Stiklastaðir, he meets a farmer's son, who tells the story of their meeting in direct speech. When the story is finished we read: *Þessa frásǫgn vissi Magnús konungr ok aðrir menn*

---

23 The narrative of the death of Magnús the Good begins in a similar way: *Nú barsk þat at er mikil tíðendi eru at segja* (*Msk.* I, 167) 'What happened now was an important event'.

í Nóregi 'This story was known by King Magnús and other men in Norway'. The farmer's son's tale is as important as the events that are told. Then we are told: *En heðan frá er sú frásǫgn um farar Haralds er hann, Haraldr, sagði sjálfr, ok þeir menn er honum fylgdu* (*Msk.* I, 84) 'But from now on the story about Haraldr's travels is what Haraldr himself and those men who went with him have told'. Although the tale of Haraldr's youthful exploits has seemed to some scholars to be maladroitly situated in the saga, it deserves closer attention here: the author of the saga assumes that everything that comes after this point in the saga ('But from now on the narrative …') is not a description of events that occurred long ago but rather a narrative that is occurring exactly at that moment, where Haraldr tells the Norwegians about his life.[24] Allusions are thus woven into the narrative to emphasise that he is the one who is telling the tale. It is said that events are described according to his 'story,' and when certain events from his life are related we are told that *hann segir sjálfr* 'he himself states' (*Msk.* I, 94). Thus, Haraldr's story of his youth in Constantinople is a story of events rather than the events themselves. In this narrative there are other narratives that replace events. Haraldr explains at some length his plan to defeat the third city in Sicily and the event itself is then played out as a repetition of his plan (*Msk.* I, 102–106).[25]

Morkinskinna and several other kings' sagas contain many skaldic verses.[26] Thus, one distinct literary genre is contained within another; poems are preserved in stories. And, of course, they are not just stored there but play an important part in the story. Verses in kings' sagas are sometimes equivalent to footnotes in a doctoral dissertation nowadays wherein references or quotations are used to validate a method or prove a

---

24 Finnur Jónsson (*Morkinskinna*, p. xv) regarded this narrative strategy as strange.

25 Throughout the saga similar narratives occur in which we are first told of the plans and the events are then dramatised; they represent an artful repetition, a 'showing' of the previous narrative 'telling' (*Msk.* I, 135, 233). The same method is employed in *Brennu-Njáls saga* (*ÍF* 12, pp. 58–65) when Gunnarr adopts the disguise of Kaupa-Héðinn. First Njáll narrates everything that will happen, and then the events themselves prove to be a repetition and confirmation of what Njáll has predicted.

26 These have recently been edited, see *Skaldic Poetry of the Scandinavian Middle Ages II: Poetry from the Kings' Sagas 2*, ed. Kari Ellen Gade.

point.[27] But the verses sometimes record important events in the narrative, and sometimes even serve as their core.[28]

The Arnórr Earls' Poet episode deals with the oral presentation of poems, and the conflict turns upon what an asset an excellent poem can be. Four of the stanzas of the *drápa* are recited directly, with the words of the king interspersed. But before Arnórr recites the poem we are told: *Þá kveðr skáldið þetta* (*Msk.* I, 143) 'Then the poet recites this'. This sober sentence serves to add further attention to the power of the poem, which is a *hrynhend drápa* 'flowing metre poem', perhaps the first of its kind. The impact of the poem can further be seen in Haraldr's repeated interruptions as the poem is recited (see part II, chapter 3). At the end Haraldr predicts that the poem will live on *'meðan Norðrlǫnd eru byggð'* (*Msk.* I, 146) '"as long as the northern lands are populated"'. This is a formidable claim but there is no reason to doubt Haraldr's seriousness and, of course, his bitter disappointment over the difference between the poems devoted to both himself and Magnús, respectively. He is almost inconsolable until Arnórr promises to compose an *erfidrápa* 'funeral poem' for him (*Msk.* I, 146), and stanzas from it appear widely throughout the saga (*Msk.* I, 70–76, 248–250, 309–310, 312–313, 318–319, 322–323).

Morkinskinna is full of kings composing poems and playing other kinds of games with verse. Haraldr the Severe is a patron of poets and himself a poet; in addition to the poem that he addresses to Úlfr the Wealthy, he composes 16 verses *ok eitt niðrlag at flestum* 'with the same refrain in many of them' and dedicates them to his lover, but only six of them appear in the saga (*Msk.* I, 114–117; see part III, chapter 3).[29] And, of course, Haraldr dies, while the poetry lives on. In the Giffarðr episode (*Msk.* II, 53–56) the 'praise poem' of Eldjárn from Húsavík is submitted to the English city ruler for interpretation and near the end of the saga

27 See especially Bjarni Einarsson, 'On the rôle of verse in saga-literature.' He puts it this way: 'In the main, Sagas of Kings quote stanzas as evidence and these stanzas are mostly from poems in praise of the king or chief in question, made by their court poets or some contemporary scald' (p. 119). Other verses, on the other hand, are, primarily 'included as part of the artistic fabric of the saga' (p. 119).

28 Bjarni Einarsson ('On the rôle of verse in saga-literature,' p. 121) claims that 155 verses in *Morkinskinna* are cited to establish truth or confirm accounts, while sixty-seven serve as links in the narrative chain.

29 On these verses, see Gudlaug Nedrelid, 'Kor mange kunstar kunne kong Harald?'

there are tales about Einarr Skúlason making verse (*Msk.* II, 221–225). A
similar spirit prevails at the court of Haraldr the Severe; a playful king lays
down a test for his poet in order to amuse himself. The kings in *Morkinskinna* are always ready for a game. When Ívarr Ingimundarson does not
want to tell King Eysteinn what is bothering him, the king is immediately
ready to play a guessing game: '*Ek mun þá geta til*' (*Msk.* II, 103) '"Then
I will guess"'. It is said that King Magnús Barelegs composed a poem for
the emperor's daughter, who thought him *sæmiligr* (*Msk.* II, 62) 'becoming'. He also composes, for fun, part of a verse about the cowardly knight
Giffarðr (*Msk.* II, 53). Sigurðr the Crusader answers in verse (*Msk.* II,
137–138) and exchanges verses with the Icelandic poet Þórarinn Short-
cloak (*Msk.* II, 134–135). The saga also includes a verse by King Sigurðr
the Noisy (*Msk.* II, 193). Haraldr the Severe, Magnús Barelegs and Sigurðr the Crusader are tough customers and known for their waging of war
in foreign lands.[30] In *Morkinskinna* poems are often part of those battles,
woven in as verses that authenticate the narrative (for example, *Msk.* II,
38–50), or we are told that men spouted stanzas at each other (see, for
example, *Msk.* II, 53–54). We may scarcely find a description of battle in
Morkinskinna in which poems do not occupy pride of place. Then it happens that men answer for themselves in verse. Prose and poetry are woven
together in an organic whole and neither can exist without the other. Thus
Eysteinn Haraldsson often refers matters to Einarr Skúlason during his
meetings with Ingi, and Einarr answers in verse, as might be expected of
a great poet (*Msk.* II, 235–236).

The verses provide a perspective on great events. In the narrative of the
invasion of England and Haraldr the Severe's death there are twenty-two
verses (*Msk.* I, 299–323). But a considerable part of *Morkinskinna* occurs
in the king's court where attention is directed towards daily troubles rather
than great events. Then the verses also play a role, both in the reign of
Haraldr the Severe and those of other kings. Haraldr pays special attention
to poetry and eagerly exchanges verses with his men. In his disputes with
Sveinn Úlfsson he decides that Sveinn has deceived him and expresses his
displeasure with a *dróttkvætt* line: *Logit hefr Baldr at Baldri* (*Msk.* I, 196)
'Baldr [Sveinn] has lied to Baldr [Haraldr]'. The poet Þjóðólfr Arnórsson

30 Andersson, 'The Politics of Snorri Sturluson,' p. 58.

is present and completes the verse. Clearly, this brief episode is considered no less worthy of reporting than the outcome of the battle.

The tale of Sneglu-Halli provides many examples of verses in the daily life of the courtiers, and once again Þjóðólfr makes an appearance. During a stroll through the town the king and his men overhear a dispute between a tanner and blacksmith. The king orders Þjóðólfr to compose some verses about the incident, but Þjóðólfr finds the subject matter too lightweight. The king then stipulates rules for the poem:

> 'er nǫkkverju meiri vandinn á en þú ætlar. Þú skalt gøra af þeim nǫkkvat aðra menn en þeir eru; lát annan vera Geirrǫð jǫtun en annan Þór.' (*Msk.* I, 271).

> 'there is more to the matter than you think. You shall turn them into different characters. Have the one be the giant Geirrǫðr and the other Þórr'.

When Þjóðólfr has accomplished the task and composed some excellent verses (in which Þórr of the bellows is the blacksmith and Geirrǫðr is the tanner of hides) the king demands other verses in which the characters become Sigurðr Fáfnisbani 'the Dragonslayer' and Fáfnir. The tanner then becomes the carving dragon of hides or the snake of cattle leather while the blacksmith becomes Sigurðr of the sledge-hammer and the king of tongs. Thus in this game mythical heroes and monsters are caught up in the daily quarrels of ordinary people. The poet is able to meet these demands and amuse the culturally-minded king who finds great sport in such poetic creativity. As a reward Þjóðólfr receives a golden ring from the king's finger and is the life and soul of the party at court: *of kveldit var tíðrætt of vísurnar (Msk.* I, 272) 'in the evening the stanzas were much discussed'. By composing verse Þjóðólfr earns the goodwill of the king and popularity among the courtiers and the author of *Morkinskinna* finds this something worth dwelling on. The spat between the blacksmith and the tanner would carry no clear historical significance according to the nineteenth and early twentieth century views concerning kings' sagas, but here Þjóðólfr's verses on the subject are related in full.

Later Halli torments the bully Einarr the Fly about paying compensation for Halli's kinsman, but Einarr is, of course, said never to have paid such compensation (the one necessary condition for the status of an *ójafn-aðarmaðr*). Halli then threatens him with insulting verse:

> [Halli] þokar þá frá hásætinu ok umlar við fyrir munni sér, svá at eigi nam orða skilin, en allir heyrðu at hann muðl-aði nǫkkvat. Þá mælti konungr: 'Gør svá vel, Einarr, sem ek bið; bœt honum nǫkkverju. Hann svífsk enkis, ok er þér verri einn kviðlingr ef eptir verðr munaðr, sem hætt er ef upp kemr at eigi falli niðr, slíkr maðr sem þú ert; því at mit megum sjá hverja setning hann hefir á, ok er þetta engi draumr er hann sagði, því at þetta mun hann enda. Ok eru dœmi til þess at níðit hefir bitit enn ríkari menn en þú ert, ok mun þat aldri niðr falla meðan Norðrlǫnd eru byggð.' (*Msk.* I, 280–281).

> [Halli] went away from the high seat and mumbled something so that the words were not understood, even though everyone heard that he had mumbled something. Then the king said: 'Please, Einarr, do as I say: give him something in compensation; there is nothing he won't do, and you will be worse off for one little ditty if it is long remembered, as is possible; once such a poem about a man like you is uttered, it will not be easily forgotten, for we can see what he intends to say. This is no idle threat that he has made, and he will carry out what he says; there are examples of curses affecting more powerful men than you, and it will never be forgotten as long as the northern lands are populated.'

The power of the word is greater than any ruthless killer like Einarr can contend with; if Halli composes a libellous verse and it catches on, it will exist forever. Ditties are more enduring than the deeds, and in the hands of Halli they are powerful weapons.[31]

The final part in the story of Haraldr the Severe up to the fateful invasion of England is comprised of three episodes about poetry, stories and

---

31 On literature as cultural capital, see Torfi H. Tulinius, 'Snorri og bræður hans: Framgangur og átök Sturlusona í félagslegu rými þjóðveldisins,' pp. 55–58; 'Virðing í flóknu samfélagi,' pp. 80–89.

entertainment at court. In these episodes the king's much discussed admiration for poetry is revealed and his personal characterisation achieves additional complexity. At the same time a portrait of the fellowship at court is presented, and the saga listeners are drawn somewhat nearer to the position of the Icelanders who were actually there. But although these stories about poetry serve a variety of narrative and thematic purposes, they are primarily about poetry – an art whose main preoccupation is itself.

In 1263, some forty years after *Morkinskinna* was written, Hákon Hákonarson lay dying; the saga had probably been put together in the first years of his reign. In the story of Hákon it is said that at his death books were read to him, first in Latin and then in Norwegian. One of the works read to him was *konungatal fra Halfdani suarta ok siþan fra ollum Noregs konungum huerium eftir annan*[32] 'a list of kings from Hálfdan the Black and then about all of Norway's kings one after another'. Here we have the same feature that occurs throughout *Morkinskinna*: in one king's saga we are told about the reading of other kings' sagas. The saga man tells about other readings of sagas where the king himself is a listener.

Hákon Hákonarson placed great emphasis on learning, wisdom and patronage of culture and art. His manner on his deathbed is in keeping with the rest of his life; the cultured king listens to a good saga even when near his death.[33] Like Haraldr the Severe and his grandfather Sverrir, Hákon employed in his service many poets, including Snorri Sturluson and his nephews Sturla and Óláfr but also some mysterious figures such as Játgeirr Torfason and Óláfr Leggsson, whose poetry is almost or altogether forgotten.[34] When such a king rules the land, the artistry of poets such as

---

32 *Flateyjarbók: En Samling af norske Konge-sagaer med indskudte mindre Fortællinger om Begivenheder i og udenfor Norge samt Annaler* 3, p. 229

33 Lönnroth (*Den dubbla scenen: Muntlig diktning från Eddan till ABBA*, pp. 56–57) interprets this narrative in a similar manner as here, but lays a little more emphasis on the formality of the recitation; it is almost a religious ceremony.

34 See especially Bjarne Fidjestøl, '"Har du høyrt eit dyrare kvæde?" Litt om økonomien bak den eldste fyrstediktinga.' On the cultural position of skalds, see Guðrún Nordal, *Tools of Literacy: The Role of Skaldic Verse in Icelandic Textual Culture of the Twelfth and Thirteenth Centuries* pp. 117–195; Bjarni Einarsson, *Skáldasögur: Um uppruna og eðli ástarskáldasagnanna fornu*; 'The Lovesick Skald: A Reply to Theodore M. Andersson'; *To skjaldesagaer: En analyse af Kormáks saga og Hallfreðar saga*; An-

Sigvatr, Arnórr the Earls' Poet and Einarr Skúlason is an admission ticket to a higher place, as happens when Ásu-Þórðr composes a poem about Víðkunnr Jónsson in order to demonstrate his 'faith' with him (*Msk.* II, 109).[35]

The poems and tales in the saga are important both to the overall picture of the society in *Morkinskinna* and to the identity of the Icelandic poet. The central focus, however, is upon the relations between the poet and the king, which rises to a symbolic level in the Hreiðarr the Simple episode. Hreiðarr recites a poem for the king that symbolises the poet's own life. The poem is *allundarligt, fyrst kynligast en því betra er síðarr er* (*Msk.* I, 164) 'a remarkable performance, at first strange but then better as it developed'. Hreiðarr's life is also at first strange but improves over time. By having the poem signify growth and maturation in the life of the simple Icelander, the author perhaps introduces the notion that in art all human life is implicit.

Poems and stories in *Morkinskinna* lie at the heart of society and of the self-image of the saga; they also represent a third form of the saga, the picture of the picture. *Morkinskinna* is not just about its author and his fellowship, but is also a story about stories.

---

dersson, 'Skalds and Troubadours'; Alison Finlay, 'Skalds, Troubadours and Sagas'; Sigurður Nordal *Íslenzk menning* 1, pp. 233–277; Russell Poole, *Viking Poems on War and Peace*.

35 Admission is not always granted in an entirely straitforward manner, however, as attested in an amusing story about Sigvatr the poet and Ívarr, Hákon's father. When Sigvatr recites a poem in his honour, Ívarr says: 'Þat verðr yðr mjǫk opt skáldunum þá er konungi leiðisk of skvaldr yðart þá leiti þér undan ok vilið draga fé af búǫndum.' (*Msk.* I, 241). '"This is what often happens to you poets when the king gets tired of your blathering – then you slink off and attempt to gouge money out of farmers"'. The narrative is humorous, as Ívarr seeks to conceal his obvious longing for poetic flattery with dissimulation and ill-temper.

2. Confronting the Past

The arrival of the present

Morkinskinna is a surprisingly 'young' text given how old it actually is. Although its action is set in the past, considerable modernity also casts a shadow over the text. Past and present coexist.[1] Lars Lönnroth has pointed out that in the flyting between the brothers Eysteinn the elder and Sigurðr the Crusader many new values find expression.[2] A *senna*, a traditional literary genre involving the formal exchange of insults, is set in a new courtly context, and civilised values win the day at the expense of the old Viking mentality. As Lönnroth acknowledges, however, the matter is far from simple. Although he sees Sigurðr as a representative of Viking con-

---

1 Susanne Kramarz-Bein, '"Modernität" der Laxdœla saga,' p. 421; Stefanie Würth, 'Die Temporalität der *Laxdœla saga*,' pp. 295–308.
2 Lars Lönnroth, *Den dubbla scenen: Muntlig diktning från Eddan till ABBA*, p. 68. *I berättelsen om kungarnas manjämning är däremot tendensen hövisk, såväl i Morkinskinna som i Heimskringla; meningen är att det gamla råbarkade manjämningsidealet, som personiferas av kung Sigurd, skall framsällas som underlägset den nya tidens mer civiliserade och höviska ideal, som personifieras av kung Östen. Vad som sker under kungarnas dispyt är nämligen att Sigurds vikingadåd … visar sig komma till korta i jämforelse med hemmasittarens, kun Östens, fredliga bragder såsom byggande av kyrkor och hamnar, klok rättskipning osv. Kulturen vinner manjämningen på vikinga-andans bekostnad. Ett gammalt mönster har därmed givits en helt ny mening, liksom när en psalm görs om till socialistisk kampsång eller en dryckevisa förvandlas till nykterhetspropaganda* 'In the tale of the contest of the kings there is, however, a courtly tendency, in *Morkinskinna* as well as in *Heimskringla*; the meaning is that the old crude man-comparison ideal, personified by King Sigurðr, will be portrayed as inferior to the new age's more civilised and courtly ideal, as embodied by King Eysteinn. What happens in the kings' contest is that Sigurðr's Viking deeds … prove to be inadequate when compared with the peaceful exploits of King Eysteinn, who remained at home and promoted the building of churches and harbours, the judicious administration of justice and so forth. Civilisation wins out over the old Viking mentality. An old framework has thus been given a whole new meaning, as when a psalm is turned into a song of socialist struggle or a drinking song is transformed into abstentionist propaganda'.

sciousness, Sigurðr regards his ability to ride in tournaments as a virtue (*Msk.* II, 132).[3] Eysteinn, the representative of the new culture, uses the word *gullhálsarnir* 'golden-necked ones' as a sarcastic reference to the extravagantly dressed men surrounding Sigurðr and in so doing speaks as a typical representative of European conservatism.[4]

Concepts of modernity and tradition are complex and evasive.[5] Brian Stock has challenged the assumption that modernism should be equated with change, and tradition with stagnation. Modernism often grows out of tradition or is disguised as tradition, and it is often the case that few things are more modern than those that derive from tradition.[6] Ole Bruhn recognises in Earl Rǫgnvaldr the Holy of the Orkneys just such a contemporary traditionalism.[7] The twelfth century was marked by conflicts between the old and the new. There then emerged those who regarded old knowledge as obsolete, as opposed to the general view of moderns as dwarfs standing on the shoulders of giants.[8] The boundaries between the old and the new were not so sharply drawn. Susanne Kramarz-Bein considers that *Laxdæla saga* devotes itself to accommodating the new fashions and emphases of

3   Ibid. On 'turniment', see Niels M. Saxtorph *et al.*, 'Turnering,' pp. 71–73; Maurice H. Keen, *Chivalry*, pp. 83–101; Juliet Vale, 'Violence and the Tournament,' pp. 143–158.

4   On these views see C. Stephen Jaeger, *The Origins of Courtliness: Civilizing Trends and the Formation of Courtly Ideals 939–1210*, pp. 176–195; Allen J. Frantzen, *Before the Closet: Same-Sex Love from Beowulf to Angels in America,* pp. 235–47; E. Jane Burns, 'Refashioning Courtly Love: Lancelot as Ladies' Man or Lady/Man?,' pp. 111–134, 116–117.

5   Brian Stock, *Listening for the Text. On the Uses of the Past*, p. 33: 'Tradition and modernity are the most troubling concepts in cultural analysis. We are never quite sure what they mean.' See Elisabeth Gössmann, '"Antiqui" und "Moderni" im 12. Jahrhundert,' pp. 40–57; Wilfried Hartmann, '"Modernus" und "Antiquus": Zur Verbreitung und Bedeutung dieser Bezeichnungen in der wissenschaftlichen Literatur vom 9. bis zum 12. Jahrhundert,' pp. 21–39.

6   Stock, 'Tradition and Modernity: Models from the Past,' pp. 33–44; *Listening for the Text*, pp. 159–71; *The Implications of Literacy. Written Language and Models of Interpretation in the Eleventh and Twelfth Centuries*, pp. 517–521.

7   Ole Bruhn, 'Earl Rognvald and the Rise of Saga Literature,' pp. 240–242; *Tekstualisering: Bidrag til en litterær antropologi*, pp. 206–213

8   Jaeger, *The Envy of Angels: Cathedral Schools and Social Ideals in Medieval Europe, 950–1200* (Philadelphia, 1994), pp. 217–36. A similar meaning is implicit in the formula 'alþýðan er gjörn til nýjungarinnar' '"the common people are eager for change"', which can be found both in *Rómverja saga* and *Heimskringla* (Vol. 2, p. 46).

the thirteenth century, although the work itself is a saga about times past.[9] *Morkinskinna* is 'young' in much the same way and this youthful spirit reveals itself not least in the description of society.[10]

This does not mean, of course, that old culture and traditions are completely ignored. In *dróttkvætt* poems, and indeed in all poetry, there is a wealth of culture, both for the poets themselves and the kings who employ them. Haraldr the Severe requires that the poet Þjóðólfr entertain him by composing verse about an argument between a blacksmith and a tanner; he must present them first as the giant Geirrøðr and Þórr (as in mythological poetry), and then as Sigurðr and Fáfnir (as in heroic poetry) (*Msk.* I, 271–272). The interest in pre-conversion tradition is great even though it is incorporated into the conceptual world of Christianity. Thus Sigurðr the Dragonslayer and Þórr reemerge as standard courtly amusements.

Vésteinn Ólason characterises the depiction of society in *Brennu-Njáls saga* in these terms: '[*Brennu-*]*Njáls saga* deals with a lost world which will never return. The seeds of its destruction lay in its foundations, yet from those same seeds had grown a mighty tree'.[11] The saga turns on the recent disappearance of the social order of the Icelandic Commonwealth, of old customs and habits. A breeze of sadness wafts over the narrative; it is a tragedy, whereas *Morkinskinna* is not. *Morkinskinna* tells of old customs, and old poems enjoy an honoured place in the narrative. Nevertheless, it is an optimistic text about modern times. It depicts not so much a society about to disappear or die but rather a new world of towns, politeness, courtly life and courtly customs, a civilisation that was destined to leave its mark on the centuries to come. *Morkinskinna* is marked by a kind of modern traditionalism – it features tradition as a precursor of modernity.[12]

9   Kramarz-Bein, '"Modernität" der Laxdœla saga.' *Laxdæla Saga* has long been associated with new customs (see Ármann Jakobsson, 'Konungasagan Laxdæla'). Kramarz-Bein explores the 'modern' nature of the saga and its evident interest in fashion and artefacts of all kinds.

10 Aaron J. Gurevich (*Categories of Medieval Culture*, p. 136) considers that courtly poetry is generally preoccupied with the present. This can be seen, for example, in the extensive use of the historic present.

11 Vésteinn Ólason, *Dialogues with the Viking Age: Narration and Representation in the Sagas of the Icelanders*, p. 204.

12 Preben Meulengracht Sørensen ('Modernitet og traditionalisme: Et bidrag til is-

King Hákon's cultural revolution

In *Morkinskinna*, the military campaigns and the amorous dealings of kings are interwoven. Magnús the Good is fostered by the king and queen of Russia after a marital spat between the royal couple. Haraldr the Severe falls into disfavour in Constantinople after rejecting Zóe the Powerful. The disputes between Hákon Ívarsson and Haraldr the Severe are simultaneously a power struggle and a love story. Repeatedly the narrative stops to turn from the affairs of state to the private matters of the king's men, in the same way as King Eysteinn Magnússon takes the time to attend to both in the tale of Ívarr Ingimundarson.

Morkinskinna was written about 1220. It is a branch in the tree of kings' sagas but shaped in its growth by the ethics and attitudes of court life. In the widest sense it may be considered a part of courtly literature.[13] At that time secular literature in the south of Europe seemed to primarily concentrate on private matters relating to the individual. But it is not only the preoccupation with the individual that is reminiscent of chivalric literature. *Morkinskinna*'s sustained interest in pomp and splendour also reflects the priorities of courtly literature. Courtly society is based on knightly ideals, its traditions, customs and social relations. The structure of *Morkinskinna* is modelled on an aesthetic comparable to that of romance literature in the twelfth and thirteenth centuries, also including loan words from the courtly world: *riddari* 'knight', *burdeigja* 'prance', *turniment* 'tournament', and this influence causes the work to differ from older kings' sagas, *Historia de antiquitate regum Norwagiensium*, *Óláfs saga Tryggvasonar* or *Ágrip* for example.[14]

---

lændingesagaernes litteraturhistorie, med en diskussion af Fóstbræðra sagas alder') has discussed the connection between tradition and innovation, especially in the *Íslendingasögur*. He identifies an increasing respect for tradition. This view corresponds with the evident fondness for modernity identifiable in earlier sagas such as *Laxdæla saga* and *Morkinskinna*.

13 If defined narrowly, courtly literature comprises only texts that were actually composed at court, but a broader definition is more useful (J. David Burnley, *Courtliness and Literature in Medieval England*, pp. 122–47).

14 *Sverris saga*, however, is characterised by an interest in the relations between kings and their retainers, and *Morkinskinna*'s extensive use of poems finds a parallel in the *Oldest Saga of St Óláfr*. Already around and even before 1200 experiments in

In 1217 a thirteen-year-old boy became the King of Norway and ruled until 1263. In all likelihood *Morkinskinna* was compiled in the first years of Hákon Hákonarson's reign. Though its intended audience was clearly Icelandic, it is likely that King Hákon's court also featured prominently in the thoughts of the saga author. Not long afterwards a momentous event in Norse literary history occurred:

> Var þá liðit frá hingatburði Christi 1226 ár, er þessi saga var á norrænu skrifuð eptir befalningu ok skipan virðuligs herra Hákonar kóngs.[15]

> At this time 1226 years since the birth of Christ had passed when this saga was written in the Norse language following the command and order of the noble King Hákon.

Reference is also made to King Hákon in *Elís saga*, *Ívens saga*, *Möttuls saga* and *Strengleikar*, a collection of *lais* traditionally attributed to Marie de France.[16] The king's activity as a patron of translations is a sign of the impulse to promote a varied literary experience at the Norwegian court. *Ívens saga* and *Tristrams saga* were translated from *romans courtois*, with the former work a translation of a poem by Chrétien de Troyes, the originator of the romance tradition in France. *Elís saga* is a translation of a *chanson de geste*, and courtly poetry and heroic poetry are two of the chief branches of courtly literature of this time. The horizon broadens even more with the translation of the *lais* of Marie de France and of *fabliaux* such as *Möttuls saga*. These five translations ascribed to King Hákon thus provide

---

saga writing had begun that subsequently nourished the Icelandic saga tradition. See Kari Ellen Gade, 'Poetry and its changing importance in medieval Icelandic culture,' pp. 69–70. In fragments of the *Oldest Saga* (*Otte Brudstykker af den ældste Saga om Olav den hellige*) there are both *þættir* and poems, and its form may have resembled *Morkinskinna*. See Louis-Jensen, 'Syvende og ottende brudstykke: Fragmentet AM 325 IV a 4to'; Jónas Kristjánsson, *Um Fóstbrœðrasögu* pp. 151–190; 'The Legendary Saga,' pp. 281–293.

15 *Tristrams saga ok Ísöndar*, p. 28. See Sverrir Tómasson, 'Hvenær var Tristrams sögu snúið?'

16 *Möttuls saga*, p. 6; *Ívens saga*, p. 98; *Elis saga ok Rosamundu*, p. 116; *Strengleikar: An Old Norse Translation of Twenty-One Old French Lais, Edited from the Manuscript Uppsala De la Gardie 4–7–AM 666 b, 4°*, p. 4.

a richly varied portrait of foreign courtly literature. It seems likely that he wished to promote this literature among his Norse subjects and that his purpose was in part a pragmatic one.[17]

Another purpose was to entertain. The translations bear witness to the taste of a young man who was touched by the tragic emotional poetry of *Tristrams saga*, but also enjoyed comic *fabliaux* tales such as *Möttuls saga*. King Hákon was just over twenty years old and newly married when *Tristrams saga* was translated, and at the royal court there was much interest in matters of love.[18] Hákon was not, of course, the first Norwegian king to show an interest in poetry. In *Morkinskinna* we may see various examples of kings as patrons of poets, and Hákon followed suit. When Snorri Sturluson went to Norway in 1218, he composed a poem for King Hákon and the then Earl Skúli, the latter of whom gets greater coverage in the poem – the *Háttatal*, which represents a third of the *Prose Edda* and was perhaps the beginning of Snorri's writing of kings' sagas.[19]

---

17 See Fidjestøl, 'Erotisk lesnad ved Håkon Håkonssons hoff,' pp. 72–76; Eyvind Fjeld Halvorsen, 'Norwegian Court Literature in the Middle Ages'; Halvorsen, *The Norse Version of Chanson de Roland*, pp. 1–31. Since Meissner (*Die Strengleikar: Ein Beitrag zur Geschichte der altnordischen Prosalitteratur*, p. 119) scholarship on Norse translations of romances in the thirteenth century has tended to emphasise their didactic importance: Geraldine Barnes, 'The riddarasögur and mediæval European literature'; Barnes, 'Arthurian Chivalry in Old Norse'; Barnes, 'Some current issues in riddarasögur research'; Susanne Kramarz-Bein, 'Höfische Unterhaltung und ideologisches Ziel: Das Beispiel der altnorwegischen Parcevals saga'; Sverrir Tómasson, '"Ei skal haltr ganga": Um Gunnlaugs sögu ormstungu'; Paul Bibire, 'From Riddarasaga to Lygisaga: The Norse Response to Romance,' pp. 57 and 62. However, many scholars favour the idea that these works sought both to entertain and inform. See Kalinke, *King Arthur North-by-Northwest: The matière de Bretagne in Old Norse-Icelandic Romances*, pp. 20–45; Gerd Wolfgang Weber, 'The decadence of feudal myth – towards a theory of riddarasaga and romance,' pp. 428–453. Kalinke states: 'To attribute solely didactic considerations to Hákon's interest in making French literature available in the Norwegian language seems too facile an explanation: that would mistake the nature of the translated romances as well as the sophistication, the intelligence, and capacity for amusement of the Norwegian court' (p. 21).

18 Fidjestøl, 'Erotisk lesnad ved Håkon Håkonssons hoff,' p. 82; Georges Duby, 'The Culture of the Knightly Class: Audience and Patronage'.

19 On the *dróttkvæði* tradition in the thirteenth century and its aesthetic, see Guðrún Nordal, *Tools of Literacy: The Role of Skaldic Verse in Icelandic Textual Culture of the Twelfth and Thirteenth Centuries*.

Translations sponsored by King Hákon show that he was not only interested in the art of a bygone era but that he desired to promote courtly literature of more recent times and to be a modern king. In Sturla Þórðarson's *Hákonar saga* he is described in comparison with the model kings of the thirteenth century, Saint Louis in France, King Alfonso X of Castile and Frederick II, the Holy Roman Emperor. These were all Christian kings who went to great lengths to bring peace and to introduce the rule of law to their respective countries. All supported the church and Christianity and regarded wisdom as their chief virtue. Frederick II was in fact considered so wise and learned that he was named *stupor mundi* 'wonder of the world'. Hákon maintained good relations with Frederick II and sought to be associated with other learned kings on the continent. His daughter was given in marriage to a prince of Castile and he sent falcons to the Sultan of Tunisia. He was tireless in building halls and churches. He intended Norway to be a civilized kingdom like those in southern Europe.[20]

The newly translated romances could serve as a source of instruction as to how courtly men in southern Europe behaved. They portrayed a new taste. Hákon did not stop there, however. It may be that he promoted the writing of the *Konungs skuggsjá*, *Speculum regale*, or 'King's mirror', intending it for his sons.[21] The notion that *Fagrskinna* was heavily influenced by Hákon is an old one.[22] Whatever the case, Hákon Hákonarson

---

20 The last part of *Hákonar saga* deals with his positive dealings with other magnates; there is praise of the Pope, for example, and much space is spent on the Spanish marriage of Hákon's daughter. On the friendship between Hákon and Frederick II, see *Hákonar saga Hákonarsonar etter Sth. 8 fol., AM 325 VIII, 4o og AM 304,4 4o*, pp. 84, 98, 136 and 154. Between them was *hínn mefti felaghſkapr* (p. 154) 'the greatest fellowship'. On Hákon's attempts to improve morals and on his overall foreign policy aims, see, among others, Ármann Jakobsson, 'Hákon Hákonarson – friðarkonungur eða fúlmenni?,' pp. 179–184; Fidjestøl, 'Erotisk lesnad ved Håkon Håkonssons hoff,' p. 83; Meissner, *Die Strengleikar*, pp. 105–135; Richard I. Lustig, 'Some views on Norwegian foreign service, 1217–1319'; Bagge, *From Gang Leader to the Lord's Anointed: Kingship in Sverris saga and Hákonar saga Hákonarsonar*, pp 121–128 and passim.
21 On *Konungsskuggsjá*, see Ármann Jakobsson, *Í leit að konungi*, p. 88 and citations there; Kramarz-Bein, 'Zur Darstellung und Bedeutung der Höfischen in der Konungs skuggsjá'; Einar Már Jónsson, *Le miroir: Naissance d'un genre littéraire*; Einar Már Jónsson, 'Staða Konungsskuggsjár í vestrænum miðaldabókmenntum.'
22 Gustav Indrebø, *Fagrskinna: Avhandlinger fra Universitetets historiske seminar*, pp. 275–284; Bjarni Einarsson, *Fagrskinna – Nóregs konunga tal*, ÍF 29, pp. cxxiii–v.

was a patron of learning and art until he died. On his deathbed he had sagas read to him, among them kings' sagas and finally the saga of his grandfather Sverrir (see part V, chapter 1). In his old age Hákon appears to have been interested in kings' sagas, whereas in his youth he had enjoyed romances.[23] His descendants shared this interest in foreign literature. *Barlaams saga ok Jósafats* is attributed to his son, while his grandson Hákon Magnússon is said to have had *venda morgum riddara sogum jnorænu ur girzsku ok franzeisku mali* 'translated many chivalric romances into Norwegian from the Greek and French languages'.[24]

Morkinskinna was composed before the translation campaign initiated by the Norwegian kings, but in it we find the same elements, and these were apparent in Iceland even earlier. The influence that aristocratic culture from the south exercised upon Nordic culture did not, of course, begin with a single translation in 1226, and it is unlikely that it would have occurred to the king to begin such translation activity if the seeds of European courtly culture had not reached Norway and Iceland long before. *Morkinskinna* clearly reveals that southern courtly culture had begun to shape northern ideology before 1220, and we need not be surprised at this.[25]

23 Fidjestøl, 'Erotisk lesnad ved Håkon Håkonssons hoff,' pp. 72–73.
24 *Viktors saga ok Blávus*, p. 3. Bibire ('From Riddarasaga to Lygisaga: The Norse Response to Romance,' p. 56) thinks that this represents an increase in the production of works. On Hákon the young and Barlaams saga, see *Biskupa sögur*, Vol. 2, p. 54. Compare Ole Widding, 'Et norsk fragment af Barlaams saga'; Widding, 'Om fragmenter af Barlaams saga ok Josaphats: Holm 12 fol. V og NoRA 64'; Odd Einar Haugen, 'Om tidsforholdet mellom Stjórn og Barlaams ok Josaphats saga'; Haugen, 'Buddha i Bjørgvin: Den norrøne soga om kongssonen Josaphat og munken Barlaam'; Reidar Astås, 'Barlaams ok Josaphats saga i nærlys'; Astås, 'Romantekst på vandring: Barlaams og Josaphats saga fra India til Island'; Haugen, 'Barlaam og Josaphat i ny utgåve.'
25 The intellectual and artistic influence of the courtly world long before the translation of *Tristrams saga* is well attested: among others, Clover, *The Medieval Saga*, pp. 148–188; Bibire, 'From Riddarasaga to Lygisaga: The Norse Response to Romance,' pp. 58–59, 62. Andersson ('Composition and Literary Culture in Þiðreks saga') and Stefanie Würth (*Der 'Antikenroman' in der isländischen Literatur des Mittelalters: Eine Untersuchung zur Übersetzung und Rezeption lateinischer Literatur im Norden*. pp. 126–135) have discussed the forerunners of the romances, older translations of secular sagas that share some similarities with French romances. Paul V. Rubow ('Den islandske Familieroman'; 'De islandske Sagaer') and Bjarni Einarsson,

But despite its flirtation with these innovations, *Morkinskinna* stands on the old foundation of the art of skaldic poetry and historiography; the courtly element is only one of the work's many roots. In the saga, epic weight and the mystery of romance are combined.[26] Its aesthetic may be influenced by that of skaldic poetry (see part II, chapter 3), and the work is itself framed by skaldic verse. Between the poems and the saga an intangible connection exists. Poets enjoy pride of place in *Morkinskinna*, as in some Sagas of Icelanders that are considered amongst the eldest, for example *Egils saga*, *Kormáks saga* and *Hallfreðar saga*.[27] Although it is difficult to point to any specific relationship between *Morkinskinna* and the oldest Sagas of Icelanders, the saga was composed near the beginning of the period during which Sagas of Icelanders were first written down. In *Morkinskinna* we find the private lives of its characters and the theme of love treated in much the same was as they are in these sagas, in which the many poems and exploration of the relationships between Icelanders with a king are principal features. More importantly, however, these are long and complex sagas in which direct speech, staging and dramatisation are prominent. None of these elements was completely innovative, but

(*Skáldasögur: Um uppruna og eðli ástarskáldasagnanna fornu*, as well as in other works) stressed the influence of romances on the *Íslendingasögur*, a view that was not universally accepted. Ideas about European influence on medieval Icelandic literature are reviewed by Lars Lönnroth (*The European sources of Icelandic saga-writing: an essay based on previous studies*) and Mattias Tveitane ('Europeisk påvirkning på den norrøne sagalitteraturen: Noen synspunkter').

26 W.P. Ker (*Epic and Romance: Essays on Medieval Literature*, p. 4) describes this main genre of medieval narrative literature thus: 'Whatever Epic may mean, it implies some weight and solidity; Romance means nothing, if it does not convey some notion of mystery and fantasy.' In fact, medieval Norse sagas are always a mixture of foreign forms, for example saints' lives and romances (Kathryn Hume, 'Structure and Perspective: Romance and Hagiographic Features in the Amicus and Amelius Story').

27 Ursula Dronke ('The Poet's Persona in the Skalds' Saga,' p. 23) goes so far as to say: 'Without the poets, I suspect, we should have had no Icelandic saga.' Clunies Ross ('The Skald Sagas as a Genre: Definitions and Typical Features,' pp. 40–43) points to the variety of similarities between skáld sagas and kings' sagas, and others have discussed the similarities between these sagas and *þættir* (see, among others, Poole, 'Introduction,' p. 16; John Lindow, 'Skald Sagas in their Literary Context 1: Related Icelandic Genres,' pp. 218–231). As Lindow notes: 'it would be fair to say that the kings' sagas of *Morkinskinna* and *Flateyjarbók*, but not those of *Heimskringla*, share important thematic aims with some of the skalds' sagas' (p. 231).

most of the dominant characteristics of the Sagas of Icelanders may also be found in *Morkinskinna*. The translated romances also deal with private lives and love and service to a king. The structure of *Morkinskinna* also stands very close to this tradition (see part II, chapters 1 and 2). Paul Bibire has discussed the difference between translated romances and the indigenous romances that later came into prominence. He regards the Sagas of Icelanders as the true heirs of translated romances.[28] The same applies to the legendary sagas, but the difference between the traditional legendary sagas and the traditional romances is to be found in their subject matter rather than their structure or ideas.[29]

Morkinskinna, unlike *Tristrams saga* or the sagas of Kormákr, Kjartan or Gunnlaugr, is not tragic. The pre-eminent theme is not love but rather kings and their relationships with their subjects. This topic lies at the core of the tradition of the kings' sagas, yet they are not really a coherent literary genre. Some are of a summary nature, while others, like *Morkinskinna*, are characterised by their dramatic and episodic features. Some occur in the misty reaches of the past, while others are near contemporary sagas. The number of poems differs from work to work.[30] Saxo Grammaticus's *Gesta Danorum* resembles *Morkinskinna*, to some degree, in its interest in the immediately recent past. Both authors also seem to embrace the inter-

28 Bibire ('From Riddarasaga to Lygisaga: The Norse Response to Romance,' pp. 64–74) notes: 'It is not the Icelandic Secondary Romances which inherit from Primary Romance the pursuit of honour or of adulterous love, and the tragic outcome which can ensue. It is Kormakr or Kjartan who is the true heir of Tristram, and it is the *Íslendinga sögur* which have assumed within their ample range the true functions of European romance' (p. 73).

29 Distinctive features shared by legendary sagas ('sagas of antiquity') and romances are various (see Ármann Jakobsson, 'Le Roi Chevalier. The Royal Ideology and Genre of Hrólfs saga kraka'; Peter Hallberg, 'Some Aspects of the Fornaldarsögur as a Corpus.' On the indigenuous romances, see Margaret Schlauch, *Romance in Iceland*; Jürg Glauser, *Isländische Märchensagas: Studien zur Prosaliteratur im spätmittelalterlichen Island*; Astrid van Nahl, *Originale Riddarasögur als Teil altnordischer Sagaliteratur*; Matthew James Driscoll, *The Unwashed Children of Eve: The Production, Dissemination and Reception of Popular Literature in Post-Reformation Iceland*.

30 Ole Bruhn (*Tekstualisering: Bidrag til en litterær antropologi*, pp. 214–223) discusses various issues associated with kings' sagas as a literary genre and his discussion shows how little the formal characteristics of the genre have been discussed (Ármann Jakobsson, 'King and Subject in Morkinskinna,' pp. 102–103).

lace aesthetic. Saxo's treatment of older poetry shows this – he recreates the poems as Latin hexameters, and augments his material extensively. The same applies to his prose sources, for Saxo shares with the author of *Morkinskinna* a love of detail not found in other works drawing on the same material.[31]

The kings' sagas are not untouched by foreign influence, even if they do not have clear models, least of all the longest and the most detailed of them. It is probably impossible to find any medieval Icelandic saga that is free from foreign influence. Nevertheless, Icelandic sagas have their own shape and character, and no foreign literary works are quite like them. *Morkinskinna* largely describes a foreign society. It is subject to influences from southern European court culture, including romances, one of the saga's roots. Another lies in the past, in the Norse poetic tradition that had occupied pride of place among Icelanders. The saga deals with skaldic verse and skaldic poets, and is full of such verse. The sources of *Morkinskinna*, on the other hand, can be found in other kings' sagas, and its author is a writer of history like those who preceded him: Theodoricus the Monk, Eiríkr Oddsson and the authors of *Ágrip*, *Orkneyinga saga* and *Jómsvíkinga saga*. Perhaps none had greater influence on him than the authors of *The Oldest Saga of St. Óláfr* and *Sverris saga*, each in his own way. Three streams run together into one work, *Morkinskinna*, and all of the confluence is evident further downstream in the Sagas of Icelanders.

Morkinskinna emerged during a period of upheaval in Icelandic saga writing. Under the influence of interlace aesthetics the author created a detailed and artistic narrative out of a strong and long-standing tradition, partially romantic in spirit but governed by the critical sense of a historian who believes that some knowledge can be derived from the saga even as, at the same time, it can be enjoyed as an entertaining and lively narrat-

---

31 On Saxo's aesthetics see Eric Christiansen, 'The place of fiction in Saxo's later books,' in *Saxo Grammaticus: A Medieval Author Between Norse and Latin Culture*, pp. 27–37; Karsten Friis-Jensen, *Saxo Grammaticus as a Latin Poet: Studies in the Verse Passages of the Gesta Danorum*, pp. 29–63; Inge Skovgaard Petersen, *Da Tidernes Herre var nær: Studier i Saxos historiesyn*, pp. 61–178; Kurt Johannesson, *Saxo Grammaticus: Komposition och världsbild i Gesta Danorum*.

ive.[32] *Morkinskinna* is a complex work, not least due to the myriad artistic streams that converged at the time of its composition and served to influence its structure.

A man of letters

The word *author* has frequently been used in this book, and it is now time to examine the term more closely. Though not necessarily stated outright, thus far I have assumed the existence of an individual author behind *Morkinskinna*, one who carefully created its structure, portrait of society and meaning, even though he defines himself as a writer of history. It was not so long ago that Finnur Jónsson believed that there was no conscious author in *Morkinskinna*.[33] In the kind of analysis attempted in the present volume, however, we need to discuss the idea of an author for *Morkinskinna*, and that, in turn, necessitates defining what the term means in this context.

When the author of *Morkinskinna* is mentioned here, I have been following a trend in literary scholarship in which several kinds of authors are spoken of, among them the implied author, by which is meant the author in the text whose voice we seem from time to time to hear.[34] The implied author is obviously similar to the narrator, but existence of the former does not depend upon point of view, the 'I' or the 'we' in the text. It is a sense of there being a human intelligence in and behind the text, the sense of a personality telling us what we as readers process and listeners hear. When, out of narratological necessity (that is, the need to interpret the saga text clearly), the word 'author' has been used in this book, I mean the author as constructed in the work. This sense of *author* is useful, for it allows the word to be used without calling up a real flesh-and-blood author – whoever he is or whether he is one man or many.

32 Andersson and Gade (*Morkinskinna*, p. 83) put it well: 'Whatever came before *Morkinskinna* looks parochial by comparison, and whatever came afterward was obliged to take the wider parameters into account.'
33 Finnur Jónsson, ed. *Morkinskinna*, p. xl (see part I, chapter 2).
34 Seymour Chatman, *Story and Discourse: Narrative Structure in Fiction and Film*, pp. 147–151; Shlomith Rimmon-Kenan, *Narrative Fiction: Contemporary Poetics*, pp. 86–105.

In modern narratology an author is assumed to lie behind a text, and, of course, modern fictional works as a general rule have a specific, identifiable author. This assumption applies less well to a work such as *Morkinskinna*. Like other sagas its origins lie in the events that are narrated, and narratives about these events have sometimes existed beyond living memory.[35] The creation of works of this nature is based on a formulaic process, which does not, as has often been assumed, especially in the early days of oral-formulaic theory (the 1960s), rule out the creative imagination, whether intentionally so or otherwise. The author of a saga is a collector who chooses material for his narrative, arranges it and creates new contexts. He may be compared to the last master builder of a large cathedral, the individual who places his hand on the finished structure.[36] In all likelihood the part played by the last master will be very significant. *Morkinskinna* is a massive work, with a much greater store of information than all the previous works deriving from the same material. In the extant saga an artistic whole has been created out of this raw material.

Did this author work alone or may we imagine a committee of writers behind the saga?[37] In *Morkinskinna* the narrator sometimes speaks in his work in the first person, but we must no more confuse him with the author himself than we would with the narrator in a traditional epic work, even though a saga audience might not have distinguished between them. This 'I' pronoun appears several times in the saga (e. g. *Msk.* I, 162, 316, II, 70, 102, 210, 234), as does the plural 'we' (*Msk.* II, 66).

The presence of the narrator is apparent in those chapters that are borrowed from *Hryggjarstykki*, where it is explained how and why the small events in Sigurðr the Noisy's escape found their way into the narrative: *því er þess getit hversu hann bjó um eldsvirkit at þat þótti hugkvæmliga gǫrt at búa svá um at aldregi vættisk* (*Msk.* II, 207) 'it has been mentioned how

---

35 Similarly, the saga does not cease to be oral simply because it was committed to writing; even after that point, whenever it occurred, it must have been read out to many listeners, many of whom will not have been functionally literate.

36 This much-used metaphor can be traced back to C. S. Lewis, *The Discarded Image: An Introduction to Medieval and Renaissance Literature*, p. 31.

37 This possibility has been discussed in connection with *Heimskringla*. See Diana Whaley, *Heimskringla: An Introduction*, p. 18; Jonna Louis-Jensen, 'Heimskringla – Et værk af Snorri Sturluson?' pp. 230–245; Kolbrún Haraldsdóttir, 'Der Historiker Snorri: Autor oder Kompilator?,' pp. 97–108.

he took care of his tinderbox, because it seemed so ingeniously made that it would not get wet'. Reasonably enough, Peter Hallberg thought it unlikely that the author is here speaking in his own voice.[38] Nevertheless, in the text we can repeatedly sense the presence of a saga author who adopts the guise of a critical writer of history, less reticent in coming forward in his own person than are the authors of the Sagas of Icelanders.[39] When the narrative pauses to describe King Haraldr the Severe, the saga author mentions that more sagas about Haraldr exist than are related in *Morkinskinna*:

> kemr mest til þess ófróðleikr várr ok þat með at vér viljum eigi rita vitnisburðarlausar sǫgur, þótt vér hǫfum heyrt þær frásagnir, því at oss þykkir betra at heðan af sé við aukit heldr en þetta sama þurfi aptr at taka. (*Msk.* I, 205).

> this results mostly from our ignorance and from our unwillingness to write down unsubstantiated tales that we have heard, because it seemed better to us from here on to add matter rather than having to take things back.

This is a literary motif, *pauca ex multis* 'a selection of examples'.[40] The author steps forward in the first person and describes his own working methods and clearly expects to be criticized for including too little in his work rather than too much, although in fact it has turned out otherwise,[41] as we have seen in earlier chapters of this book.

The narrative of the relations between Haraldr the Severe and Finnr Árnason that includes the *fabliau*-like tale about Sveinn Úlfsson and the old lady in the cottage deserves some attention. Perhaps the author thought it risky to record insults directed at kings. Before the remarks by Finnr are

---

38 Hallberg, 'Hryggjarstykki: Några anteckningar,' p. 120.

39 The willingness of *Íslendingasögur* authors to project themselves into the narrative varies. Paul Schach ('Some Forms of Writer Intrusion in the Íslendingasögur') identifies some kinds of authorial intrusions and considers them more common in the earliest days of saga writing. *Morkinskinna* probably dates from those times (around 1220).

40 Sverrir Tómasson, *Formálar íslenskra sagnaritara á miðöldum: Rannsókn bókmenntahefðar*, pp. 236–238.

41 Finnur Jónsson, ed. *Morkinskinna*, pp. xxxv–xl.

quoted in the saga, they are called *skrǫk* 'a fib', and this word is accompanied by a psychological explanation: *Þá mælti Fiðr jarl orðskrǫk þat er síðan er uppi haft ok frá segir hversu reiðr hann var, er hann fekk eigi stillt orðum sínum* (*Msk.* I, 251) 'Then Finnr uttered the falsehood that has survived and is preserved as an example of how angry he was that he could not control his words'. Directly afterwards comes the tale of Sveinn and the old woman, which is of a completely different character – unlike Finnr's royal insults those of the old woman result from simple-mindedness and not viciousness or anger. She calls the king *haltan ok ragan* 'lame and cowardly' without realising that he is sitting right in front of her. Then the author thinks it appropriate to explain why the tale is told at all and offers the saga listener this explanation: *Þetta er gamans frásǫgn ok eigi sǫguligt eins kostar, nema fyr þá sǫk at hér er lýst grein speki ok óvizku* (*Msk.* I, 252) 'This is a story told for pleasure and not particularly historical, except for the fact that here is presented the difference between wisdom and ignorance'. This author's note clearly states the exemplary function of the tale, similar to those episodes discussed above, and goes on to say that everybody since that time has regarded Finnr's remark as *barnsorð* (*Msk.* I, 253) 'the words of a child'.

The 'we' figure appears in Magnús Barelegs's last battle and mentions that he cannot explain fully all the king's battle tactics (*Msk.* II, 66). Later it is said that the narrative of the king's death is best told by the man who followed him the longest:

> kunni engi frá því glǫggra at segja en Víðkuðr Jóansson, því at hann hafði einna manna bazt fylgt konungi ok flýði eigi fyrr, sem áðr gat ek, en konungi var ráðinn bani ok konungr sjálfr bað hann flýja. (*Msk.* II, 70).

> No one could tell the tale more fully than Víðkunnr Jóansson because of all men he had best followed the king and did not flee, as I earlier stated, before the king was struck down and the king himself ordered him to flee.

Here the author speaks as an objective historian even if in the first person. In adventure stories, where the story rather than the source of the information is paramount, such authorial intrusions as this would seem egregious.

The author's position on any issue is sometimes made clear although he does not speak in his own voice.[42] Rumour is often used to judge the proceedings, as in the Sagas of Icelanders. Hreiðarr Grjótgarðsson is said to have followed his lord well *ok gott er hverjum er slíkan orðróm getr* (*Msk.* II, 203) 'and it is good for everyone to receive such praise'. Here the author himself has the final word. Likewise the reactions of the general public tell the story of Hallvarðr Gunnarsson, the killer of Sigurðr Dandy-hat: *var hann skotinn í lopti einu, ok harmaði hann engi maðr* (*Msk.* II, 233–234) 'he was shot in an upstairs chamber and nobody mourned his passing'. The punishment of Tryggvi Óláfsson's killer is described thus: *eptir þat lét konungr festa hann upp á gálga ok hreinsaði svá landit, en hefndi konungs* (*Msk.* I, 289) 'afterwards the king had him hanged on a gallows and thus the land was cleansed and the king avenged'. The use of the word *hreinsa* 'cleanse' shows that the punishment is viewed positively. When a particular crime breaks God's law the author is not afraid to take a position. He expresses himself in no uncertain terms about the execution of Bishop Reinaldr: *er glíklegt at þetta óverkan hafi dregit Nóreg til mikillar ógiptu ok þeim er gerðu ok fellu með í bann ok Guðs reiði* (*Msk.* II, 162) 'it is probable that this crime condemned Norway to much misfortune, and those who did the deed were excommunicated and suffered God's wrath'.

Although there is an authorial presence in the work and the narrator speaks now and then in the first person, this does not mean that there was an individual author. No such claim is being made here. A clear authorial sensibility may nevertheless be found in the work, and this sensibility is a creation of traditional narrative art, and not an invention of twentieth-century academic scholars. Thus it is safe to refer to the 'author' of *Morkinskinna*, if all that is meant is the author in the text, the implied author. That author does not have to be, and in the Middle Ages rarely was, an individual person. But it is no less likely for *Morkinskinna* than for any other Old Icelandic saga that a flesh-and-blood author is responsible for the work.

Aside from all this, attitudes to authorship were very different at the time than now. Medieval texts were not the immutable or sole possession of their authors. It is not possible to focus on an 'original' text that is the final product of an author. This does not mean that we must discontinue the search for the most authentic text or that there are no differences among scribes, redactors and authors. But even those who considered themselves authors did not commit to vellum only their own words.[43] It is difficult to estimate the contribution of scribes to the creation of the extant text of *Morkinskinna*, but there is no evidence to suggest that the scribes of the oldest extant manuscript (GKS 1009 fol) have added more to the material than scribes generally do. They were creating another work of art, the book now known as *Morkinskinna*.

What kind of man was the 'author' of *Morkinskinna*? The implied author is in his own way a self-effacing individual, since he dresses himself in the guise of the historian who seems to make ancient lore available in an objective fashion. But although sagas are expressed objectively, all history writing and all narratives have a purpose, whether medieval or modern, and the instinct for unity and coherence in the saga was then strong. Historical writings will always bear the mark of their authors, and with respect to *Morkinskinna* we can sense much about its author even though his identity will always be unknown.

We may think of the author of *Morkinskinna* as an Icelandic man of letters who had served a Norwegian king. From the saga we may infer a love of things both Icelandic and exotic, a fondness for poetry and *exempla*. The author of *Morkinskinna* may be conceived as a man of ideas who believed equally in the inherent authority of a king and the doctrines of the church, although in his saga there is less interest in spiritual than in secular matters. He had an interest in the relationships between people, their emotions, and the private and social lives that he had seen being forged in Norway. All of this may be inferred from his text, but no attempt will be made here to come up with the author's name.

---

43 Sverrir Tómasson, *Formálar íslenskra sagnaritara á miðöldum*, pp. 180–194; A.J. Minnis, *Medieval Theory of Authorship: Scholastic Literary Attitudes in the Later Middle Ages*; Per Nykrog, 'The Rise of Literary Fiction.'

WE TELL OURSELVES STORIES

An Icelander ventures out into the world

In the discussion thus far the tale of Ívarr Ingimundarson has been mentioned on several occasions. This story portrays a society that revolves around a king, his retainers, feasts, joy and poetry. Though the roles of courtier and poet are explored, the king's activities are paramount. The Ívarr episode deals with the private life of the poet, but the primary subject is the friendship between the poet and the king who helps him overcome the pangs of unrequited love. This brief story seems unimportant in the larger scheme of eleventh- and twelfth-century Norwegian history. Although the particular value of the tale is limited, its general application is much more significant. Focusing closely upon the nature of the solution to Ívarr's problem rather than the specific nature of the problem itself, the episode is basically a dramatic narrative used to illustrate a general point over and above its particular characters and events – in short, an *exemplum*. Such is true about many other narratives in the saga; the shorter and more unremarkable they seem, the more important they can be.

This is also apparent in the episode of Arnórr the Earls' Poet wherein neither battles nor important matters of state are described, merely the composition and oral delivery of a poem. Focusing, however, on the power of kingship, two kings are compared; one of them radiates stability and moderation, the other repeatedly interrupts the poet's delivery and obviously has a hard time coping with the comparison. Arnórr's steady hand, succeeding in favouring one king without insulting the other, in dealing with kings is exemplary. Highlighting Arnórr as an Icelander the story promotes the notion that as courtiers Icelanders are at least as accomplished as others, and sometimes more so. This episode draws a portrait of a courtly society in which the behaviour of people obeys clear but complex rules, and wherein competition also plays an important role, in this instance competition between two kings. Finally, the tale turns on the art of poetry and its value in society. The tale also includes stanzas from Arnórr's celebrated poem *Hrynhenda*. In this way one work of art is woven into another.

Competition also plays an important role in the brief episode of Brandr the Bountiful, at first a seemingly modest tale about a trick played by the king upon an Icelandic retainer. Haraldr contrives a series of tests that

Brandr must pass, but it turns out that the king himself is also required to pass a test and in this Brandr helps him. The tale deals primarily with the importance of moderation for a just king and links up with many other narratives involving moderation to be found throughout *Morkinskinna*. The Brandr episode is a tale about royal power in general but is also a character portrait of Haraldr. The role of a courtier is difficult, as is clearly revealed in the tale. Both the poet Þjóðólfr and Brandr are in danger of falling out of favour if they do not pass the king's test. This test is nonetheless a game – and the game is important in the courtly society described in *Morkinskinna*. A game can both be child's play and art and, of course, it can have serious consequences for the players. Brandr delivers no poem but his performance, when he unwaveringly continues his work without a word passing his lips as he yields up his gifts to the king as requested, is no less artful. We may notice how the tale characterises Haraldr: he must be intelligent enough to interpret Brandr's actions properly. A less subtle king might have misinterpreted Brandr's conduct and reacted rather differently.

In the tale in which the king and the fisherman exchange extemporaneous and coarse compositions, the game element is also very important (see part III, chapter 2). Ditties fly back and forth, and riddles are wrestled with. King Haraldr's delight in play, competition and art are apparent, and while the fisherman is quick to respond, he shows respect for the king. He is not an Icelander, however, whereas Þjóðólfr is; even though he is a poet he is slow to counter the king's banter, and though he is an insider at court he is sensitive to slights. The repeated practical jokes played on Þjóðólfr serve not only to characterise the king but also to confirm that the king's court is no place for the faint of heart. The fisherman makes use of the power of words; eloquence secures him the backing of the king. Words are a resource of great value at court. This is also apparent in the episode about Stúfr the Blind, in which once again we see how a clever retainer can make insinuations against a touchy king without insulting him. Stúfr plays the same game as Arnórr the Earls' Poet had previously done, but King Haraldr's emotional control has improved in the meantime – it matures as the saga develops, and we learn just how important a virtue this is for a king; Haraldr is a man of justice when and if he keeps a tight reign on his temper. In the Stúfr episode we see that access to the court is neither quick nor easy. Stúfr succeeds in entering the king's service, and his countrymen are honoured.

These short tales are all set in the days of Haraldr the Severe, but the same narrative pattern reoccurs after Haraldr's death, as in the tale of Ívarr occuring at the court of King Eysteinn Magnússon, and the Þórarinn Shortcloak episode at Sigurðr the Crusader's. In each tale a tough courtly society is described wherein poetry has pride of place and Icelanders exploit this situation. The same is true of the Einarr Skúlason episode, a single tale made up of three narratives. Their main point is the position of the art of skaldic poetry in a new society where other arts have become influential. At the same time we meet an Icelander who enjoys the support of the king because of his art, and we meet a king who supports the poet. The tales occur in a municipal setting where many people are on the stage and where there is sufficient time for fun and games.

It is thus clear that such brief tales in *Morkinskinna* can be very meaningful indeed, most commonly in their exploration of the nature of political power. One after another kings are shown in the light of their retainers and their popularity, joy in play and magnanimity are all emphasised. The import of moderation is stressed again and again. Repeated comparison between two kings (or a single king and his chieftains) shows that friction is the inevitable result in a kingdom when more than one person shares power. Such comparisons also illuminate royal power and the role of the king. Thus, far from superfluous to the main narrative thread, these short episodes represent the essence of the saga's *raison d'être*.

In *Morkinskinna*, society is represented as a static entity, even though the narrative covers 125 years. The backdrop is essentially the same in the tales mentioned above. Society is opulent, and emphasis is placed upon the superficial, upon the joyous merrymaking. Our gaze, however, is directed at private lives and people's feelings, and we are made aware of what a hard and competitive world the court is. The society of *Morkinskinna* is unusual and probably more like the one with which the author and his audience were familiar than any Norwegian society during the years in which the events of the saga were purported to have taken place.

Icelanders are ubiquitous in *Morkinskinna*. When Haraldr the Severe is thrown into a dungeon in Constantinople, there are two Icelanders with him, Úlfr the Marshall and Halldórr Snorrason. Úlfr dies just before the

Haraldr's final military campaign (in England), and his death is one of many omens indicating the eventual outcome of the expedition. Halldórr becomes estranged from the king, and returns to Iceland, where for the rest of his life he dines out on stories involving the king and himself. A young Icelander absorbs these stories and later entertains the king by repeating them. The narrative ends with Halldórr named as their source. No one who reads the story without the frame narrative of the saga would understand this reference, but the audience of *Morkinskinna* recognises an old friend. Poetry is the glue that binds things together in *Morkinskinna*. Early in the saga the poet Sigvatr gives Magnús the Good some insight into the error of his ways. Shortly before the end of the saga Einarr Skúlason recites some skaldic verses that no one can properly remember. In between lies many a tale. Haraldr the Severe tells Magnús the Good about his travels abroad, and at the same time the narrator of *Morkinskinna* tells the saga audience the very same tale. Much later Einarr Paunch-Shaker falls asleep while the king is telling this story, and even later a young Icelander appears on the scene ready to pass on this same tale to the king, directly from the mouth of Halldórr Snorrason.

Those narratives that appear least significant are in fact the most arresting. Like all *exempla* they preserve general knowledge. Trivial everyday events acquire a symbolic and universal dimension, since everything in life is analogous, and out of small incidents larger truths can be inferred. These analogies thus take on the character of proverbs and maxims in which truth is distilled in a few words. Like all historical writings *Morkinskinna* deals with individual past events. But the author's obligation to tell the truth is accompanied by the licence to extrapolate wisdom from the saga. The saga contains symbolic tales that have more than one meaning – they transmit truths about individuals and all men, about society and the world at large, and about the power of kings – in which the saga writer moves between the particular and the general. We may see polished symbolic thought where many things are referred to simultaneously. The saga is not just the history of Norway but also a saga of the figure of the poet himself. We see this in the many restatements of the saga's principal themes: the power of kings, the relations between kings and retainers, sophisticated Icelandic court poets with the riches of skaldic artistry in their intellectual baggage, poor and simple Icelanders and other deracinated greenhorns on the courtly stage, the harshness of court life, its delights and high spirits, its pomp and splendour, its adventures, the faraway lands and stories and poems. All the major themes of *Morkinskinna* could be found in the experiences of an Icelandic poet who has spent part of his life in a Norwegian royal court, a life story probably close to that of an imagined author of *Morkinskinna*.

The society purportedly described in *Morkinskinna* is that of eleventh- and twelfth-century Norway, but the saga nevertheless carries a clear imprint of the society that was developing in thirteenth-century Europe. Despite his interest in the past and its traditions, the author of *Morkinskinna* approaches the saga with the present in mind.[44] Most of the narrative literature in twelfth- and thirteenth-century Iceland dealt with history, notably that of the Viking and heroic ages, but the spirit of the sagas ought rather to be associated with contemporary feudalism and chivalric morality. The sagas reflect, to only a limited extent, a pan-Germanic heritage; a more potent influence on their presentation of the past is the world of chivalric romance. In the literary culture of European feudal society all sorts of ancient figures reappeared as medieval knights: Achilles and Hector, Alexander the Great, Caesar, the biblical King David, King Arthur and Charlemagne. All are depicted as medieval contemporaries who honour the ideals and customs of knights, but are nevertheless mightier and more remarkable than any contemporary figures. They all become part of a common past that was still alive in contemporary medieval days, rather as time works in fairy tales.[45] Present and past do not remain as two worlds but

44 This is typical of medieval historiography. Despite an interest in things new, medieval historians sometimes failed to distinguish clearly between present and past. As Peter Burke puts it (*The Renaissance Sense of the Past*, p. 1): 'Medieval men lacked a sense of the past being different in quality from the present. They did not deny that in some ways the past was unlike the present … [b]ut they did not take the difference very seriously.'

45 Ibid., pp. 1–6; Werner Paravicini, *Die ritterlich-höfische Kultur des Mittelalters*, pp. 18 and 28; Keen, *Chivalry*, pp. 102–24. See also Roberta Frank, 'Germanic Legend in Old English Literature,' p. 88. The champions named here came to Iceland in translated sagas, as Würth (*Der 'Antikenroman' in der isländischen Literatur des Mittelalters: Eine Untersuchung zur Übersetzung und Rezeption lateinischer Literatur im Norden*) points out.

rather become one. The more distant the past, the more eagerly it was compared to the knightly society familiar to the author.[46]

Medieval literature, ideas, and society were a seamless whole that could not be broken down into constituent elements. The intellectual world of *Morkinskinna* fashioned itself on the society that was described in the saga, a courtly society that began to take shape in the twelfth and thirteenth centuries. The Middle Ages were a time of change. Norbert Elias and Stephen Jaeger have described how society developed gradually in the direction that we call 'civilisation', with increasingly formalised rules of behaviour. It was not just about new dining customs, sleeping arrangements and bathing habits, but also about new attitudes towards other classes, and towards life and death. Although they agree about the notion of gradual development, Elias argues that social development generates ideas and culture, whereas Jaeger is more inclined to stress the influence of culture on the development of society. Whatever the case, it is clear that early in the thirteenth century, when *Morkinskinna* was created, new norms were emerging in medieval chivalric society.

Jaeger argues that it was clerics who took the initiative in creating a new chivalric image and their teaching exerted a strong influence on courts and in cathedral schools. Cultural innovations first established themselves in royal courts, before extending their influence more generally into the lives of men of rank and property. The new ideal was the Christian and cultured courtier; the knight, who was a lion on the battlefield and a lamb in the chamber. Among the qualities of the new chivalric ideal were magnanimity, knowledge, eloquence and wit. Knights were obliged to dress stylishly, to express themselves well, and, above all, to show moderation in all situations. They could learn how to behave properly from reading chivalric romances, and these were works that clerics had played a significant role in creating. Jaeger suggests that these narratives did not so much reveal an existing courtly morality as proclaim a new one. Among

---

46 As William Brandt (*The Shape of Medieval History: Studies in Modes of Perception*, p. xv) has pointed out, medieval history writers are just as favourably disposed towards their own period as are modern historians: 'medieval chronicles have little of the antiquarian about them. They were written for their own time without much concern for the past.'

the values promoted were moderation, adoration of women, peacefulness and *amour courtois*.[47]

If royal courts were viewed in light of the new courtly society, they could be thought of as peaceful places where the monarch protected others, where formality reigned and order was rarely upset, where each courtier had his role and place, and conflicts were rare. Elias and Jaeger agree that actual court life bore little resemblance to such an idealised vision. In reality, there were fierce rivalries and much violence, and it would have been absolutely essential to exercise restraint in order not to reveal one's own intentions. Courtiers needed to preserve a dignified exterior.[48]

Morkinskinna depicts a harsh courtly world in which men needed to defend their honour and position in society every bit as much as they needed to in the old Icelandic Commonwealth society. The royal court was nevertheless a different world. The Commonwealth was beginning to unravel at the time when the Sagas of Icelanders were being composed, whereas *Morkinskinna* describes a social system that was on the rise, a European court society. The difference was primarily that the power struggle was associated with a new idealised view of man, which would later find expression in the *riddarasögur* 'romance sagas'.[49] *Morkinskinna* purports to deal with times long past, but it also depicts a society that is still being formed: a new age.

47 Norbert Elias, *The Civilizing Process*; Jaeger, *The Origins of Courtliness*; Jaeger, *The Envy of Angels*, pp. 21–117
48 On the nature and culture of feudalism, see, among others, Georges Duby, *The Three Orders: Feudal Society Imagined*; Paravicini, *Die ritterlich-höfische Kultur des Mittelalters*; Joachim Bumke, *Höfische Kultur: Literatur und Gesellschaft im hohen Mittelalter*, Vols. 1–2; Keen, *Chivalry*; Marc Bloch, *Feudal Society*; F.L. Ganshof, *Feudalism*; Elias, *The Court Society*; Elias, *The Civilizing Process*; Jaeger, *The Origins of Courtliness*; Jaeger, *The Envy of Angels*; Fredric L. Cheyette, ed. *Lordship and Community in Medieval Europe: Selected Readings*; Robert Hanning, *The Individual in Twelfth-Century Romance*; J. David Burnley, *Courtliness and Literature in Medieval England*.
49 Paul Bibire ('From Riddarasaga to Lygisaga: The Norse Response to Romance,' p. 73) notes that only to a limited extent are later romances the descendants of the translations. Nevertheless wish-fulfilment tales tend to be set in courts: 'Romance is probably the only vehicle available for this idealised expression of human achievement and fulfilment within society, because the metaphor of the courtly world was (and possibly remains) the only available idealisation of society.'

The saga closely examines this new society with courtliness as its ideal, but focuses, no less, on the Icelander who is part of that court. What is the Icelander's place in this new world? The saga involves a quest for an identity for both author and audience, an identity in which both a king and poetry play a part. This search binds together a work that moves from Magnús the Good to Ingi Haraldsson, and a work in which figures disappear constantly from the stage and new ones assume their places. Time passes, but when it pauses on stage, we see there a courtly society and within it the man; on the one hand a courtier who is sometimes an Icelander, and on the other hand a king. And we see the narrative: saga, poem and language itself.

The saga is sometimes serious in tone, sometimes adventurous. It speaks of a king who was not alone in the world but rather at the head of a court where there were skalds and entertainments. It speaks of a king of the Icelanders. It speaks of an Icelander who travelled widely in the world, sometimes with polar bears or with filthy hands, sometimes with wise-cracking ditties but more often poetry on his lips. It speaks of an Icelander who makes the Norwegian court his own society and the Norwegian king his leader. There he found a place for Iceland in this new world.

Conclusion

A maker of myths

At the beginning of this book it was suggested that *Morkinskinna* is an interesting work that has been insufficiently appreciated, an important saga in its own right, irrespective of its influence on *Fagrskinna*, *Heimskringla* and other sagas. *Morkinskinna* deserves be taken on its own terms, for its ideas and its narrative artistry. Accordingly, the links between *Morkinskinna* and other works do not loom large in my analysis; the main emphasis is on the saga itself as a work of narrative art.

How and when *Morkinskinna* achieved its present form will no doubt remain a mystery. Most of the evidence, however, points to a date around 1220. For a long time it was thought that the extant text was the result of additions having been made to an *ur-Morkinskinna,* even though scholars could never agree on the exact nature of the material that had been added, and no definitive conclusions concerning these putative additions and interpolations have emerged. When the evidence is analysed, there is little reason to believe that *Morkinskinna* has changed much from its original form to the version that appears in the extant manuscripts. We may also conclude that the present text of *Morkinskinna* was Icelandic, that it was put together around 1220, and that it served as a source for both *Fagrskinna* and *Heimskringla*.

Morkinskinna is an organically complete saga, no less so than those two later works. Its aesthetics are complex, but perfectly in tune with the spirit of the time. Much of the material that an earlier generation of scholars regarded as alien or superfluous may be said to have a rightful place in the multi-stranded narrative texture of the saga. The structure of *Morkinskinna* proves to be by no means haphazard or clumsy but is rather perfectly consistent with the aesthetic priorities of the historian who was its author. The form and themes of the saga are closely integrated. Much of the material previously considered extraneous to the saga in fact contributes meaningfully to what the saga posits about society, royal power and the position of Icelanders in the Norwegian court. By analysing *Morkin-skinna* in its entirety, including its material about Icelanders and other allegedly extraneous sections, the present study seeks to present the saga in a new light.

All told relatively little attention had been paid to making sense of the work's structure and themes, and, for this reason, there is relatively little earlier scholarship in this area from which to draw. Scholars who have engaged with the saga to any extent have concentrated primarily on its origins and the complexities that result from the speculation about the nature of the *ur-Morkinskinna*. For this reason this new study is both an introduction to and an interpretation of *Morkinskinna*. When the overall ideology of the saga is examined, no theme looms larger than courtly society (which is always the same throughout the saga), and its ideals. On this narrative stage we encounter the two principal characters of a work that explores the idea of a courtier serving a king, and their relationship reflects the fundamental nature of *Morkinskinna*: it is an Icelandic work of art about Norwegian kings.

The present discussion assumes that *Morkinskinna* does not simply deal with isolated dramatic episodes drawn from the characters' lives but functions rather as didactic history with an ideological purpose. If this hypothesis is accepted, then some of the work's so-called 'digressions' may be regarded as *exempla* that lie at the heart of the narrative; they treat issues that are central to the saga as a whole, and are so intertwined with the core of the work that it would be difficult to separate them. Among these topics are the nature of royal power, the relationship between kings and subjects and their duties towards the king, the ethos of courtly society, the place of Icelanders in the Norwegian courts and the value of poetry and storytelling. All these issues could have impacted on the life of a single person, an Icelander who travelled to Norway and served the king as a poet and courtier. There is no need to give such an individual a name. His spirit pervades *Morkinskinna*.

There are two perspectives discernible in the saga. One is that of the Norwegian court, the king and his men. The other is the same Norwegian court as viewed from the bleak rocky outcrop on the edge of the Arctic Circle – the court as seen through the clear eye of an Icelandic guest. Although the saga takes place almost exclusively on the exotic Norwegian courtly stage, two societies remain in focus: the wealthy and courtly mainland kingdom, and the distant land to which the author and his listeners trace their origins and which they have by no means forgotten – the agrarian society of Iceland. The audience of *Morkinskinna* could have been twofold: members of the Norwegian royal court, which also functions as a kind of character in the saga, and the Icelanders for whom the saga was written and who are also represented by the work's more traditional characters. The work was intended not only for Icelanders based in the court but also for their fellow countrymen who were back home on their volcanic island in the north Atlantic, and only able to travel abroad in their imagination, under the stimulus provided by works such as *Morkinskinna* and other sagas. That Icelandic audience played its full part in helping to create *Morkinskinna*'s colourful picture of a refined and exotic world. It is also because of this that one of the saga's principal stories deals with how Icelanders gained a foothold in this world.

Otherness is an important theme of the saga. The Icelanders in the saga are not at home but in another land. This expatriate mindset is an energising force in *Morkinskinna*. Those who have been at court for a long time have a view of two worlds. Every Icelandic courtier is really two individuals. On the one hand he is a sophisticated man of the world, perhaps a poet who even disguises and rejects his Icelandic origins and makes it difficult for newcomers at court. Behind this guise, however, is a youth spent in grinding Icelandic poverty and privation. The tale of Sneglu-Halli presents this dichotomy in the personage of Þjóðólfr Arnórsson. We might say that his is the story of every Icelandic courtier in Norway.

In its form, style and substance *Morkinskinna* represents a distillation of south European aristocratic literature. It seems to stem from someone who knew courtly culture from the inside. It deals in a real sense with the courtiers of the king. But it has many roots. It follows in the wake of other sagas about Norwegian kings and it contains skaldic poetry that could have influenced its structure as much as foreign models. Skaldic poets and saga authors are bearers of the tradition. Sagas like *Morkinskinna* deal with times, customs and people that are no more. But although it looks to the past, the saga also presents the present and the future on its stage, because the society under the microscope is thirteenth-century courtly society. It was at this time that Scandinavia welcomed southern European culture with open arms, with Hákon Hákonarson in the vanguard. He was young when *Morkinskinna* was composed, but he later took great pains to introduce chivalric literature to the Norse-speaking world.

Morkinskinna is an example of another kind of reaction to the new reality. It is grounded in the old narrative and poetic traditions. Yet, although *Morkinskinna* is a text about the past, there is no apparent nostalgia expressed for former times, no tears shed over the passing of the world of the saga, the world that was. On the contrary, *Morkinskinna* deals with the present and the challenges confronting both its author and the audience for whom it was written. The interest in courtly society was a creative one, as was the attitude towards historical material, notably that relating to the recent history of Norway. Thus, *Morkinskinna* preserves not only myths about the past but also about the new world, about courtly society. It would be a new world for a provincial Icelander. The author of *Morkinskinna* is like an explorer who has discovered a new world on his travels and it does not matter that others have already been there. Then he brings this world home to his audience in Iceland. This world lies partially concealed in *Morkinskinna* under two centuries of Norwegian history: the new society, the king whom the poet serves, the courtier, and the artistry that is his weapon.

Thus, the saga revolves around identity. All Icelanders, all courtiers and all the poets in the saga could be aspects of an author, who in his time filled each of these roles. The other kings in the narrative derive their existence from the author's familiarity with the kings whom he served. Poets create their own world in language in order to compare it with their experience of the real thing; they understand the world and explain it to others. They do not always need to create new events or persons, for sometimes they disguise themselves as a writer of sagas and derive their characters from the actual world. The author of *Morkinskinna* does just this, but teasingly he always reminds us of the costume that he has adopted.

Morkinskinna was not situated within any clearly defined aesthetic or tradition. It is in fact like no other saga. *Morkinskinna* is contradictory, and not simply because in it we find a combination of traditional values and the ideals of a new society. The saga ranges over the world, but deals with the place of the Icelander in that world. The author is an idealist who narrates *exempla* in order to teach moral lessons, but he is also an adventurer who loves narrative for its own sake. It is pointless to brood too much about the contradictions in the saga. Its author knows that he is in disguise and that there is nothing simple in the behaviour of any human being.

Snorri Sturluson was a guest at court at the time *Morkinskinna* was being composed. His interest in the kings of Norway was the same as that of the author of *Morkinskinna* but the works they created are dissimilar. Snorri became the poet of the king and Earl Skúli, he was their vassal, and may even have dreamed of being the Earl of Iceland. Despite his great knowledge of ancient customs, Snorri Sturluson did not remain untouched by the modern age, as *Heimskringla* confirms. Though *Heimskringla* and *Morkinskinna* march to their respective and distinctive drums, they both deal with Icelanders and royal power.

By about 1220 the king of Norway had become a kind of yardstick for Icelanders. Their power struggles began to involve him to an ever increasing extent. No extant Norwegian historical writings are as extensive as the sagas that Icelanders composed about Norwegian kings in this period, four decades before the nation submitted to the king. In no other saga of the Norwegian kings are Icelanders as prominent as in *Morkinskinna*. Nevertheless, the kings are the protagonists of the story. In the life of every poet in thirteenth-century courtly society, one man reigns supreme, and that is the king; without him there would be no saga. But the king is not alone, and *Morkinskinna* is not primarily about one man but about men, and its author is particularly interested in the complications that arise in the dealings between them. He serves these ends best by analysing these interpersonal relations and setting them on a stage for all to observe.

Bibliography

Primary Sources

Adam of Bremen. *Hamburgische Kirchengeschichte*. Ed. Bernard Schmeidler. Monumenta Germaniae Historica, Scriptores rerum Germanicarum 2, 3rd edn. Hannover, 1917.

Aristotle. *Poetics*. Ed. and trans. Stephen Halliwell. London, 1995.

Ágrip af Nóregskonunga sǫgum. Ed. Bjarni Einarsson. Íslenzk fornrit 29. Reykjavík, 1985.

Árni Magnússon. *Brevveksling med Torfæus (Þormóður Torfason)*. Ed. Kristian Kålund. Copenhagen, 1916.

Bandamanna saga. Ed. Guðni Jónsson. Íslenzk fornrit 7. Reykjavík, 1936.

Bjarnar saga Hítdælakappa. Ed. Sigurður Nordal and Guðni Jónsson. Íslenzk fornrit 3. Reykjavík, 1938.

Brands þáttur ǫrva. Ed. Einar Ólafur Sveinsson. Íslenzk fornrit 4. Reykjavík, 1935.

Brennu-Njáls saga. Ed. Einar Ólafur Sveinsson. Íslenzk fornrit 12. Reykjavík, 1954.

Codex Frisianus (Sagas of the Kings of Norway). MS. No. 45 fol. in the Arnamagnæan Collection in the University Library of Copenhagen. Ed. Halldór Hermannsson. Corpus codicum Islandicorum medii aevi 4. Copenhagen, 1932.

Codex Frisianus: En Samling af norske Konge-sagaer. Ed. C.R. Unger. Christiania [Oslo], 1871.

Danakonunga sǫgur. Ed. Bjarni Guðnason. Íslenzk fornrit 35. Reykjavík, 1982.

The Ecclesiastical History of Orderic Vitalis II (Books III and IV) and V (Books IX and X). Ed and trans. Marjorie Chibnall. Oxford Medieval Texts. Oxford, 1968 and 1975.

Edda Snorra Sturlusonar. Ed. Finnur Jónsson. Copenhagen, 1931.

Egils saga Skalla-Grímssonar. Ed. Sigurður Nordal. Íslenzk fornrit 2. Reykjavík, 1933.

Eirik the Red and Other Icelandic Sagas. Ed. and trans. Gwyn Jones. London, 1961.

Bibliography

Eliot, George. *Felix Holt, the Radical.* Edinburgh and London, 1866.

Elis saga ok Rosamundu. Ed. Eugen Kölbing. Heilbron, 1881.

Einarr Skúlason's Geisli: a critical edition. Ed. Martin Chase. Toronto, 2005.

Erex saga. Norse Romance II: Knights of the Round Table. Ed. and trans. Marianne E. Kalinke. Arthurian Archives 4. Cambridge, 1999.

Eyrbyggja saga. Ed. Einar Ólafur Sveinsson. Íslenzk fornrit 4. Reykjavík, 1935.

Fagrskinna. Nóregs kononga tal. Ed. Finnur Jónsson. Copenhagen, 1902.

Fagrskinna-Nóregs konungatal. Ed. Bjarni Einarsson. Íslenzk fornrit 29. Reykjavík, 1985.

Fjörutíu Íslendinga-þættir. Ed. Þorleifur Jónsson. Reykjavík, 1904.

Flateyjarbok. En Samling af norske Konge-sagaer med indskudte mindre Fortællinger om Begivenheder i og udenfor Norge samt Annaler 1–3. Ed. Guðbrandur Vigfússon and C.R. Unger. Oslo, 1860–1868.

Flateyjarbók. 1–4. Ed. Finnbogi Guðmundsson, Vilhjálmur Bjarnar and Sigurður Nordal. Akranes, 1944–1945.

Fornmanna sögur eptir gömlum handritum útgefnar að tilhlutun hins kónungliga norræna fornfræða félags 1–12. Copenhagen, 1831–1832.

Fóstbrœðra saga. Ed. Björn K. Þórólfsson and Guðni Jónsson. Íslenzk fornrit 6. Reykjavík, 1943.

Færeyinga saga. Ed. Ólafur Halldórsson. Reykjavík, 1987.

Gísls þáttr Illugasonar. Ed. Sigurður Nordal and Guðni Jónsson. Íslenzk fornrit 3. Reykjavík, 1938.

Gísls þáttr Illugasonar. Ed. Peter Foote. Íslenzk fornrit 15. Reykjavík, 2003.

Grettis saga Ásmundarsonar. Ed. Guðni Jónsson. Íslenzk fornrit 7. Reykjavík, 1936.

Gull-Ásu-Þórðar þáttr. Ed. Jón Jóhannesson. Íslenzk fornrit 11. Reykjavík, 1950.

Gunnlaugs saga ormstungu. Ed. Sigurður Nordal and Guðni Jónsson. Íslenzk fornrit 3. Reykjavík, 1938.

Halldórs þáttr Snorrasonar II. Ed. Einar Ólafur Sveinsson. Íslenzk fornrit 5. Reykjavík, 1934.

Hákonar saga Hákonarsonar etter Sth. 8 fol., AM 325 VIII,4° og AM 304,4°. Ed. Marina Mundt. Oslo, 1977.

Hálfs saga ok Hálfsrekka. Ed. A. Le Roy Andrews. Halle, 1909.

Heiðarvíga saga. Ed. Sigurður Nordal and Guðni Jónsson. Íslenzk fornrit 3. Reykjavík, 1938.

Bibliography

Heimskringla 1–3. Ed. Bjarni Aðalbjarnarson. Íslenzk fornrit 26–28. Reykjavík, 1941–1951.

Hemings þáttr Áslákssonar. Ed. Gillian Fellows Jensen. Editiones Arnamagnæanæ B, 3. Copenhagen, 1962.

Hirdskråen: Hirdloven til Noregs konge og hans håndgangne menn, etter AM 322 fol. Ed. Steinar Imsen. Oslo, 2000.

Hrólfs saga kraka. Ed. Desmond Slay. Editiones Arnamagnæanæ B, 1. Copenhagen, 1960.

Hulda. Sagas of the Kings of Norway 1035–1177: Manuscript no. 66 fol. in the Arnamagnæan Collection. Ed. Jonna Louis-Jensen. Copenhagen, 1968.

Hungrvaka. Ed. Ásdís Egilsdóttir. Íslenzk fornrit 16. Reykjavík, 2002.

ÍF = Íslenzk fornrit.

Íslendingabók. Ed. Jakob Benediktsson. Íslenzk fornrit 1. Reykjavík, 1968.

Íslendinga sögur 1–13. Ed. Guðni Jónsson. Reykjavík, 1953.

Íslendinga sögur 1–9. Ed. Grímur M. Helgason and Vésteinn Ólason. Hafnarfjörður, 1968–1976.

Íslendinga sögur og þættir 1–2. Ed. Bragi Halldórsson, Jón Torfason, Sverrir Tómasson and Örnólfur Thorsson. Reykjavík, 1985–1986.

Íslendinga þættir. Ed. Guðni Jónsson. Reykjavík, 1935.

Ívens saga. Norse Romance II: Knights of the Round Table. Ed. and trans. Marianne E. Kalinke. Arthurian Archives 4. Cambridge, 1999.

Karlamagnús saga og kappa hans 1–3. Ed. Bjarni Vilhjálmsson. Reykjavík, 1954.

Króka-Refs saga. Ed. Jóhannes Halldórsson. Íslenzk fornrit 14. Reykjavík, 1959.

Laxdæla saga. Ed. Einar Ól. Sveinsson. Íslenzk fornrit 5. Reykjavík, 1934.

Ljósvetninga saga. Ed. Björn Sigfússon. Íslenzk fornrit 10. Reykjavík, 1940.

Medieval Literary Criticism. Ed. O. B. Hardison, Jr., Alex Preminger, Kevin Kerrane and Leon Golden. New York, 1974.

Monumenta Historica Norvegiæ: Latinske kildeskrifter til Norges historie i middelalderen. Ed. Gustav Storm. Christiania, 1880.

Morkinskinna. Pergamentsbog fra første halvdel af det trettende aarhundrede indeholdende en af de ældste optegnelser af norske kongesagaer. Ed. C. R. Unger. Christiania, 1867.

Morkinskinna. Ed. Finnur Jónsson. Copenhagen, 1932.

Morkinskinna: MS. No. 1009 fol. in the Old Royal collection of The Royal Library, Copenhagen. Ed. Jón Helgason. Copenhagen, 1934.

Bibliography

Morkinskinna: The Earliest Icelandic Chronicle of the Norwegian Kings (1030–1157). Ed. and trans. Theodore M. Andersson and Kari Ellen Gade. Islandica 51. Ithaca and London, 2000.

Morkinskinna: Norske kongesoger 1030–1157. Trans. Kåre Flokenæs. Stavanger, 2001.

Msk. = *Morkinskinna* I–II. Ed. Ármann Jakobsson and Þórður Ingi Guðjónsson. Íslenzk fornrit 23–24. Reykjavík, 2011.

Möttuls saga. Norse Romance II: Knights of the Round Table. Ed. and trans. Marianne E. Kalinke. Arthurian Archives 4. Cambridge, 1999.

Odds þáttr Ófeigssonar. Ed. Guðni Jónsson. Íslenzk fornrit 7. Reykjavík, 1936.

Olafs saga hins helga. Die 'Legendarische Saga' über Olaf den Heiligen (Hs. Delagard. saml. nr. 8^{II}). Ed. Anne Heinrichs, Doris Janshen, Elke Radicke and Hartmut Röhn. Heidelberg, 1982.

Orkneyinga saga. Ed. Finnbogi Guðmundsson. Íslenzk fornrit 34. Reykjavík, 1965.

Otte Brudstykker af den ældste Saga om Olav den hellige. Ed. Gustav Storm. Christiania [Oslo], 1893.

Ólafs saga Tryggvasonar en mesta 1–3. Ed. Ólafur Halldórsson. Editiones Arnamagnæanæ A, 1–3. Copenhagen, 1958–2000.

Palæografisk Atlas. Oldnorsk-islandsk afdeling. Copenhagen, 1905.

Saga Ólafs konungs hins helga – Den Store Saga om Olav den Hellige. Efter Pergamenthåndskrift i Kungliga Biblioteket i Stockholm Nr. 2 4to med varianter fra andre håndskrifter. Ed. Oscar Albert Johnsen and Jón Helgason. Oslo, 1941.

Samlestrarbókin: Úr safni Steingríms Arasonar. Ed. Gunnar Guðmundsson and Jónas Guðjónsson. Reykjavík, 1972.

Saxo Grammaticus. *Gesta Danorum – Danmarkshistorien* I–II. Ed. Karsten Friis-Jensen, trans. Peter Zeeberg. Copenhagen, 2005.

Sex sögu-þættir. Ed. Jón Þorkelsson. Reykjavík, 1855.

Sigurd Ranessöns Proces. Ed. Gustav Storm. Christiania, 1877.

Skaldic Poetry of the Scandinavian Middle Ages II: Poetry from the Kings' Sagas 1–2. Ed. Kari Ellen Gade. Turnhout, 2009.

Sneglu-Halla þáttr. Ed. Jónas Kristjánsson. Íslenzk fornrit 9. Reykjavík, 1956.

Strengleikar. An Old Norse Translation of Twenty-one Old French Lais. Edited from the Manuscript Uppsala De la Gardie 4–7 – AM 666 b, 4°. Ed. Robert Cook and Mattias Tveitane. Oslo, 1979.

Bibliography

Sturlunga saga Vols. 1–2. Ed. Jón Jóhannesson, Magnús Finnbogason and Kristján Eldjárn. Reykjavík, 1946.

Stúfs saga: Gefin út í firsta sinn eftir handritunum. Ed. Björn M. Ólsen. Fylgirit Árbókar Háskóla Íslands 1912. Reykjavík, 1912.

Stúfs þáttr. Ed. Einar Ólafur Sveinsson. Íslenzk fornrit 5. Reykjavík, 1934.

Sverris saga. Ed. Þorleifur Hauksson. Íslenzk fornrit 30. Reykjavík, 2007.

Tristrams saga ok Ísöndar. Norse Romance I: The Tristan Legend. Ed. and trans. Peter Jorgensen. Arthurian Archives 3. Cambridge, 1999

Two Icelandic Stories: Hreiðars þáttr. Orms þáttr. Ed. Anthony Faulkes. Viking Society for Northern Research Text Series 4. London, 1967.

Utvalgte þættir fra Morkinskinna. Ed. Tor Ulset. Nordisk filologi 14. Oslo, 1978.

Vatnsdæla saga. Ed. Einar Ól. Sveinsson. Íslenzk fornrit 8. Reykjavík, 1939.

Viktors saga ok Blávus. Ed. Jónas Kristjánsson. Reykjavík, 1964.

Víglundar saga. Ed. Jóhannes Halldórsson. Íslenzk fornrit 14. Reykjavík, 1959.

William of Malmesbury. *Gesta regum Anglorum – The History of the English Kings* I. Ed. R. A. B. Mynors *et al*. Oxford, 1998.

Þorgils saga ok Hafliða. Ed. Ursula Brown. London, 1952.

Þorvarðar þáttr Krákunefs. Ed. Guðni Jónsson. Íslenzk fornrit 6. Reykjavík, 1943.

Secondary Sources

Aalbæk-Nielsen, Kaj. *Kærlighed i middelalderen*. Copenhagen, 1999.

Agnes S. Arnórsdóttir. *Konur og vígamenn: Staða kynjanna á Íslandi á 12. og 13. öld*. Reykjavík, 1995.

Akehurst, F. R. P. and Stephanie Cain Van D'Elden, ed. *The Stranger in Medieval Society*. Medieval Cultures 12. Minneapolis, 1998.

Albeck, Gustav. *Knytlinga: Sagaerne om Danmarks konger*. Copenhagen, 1946.

Althoff, Gerd. 'Friendship and Political Order.' In *Friendship in Medieval Europe*, pp. 91–105. Ed. Julian Haseldine. Sutton, 1999.

Andersson, Theodore M. 'The Doctrine of Oral Tradition in the Chanson de geste and Saga.' *Scandinavian Studies* 34 (1962), 219–236.

—. *The Problems of Icelandic Saga Origins: A Historical Survey*. New Haven and London, 1964.

—. *The Icelandic Family Saga: An Analytic Reading*. Cambridge, Massachusetts, 1967.

Bibliography

—. 'Skalds and Troubadours.' *Mediaeval Scandinavia* 2 (1969), 7–41.

—. 'Splitting the Saga.' *Scandinavian Studies* 47 (1975), 437–441.

—. 'King's Sagas (Konungasögur).' *Old Norse-Icelandic Literature. A Critical Guide*, pp. 197–238. Ed. Carol J. Clover and John Lindow. Islandica XLV. Ithaca, 1985.

—. 'Snorri Sturluson and the saga school at Munkaþverá.' *Snorri Sturluson: Kolloquium anläßlich der 750. Wiederkehr seines Todestages*, pp. 9–25. Ed. Alois Wolf. Tübingen, 1993.

—. 'The Politics of Snorri Sturluson.' *Journal of English and Germanic Philology* 93 (1994), 55–78.

—. 'Composition and Literary Culture in Þiðreks saga.' *Studien zum Altgermanischen: Festschrift für Heinrich Beck*, pp. 1–23. Ed. Heiko Uecker. Ergänzungsbände zum Reallexikon der Germanischen Altertumskunde 11. Berlin and New York, 1994.

—. 'The Literary Prehistory of Eyjafjǫrðr.' *Samtíðarsögur, Forprent: Níunda alþjóðlega fornsagnaþingið á Akureyri 31. 7–6.8.* 1994, pp. 16–30. Reykjavík, 1994.

—. 'The Unity of Morkinskinna.' *Sagas and the Norwegian Experience. Preprints. 10. Internasjonale Sagakonferanse, Trondheim 3.–9. august* 1997, pp. 1–10. Trondheim, 1997.

—. 'The Continuation of *Hlaðajarla saga.' *Journal of English and Germanic Philology* 97 (1998), 155–167.

—. 'The King of Iceland.' *Speculum* 74 (1999), 923–934.

—. 'Why do Americans say "Family Sagas"?' In *Gudar på jorden: Festskrift til Lars Lönnroth*, pp. 297–307. Ed. Stina Hansson and Mats Malm. Stockholm, 2000.

—. 'Skald Sagas in their Literary Context 3: The Love Triangle Theme.' *Skaldsagas: Text, Vocation, and Desire in the Icelandic Sagas of Poets*, pp. 272–284. Ed. Russell Poole. Ergänzungsbände zum Reallexikon der Germanischen Altertumskunde 27. Berlin and New York, 2001.

Andersson, Theodore M. and Kari Ellen Gade. 'Introduction.' *Morkinskinna: The Earliest Icelandic Chronicle of the Norwegian Kings (1030–1157)*. Islandica 51. Ithaca and London, 2000.

Astås, Reidar. 'Barlaams ok Josaphats saga i nærlys.' *Maal og minne* (1990), 124–152.

—. 'Romantekst på vandring: "Barlaams og Josaphats saga" fra India til Island.' *Edda* 90 (1990), 3–13.

Bibliography

Auður G. Magnúsdóttir. *Frillor och fruar: Politik och samlevnad på Island 1120–1400.* Avhandlinger från Historiska Institutionen i Göteborg 29. Göteborg, 2001.

Ármann Jakobsson. 'Sannyrði sverða: Vígaferli í Íslendinga sögu og hugmyndafræði sögunnar.' *Skáldskaparmál* 3 (1994), 42–78.

——. 'Hákon Hákonarson – friðarkonungur eða fúlmenni?' *Saga* 33 (1995), 166–185.

——. *Í leit að konungi: Konungsmynd íslenskra konungasagna.* Reykjavík, 1997.

——. 'Konge og undersåt i Morkinskinna.' *Sagas and the Norwegian Experience: Preprints. 10. Internasjonale Sagakonferanse, Trondheim 3.–9. august 1997,* pp. 11–21. Trondheim, 1997.

——. 'History of the Trolls? Bárðar saga as an historical narrative.' *Saga-Book of the Viking Society* 25 (1998), 53–71.

——. 'Konungasagan Laxdæla,' *Skírnir* 172 (1998), 357–383.

——. 'King and Subject in Morkinskinna.' *Skandinavistik* 28 (1998), 101–117.

——. 'Le Roi Chevalier. The Royal Ideology and Genre of Hrólfs saga kraka.' *Scandinavian Studies* 71 (1999), 139–166.

——. 'Rundt om kongen: En genvurdering af Morkinskinna.' *Maal og minne* (1999), 71–90.

——. 'The rex inutilis in Iceland.' *Majestas* 7 (1999), 41–53.

——. 'Royal pretenders and faithful retainers: The Icelandic vision of kingship in transition.' *Gardar* 30 (1999), 47–65.

——. 'The Individual and the Ideal: The Representation of Royalty in Morkinskinna.' *Journal of English and Germanic Philology* 99 (2000), 71–86.

——. 'Ekki kosta munur: Kynjasagan Njála.' *Skírnir* 174 (2000), 21–48.

——. 'Kongesagaen som forsvandt: Nyere kongesagastudier med særligt henblik på Morkinskinna.' In *Den nordiske renessansen i høymiddelalderen,* pp. 65–81. Ed. Jón Viðar Sigurðsson and Preben Meulengracht Sørensen. Tid og Tanke 6. Oslo, 2000.

——. 'Um uppruna Morkinskinnu: Drög að rannsóknarsögu.' *Gripla* 11 (2000), 221–245.

——. 'The Amplified Saga: Structural Disunity in Morkinskinna.' *Medium Aevum* 70 (2001), 29–46.

——. 'Dulargervið.' In *Sagnaheimur: Studies in Honour of Hermann Pálsson on his 80th birthday, 26th May 2001,* pp. 1–12. Ed. Ásdís Egilsdóttir and Rudolf Simek. Studia Medievalia Septentrionalia 6. Vienna, 2001.

Bibliography

—. 'Strukturelle Brüche in der Morkinskinna.' In *Arbeiten zur Skandinavistik*. *14. Arbeitstagung der deutschsprachigen Skandinavistik. 1.-5. 9. 1999 in München*, pp. 389–400. Ed. Annegret Heitmann. Texte und Untersuchungen zur Germanistik und Skandinavistik 48. Frankfurt, 2001.

—. *Staður í nýjum heimi: Konungasagan Morkinskinna*. Reykjavík, 2002.

—. 'Den kluntede afskriver: Finnur Jónsson og Morkinskinna.' *Opuscula* 11 (2003), 289–306.

—. 'Konungurinn og ég: Sjálfsmynd Íslendings frá 13. öld.' *Þjóðerni í þúsund ár?*, pp. 39–55. Ed. Jón Yngvi Jóhannsson *et al.* Reykjavík, 2003.

—. 'The Hunted Children of Kings: A Theme in the Old Icelandic Sagas.' *Scandinavica* 43 (2004), 5–27.

—. 'Munnur skáldsins: Um vanda þess og vegsemd að vera listrænn og framgjarn Íslendingur í útlöndum.' *Ritmennt* 10 (2005), 63–79.

—. 'Royal Biography,' In *A Companion to Old Norse-Icelandic Literature and Culture*, pp. 388–402. Ed. Rory McTurk. Blackwell companions to literature and culture 31. Oxford, 2005.

—. 'Textreferenzen in der Morkinskinna: Geschichten über Dichtung und Geschichten,' *Skandinavistik* 37 (2007), 118–130.

—. 'Laxdæla dreaming: a saga heroine invents her own life.' *Leeds studies in English* (2008), 33–51.

—. 'En plats i en ny värld: Bilden av riddarsamhället i Morkinskinna,' *Scripta Islandica* 59 (2008), 27–46.

—. 'Food and the North-Icelandic Identity in 13th century Iceland and Norway.' In *Images of the North: Histories – Identities – Ideas*, pp. 69–79. Ed. Sverrir Jakobsson. Studia Imagologica 14. Amsterdam and New York, 2009.

—. 'Friðkolla,' In *Margarítur, hristar Margréti Eggertsdóttur fimmtugri 25. nóvember 2010*, pp. 12–13. Reykjavík, 2010.

—. 'Um hvað fjallaði Blágagladrápa?,' *Guðrúnarstikki kveðinn Guðrúnu Nordal fimmtugri 27. september 2010*, pp. 11–14. Reykjavík, 2010.

—. 'Morkinskinna', In *The Oxford Dictionary of the Middle Ages* Vol. 3, p. 1196. Ed. Robert E. Bjork. Oxford, 2010.

—. 'The Life and Death of the Medieval Icelandic Short Story.' *Journal of English and Germanic Philology* 112 (2013), 257–291.

—. 'Image is Everything: The Morkinskinna Account of King Sigurðr of Norway's Journey to the Holy Land,' *Parergon* 30.1 (2013), 121–40.

—. 'The Madness of King Sigurðr: Narrating Insanity in an Old Norse Kings' Saga.' *Studies in Early Medicine* 3 (2014). (forthcoming)

Bibliography

—. *Íslendingaþættir: Saga hugmyndar.* Studia Islandica 63. Reykjavík 2014. (forthcoming)

Ásdís Egilsdóttir. *Þættir: Einkenni og staða innan íslenskra miðaldabókmennta.* University of Iceland, 1982.

—. 'Af óskynlegum Íslendingi.' In *Orðaforði heyjaður Guðrúnu Kvaran 21. júlí 1993*, pp. 11–13. Reykjavík, 1993.

—. 'Um biskupasögur.' In *Biblían og bókmenntirnar: Rit helgað minningu séra Jakobs Jónssonar. dr. theol*, pp. 39–54. Studia theologica islandica 9. Reykjavík, 1994.

—. 'Drekar, slöngur og heilög Margrét.' In *Heiðin minni: Greinar um fornar bókmenntir*, pp. 241–256. Ed. Haraldur Bessason and Baldur Hafstað. Reykjavík, 1999.

Bagerius, Henric. 'Vita vikingar och svarta sköldmör: Föreställningar om sexualitet i Snorre Sturlassons kungesagor.' *Scripta Islandica* 48 (1997), 13–38.

Bagge, Sverre. 'Theodoricus Monachus – Clerical Historiography in Twelfth-Century Norway.' *Scandinavian Journal of History* 14 (1989), 113–133.

—. 'Kvinner i politikken i middelalderen.' *Middelalderkvinner – liv og virke*, pp. 5–30. Ed. Ingvild Øye. Onsdagskvelder i Bryggens museum 4. Bergen, 1989.

—. 'Harald Hardråde i Bysants: To fortellinger, to kulturer.' In *Hellas og Norge: Kontakt, komparasjon, kontrast*, pp. 169–192. Ed. Øivind Andersen and Tomas Hägg. Bergen, 1990.

—. *Society and Politics in Snorri Sturluson's Heimskringla.* Berkeley, 1991.

—. *From Gang Leader to the Lord's Anointed: Kingship in Sverris saga and Hákonar saga Hákonarsonar.* The Viking Collection 8. Odense, 1996.

—. 'Icelandic Uniqueness or a Common European Culture? The Case of the Kings' Sagas.' *Scandinavan Studies* 69 (1997), 418–442.

—. *Mennesket i middelalderens Norge: Tanker, tro og holdninger 1000–1300.* Oslo, 1998.

Bakhtin, Mikhail, trans. Hélène Iswolsky. *Rabelais and His World.* Bloomington, 1984.

Barnes, Geraldine. 'The riddarasögur and mediæval European literature.' *Mediaeval Scandinavia* 8 (1975), 140–158.

—. 'Arthurian Chivalry in Old Norse.' *Arthurian Literature* 7 (1987), 50–102.

357

—. 'Some current issues in riddarasögur research.' *Arkiv för nordisk filologi* 104 (1989), 73–88.

Barthes, Roland, trans. Richard Howard. 'The Discourse of History.' In *The Rustle of Language*, pp. 127–140. Oxford, 1986.

Beck, Heinrich. 'Hit óarga dýr und die mittelalterliche Tiersignificatio.' In *Saga og språk: Studies in language and literature*, pp. 97–111. Ed. John M. Weinstock. Austin, 1972.

Bédier, Joseph. *Le roman de Tristan et Iseut*. Paris, 1920.

Benton, John. 'Consciousness of Self and Perceptions of Individuality.' In *Renaissance and Renewal in the Twelfth Century*, pp. 263–295. Ed. Robert L. Benson, Giles Constable, and Carol D. Lanham. Oxford, 1982.

Berger, Alan J. 'The Textual History of Þinga saga.' *Arkiv för nordisk filologi* 94 (1979), 50–56.

—. '*Heimskringla* and the Compilations.' *Arkiv för nordisk filologi* 114 (1999), 5–15.

—. '*Heimskringla* is an abbreviation of Hulda-Hrokkinskinna.' *Arkiv för nordisk filologi* 116 (2001), 65–69.

Bergljót S. Kristjánsdóttir, Sverrir Tómasson, and Ármann Jakobsson. 'Andmælaræður við doktorsvörn Ármanns Jakobssonar 1.2.2003.' *Gripla* 14 (2003), 285–322.

Bibire, Paul. 'From Riddarasaga to Lygisaga: The Norse Response to Romance.' In *Les sagas de chevaliers (Riddarasögur): Actes de la Ve Conférence Internationale sur les Sagas (Toulon. Juillet 1982)*, pp. 55–74. Ed. Régis Boyer. Toulon, 1982.

Bisgaard, Lars. *Tjenesteideal og fromhedsideal: Studier i adelens tænkemåde i dansk senmiddelalder*. Aarhus, 1988.

Bjarni Aðalbjarnarson. *Om de norske kongers sagaer*. Skrifter utgitt av Det Norske Vitenskaps- Akademi i Oslo II. Hist.-filos. klasse. 1936. no. 4. Oslo, 1937.

Bjarni Einarsson. *Skáldasögur. Um uppruna og eðli ástarskáldasagnanna fornu*. Reykjavík, 1961.

—. 'The Lovesick Skald: A Reply to Theodore M. Andersson.' *Mediaeval Scandinavia* 4 (1971), 21–41.

—. 'On the rôle of verse in saga-literature.' *Mediaeval Scandinavia* 7 (1974), 118–125.

—. 'On the status of Free Men in Society and Saga.' *Mediaeval Scandinavia* 7 (1974), 45–55.

Bibliography

—. *Litterære forudsætninger for Egils saga*. Rit Stofnunar Árna Magnússonar 8. Reykjavík, 1975.

—. *To skjaldesagaer: En analyse af Kormáks saga og Hallfreðar saga*. Bergen, 1976.

Bjarni Guðnason. 'Þættir.' In *Kulturhistorisk leksikon for nordisk middelalder fra vikingetid til reformationstid* Vol. 20 (1976), cols. 405–410.

—. *Fyrsta sagan*. Studia Islandica 37. Reykjavík, 1978.

—. *Túlkun Heiðarvígasögu*. Studia Islandica 50. Reykjavík, 1993.

Björn Gíslason. 'Klám og gróteska í Sneglu-Halla þætti.' *Mímir* 47 (1999), 33–42.

Björn M. Ólsen. *Um Íslendingasögur: Kaflar úr háskólafyrirlestrum*. Ed. Sigfús Blöndal and Einar Ól. Sveinsson. Safn til sögu Íslands og íslenzkra bókmennta VI, 3. Reykjavík, 1937–39.

Blaisdell, Foster W. Jr. 'The Figure of the King: Arthur vs. Hrólf.' *Fourth International Saga Conference, München, July 30th – August 4th, 1979*. München, 1979.

Bloch, R. Howard. *Etymologies and Genealogies: A Literary Anthropology of the French Middle Ages*. Chicago and London, 1986.

Bloch, Marc, trans. L. A. Manyon. *Feudal Society*. London and Henley, 1961.

Boberg, Inger M. *Motif-Index of Early Icelandic Literature*. Bibliotheca Arnamagnæana 27. Copenhagen, 1966.

Bogi Th. Melsteð. 'Töldu Íslendingar sig á dögum þjóðveldisins vera Norðmenn?' *Afmælisrit til dr. phil. Kr. Kålunds bókavarðar við Safn Árna Magnússonar 19. ágúst 1914*, pp. 16–33. Copenhagen, 1914.

Bouman, A. C. *Patterns in Old English and Old Icelandic Literature*. Leiden, 1962.

Bourdieu, Pierre. *Distinction: a social critique of the judgement of taste*. London and New York, 1984.

Brandt, William. *The Shape of Medieval History: Studies in Modes of Perception*. New Haven, 1966.

Brooke, Christopher Nugent Lawrence. *The Medieval Idea of Marriage*. Oxford, 1989.

Bruhn, Ole. 'Earl Rognvald and the Rise of Saga Literature.' In *The Viking Age in Caithness, Orkney and the North Atlantic: Select Papers from the Proceedings of the Eleventh Viking Congress, Thurso and Kirkwall, 22 august–1 september 1989*, pp. 240–247. Ed. Colleen E. Batey, Judith Jesch and Christopher D. Morris. Edinburgh, 1993.

Bibliography

Bruhn, Ole. *Tekstualisering: Bidrag til en litterær antropologi.* Aarhus, 1999.

Brünger, Tanja. "'Hugkvæmir og höfðingjadjarfir": Urteile und Vorurteile über Isländer in zwei Kurzerzählungen des 13. Jahrhunderts.' *Skandinavistik* 29 (1999), 36–52.

Bull, Edvard. 'Håkon Ivarssons saga.' *Edda* 27 (1927), 33–44.

Bumke, Joachim. *Studien zum Ritterbegriff im 12. und 13. Jahrhundert.* Heidelberg, 1964.

—. *Höfische Kultur: Literatur und Gesellschaft im hohen Mittelalter* 1–2, 3rd edn. München, 1986.

—. 'Höfischer Körper – Höfische Kultur.' In *Modernes Mittelalter: Neue Bilder einer populären Epoche*, pp. 67–102. Ed. Joachim Heinzle. Frankfurt am Main and Leipzig 1994.

Burke, Peter. *The Renaissance Sense of the Past.* London, 1969.

—. *History and Social Theory.* Cambridge, 1992.

—. 'Humanism and Friendship in Sixteenth-Century Europe.' In *Friendship in Medieval Europe*, pp. 262–274. Ed. Julian Haseldine. Sutton, 1999.

Burnley, J. David. *Courtliness and Literature in Medieval England.* London, 1998.

Burns, E. Jane. *Bodytalk: When Women Speak in Old French Literature.* Philadelphia, 1993.

—. 'Refashioning Courtly Love: Lancelot as Ladies' Man or Lady/Man?' In *Constructing Medieval Sexuality*, 111–134. Ed. Karma Lochrie, Peggy McCracken and James A. Schultz. Minneapolis and London, 1997.

Burrow, J. A. *Medieval Writers and their Work: Middle English Literature and its Background 1100–1500.* Oxford, 1982.

Butler, Judith. *Gender Trouble: Feminism and the Subversion of Identity.* New York and London, 1990.

Bynum. Caroline Walker. 'Did the XIIth Century discover the individual?' *Journal of Ecclesiastical History* 31 (1980), 1–17.

—. *Jesus as Mother: Studies in the Spirituality of the High Middle Ages.* Berkeley, 1982.

Bååth, Albert Ulrich. *Studier öfver kompositionen i några isländska ättsagor.* Lund, 1885.

Caie, Graham D. 'A City Built to Music: An Introduction to the Story of Arthur.' In *The Vitality of the Arthurian Legend: A Symposium*, pp. 13–23. Ed. Mette Pors. Odense, 1988.

Cantor, Norman F. *Inventing the Middle Ages: The Lives, Works, and Ideas of the Great Medievalists of the Twentieth Century*. New York, 1991.

Chatman, Seymour, *Story and Discourse: Narrative Structure in Fiction and Film*. Ithaca and London, 1978.

Chesnutt, Michael. 'Haralds saga Maddaðarsonar.' In *Speculum Norroenum: Norse Studies in Memory of Gabriel Turville-Petre*, pp. 33–55. Ed. Ursula Dronke *et al*. Odense, 1981.

Cheyette, Fredric L., ed. *Lordship and Community in Medieval Europe: Selected Readings*. New York, 1968.

Christiansen, Eric. 'The place of fiction in Saxo's later books.' In *Saxo Grammaticus: A Medieval Author Between Norse and Latin* Culture, pp. 27–37. Ed. Karsten Friis-Jensen. Copenhagen, 1981.

Clanchy, Michael T. *From Memory to Written Record: England. 1066–1307*. London, 1979.

Clover, Carol J. 'Scene in Saga Composition.' *Arkiv för nordisk filologi* 89 (1974), 57–83.

—. 'Hárbarðsljóð as Generic Farce.' *Scandinavian Studies* 51 (1979), 124–145.

—. 'The Language of Interlace: Notes on Composition in Saga and Romance.' *Fourth International Saga Conference, München, July 30th – August 4th, 1979*. Munich, 1979.

—. 'The Germanic Context of the Unferþ Episode,' *Speculum* 55 (1980), 444–468.

—. *The Medieval Saga*. Ithaca, 1982.

Clunies Ross, Margaret. 'The Development of Old Norse Textual Worlds: Genealogy as a Principle of Literary Organisation in Early Iceland.' *Journal of English and Germanic Philology* 92 (1993), 372–385.

—. 'From Iceland to Norway: Essential Rites of Passage for an Early Icelandic Skald.' *alvíssmál* 9 (1999), 55–72.

—. 'The Skald Sagas as a Genre: Definitions and Typical Features.' In *Skaldsagas: Text, Vocation, and Desire in the Icelandic Sagas of Poets*, 25–49. Ed. Russell Poole. Ergänzungsbände zum Reallexikon der Germanischen Altertumskunde 27. Berlín and New York, 2001.

Cohen, Jeffrey Jerome. *Of Giants: Sex, Monsters, and the Middle Ages*. Medieval Cultures 17. Minneapolis and London, 1999.

Contamine, Philippe, trans. Michael Jones. *War in the Middle Ages*. Oxford, 1985. (Original: *La Guerre au Moyen Age*. París, 1980.)

Cook, Robert. 'The Reader in Grettis saga.' *Saga-Book of the Viking Society* (1984–85), 133–154.

Cormack, Margaret. '*Heimskringla, Egils saga*, and the daughter of Eiríkr blóðöx.' In *Sagas and the Norwegian Experience: Preprints: 10. Internasjonale Sagakonferanse, Trondheim 3.–9. august 1997*, pp. 139–148. Trondheim, 1997.

Crane, Susan. 'Knights in Disguise: Identity and Incognito in Fourteenth-Century Chivalry.' In *The Stranger in Medieval Society*, pp. 63–79. Ed. F.R.P. Akehurst and Stephanie Cain Van D'Elden. Medieval Cultures 12. Minneapolis, 1998.

Crouch, David. *The Image of the Aristocracy in Britain, 1000–1300*. London and New York 1992.

Curtius, Ernst Robert. 'Zur interpretation des Alexiusliedes.' *Zeitschrift für romanische Philologie* 56 (1936), 113–137.

—, trans. Willard R. Trask. *European Literature and the Latin Middle Ages*. Princeton 1973. (Original: *Europäisches Literatur und lateinisches Mittelalter*. Bern, 1948.)

Damsholt, Nanna. *Kvinnebilledet i dansk højmiddelalder*. Copenhagen, 1985.

Danielsson, Tommy. *Om den isländska släktsagans uppbyggnad*. Skrifter utgivna af Literaturvetenskapliga institutionen vid Uppsala universitet 22. Uppsala, 1986.

—. 'Magnús berfættrs sista strid.' *Scripta Islandica* 39 (1988), 44–70.

—. *Sagorna om Noregs kungar: Från Magnús góði till Magnús Erlingsson*. Södertälje, 2002.

Darnton, Robert. 'History of Reading.' In *New Perspectives on Historical Writing*, pp. 140–67. Ed. Peter Burke. Cambridge, 1991.

Davis, Natalie Zemon. *Society and Culture in Early Modern France: Eight Essays*. Stanford, 1975.

Davíð Erlingsson. 'Saga gerir mann: Hugleiðing um gildi og stöðu hugvísinda.' *Skírnir* 166 (1992), 321–345.

—. 'Fótaleysi göngumanns: Atlaga til ráðningar á frumþáttum táknmáls í sögu af Hrólfi Sturlaugssyni, ásamt formála.' *Skírnir* 170 (1996), 340–356.

—. 'Bakrauf og bakrauf.' *Skírnir* 171 (1997), 401–411.

—. 'Manneskja er dýr og henni er hætt: Um nykrað.' *Gripla* 10 (1998), 49–61.

Doxey, Gary B. 'Norwegian Crusaders and the Balearic Islands.' *Scandinavian Studies* 68 (1996), 139–160.

Bibliography

Driscoll, Matthew James. *The Unwashed Children of Eve: The Production, Dissemination and Reception of Popular Literature in Post-Reformation Iceland*. Enfield Lock, Middlesex, 1997.

Dronke, Peter. *Poetic Individuality in the Middle Ages: New Departures in Poetry 1100–1150*. Oxford, 1970.

Dronke, Ursula. 'The Poet's Persona in the Skalds' Saga.' *Parergon* 22 (1978). 23–28.

—. *The role of sexual themes in Njáls Saga: The Dorothea Coke Memorial Lecture in Northern Studies, University College London, 27 May 1980*. London, 1981.

Duby, Georges. 'Les "jeunes" dans la société aristocratique dans la France du Nord-Ouest au XIIe siècle.' *La Société chevaleresque. Hommes et structures du Moyen Age (I)*. Paris 1979, 129–142. (Previously printed in *Annales, Economies-Sociétés-Civilisations* 19 (1964), 835–846.)

—. 'The Diffusion of Cultural Patterns in Feudal Society.' *Past and Present* 39 (1968), 3–10.

—. 'The Culture of the Knightly Class: Audience and Patronage.' *Renaissance and Renewal in the Twelfth Century*, pp. 248–262. Ed. Robert L. Benson, Giles Constable and Carol D. Lanham. Oxford, 1982.

—, trans. Elborg Forster. *Medieval Marriage. Two Models from Twelfth-Century France*. Baltimore and London, 1978.

—, trans. Arthur Goldhammer. *The Three Orders: Feudal Society Imagined*. Chicago and London, 1980. (Original: *Les trois ordres ou l'imaginaire du féodalisme*. Paris, 1978.)

—. *Le chevalier, la femme et le prêtre: Le mariage dans la France féodale*. Paris, 1981.

—, trans. Arthur Goldhammer. 'Communal Living.' *A History of Private Life II: Revelations of the Medieval World*, pp. 35–85. Ed. Georges Duby. Cambridge and London, 1988. (Original: *Histoire de la vie Privée 2: De l'Europe féodale à la Renaissance*. Paris, 1985.)

—, trans. Jane Dunnett. *Love and Marriage in the Middle Ages*. Cambridge, 1994. (Original: *Mâle moyen age*. Paris, 1988.)

Dundes, Alan. *The Morphology of North American Indian Folktales*. FF Communications, 195. Helsinki, 1964.

Ebel, Else. *Der Konkubinat nach altwestnordische Quellen: Philologische Studien zur sogenannten 'Friedelehe'*. Ergänzungsbände zum Reallexikon der Germanischen Altertumskunde 8. Berlin and New York, 1993.

Bibliography

Eco, Umberto, trans. William Weaver. 'The Return of the Middle Ages.' In *Faith in Fakes: Travels in Hyperreality*, pp. 61–85. London, 1986.

Einar Már Jónsson. 'Staða Konungsskuggsjár í vestrænum miðaldabókmenntum.' *Gripla* 7 (1990), 323–354.

—. *Le miroir: Naissance d'un genre littéraire*. Paris, 1995.

Einar Gunnar Pétursson. *Eddurit Jóns Guðmundssonar lærða. Samantektir á Eddu og Að fornu í þeirri gömlu norrænu kölluðust rúnir bæði ristingar og skrifelsi: Þættir úr fræðasögu 17. aldar. I. Inngangur*. Reykjavík, 1998.

Einar Ólafur Sveinsson. *Verzeichnis isländischer Märchenvarianten*. FF Communications 83. Helsinki, 1929.

Elias, Norbert, trans. Edmund Jephcott. *The Civilizing Process*. Oxford, 1994. (Original: *Über den Prozess der Zivilisation*. Basel, 1939.)

—, trans. Edmund Jephcott. *The Court Society*. Oxford, 1983. (Original: *Die höfische Gesellschaft: Untersuchungen zur Soziologie des Königtums und der höfischen Aristokratie*. 1969.)

Fentress, James and Chris Wickham. *Social Memory*. Oxford, UK and Cambridge, Mass., 1992.

Fichtner, Edward G. 'Gift Exchange and Initiation in the Auðunar þáttr vestfirzka.' *Scandinavian Studies* 51 (1979), 249–272.

Fidjestøl, Bjarne, 'Tåtten om Harald Hardråde og fiskaren Þorgils.' *Maal og minne* (1971), 34–49.

—. 'Ut no glytter dei fagre droser: Om kvinnesynet i norrøn litteratur.' *Syn og segn* 82 (1976), 464–472.

—. 'Arnórr Þórðarson: Skald of the Orkney Jarls.' In *The Northern and Western Isles in the Viking World: Survival, Continuity and Change*, pp. 239–257. Ed. Alexander Fenton and Hermann Pálsson. Edinburgh, 1984.

—. 'Erotisk lesnad ved Håkon Håkonssons hoff.' *Middelalderkvinner – liv og virke*, pp. 72–89. Ed. Ingvild Øye. Onsdagskvelder i Bryggens museum 4. Bergen, 1989.

—, trans. Peter Foote. 'The king's skald from Kvinesdal and his poetry.' In *Selected Papers*, pp. 68–92. Ed. Odd Einar Haugen and Else Mundal. The Viking Collection 9. Odense, 1997. (Original: 'Kongsskalden frå Kvinesdal og diktinga hans,' *Rikssamling på Agder*, pp. 7–31. Kristiansand, 1976.)

Fineman, Joel. 'The History of the Anecdote: Fiction and Fiction.' In *The New Historicism*, pp. 49–76. Ed. H. Aram Veeser. New York and London 1989.

Finlay, Alison, 'Skalds, Troubadours and Sagas.' *Saga-Book of the Viking Society* 24 (1995), 105–153.

—. 'Kings and Icelanders in Poets' Sagas and Þættir.' In *Sagas and the Norwegian Experience. Preprints. 10. Internasjonale Sagakonferanse, Trondheim 3.–9. august 1997.* Trondheim 1997, 159–168.

—. 'Pouring Óðinn's Mead: An Antiquarian Theme?' In *Old Norse Myths, Literature and Society. Proceedings of the 11th International Saga Conference, 2–7 July 2000, University of Sydney*, pp. 85–99. Ed. Geraldine Barnes and Margaret Clunies Ross. Sydney, 2000.

—. 'Skald Sagas in their Literary Context 2: Possible European Contexts.' In *Skaldsagas: Text, Vocation, and Desire in the Icelandic Sagas of Poets*, pp. 232–271. Ed. Russell Poole. Ergänzungsbände zum Reallexikon der Germanischen Altertumskunde 27. Berlín and New York, 2001.

Finnur Jónsson, *Den oldnorske og oldislandske Litteraturs Historie* Vol. II, 2. Copenhagen: 1901.

—. 'Tilnavne i den islandske Oldlitteratur.' *Aarbøger for nordisk Oldkyndighed og Historie* (1907), 161–381.

—. 'Rögnvald jarls Jorsalfærd.' *(Norsk) Historisk tidsskrift* IV:8 (1912–13), 151–165.

—. 'Flateyjarbók.' *Aarbøger for nordisk Oldkyndighed og Historie* (1927), 139–190.

—. 'Indledning.' *Morkinskinna.* Ed. Finnur Jónsson. Samfund til udgivelse af gammel nordisk litteratur 53. Copenhagen, 1932.

Fleischhauer, Wolfgang. *Kalf Arnason: Die Berührungen zwischen Heldenlied und Königssaga.* Cologne, 1938.

Foote, Peter. 'Notes on the Prepositions OF and UM(B) in Old Icelandic and Old Norwegian Prose,' *Studia Islandica* 14 (1955), 41–83.

—. *On the Saga of the Faroe Islanders: An Inaugural Lecture delivered at University College London.* London, 1964.

—. 'Aachen, Lund, Hólar.' In *Les relations littéraires Franco-Scandinaves au moyen âge: Actes du College de Liège (avril 1972)*, pp. 53–76. Paris, 1972.

—. 'Latin rhetoric and Icelandic poetry: Some contacts.' *Saga och sed* (1982), 107–127.

Foucault, Michel, trans. Alan Sheridan. *Discipline and Punish: The Birth of Prison.* London, 1977. (Original: *Surveiller et punir: naissance de la prison.* Paris, 1976.)

Fowler, Alastair. *Kinds of Literature: An Introduction to the Theory of Genres and Modes.* Oxford, 1982.

Frank, Roberta. 'Why Skalds Address Women.' In *Poetry in the Scandinavian Middle Ages: The Seventh International Saga Conference, Spoleto, 4–10 September 1988*, pp. 67–83. Ed. Teresa Pàroli. Spoleto, 1990.

——. 'Germanic Legend in Old English Literature.' In *The Cambridge Companion to Old English Literature*, pp. 88–106. Ed. M. Godden and M. Lapidge. Cambridge, 1991.

Frantzen, Allen J. *Before the Closet: Same-Sex Love from Beowulf to Angels in America*. Chicago and London, 1998.

Friis-Jensen, Karsten. *Saxo Grammaticus as a Latin Poet: Studies in the Verse Passages of the Gesta Danorum*. Rome, 1987.

Gade, Kari Ellen. 'Hanging in Northern Law and Literature.' *Maal og minne* (1985), 159–183.

——. 'The Naked and the Dead in Old Norse Society.' *Scandinavian Studies* 60 (1988), 219–245.

——. 'Einarr Þambarskelfir's Last Shot,' *Scandinavian Studies* 67 (1995), 153–162.

——. 'Einarr Þambarskelfir, Again,' *Scandinavian Studies* 67 (1995), 547–550.

——. '1236: Óraekja meiddr ok heill gǫrr,' *Gripla* 9 (1995), 115–132.

——. 'Northern Lights on the Battle of Hastings' *Viator* 28 (1995), 65–81.

——. 'Kaupangr – Þrándheimr – Niðaróss: On the dating of the Old Norse kings' sagas,' *Maal og minne* (1998), 41–60. (Previously printed in *Sagas and the Norwegian Experience. Preprints. 10. Internasjonale Sagakonferanse, Trondheim 3.–9. august 1997*, pp. 169–178. Trondheim, 1997.)

——. 'Poetry and its changing importance in medieval Icelandic culture.' In *Old Icelandic Literature and Society*, pp. 61–95. Ed. Margaret Clunies Ross. Cambridge Studies in Medieval Literature 42. Cambridge, 2000.

——. 'Morkinskinna's Giffarðsþáttr: Literary fiction or historical fact?' *Gripla* 11 (2000), 181–198.

Ganshof, F.L., trans. Philip Grierson. *Feudalism*. London, 1952. (Original: *Qu'est-ce que la féodalite?* Bruxelles, 1944)

Gaunt, Simon, *Gender and genre in medieval French literature*. Cambridge, 1995.

Gelsinger, Bruce E. 'The Battle of Stamford Bridge and the Battle of Jaffa: A Case of Confused Identity?' *Scandinavian Studies* 60 (1988), 13–29.

Gimmler, Heinrich, *Die Thættir der Morkinskinna: Ein Beitrag zur Überlieferungsproblematik und zur Typologie der altnordischen Kurzerzählung*. Frankfurt am Main 1976.

Bibliography

Glauser, Jürg. 'Erzähler – Ritter – Zuhörer: Das Beispiel der Riddarasögur: Erzählkommunikation und Hörergemeinschaft im mittelalterlichen Island,' In *Les sagas de chevaliers (Riddarasögur)*. Actes de la Ve Conférence Internationale sur les Sagas (Toulon, Juillet 1982), pp. 93–119. Ed. Régis Boyer. Toulon, 1982.

—. *Isländische Märchensagas: Studien zur Prosaliteratur im spätmittelalterlichen Island*. Beiträge zur nordischen Philologie 12. Basel and Frankfurt am Main, 1983.

Goffman, Erving. *The Presentation of Self in Everyday Life*. New York, 1959.

Gramsci, Antonio. *Selections from the Prison Notebooks*. Ed. and trans. Quentin Hoare and Geoffrey Nowell-Smith. New York, 1971.

Greenblatt, Stephen. *Marvelous Possessions: The Wonder of the New World*. Oxford, 1991.

Guðbrandur Vigfússon. 'Prolegomena.' In *Sturlunga saga*. 2 vols. Vol. I. pp. xvii–ccxiv. Ed. Guðbrandur Vigfússon. Oxford, 1878.

Guðni Jónsson. 'Formáli.' *Íslendinga þættir*. Reykjavík, 1935.

—. 'Formáli.' Íslenzk fornrit 7. Reykjavík, 1936.

—. 'Formáli.' Íslenzk fornrit 6. Ed. Björn K. Þórólfsson and Guðni Jónsson. Reykjavík, 1943.

—. *Konungasögur 1: Ólafs saga Tryggvasonar eftir Odd munk. Helgisaga Ólafs Haraldssonar. Brot úr Elztu sögu*. Reykjavík, 1957.

Guðrún Ása Grímsdóttir. 'Um sárafar í Íslendinga sögu Sturlu Þórðarsonar.' In *Sturlustefna: Ráðstefna haldin á sjö alda ártíð Sturlu Þórðarsonar sagnaritara 1984*, pp. 184–203. Ed. Guðrún Ása Grímsdóttir and Jónas Kristjánsson. Rit Stofnunar Árna Magnússonar á Íslandi 32. Reykjavík, 1988.

—. 'Fornar menntir í Hítardal: Eilítið um íslenska tignarmenn and ættartölurit á 17. öld.' *Ný saga* 7 (1995), 43–52.

Guðrún Nordal. '"Eitt sinn skal hverr deyja." Dráp og dauðalýsingar í Íslendinga sögu.' *Skírnir* 163 (1989), 72–94.

—. *Tools of Literacy: The Role of Skaldic Verse in Icelandic Textual Culture of the Twelfth and Thirteenth Centuries*. Toronto, 2001.

—. 'Samhengið í íslenskum fornbókmenntum.' In *Sagnaheimur: Studies in Honour of Hermann Pálsson on his 80th birthday, 26th May 2001*, pp. 91–106. Ed. Ásdís Egilsdóttir and Rudolf Simek. Studia Medievalia Septentrionalia 6. Vienna, 2001.

Bibliography

Gunnar Karlsson. 'Kenningin um fornt kvenfrelsi á Íslandi.' *Saga* 24 (1986), 45–77.

—. 'Siðamat Íslendingasögu.' In *Sturlustefna: Ráðstefna haldin á sjö alda ártíð Sturlu Þórðarsonar sagnaritara 1984*, pp. 204–221. Ed. Guðrún Ása Grímsdóttir and Jónas Kristjánsson. Rit Stofnunar Árna Magnússonar á Íslandi 32. Reykjavík, 1988.

Gurevich, Aaron J., trans. G.L. Campbell. *Categories of Medieval Culture*. London, 1985. (Original: *Kategorii srednevekovi kultury*. Moskva, 1972.)

—, trans. Erhard Glier. *Das Individuum im europäischen Mittelalter*. Munich, 1994.

—, trans. Katharine Judelson. *The Origins of European Individualism*. Oxford, 1995.

Gurevich, Elena. 'Skaldic Praise Poetry and Macrologia: some observations on Óláfr Þórðarson's use of his sources.' In *Old Norse Myths, Literature and Society: Proceedings of the 11th International Saga Conference, 2–7 July 2000*, University of Sydney, pp. 100–108. Ed. Geraldine Barnes and Margaret Clunies Ross. Sydney, 2000.

Gössmann, Elisabeth. '"Antiqui" und "Moderni" im 12. Jahrhundert.' In *Antiqui et Moderni: Traditionsbewußtsein und Fortschrittbewußtsein im späten Mittelalter*, pp. 40–57. Ed. Albert Zimmermann. Miscellanea Mediaevalia 9. Berlin 1974.

Habermas, Jürgen, trans. Thomas Burger. *The Structural Transformation of the Public Sphere: An Inquiry into a Category of Bourgeois Society*. Cambridge, Mass. 1989. (Original: *Strukturwandel der Öffentlichkeit*. Darmstadt and Neuwied, 1962.)

Hagland, Jan Ragnar. 'Olavslegender frå Bysants.' In *Hellas og Norge: Kontakt, komparasjon, kontrast*, pp. 193–210. Ed. Øivind Andersen and Tomas Hägg. Bergen, 1990.

Hallberg, Peter. 'Hryggjarstykki: Några anteckningar.' *Maal og minne* (1979), 113–121.

—. 'Some Aspects of the Fornaldarsögur as a Corpus.' *Arkiv för nordisk filologi* 97 (1982), 1–35.

Halsall, Guy. 'Violence and society in the early medieval west: an introductory survey,' In *Violence and Society in the Early Medieval West*, pp. 1–45. Ed. Guy Halsall. Woodbridge, Suffolk, 1998.

Halvorsen, Eyvind Fjeld. *The Norse Version of Chanson de Roland*. Bibliotheca Arnamagnæana 19. Copenhagen, 1959.

Bibliography

——. 'Fagrskinna,' *Kulturhistorisk leksikon for nordisk middelalder fra vikingtid til reformasjonstid* Vol. 4 (1959), cols. 139–140.

——. 'Riddersagaer.' *Kulturhistorisk leksikon for nordisk middelalder fra vikingtid til reformasjonstid* Vol. 14 (1969), cols. 175–183.

——. 'Norwegian Court Literature in the Middle Ages.' *Orkney Miscellany* 5 (1973), 17–26.

Hanning, Robert. *The Individual in Twelfth-Century Romance*. New Haven, 1977.

Harris, Joseph. *The King and the Icelander: a Study in the Short Narrative Forms of Old Icelandic Prose*. Ph.D.-Dissertation. Harvard, 1969.

——. 'Genre and Narrative Structure in Some Íslendinga þættir.' *Scandinavian Studies* 44 (1972), 1–27.

——. 'Genre in Saga Literature: A Squib.' *Scandinavian Studies* 47 (1975), 427–436.

——. 'Ǫgmundar þáttr dytts ok Gunnars helmings: Unity and Literary Relations.' *Arkiv för nordisk filologi* 90 (1975), 156–182.

——. 'Theme and Genre in some Íslendinga þættir.' *Scandinavian Studies* 48 (1976), 1–28.

——. 'The King in Disguise. An International Popular Tale in Two Old Icelandic Adaptions.' *Arkiv för nordisk filologi* 94 (1979), 57–81.

——. 'Þættir.' *Dictionary of the Middle Ages* 12 (1989), 1–6.

——. 'Gender and genre: short and long forms in the saga literature.' In *The Making of the Couple: The Social Function of Short-form Medieval Narrative. A Symposium*, pp. 43–66. Ed. Flemming G. Andersen and Morten Nøjgaard. Odense, 1991.

Harris, Richard L. 'The Proverbs of Morkinskinna: A Preliminary Survey.' *International Congress on Medieval Studies. 10 May 2007, Kalamazoo*.

Hartmann, Wilfried. '"Modernus" und "Antiquus": Zur Verbreitung und Bedeutung dieser Bezeichnungen in der wissenschaftlichen Literatur vom 9. bis zum 12. Jahrhundert.' *Antiqui et Moderni: Traditionsbewußtsein und Fortschrittbewußtsein im späten Mittelalter*, pp. 21–39. Ed. Albert Zimmermann. Miscellanea Mediaevalia 9. Berlín, 1974.

Haugen, Odd Einar. 'Om tidsforholdet mellom Stjórn og Barlaams ok Josaphats saga.' *Maal og minne* (1983), 18–28.

——. 'Buddha i Bjørgvin: Den norrøne soga om kongssonen Josaphat og munken Barlaam.' *Syn og segn* (1986), 263–270.

——. 'Barlaam og Josaphat i ny utgåve.' *Maal og minne* (1991), 1–24.

Bibliography

Heffernan, Thomas J. *Sacred Biography: Saints and their Biographers in the Middle Ages*. Oxford, 1988.

Heinrichs, Anne, '"Intertexture" and its Functions in Early Written Sagas: a Stylistic Observation of Heiðarvíga saga, Reykdæla saga and the Legendary Olafssaga.' *Scandinavian Studies* 48 (1976), 127–145.

—. 'Wenn ein König liebeskrank wird: Der Fall Óláfr Haraldsson.' In *Die Aktualität der Saga: Festschrift für Hans Schottmann*, pp. 27–51. Ed. Stig Toftgaard Andersen. Ergänzungsbände zum Reallexikon der Germanischen Altertumskunde 21. Berlin and New York 1999.

Heinrichs, Heinrich Matthias. 'Die Geschichte vom sagakündigen Isländer (Íslendings þáttr sǫgufróða): Ein Beitrag zur Sagaforschung.' In *Literaturwissenschaft und Geschichtsphilosophie: Festschrift für Wilhelm Emrich*, pp. 225–231. Ed. Helmut Arntzen, Bernd Balzer, Karl Pestalozzi and Rainer Wagner. Berlin, 1975.

Helga Kress. 'Bróklindi Falgeirs: Fóstbræðrasaga og hláturmenning miðalda.' *Skírnir* 161 (1987), 271–286.

—. 'Staðlausir stafir: Um slúður sem uppsprettu frásagnar í Íslendingasögum.' *Skírnir* 165 (1991), 130–156.

—. *Máttugar meyjar: Íslensk fornbókmenntasaga*. Reykjavík, 1993.

Helgi Þorláksson. 'Draumar Dalamanns.' In *Fjölmóðarvíl til fagnaðar Einari G. Péturssyni fimmtugum 25. júlí 1991*, pp. 43–49. Reykjavík, 1991.

—. 'Virtir menn og vel metnir.' In *Sæmdarmenn: Um heiður á þjóðveldisöld*, pp. 15–22. Ed. Helgi Þorláksson *et al*. Reykjavík, 2001.

Heller, Rolf. *Die literarische Darstellung der Frau in den Isländersagas*. Saga 2. Halle (Saale), 1958.

Hermann Pálsson, *Sagnaskemmtun Íslendinga*. Reykjavík, 1962.

—. 'Brands þáttur örva.' *Gripla* 7 (1990), 117–130.

—. 'Hirðskáld í spéspegli.' *Skáldskaparmál* 2 (1992), 148–169.

—. 'Mannfræði, dæmi, fornsögur.' In *Twenty-Eight Papers Presented to Hans Bekker-Nielsen on the Occasion of his Sixtieth Birthday 28 April 1993*, pp. 303–322. Ed. Jørgen Højgaard Jørgensen and Elmer H. Atonsen. Odense, 1993.

Heusler, Andreas. 'Die Anfänge der isländischen Saga.' *Abhandlungen der Königlich Preussischen Akademie der Wissenschaften 1913. Phil.-hist. Klasse. no. 9.* Berlin, 1913.

—. *Die Geschichte vom weisen Njal*. Jena, 1914.

Bibliography

Holbek, Bengt. *Interpretation of Fairy Tales: Danish Folklore in a European Perspective*. FF Communications 239. Helsinki, 1987.

Holbek, Bengt. *Tolkning af trylleeventyr*. Copenhagen, 1989.

Holm-Olsen, Ludvig. 'En replikk i Harald Hardrådes saga.' *Maal og minne* (1959), 35–41.

Holtsmark, Anne, 'Harald Gille, en sending,' *Arkiv för nordisk filologi* 77 (1962), 84–89.

—. 'Kattar Sonr.' *Saga-Book of the Viking Society* 16 (1963–64), 144–155.

—. 'Kongesaga,' *Kulturhistorisk leksikon for nordisk middelalder fra vikingtid til reformasjonstid* Vol. 9 (1964), cols. 41–46.

—. 'Hryggiarstykki.' *(Norsk) Historisk tidsskrift* 45 (1966), 144–155.

Hreinn Benediktsson. *Early Icelandic Script as Illustrated in Vernacular Texts from the Twelfth and Thirteenth Centuries*. Icelandic Manuscripts, series in folio 2. Reykjavík, 1965.

Hughes, Shaun F.D. 'The Battle of Stamford Bridge and the Battle of Bouvines.' *Scandinavian Studies* 60 (1988), 30–76.

Huizinga, Johan, trans. F. Hopman. *The Waning of the Middle Ages: A Study of the Forms of Life, Thought, and Art in France and the Netherlands in the Fourteenth and Fifteenth Centuries*. Harmondsworth, 1976. (Original: *Herfsttij der Middeleeuwen*. Haarlem, 1919.)

—. *Homo ludens: A Study of the Play Element in Culture*. London, 1970.

Hume, Kathryn. 'Structure and Perspective: Romance and Hagiographic Features in the Amicus and Amelius Story.' *Journal of English and Germanic Philology* 69 (1970), 89–107.

—. 'Beginnings and Endings in the Icelandic Family Sagas.' *Modern Language Review* 68 (1973), 593–606.

—. 'The Thematic Design of Grettis saga.' *Journal of English and Germanic Philology* 73 (1974), 469–486.

Hødnebø, Finn. 'Morkinskinna.' *Kulturhistorisk leksikon for nordisk middelalder fra vikingtid til reformasjonstid* 11 (1966), cols. 703–704.

Indrebø, Gustav, *Fagrskinna: Avhandlinger fra Universitetets historiske seminar*. Christiania, 1917.

—. 'Aagrip.' *Edda* 17 (1922), 18–65.

—. 'Harald Hardraade i Morkinskinna.' In *Festskrift til Finnur Jónsson 29. maj 1928*, pp. 173–80. Ed. Johannes Brøndum-Nielsen *et al*. Copenhagen, 1928.

—. 'Nokre merknader til den norröne kongesoga.' *Arkiv för nordisk filologi* 54 (1939), 58–79.

Bibliography

Jaeger, C. Stephen. *The Origins of Courtliness: Civilizing Trends and the Formation of Courtly Ideals 939–1210.* Philadelphia, 1985.

—. *The Envy of Angels: Cathedral Schools and Social Ideals in Medieval Europe, 950–1200.* Philadelphia, 1994.

—. *Ennobling Love: in Search of a Lost Sensibility.* Philadelphia, 1999.

Jakobsen, Alfred. 'Om forholdet mellom Fagrskinna og Morkinskinna,' *Maal og minne* (1968), 47–58.

—. 'Om Fagrskinna-forfatteren.' *Arkiv för nordisk filologi* 85 (1970), 88–124.

—. 'Tåtten om Måne skald.' *Maal og minne* (1981), 167–172.

—. 'Har det eksistert en skriftlig saga om Tore Hund og hans ætt?' *Maal og minne* (1988), 1–12.

Jameson, Fredric. *The Political Unconscious: Narrative as a socially symbolic act.* Ithaca and New York, 1981.

Jauss, Hans Robert. *Alterität und Modernität der mittelalterlichen Litteratur: Gesammelte Aufsätze 1956–1976.* Munich, 1977.

Jochens, Jenny. 'Consent in Marriage: Old Norse Law, Life, and Literature.' *Scandinavian Studies* 58 (1986), 142–176.

—. 'The Female Inciter in the Kings' Sagas' *Arkiv för nordisk filologi* 102 (1987), 100–119.

—. 'The Politics of Reproduction: Medieval Norwegian Kingship.' *The American Historical Review* 92 (1987), 327–349.

—. *Women in Old Norse Society.* Ithaca and London, 1995.

—. *Old Norse Images of Women.* Philadelphia, 1996.

—. 'Representations of Skalds in the Sagas 2: Gender Relations.' In *Skaldsagas: Text, Vocation, and Desire in the Icelandic Sagas of Poets,* pp. 309–332. Ed. Russell Poole. Ergänzungsbände zum Reallexikon der Germanischen Altertumskunde 27. Berlin and New York, 2001.

Johannesson, Kurt. *Saxo Grammaticus: Komposition och världsbild i Gesta Danorum.* Stockholm, 1978.

Johnsen, Arne Odd. *Studier vedrørende kardinal Nicolaus Brekespear legasjon til Norden.* Oslo, 1945.

Joseph, Herbert S. 'The Þáttr and the Theory of Saga Origins.' *Arkiv för nordisk filologi* 87 (1972), 86–96.

Jón Hnefill Aðalsteinsson. 'Íslenski skólinn.' *Skírnir* 165 (1991), 103–129.

Jón Helgason. 'Introduction.' *Morkinskinna. MS. No. 1009 fol. in the Old Royal collection of The Royal Library, Copenhagen.* Corpus codicum Islandicorum medii aevi 6. Copenhagen, 1934.

Bibliography

—. 'Bókasafn Brynjólfs biskups.' *Landsbókasafn Íslands: Árbók* (1946–47), 115–147.

—. *Handritaspjall*. Reykjavík, 1958.

Jón Viðar Sigurðsson. *Frá goðorðum til ríkja: Þróun goðavalds á 12. og 13. öld.* Sagnfræðirannsóknir 10. Reykjavík, 1989.

—. 'Friendship in the Icelandic Commonwealth.' In *From Sagas to Society: Comparative Approaches to Early Iceland*, pp. 205–215. Ed. Gísli Pálsson. Enfield Lock, Middlesex, 1992.

—. *Goder og maktforhold på Island i fristatstiden*. Oslo, 1993.

—. 'Forholdet mellom frender, hushold og venner på Island i fritatstiden.' *(Norsk) Historisk tidskrift* 74 (1995), 311–330.

—, trans. Jens Lundskær-Nielsen. *Chieftains and Power in the Icelandic Commonwealth*. The Viking Collection 12. Odense, 1999.

—. *Norsk historie 800–1300: Frå høvdingmakt til konge- og kyrkjemakt*. Oslo, 1999.

Jón Þorkelsson. 'Morkinskinna (ritdómur).' *Norðanfari* 7 (1868), 66–67.

Jónas Kristjánsson. *Um Fóstbræðrasögu*. Rit Stofnunar Árna Magnússonar 1. Reykjavík, 1972.

—. 'The Legendary Saga.' In *Minjar og menntir. Afmælisrit helgað Kristjáni Eldjárn 6. desember 1976*, pp. 281–293. Ed. Guðni Kolbeinsson. Reykjavík, 1976.

—. 'Bókmenntasaga.' *Saga Íslands* Vol. 3, pp. 261–350. Reykjavík, 1978.

Kaeuper, Richard W. 'Chivalry and the "Civilizing Process".' In *Violence in Medieval Society*, pp. 21–35. Ed. Richard W. Kaeuper. Woodbridge, Suffolk, 2000.

Kaiser, Charlotte. *Krankheit und Krankheitsbewältigung in den Isländersagas: Medizinhistorischer Aspekt und erzähltechnische Funktion*. Cologne, 1998.

Kalinke, Marianne E. 'Amplification in *Möttuls saga*: Its Function and Form.' *Acta Philologica Scandinavica* 32 (1979), 239–255.

—. *King Arthur North-by-Northwest: The matière de Bretagne in Old Norse-Icelandic Romances*. Bibliotheca Arnamagnæana 37. Copenhagen, 1981.

—. 'The Foreign Language Requirement in Medieval Icelandic Romance.' *Modern Language Review* 78 (1983), 850–861.

—. 'Sigurðar Saga Jórsalafara: The Fictionalization of Fact in Morkinskinna.' *Scandinavian Studies* 56 (1984), 152–167.

Bibliography

—. 'The Misogamous Maiden Kings of Icelandic Romance.' *Scripta Islandica* 37 (1986), 47–71.

—. *Bridal-Quest Romance in Medieval Iceland.* Islandica 46. Ithaca and London, 1990.

Keen, Maurice H. *Chivalry.* New Haven, 1984.

—. *Nobles, Knights and Men-at-Arms in the Middle Ages.* London, 1996.

Kellermann, Wilhelm. *Aufbaustil und Weltbild Chrestiens von Troyes im Percevalroman.* Beihefte zur Zeitschrift für Romanische Philologie 87. Halle/Saale, 1936.

Ker, W. P. *Epic and Romance: Essays on Medieval Literature.* London, 1926.

Kjeldsen, Alex Speed. *Et mørt håndskrift og dets skrivere: Filologiske studier i kongesagahåndskriftet Morkinskinna.* Phd. thesis at Nordisk Forskningsinstitut, University of Copenhagen, 2010.

Klaniczay, Gabor, trans. Susan Singerman, ed. Karen Margolis. *The Uses of Supernatural Power: The Transformation of Popular Religion in Medieval and Early-Modern Europe.* Cambridge, 1990.

Koht, Halvdan. 'Kong Sigurd på Jorsal-ferd.' *Norsk Historisk tidsskrift* V:5 (1924), 153–168.

Koht, Halvdan. 'Var Magnus den Gode skald?' *Norsk Historisk tidsskrift* V:6 (1927), 576–578.

Kolbrún Haraldsdóttir. 'Der Historiker Snorri: Autor oder Kompilator?' In *Snorri Sturluson: Beiträge zu Werk und Rezeption*, pp. 97–108. Ed. Hans Fix. Ergänzungsbände zum Reallexikon der Germanischen Altertumskunde 18. Berlín and New York, 1998.

Krag, Claus. 'Harald Hardrådes ungdomsår og kongesagaene: Forholdet mellom sagaprosa, skaldekvad og muntlig tradisjon.' *Collegium medievale* 11 (1998), 9–31.

Kramarz-Bein, Susanne. '"Modernität" der Laxdœla saga.' In *Studien zum Altgermanischen: Festschrift für Heinrich Beck*, pp. 421–442. Ed. Heiko Uecker. Ergänzungsbände zum Reallexikon der Germanischen Altertumskunde 11. Berlín and New York, 1994.

—. 'Zur Darstellung und Bedeutung der Höfischen in der Konungs skuggsjá.' *Collegium medievale* 7 (1994), 51–86.

—. 'Höfische Unterhaltung und ideologisches Ziel: Das Beispiel der altnorwegischen Parcevals saga.' In *Die Aktualität der Saga: Festschrift für Hans Schottmann*, pp. 63–84. Ed. Stig Toft Andersen. Ergänzungsbände zum Reallexikon der Germanischen Altertumskunde 21. Berlín and New York, 1999.

Kvalén, Eivind. 'Tilhøvet millom Morkinskinna, Fagrskinna, Ágrip og Orkneyinga saga.' *Edda* 24, 2 (1925), 285–335.

—. *Den eldste norske kongesoga: Morkinskinna og Hryggjarstykki.* Oslo, 1925.

Kålund, Kristian, ed. *Katalog over den arnamagnæanske håndskriftsamling* Vols. 1–2. Copenhagen, 1889–94.

Kålund, Kristian, ed. *Katalog over de oldnorsk-islandske håndskrifter i Det store kongelige bibliotek og i Universitetsbiblioteket (udenfor Den arnamagnæanske samling) samt Den arnamagnæanske samlings tilvækst 1894–1899.* Copenhagen, 1900.

Lange, Wolfgang. 'Einige Bemerkungen zur altnordischen Novelle.' *Zeitschrift für deutsches Altertum* 88 (1957), 150–159.

Lassen, Annette. 'Øjets sprog: En undersøgelse af blikkets og blindhedens symbolværdi i den norrœne litteratur.' *Maal og minne* (2001), 113–134.

Lawson, M.K. *Cnut: The Danes in England in the early eleventh century.* London and New York, 1993.

Leach, Henry Goddard. *Angevin Britain and Scandinavia.* Cambridge, 1921.

Lears, T.J. Jackson. 'The Concept of Cultural Hegemony: Problems and Possibilities.' *American Historical Review* 90 (1985). 567–593.

Lewis, C.S. 'The Anthropological Approach.' In *English and Medieval Studies presented to J.R.R. Tolkien on the Occasion of his Seventieth Birthday,* pp. 219–230. Ed. Norman Davies and C.L. Wrenn. London, 1962.

—. *The Discarded Image: An Introduction to Medieval and Renaissance Literature.* Cambridge, 1964.

Leyerle, John. 'The Interlace Structure of Beowulf.' *University of Toronto Quarterly* 37 (1967), 1–17.

Liberman, Anatoly. 'Gone with the Wind: More Thoughts on Medieval Farting.' *Scandinavian Studies* 68 (1996), 98–104.

Lie, Hallvard. *Studier i Heimskringlas stil: Dialogene og talene.* Skrifter utgitt av Det Norske Vitenskaps-Akademi i Oslo II. Hist.-filos. klasse. 1936, no. 5. Oslo, 1937.

Liestøl, Knut. 'Kjetta på Dovre: Til spursmålet um pilegrimsvegar og segnvandring.' *Maal og minne* (1933), 24–48.

Lindblad, Gustaf. *Det isländska accenttecknet: En historisk-ortografisk studie with an English summary.* Lund, 1952.

Lindow, John. 'Old Icelandic þáttr: Early Usage and Semantic History.' *Scripta Islandica* 29 (1978), 3–44.

—. 'Hreiðars Þáttr heimska and AT 326: An Old Icelandic Novella and an International Folktale.' *Arv* 34 (1978), 152–179.

—. 'Þáttr.' *Medieval Scandinvia: An Encyclopedia.* Ed. Philip Pulsiano. New York and London 1993, 661–662.

—. 'Skald Sagas in their Literary Context 1: Related Icelandic Genres.' In *Skaldsagas: Text, Vocation, and Desire in the Icelandic Sagas of Poets,* pp. 218–231. Ed. Russell Poole. Ergänzungsbände zum Reallexikon der Germanischen Altertumskunde 27. Berlin and New York, 2001.

Lockertsen, Roger. 'Namnet på Trondheim by i dei eldste kjeldene.' *Maal og minne* (1999), 145–163.

Loomis, Roger Sherman. 'Arthurian Influence on Sport and Spectacle.' In *Arthurian Literature in the Middle Ages: A Collaborative History,* pp. 553–559. Ed. Roger Sherman Loomis. Oxford, 1959.

Lot, Ferdinand. *Étude sur le Lancelot en prose.* Bibliothèque de l'École des hautes Études 226. Paris, 1918.

Louis-Jensen, Jonna. 'Introduction.' In *Hulda. Sagas of the Kings of Norway 1035–1177: Manuscript no. 66 fol. in the Arnamagnæan Collection,* pp. 9–24. Ed. Jonna Louis-Jensen. Early Icelandic Manuscripts in Facsimile 8. Copenhagen, 1968.

—. 'Den yngre del af Flateyjarbók.' In *Afmælisrit Jóns Helgasonar 30. júní 1969,* pp. 235–250. Ed. Jakob Benediktsson *et al.* Reykjavík, 1969.

—. 'Et forlæg til Flateyjarbók? Fragmenterne AM 325 IV β og XI,3 4to.' *Opuscula* 4 (1970), 141–158. Bibliotheca Arnamagnæana 30.

—. 'En strofe af Bersǫglivísur.' *Opuscula* 4 (1970), 141–158. Bibliotheca Arnamagnæana 30.

—. '"Syvende og ottende brudstykke": Fragmentet AM 325 IV α 4to.' *Opuscula* 4 (1970), 31–60. Bibliotheca Arnamagnæana 30.

—. *Kongesagastudier: Kompilationen Hulda-Hrokkinskinna.* Bibliotheca Arnamagnæana 32. Copenhagen, 1977.

—. 'A Good Day's Work: Laxdæla saga, ch. 49.' *Twenty-Eight Papers Presented to Hans Bekker-Nielsen on the Occasion of his Sixtieth Birthday 28 April 1993.* Odense, 1993, 267–281.

—. 'Morkinskinna,' *Medieval Scandinavia. An Encyclopedia,* pp. 419–420. Ed. Philip Pulsiano. New York and London, 1993.

—. 'Heimskringla – Et værk af Snorri Sturluson?' *Nordica Bergensia* 14 (1997), 230–245.

Bibliography

Ludwig, Werner. *Untersuchungen über den Entwiclungsgang und die Funktion des Dialogs in der isländischen Saga.* Leipzig, 1934.

Lustig, Richard I. 'Some views on Norwegian foreign service, 1217–1319.' *Mediaeval Scandinavia* 11 (1978–79), 212–240.

Lönnroth, Lars. 'Kroppen som själens spegel – Ett motiv i de isländska sagorna.' *Lychnos* (1963–1964), 24–61.

—. 'Tesen om de två kulturerna: Kritiska studier i den isländska sagaskrivningens sociala föruttsättningar.' *Scripta Islandica* 15 (1964).

—. *The European sources of Icelandic saga-writing: an essay based on previous studies.* Stockholm, 1965.

—. 'Rhetorical Persuasion in the Sagas.' *Scandinavian Studies* 42 (1970), 157–189.

—. 'Charlemagne, Hrolf Kraki, Olaf Tryggvason: Parallels in the Heroic Tradition.' In *Les relations littéraires Franco-Scandinaves au moyen âge. Actes du College de Liège (avril 1972)*, pp. 29–52. Ed. Maurice Delbouille. Paris, 1975.

—. 'The Concept of Genre in Saga Literature.' *Scandinavian Studies* 47 (1975), 419–426.

—. *Njáls Saga: A critical introduction.* Berkeley, 1976.

—. *Den dubbla scenen: Muntlig diktning från Eddan till ABBA.* Stockholm, 1978.

—. 'The double scene of Arrow-Odd's drinking contest.' In *Medieval Narrative: A Symposium*, pp. 94–119. Ed. Hans Bekker-Nielsen *et al.* Odense, 1979.

—. 'The Man-Eating Mama of Miklagard: Empress Zóe in Old Norse Saga Tradition.' In *Kairos: Studies in Art History and Literature in Honour of Professor Gunilla Åkerström-Hougen*, pp. 37–49. Ed. Elisabeth Piltz and Paul Åström. Jonsered, 1998.

—. 'Saga and Jartegn: The appeal of mystery in saga texts.' In *Die Aktualität der Saga: Festschrift für Hans Schottmann*, pp. 111–123. Ed. Stig Toft Andersen. Ergänzungsbände zum Reallexikon der Germanischen Altertumskunde 21. Berlin and New York, 1999.

Madelung, Margaret Arent. 'Snorri Sturluson and Laxdoela: The hero's accoutrements.' In *Saga og språk. Studies in language and literature*, pp. 45–92. Ed. John M. Weinstock. Austin, 1972.

Magerøy, Hallvard. 'Skaldestrofer som retardasjonsmiddel i islendingesogene.' *Sjötíu ritgerðir helgaðar Jakobi Benediktssyni 20. júlí 1977*, pp. 586–599. Vols. 1–2. Ed. Einar G. Pétursson and Jónas Kristjánsson. Rit Stofnunar Árna Magnússonar á Íslandi 12. Reykjavík, 1977.

Manhire, William. 'The Narrative Functions of Source-References in the Sagas of the Icelanders.' *Saga-Book of the Viking Society* 19 (1975–76), 170–190.

Marold, Edith. 'The Relation Between Verses and Prose in Bjarnar saga Hítdœlakappa.' In *Skaldsagas: Text, Vocation, and Desire in the Icelandic Sagas of Poets*, pp. 75–124. Ergänzungsbände zum Reallexikon der Germanischen Altertumskunde 27. Ed. Russell Poole. Berlin and New York, 2001.

Martinez Pizarro, Joaquin. 'Kings in Adversity: A Note on Alfred and the Cakes.' *Neophilologus* 80 (1996), 319–326.

Mauss, Marcel, trans. Ian Cunnison. *The Gift: Forms and Functions of Exchange in Archaic Societies*. London, 1970. (Original: 'Essai sur le don: Forme et raison de l'échange dans les sociétés archaïques.' *L'Année Sociologique* 1,1. Paris, 1925.)

Maxwell, I.R. 'Pattern in Njáls Saga.' *Saga-Book of the Viking Society* 15 (1957–61), 17–47.

McGuire, Brian Patrick. *Friendship and Community: The Monastic Experience, 350–1250*. Kalamazoo, 1988.

McKinnell, John. 'Ögmundar þáttr: Versions, Structure and Ideology.' In *Sagnaheimur: Studies in Honour of Hermann Pálsson on his 80th birthday, 26th May 2001*, pp. 159–174. Ed. Ásdís Egilsdóttir and Rudolf Simek. Studia Medievalia Septentrionalia 6. Vienna, 2001.

McNamara, Jo Ann. 'The Herrenfrage: The Restructuring of the Gender System, 1050–1150.' In *Medieval Masculinities: Regarding Men in the Middle Ages*, pp. 3–29. Ed. Clare A. Lees. Medieval Cultures 7. Minneapolis and London, 1994.

Meissner, Rudolf. *Die Strengleikar: Ein Beitrag zur Geschichte der altnordischen Prosalitteratur*. Halle a.S. 1902.

Meister, Klaus. 'Herodotos.' *Der Neue Pauly* 5 (1998), 469–475.

Meulengracht Sørensen, Preben. *Fortælling og ære: Studier i islændingesagaerne*. Aarhus, 1993.

—. 'Modernitet og traditionalisme: Et bidrag til islændingesagaernes litteraturhistorie, med en diskussion af Fóstbrœðra sagas alder.' In *Die Aktualität der Saga: Festschrift für Hans Schottmann*, pp. 149–162. Ed. Stig Toft Andersen. Ergänzungsbände zum Reallexikon der Germanischen Altertumskunde 21. Berlin and New York, 1999.

—. 'Social institutions and belief systems of medieval Iceland (c. 870–1400) and their relations to literary production.' In *Old Icelandic Literature and*

Society, pp. 8–29. Ed. Margaret Clunies Ross. Cambridge Studies in Medieval Literature 42. Cambridge, 2000.

—. 'The Prosimetrum Form 1: Verses as the Voice of the Past.' In *Skaldsagas: Text, Vocation, and Desire in the Icelandic Sagas of Poets*, pp. 172–190. Ed. Russell Poole. Ergänzungsbände zum Reallexikon der Germanischen Altertumskunde 27. Berlin and New York, 2001.

Miller, William Ian. 'Emotions and the Sagas.' In *From Sagas to Society: Comparative Approaches to Early Iceland*, pp. 89–109. Ed. Gísli Pálsson. Enfield Lock, Middlesex, 1992.

—. *Humiliation and Other Essays on Honor, Social Discomfort, and Violence.* Ithaca and London, 1993.

—. *Eye for an Eye.* Cambridge and New York, 2006.

—. *Audun and the Polar Bear: Luck, Law, and Largesse in a Medieval Tale of Risky Business.* Medieval Law and Its Practice 1. Leiden and Boston, 2008.

Minnis, A. J. *Medieval theory of authorship: Scholastic literary attitudes in the later Middle Ages.* 2nd edn. Aldershot, 1988.

Mitchell, Stephen A. *Heroic Sagas and Ballads.* Ithaca and London, 1991.

Morris, Colin. *The Discovery of the Individual 1050–1200.* London, 1972.

Morton, Andrew Queen. *Literary Detection: How to prove authorship and fraud in literature and documents.* Epping, 1978.

Motz, Lotte. 'More Thoughts on Einar Þambarskelfir.' *Scandinavian Studies* 68 (1996), 370–372.

Mundal, Else. 'Sigurðr hrísi eller Sigurðr risi?' *Nordica Bergensia* 29 (2003), 5–13.

Mårtensson, Lasse. *Studier i AM 557 4to.* Reykjavík 2012.

Nahl, Astrid van. *Originale Riddarasögur als Teil altnordischer Sagaliteratur.* Texte und Untersuchungen zur Germanistik und Skandinavistik 3. Frankfurt am Main and Bern, 1981.

Nedrelid, Gudlaug. 'Kor mange kunstar kunne kong Harald?' In *Sagas and the Norwegian Experience. Preprints. 10. Internasjonale Sagakonferanse, Trondheim 3.–9. august 1997*, pp. 501–510. Trondheim, 1997.

Netter, Irmgard. *Die direkte Rede in den Isländersagas.* Form und Geist 36. Leipzig, 1935.

Njörður P. Njarðvík. 'Maður hét Auðun.' In *Sagnaþing helgað Jónasi Kristjánssyni sjötugum 10. apríl 1994*, pp. 611–616. Vols. 1–2. Ed. Gísli Sigurðsson, Guðrún Kvaran og Sigurgeir Steingrímsson. Reykjavík, 1994.

Bibliography

Nykrog, Per. 'The Rise of Literary Fiction.' In *Renaissance and Renewal in the Twelfth Century*, pp. 593–612. Ed. Robert L. Benson, Giles Constable and Carol D. Lanham. Oxford, 1982.

O'Donoghue, Heather. *The Genesis of a Saga Narrative: Verse and Prose in Kormaks Saga*. Oxford, 1991.

O'Keeffe, Katherine O'Brien. 'Introduction.' In *Reading Old English Texts*, pp. 1–19. Ed. Katherine O'Brien O'Keeffe. Cambridge, 1997.

Olsen, Magnus. 'Lidt om en vestnorsk stormandsæt i 12te aarh.' *Norsk Historisk tidsskrift* V:2 (1914), 181–189.

Olsen, Magnus. 'En skjemtehistorie av Harald Hardråde.' *Maal og minne* (1953), 1–22.

Olsen, Thorkild Damsgaard. 'Kongekrøniker og kongesagaer.' In *Norrøn fortællekunst: Kapitler af den norsk-islandske middelalderlitteraturs historie*, pp. 42–71. Ed. Hans Bekker-Nielsen, Thorkild Damsgaard Olsen and Ole Widding. Copenhagen, 1965.

Ólafía Einarsdóttir. 'Fagrskinnas forfattelsestidspunkt: Olaf Haraldsson – Tyskland – Håkon Håkonsson.' In *Germanisches Altertum und christliches Mittelalter: Festschrift für Heinz Klingenberg zum 65. Geburtstag*, pp. 51–89. Ed. Bela Broganyi and Thomas Krömmelbein. Hamburg, 2002.

Ólafur Halldórsson. 'Morgunverk Guðrúnar Ósvífursdóttur.' *Skírnir* 147 (1973), 125–128.

—. 'Þingmanna þáttur.' In *Sagnaþing helgað Jónasi Kristjánssyni sjötugum 10. apríl 1994*, pp. 617–640. Vols. 1–2. Ed. Gísli Sigurðsson, Guðrún Kvaran og Sigurgeir Steingrímsson. Reykjavík, 1994.

Paravicini, Werner. *Die ritterlich-höfische Kultur des Mittelalters*. Enzyklopädie deutscher Geschichte 32. Munich, 1994.

Patterson, Lee. 'On the Margin: Postmodernism, Ironic History, and Medieval Studies.' *Speculum* 65 (1990), 87–108.

Perkins, Richard. 'The Gateway to Trondheim: Two Icelanders at Agdenes.' *Saga-Book of the Viking Society* 25 (1999), 179–213.

Poole, Russell. 'Some Royal Love-verses.' *Maal og minne* (1985), 115–131.

—. *Viking Poems on War and Peace*. Toronto, 1991.

—. 'Introduction.' In *Skaldsagas: Text, Vocation, and Desire in the Icelandic Sagas of Poets*, pp. 1–24. Ed. Russell Poole. Ergänzungsbände zum Reallexikon der Germanischen Alterumskunde 27. Berlin and New York, 2001.

Power, Rosemary. 'Magnus Bareleg's Expeditions to the West.' *Scottish Historical Review* 65 (1986), 107–132.

—. 'The Death of Magnus Barelegs.' *The Scottish Historical Review* 73 (1994), 107–132.

Propp, Vladimir I., trans. Laurence A. Scott and Louis A. Wagner. *Morphology of the Folktale*. 2nd edn. Austin, Texas and London, 1968.

Reichborn-Kjennerud, Ingvald. 'Gamle sykdomsnavn.' *Maal og minne* (1942), 118–121.

Reichert, Hermann. 'King Arthur's Round Table: sociological implications of its literary reception in Scandinavia.' In *Structure and Meaning in Old Norse Literature: New Approaches to Textual Analysis and Literary Criticism*, pp. 394–414. Ed. John Lindow, Lars Lönnroth and Gerd Wolfgang Weber. The Viking Collection 3. Odense, 1986.

Riant, Paul. *Expéditions et pèlerinages des Scandinaves en Terre Sainte au temps des croisades*. Paris, 1865.

Riley-Smith, Jonathan. *The First Crusade and the Idea of Crusading*. New York and London, 2003.

Rimmon-Kenan, Shlomith. *Narrative Fiction: Contemporary Poetics*. New Accents. London and New York, 1983.

Rowe, Elizabeth Ashman. 'Cultural Paternity in the Flateyjarbók Ólafs saga Tryggvasonar.' *alvíssmál* 8 (1998), 3–28.

—. *The Development of Flateyjarbók: Iceland and the Norwegian Dynastic Crisis of 1389*. The Viking Collection 15. Odense, 2005.

Rubow, Paul V. 'Den islandske Familieroman.' *Tilskueren*. May 1928, 347–357. (Rpt. *Sagadebatt*, pp. 188–198. Ed. Else Mundal. Oslo, 1977).

—. 'De islandske Sagaer.' *Smaa kritiske Breve*, pp. 7–33. Copenhagen, 1936.

Ryding, William W. *Structure in Medieval Narrative*. The Hague and Paris, 1971.

Sandaaker, Odd. 'Ágrip og Morkinskinna: Tekshistoriske randnotar.' *Maal og minne* (1996), 31–56.

—. 'Magnus Erlingssons kroning: Ein "politiserande" sagatradisjon?' *Historisk tidsskrift* 77 (1998), 181–196.

Sandnes, Jørn. *Kniven, ølet og æren: Kriminalitet og samfunn i Norge på 1500- og 1600-tallet*. Oslo, 1990.

Sandvik, Gudmund. *Hovding og konge i Heimskringla*. Avhandlinger fra Universitetets Historiske Seminar 9. Oslo, 1955.

Bibliography

Saxtorph, Niels M., Hans H. Ronge and Finn Hødnebø. 'Turnering.' *Kulturhistorisk leksikon for nordisk middelalder fra vikingetid til reformationstid* Vol. 19 (1975), cols. 71–73.

Sayers, William. 'The Honor of Guðlaugr Snorrason and Einarr Þambarskelfir: A Reply.' *Scandinavian Studies* 67 (1995), 537–544.

Schach, Paul. 'Some Forms of Writer Intrusion in the Íslendingasögur,' *Scandinavian Studies* 42 (1970), 128–156.

——. 'Some Observations on the Generation-Gap Theme in the Icelandic Sagas.' *The Epic in Medieval Society. Aesthetics and Moral Values*, pp. 361–381. Ed. Harald Schotter. Tübingen, 1977.

Schlauch, Margaret. *Romance in Iceland*. London, 1934.

Schrodt, Richard. 'Der altnordische Beiname "Sýr".' *Arkiv för nordisk filologi* 94 (1979), 114–119.

Seip, Didrik Arup. *Trondhjems bynavn*. Trondheim, 1930.

Shahar, Shulamith, trans. Chaya Galai. *The Fourth Estate: A History of Women in the Middle Ages*. London, 1983.

Sigfús Blöndal, *Væringjasaga: Saga norræna, rússneskra og enskra hersveita í þjónustu Miklagarðskeisara á miðöldum*. Reykjavík, 1954.

Sigurður Nordal. *Om Olaf den helliges saga: En kritisk undersøgelse*. Copenhagen, 1914.

——. *Snorri Sturluson*. Reykjavík, 1920.

——. 'Snorri Sturluson: Nokkurar hugleiðingar á 700. ártíð hans.' *Skírnir* 115 (1941), 5–33.

——. *Íslenzk menning* I. Reykjavík, 1942.

——. 'Sagalitteraturen.' In *Nordisk kultur VIII: B. Litteraturhistorie B. Norge og Island*, pp. 180–273. Ed. Sigurður Nordal. Stockholm, 1953.

Sigurður Svavarsson. 'Athugun á þáttum sem bókmenntagrein með dæmi af Auðunar þætti vestfirska.' *Mímir* 29 (1981), 20–37.

Skovgaard Petersen, Inge. *Da Tidernes Herre var nær: Studier i Saxos historiesyn*. Copenhagen, 1987.

Skúli Björn Gunnarsson. 'Hið íslenska hirðfífl: Um fíflsku Sneglu-Halla og Hreiðars heimska.' *Mímir* 43 (1996), 55–63.

Skúli Thorlacius (Þórðarson). 'Einar Skulsesøns Levnets-Beskrivelse – Vita Einari, Skulii Filii.' In *Heimskringla edr Noregs Konunga Sögor, af Snorra Sturlusyni – Snorre Sturlesøns Norske Kongers Historie – Historia Regum Norvegicorum, conscripta a Snorrio Sturlæ Filio* 3, pp. 481–494. Ed. Gerhard Schöning and Skúli Thorlacius. Copenhagen, 1783.

Bibliography

Solberg, Janet L. "'Who Was That Masked Man?" Disguise and Deception in Medieval and Renaissance Comic Literature.' In *The Stranger in Medieval Society*, pp. 117–138. Ed. F. R. P. Akehurst og Stephanie Cain Van D'Elden. Medieval Cultures 12. Minneapolis, 1998.

Spacks, Patricia Meyer. *Gossip.* Chicago and London, 1985.

Spiegel, Gabrielle M. *Romancing the Past: The Rise of Vernacular Prose Historiography in Thirteenth-Century France.* Berkeley, 1993.

Stavnem, Rolf. *Stroferne i Grettis saga: Deres funktion og betydning.* Copenhagen, 2000.

Stearns, Peter N. and Carol Stearns. 'Emotionology: Clarifying the History of Emotions and Emotional Standards.' *American Historical Review* 90 (1985), 813–836.

Stefán Einarsson. 'Æfintýraatvik í Auðunar þætti vestfirzka.' *Skírnir* 113 (1939), 161–171.

Stefán Karlsson. 'Om norvagismer i islandske håndskrifter.' *Maal og minne* (1978), 87–101.

—. 'Islandsk bogeksport til Norge i middelalderen.' *Maal og minne* (1979), 1–17.

Stock, Brian. *The Implications of Literacy. Written Language and Models of Interpretation in the Eleventh and Twelfth Centuries.* Princeton, 1983.

—. 'Tradition and Modernity: Models from the Past.' *Modernité au Moyen Âge: Le défi du Passé.* Ed. Brigitte Cazelles and Charles Méla. Recherches et rencontres 1. Geneva, 1990. 33–44.

—. *Listening for the Text. On the Uses of the Past.* Baltimore and London, 1990.

Storm, Gustav. *Snorre Sturlassöns Historieskrivning: En kritisk undersögelse.* Copenhagen, 1873.

—. 'Harald Haardraade og Væringerne i de græske Keiseres Tjeneste.' *(Norsk) Historisk tidsskrift* Vol. II, 4 (1884), 354–386.

Strand, Birgit. *Kvinnor och män i Gesta Danorum.* Kvinnohistoriskt arkiv 18. Göteborg, 1980.

Strömbäck, Dag. 'The Dawn of West Norse Literature.' *Bibliography of Old Norse-Icelandic Studies* (1963), 7–24.

Svava Jakobsdóttir. *Skyggnst á bak við ský.* Reykjavík, 1999.

Sverrir Jakobsson. 'Griðamál á ófriðaröld.' In *Íslenska söguþingið 28.–31. maí 1997: Ráðstefnurit* 1. Ed. Guðmundur J. Guðmundsson and Eiríkur K. Björnsson. Reykjavík, 1998, 117–134.

—. 'Friðarviðleitni kirkjunnar á 13. öld.' *Saga* 36 (1998). 7–46.

Bibliography

—. 'Hvers konar þjóð voru Íslendingar á miðöldum?' *Skírnir* 173 (1999), 111–140.

—. 'Defining a Nation: Popular and Public Identity in the Middle Ages.' *Scandinavian Journal of History* 24 (1999), 91–101.

—. 'Uppruni nútímans á 13. öld.' *Skírnir* 174 (2000), 215–221.

—. 'Útlendingar á Íslandi á miðöldum.' *Andvari* 126 (2001), 36–51.

—. *Við og veröldin: Heimsmynd Íslendinga 1100–1400.* Reykjavík, 2005.

Sverrir Tómasson. 'Vinveitt skemmtan og óvinveitt.' In *Maukastella færð Jónasi Kristjánssyni fimmtugum 10. apríl 1974*, pp. 65–68. Reykjavík, 1974.

—. 'Hvenær var Tristrams sögu snúið?' *Gripla* 2 (1977), 47–78.

—. *Formálar íslenskra sagnaritara á miðöldum: Rannsókn bókmenntahefðar.* Rit Stofnunar Árna Magnússonar 33. Reykjavík, 1988.

—. 'Hugleiðingar um horfna bókmenntagrein.' *Tímarit Máls og menningar* 50 (1989), 211–226.

—. 'Konungasögur.' In *Íslensk bókmenntasaga* 1, pp. 358–401. Ed. Vésteinn Ólason. Reykjavík, 1992.

—. 'Skorið í fornsögu: Þankar um byggingu Hrafnkels sögu.' In *Sagnaþing helgað Jónasi Kristjánssyni sjötugum 10. apríl 1994*, pp. 787–799. Vols. I–II. Ed. Gísli Sigurðsson, Guðrún Kvaran and Sigurgeir Steingrímsson. Reykjavík, 1994.

—. '"Ei skal haltr ganga": Um Gunnlaugs sögu ormstungu.' *Gripla* 10 (1998), 7–22.

—. 'Snorri Sturluson als Hagiograph.' In *Snorri Sturluson: Beiträge zu Werk und Rezeption*, pp. 275–286. Ed. Hans Fix. Ergänzungsbände zum Reallexikon der Germanischen Altertumskunde 18. Berlin and New York, 1998.

Taylor, Alexander B. 'Eysteinn Haraldsson in the West, c. 1151: Oral Traditions and Written Record.' In *The Fourth Viking Congress, York, August 1961*, pp. 119–134. Ed. Alan Small. Aberdeen University Studies 149. Edinburgh and London, 1965.

Taylor, Arnold R. 'Auðun and the Bear.' *Saga-Book of the Viking Society* 13 (1947–48), 78–96.

Tolkien, J. R. R. 'Beowulf: the Monsters and the Critics.' *Proceedings of the British Academy* 22 (1936), 245–295.

Torfi H. Tulinius. 'Snorri og bræður hans: Framgangur og átök Sturlusona í félagslegu rými þjóðveldisins.' *Ný saga* 12 (2000), 49–60.

Bibliography

—. 'Virðing í flóknu samfélagi.' In *Sæmdarmenn: Um heiður á þjóðveldisöld*, pp. 57–89. Ed. Helgi Þorláksson *et al*. Reykjavík, 2001.

—, trans. Randi C. Eldevik. *The Matter of the North: The Rise of Literary Fiction in Thirteenth-century Iceland*. The Viking Collection 13. Odense, 2002. (Original: *La "Matière du Nord": Sagas légendaires et fiction dans la littérature islandaise en prose du XIIIe siècle*. Paris, 1995).

Turville-Petre, Gabriel. *Origins of Icelandic Literature*. Oxford, 1953.

—. *Haraldr the Hard-ruler and his Poets: The Dorothea Coke Memorial Lecture in Northern Studies delivered 1 December 1966 at University College London*. London, 1968.

Tveitane, Mattias. 'Europeisk påvirkning på den norrøne sagalitteraturen: Noen synspunkter.' *Edda* 69 (1969), 73–95.

Ullmann, Walter. *The Individual and Society in the Middle Ages*. Baltimore, 1966.

Ulset, Tor. 'Innledning.' In *Utvalgte þættir fra Morkinskinna*. Nordisk filologi 14. Oslo, 1978.

Unger, C.R. 'Forord.' In *Morkinskinna. Pergamentsbog fra første halvdel af det trettende aarhundrede. Indeholdende en af de ældste optegnelser af norske kongesagaer*. Pp. i–iv. Ed. C.R. Unger. Christiania [Oslo], 1867.

—. 'Fortale.' In *Flateyjarbok. En Samling af norske Konge-sagaer med indskudte mindre Fortællinger om Begivenheder i og udenfor Norge samt Annaler*. Vol. 3. pp. i–xxiv. Oslo, 1868.

Uspenskij, Fjodor. 'Christliche und heidnische namen im mittelalterlichen Skandinavien: *Magnús* als Name für ein illegitimes Kind des Herrschers.' In *Scandinavia and Christian Europe in the Middle Ages: Papers of the 12th International Saga Conference, Bonn/Germany, 28th July – 2nd August 2003*, pp. 506–514. Ed. Rudolf Simek and Judith Meurer. Bonn, 2003.

Vale, Juliet. 'Violence and the Tournament.' In *Violence in Medieval Society*, pp. 143–158. Ed. Richard W. Kaeuper. Woodbridge, Suffolk, 2000.

Veblen, Thorstein. *The Theory of the Leisure Class: An Economic Study of Institutions*. 4th edn. New York, 1934. (Originally published 1899)

Vésteinn Ólason. 'Íslendingaþættir.' *Tímarit Máls og menningar* 46 (1985), 60–73.

—. 'Den frie mannens selvforståelse i islandske sagaer og dikt.' In *Medeltidens födelse: Symposier på Krapperups Borg* Vol. 1, pp. 277–286. Ed. Anders Andrén. Gyllenstiernska Krapperupsstiftelsen, 1989.

—. 'Íslendingasögur og þættir.' In *Íslensk bókmenntasaga* Vol. 2. Ed. Vésteinn Ólason. Reykjavík, 1993.

—, trans. Andrew Wawn. *Dialogues with the Viking Age: Narration and Representation in the Sagas of the Icelanders.* Reykjavík, 1998. (Original: *Samræður við söguöld: frásagnarlist Íslendingasagna og fortíðarmynd.* Reykjavík, 1998).

Vinaver, Eugène. *A la recherche d'une poétique médiévale.* Paris, 1970.

—. *The Rise of Romance.* Totowa, New Jersey, 1971.

Violence and Society in the Early Medieval West. Ed. Guy Halsall. Woodbridge, Suffolk 1998.

Vogt, Wilhelm Heinrich. 'Die frásagnir der Landnámabók.' *Zeitschrift für deutsches Altertum* 58 (1921), 161–204.

Wack, Mary F. *Lovesickness in the Middle Ages: The Viaticum and Its Commentaries.* Philadelphia, 1990.

Weber, Gerd Wolfgang. 'The decadence of feudal myth – towards a theory of riddarasaga and romance.' In *Structure and Meaning in Old Norse Literature: New Approaches to Textual Analysis and Literary Criticism,* pp. 415–454. Ed. John Lindow, Lars Lönnroth and Gerd Wolfgang Weber. The Viking Collection 3. Odense, 1986.

Weber, Max. *Wirtschaft und Gesellschaft: Grundriss der Sozialökonomik.* 2nd edn. Tübingen, 1922–1927. Vols. 1–2.

Whaley, Diana. *Heimskringla: An Introduction.* Viking Society for Northern Research Text Series 8. London, 1991.

—. 'Nicknames and Narratives in the Sagas.' *Arkiv för nordisk filologi* 108 (1993), 122–146.

—. *The Poetry of Arnórr Jarlaskáld: An Edition and Study.* Westfield Publications in Medieval Studies. London, 1998.

—. 'Representations of Skalds in the Sagas 1: Social and Professional Relations.' In *Skaldsagas: Text, Vocation, and Desire in the Icelandic Sagas of Poets,* pp. 285–308. Ed. Russell Poole. Ergänzungsbände zum Reallexikon der Germanischen Altertumskunde 27. Berlin and New York, 2001.

White, Paul A. 'The Latin Men: The Norman Sources of the Scandinavian Kings' Sagas.' *Journal of English and Germanic Philology* 98 (1999), 157–169.

Widding, Ole. 'Et norsk fragment af Barlaams saga.' *Maal og minne* (1963), 37–46.

—. 'Om fragmenter af Barlaams saga ok Josaphats: Holm 12 fol. V og NoRA 64.' *Maal og minne* (1972), 93–103.

Bibliography

Wikander, Stig. 'Från indisk djurfabel till isländsk saga.' *Vetenskaps-societen i Lund: Årsbok 1964*, 89–114.

Wikström, Lars and Grethe Authén Blom. 'Torgfrid.' *Kulturhistorisk leksikon for nordisk middelalder fra vikingetid til reformationstid* Vol. 18 (1974), cols. 475–481.

Woesler, Winfried. 'Hvordan tekstfejl opstår og udbedres.' In *I tekstens tegn*, pp. 9–32. Ed. Jørgen Hunosøe and Esther Kielberg. Copenhagen, 1994.

Wolf, Alois, ed. *Snorri Sturluson: Kolloquium anläßlich der 750. Wiederkehr seines Todestages*. ScriptOralia 51. Tübingen, 1993.

Würth, Stefanie. *Elemente des Erzählens: Die Þættir der Flateyjarbók*. Basel and Frankfurt a.M. 1991.

—. *Der 'Antikenroman' in der isländischen Literatur des Mittelalters: Eine Untersuchung zur Übersetzung und Rezeption lateinischer Literatur im Norden*. Beiträge zur nordischen Philologie 26. Basel and Frankfurt, 1998.

—. 'New Historicism und altnordische Literaturwissenschaft.' In *Verhandlungen mit dem New Historicism: Das Text-Kontext-Problem in der Literaturwissenschaft*, pp. 193–208. Ed. Jürg Glauser and Annegret Heitmann. Würzburg, 1999.

—. 'Die Temporalität der *Laxdæla saga*.' In *Sagnaheimur: Studies in Honour of Hermann Pálsson on his 80th birthday, 26th May 2001*, pp. 295–308. Ed. Ásdís Egilsdóttir and Rudolf Simek. Studia Medievalia Septentrionalia 6. Vienna, 2001.

Zernack, Julia. 'Hyndlulioð, Flateyjarbók und die Vorgeschichte der Kalmarer Union.' *Skandinavistik* 29 (1999), 89–114.

Þormóður Torfason. *Orcades*. Copenhagen, 1697.

—. 'Prolegomena.' *Historia rerum Norvegicarum*. Copenhagen, 1711.

—. *Series dynastarum et regum Daniæ*. Copenhagen, 1702.

Þórhallur Guttormsson. *Brynjólfur biskup Sveinsson*. Reykjavík, 1973.

Index

Icelandic names in this index are listed by given name followed by their patronymic, e. g. Ari Einarsson.

Index

Norwegian courtier, 12,
182 n26, 198
Árni Magnússon (1663–1730), 24
Ásdís Egilsdóttir (b. 1946), 9,
160 n33, 199 n8
Áslákr hani 'the Rooster',
Norwegian courtier, 191 n33
Ásólfr jarlsfrændi 'Earl's kinsman',
30
Ásu-Þórðr of the Eastfjords, 89,
169, 208 n40, 283, 316

B

Bagge, Sverre (b. 1942), 73–4 n4,
130 n19, 164 n41, 205 n26
Bakhtin, Mikhail (1895–1975),
178 n17
Baldr, Norse god, 312
Bandamanna saga, 284 n10
Barlaams saga ok Jósafats, 324
battles, 31, 106, 142–4, 150, 153–5,
160, 165, 174–6, 203, 207–8,
215–7, 233–5, 245, 246–7, 257,
259–61, 263, 269–71, 278–9,
300–4, 307–9, 312–3, 331
Bárðr upplenzki 'the Uplander',
courtier, 271 n19
Beck, Heinrich (b. 1929), 247 n24
Bédier, Joseph (1864–1938), 79, 82
Benteinn Kolbeinsson, courtier
(d. 1138), 122
Beowulf, 79, 83
Bergman, Ingmar (1918–2007), 139
Bergþórr Másson, Icelandic
chieftain, 276
Bersǫglisvísur, 57, 108, 263, 306
Bibire, Paul, 326, 340 n49
Bible, The, 232 n6, 338
Bjarnar saga Hítdælakappa, 95 n3,
108 n28

Bjarni Aðalbjarnarson
(1908–1953), 26 n10, 29 n19,
30, 35, 42–8, 57–8, 65–6, 73,
89, 244 n18
Bjarni Einarsson (1917–2000),
50–1, 53–4, 56, 103 n18,
311 n27, 324 n25
Bjarni Guðnason (b. 1928), 88 n56
Bjǫrgvin (Bergen), 143 n9, 144–5,
234–5, 239, 279
Björn M. Ólsen (1850–1919),
64 n98, 87 n52, 89–90, 116 n5
Blágagladrápa, 118–9
Bloch, R. Howard (b. 1943), 199 n11
Boberg, Inger M. (1900–1957),
222 n13, 227,n29
Boccaccio, Giovanni (1313–1375),
90
Bosphorus, the, 165
Bourdieu, Pierre (1930–2002),
150 n16
Bragi Halldórsson (b. 1949), 93 n1
Brandr inn ǫrvi 'the Bountiful'
Vermundarson, 41–2, 195, 221,
263, 284, 288–9, 334–5
Brandt, William, 170 n4, 339 n46
Brecht, Bertold (1898–1956), 124
Brennu-Njáls saga, 16 n4, 18, 64,
82–4, 116, 124, 147 n13, 208,
223, 227 n29, 310 n25, 319
Bruhn, Ole (1947–1997), 289, 318,
326 n30
Brünger, Tanja, 287 n19
Brynjólfur Sveinsson (1605–1675),
23–4
Burke, Peter (b. 1945), 338 n44
Burnley, J. David, 256 n6
Burns, E. Jane (b. 1948), 210 n47
Butler, Judith (b. 1956), 223–4, 228
Bǫlverkr Arnórson, poet, 299

Index

Index

Ingi Bárðarson, King of Norway,
1204–1217 (1185–1217), 30,
166, 240, 304
Ingi Haraldsson, King of Norway,
1136–1161 (1134–1161), 134, 142,
200, 208 n42, 249, 252, 256–8,
262, 274, 285, 312, 341
Ingi Steinkelsson, King of Sweden,
1079–1084; 1087–1105 (d.
1105), 218–9
Ingibjǫrg ekkja 'the widow', 209
Ingibjǫrg Gothormsdóttir, Queen,
172 n5
Ingibjǫrg Halldórsdóttir, 209
Ingigerðr Ólafsdóttir, Queen of
Russia, 139, 196, 230–1, 241
Ingimarr Sveinsson, Norwegian
chieftain (d. 1134), 169–70, 283
Ingiríðr Rǫgnvaldsdóttir, Queen
(d. 1170), 142, 208 n42, 256–7,
262, 274
insanity, see madness
insults, 99, 129, 177, 180, 203, 227,
237, 242, 282–3, 286–7, 314,
317–8, 330–1
Ireland, 165, 261, 263, 274
irony, 114, 118–9, 126, 129, 132–5,
189, 226–7, 296–7
Íslendingabók, see also Ari fróði
Þorgilsson, 108
Íslendingasögur, see Sagas of
Icelanders, the
Íslendings þáttr sögufróða, 89
Ívarr hvíti 'the White', 316 n35
Ívarr Íngimundarson, poet, Ívars
þáttr Íngimundarsonar,
93–100, 103, 111, 113–6, 129–31,
170, 179, 199, 206–7, 256, 289,
312, 320, 334, 336
Ívarr skrauthanki 'Decorative

Handle' Kálfsson, Bishop of
Þrándheim, 173–4
Ívarr dynta 'the Conceited'
Starrason (d. 1139), 173–4
Ívens saga, 141 n5, 321

J

Jaeger, C. Stephen (b. 1940),
174 n10, 203 n22, 224,
289 n23, 339–40
Jakobsen, Alfred (1917–1997),
46–7, 53, 61 n90, 65 n103,
284 n10
Jameson, Fredric (b. 1934), 139 n2
Jamtaland (Jämtland), 234–5
Jarizleifr Valdamarsson, Grand
Prince of Kiev, 1016–1018;
1019–1054 (978–1054), 59–60,
101, 139, 148 n14, 180–1, 183,
196, 230–2, 244, 287
Játgeirr Torfason, poet, 315
Jerusalem, see Holy Land, the
Jesus Christ, see Christ
Jochens, Jenny (b. 1928), 205 n27,
207 n35
Johannesson, Kurt (b. 1935), 78 n8
John of Salisbury (c. 1120–1180),
189 n31
Jones, Gwyn (1907–1999), 97 n8
Jordan, river, 233
Jómsvíkinga saga, 327
Jón Helgason (1899–1986), 28, 35,
61, 74–5
Jón Loptsson (Sturlunga saga)
(1124–1197), 192 n35
Jón Sigurðarson of Austrátt,
Norwegian chieftain, 30
Jón Þorkelsson (1822–1904),
29–30, 32, 86
Jórunn Þorbergsdóttir, 280–1
Jöfraskinna, 24

397

Index

Index

(1940–2001), 287 n18, 300 n8, 319 n12

Miklagarðr, see Constantinople

Miller, William Ian (b. 1946), 121 n10

Morgan le Fay, sorceress, 81 n25

Morkere (Morcar, Mǫrukári), Earl of Northumberland, 1065–1066 (d. 1087), 165

Morkinskinna, manuscript, 11 n1, 15, 23–33, 35–6, 38–9, 40, 47–9, 67–9, 332–3

Morton, Andrew Queen (b. 1919), 62 n91

Munkaþverá, 33

Möttuls saga, 141 n5, 321–2

N

Nið (Nid), river, 143, 304

Niðarós (Nidaros) (Trondheim), 57, 120, 144–6

Njáll Þorgeirsson of Bergþórshváll (*Brennu-Njáls saga*), 310 n25

Njáls saga, Njála, see *Brennu-Njáls saga*

Norðbrikt, 132–3, 207, 216, 277–8. See also Haraldr inn harðráði

Normandy, 81, 165, 204 n24, 304

O

O'Donoghue, Heather (b. 1953), 108 n28

Oddný Jónsdóttir, 94, 130 n21

Oddr Gellisson, witness, 32, 298

Oddr Ófeigsson, Icelandic merchant, 284 n10

Oddr Snorrason, monk and saga writer, 84

old age, 145–7, 170–2, 192–3, 197, 200, 247–9, 266, 307, 324

Oldest saga of St Óláfr, see *Óláfs saga in elzta*

Orkneyinga saga, 327

Orkneys, Orkney Isles, 24, 118, 165, 269–70, 318

Orlando furioso, poem, 79 n10

Ormr inn langi 'the Long Serpent', ship, 273

Ormr Ívarsson, Norwegian chieftain, 29

Ormr Skoptason, Earl (d. 1050), 264

Ouse, River, 165

Óðinn, Norse god, 166–7

Óláfr I, Óláfr Tryggvason, King of Norway, 970–995 (935–995), 11, 216, 260

Óláfr II, Óláfr inn helgi 'the Saint' Haraldsson, King of Norway, 1015–1028 (995–1030), 11, 26, 29, 54–5, 56, 105, 106, 116–7, 141, 143, 166, 202, 205, 206 n30, 217, 219, 231–2, 257, 269, 275 n1, 280–1, 297, 304, 306

Óláfr III, Óláfr inn kyrri 'the Quiet' Haraldsson, King of Norway, 1066–1093 (1050–1093), 56, 144, 146, 150, 161, 167, 200, 219, 222 n13, 236, 239, 246, 249, 254–5, 257–8, 263, 273, 279

Óláfr inn sænski 'the Swede' Eiríksson, King of Sweden, (d. 1022), 139

Óláfr pái 'the Peacock' Hǫskuldsson (*Laxdæla saga*) (d. 1006), 243

Óláfr Leggsson, poet, 315

Index

Index